OCR GCSE FOOD PREPARATION AND NUTRITION

OCR GCSE

VAL FEHNERS
Consultant Editor: **ANITA HARDY**

HODDER EDUCATION
AN HACHETTE UK COMPANY

Author acknowledgements

Val Fehners would like to thank Adrian Fehners for his support and Katherine and Orla Webb-Sear for their photographs.

Anita Hardy would like to thank her husband Ronald Hardy for his patience, support and tolerance.

Although every effort has been made to ensure that website addresses are correct at time of going to press, Hodder Education cannot be held responsible for the content of any website mentioned in this book. It is sometimes possible to find a relocated web page by typing in the address of the home page for a website in the URL window of your browser.

Hachette UK's policy is to use papers that are natural, renewable and recyclable products and made from wood grown in sustainable forests. The logging and manufacturing processes are expected to conform to the environmental regulations of the country of origin.

Orders: please contact Bookpoint Ltd, 130 Park Drive, Milton Park, Abingdon, Oxon OX14 4SE. Telephone: (44) 01235 827720. Fax: (44) 01235 400454. Email education@bookpoint.co.uk Lines are open from 9 a.m. to 5 p.m., Monday to Saturday, with a 24-hour message answering service. You can also order through our website: www.hoddereducation.co.uk

ISBN: 978 1471 86749 1

© Val Fehners 2016

First published in 2016 by
Hodder Education,
An Hachette UK Company
Carmelite House
50 Victoria Embankment
London EC4Y 0DZ

www.hoddereducation.co.uk

Impression number   10 9 8 7 6 5 4 3 2

Year   2020 2019 2018 2017 2016

All rights reserved. Apart from any use permitted under UK copyright law, no part of this publication may be reproduced or transmitted in any form or by any means, electronic or mechanical, including photocopying and recording, or held within any information storage and retrieval system, without permission in writing from the publisher or under licence from the Copyright Licensing Agency Limited. Further details of such licences (for reprographic reproduction) may be obtained from the Copyright Licensing Agency Limited, Saffron House, 6–10 Kirby Street, London EC1N 8TS.

Cover photo © fullempty/Alamy Stock Photo

Illustrations by Aptara

Typeset in Vectora LT Std 10/13pt by Aptara Inc.

Printed in Italy

A catalogue record for this title is available from the British Library.

Contents

Acknowledgements		ii
Foreword		v
Introduction to OCR GCSE Food Preparation and Nutrition		vi

Section A: Nutrition — 1

Topic 1	The relationship between diet and health	2
Topic 2	Nutritional and dietary needs of different groups of people	21
Topic 3	Nutritional needs when selecting recipes for different groups of people	32
Topic 4	Energy balance	38
Topic 5	Protein	43
Topic 6	Fats	47
Topic 7	Carbohydrates	52
Topic 8	Vitamins	58
Topic 9	Minerals	63
Topic 10	Water	66
Topic 11	Nutrients in food	69
Section A Practice questions		85

Section B: Food — 87

Topic 1:	Food provenance: food source and supply	88
Topic 2:	Food provenance: food processing and production	103
Topic 3:	Food security	122
Topic 4:	Technological developments to support better health and food production	129
Topic 5:	Development of culinary traditions	139
Topic 6:	Factors influencing food choice	150
Section B Practice questions		162

Section C: Cooking and food preparation — 163

Topic 1:	Food science	164
Topic 2:	Sensory properties	195
Topic 3:	Food safety	202
Section C Practice questions		216

Section D: Skills requirements (preparation and cooking techniques) — 217

- **Topic 1:** Knife skills — 218
- **Topic 2:** Preparation and techniques — 224
- **Topic 3:** Cooking methods — 229
- **Topic 4:** Sauces — 230
- **Topic 5:** Set a mixture — 234
- **Topic 6:** Raising agents — 236
- **Topic 7:** Dough — 239
- **Topic 8:** Judge and manipulate sensory properties — 251
- **Section D Practice questions** — 257

Preparing for assessment — 259

- **Topic 1:** The Non-Examined Assessment (NEA) Task 1: Food Investigation Task — 260
- **Topic 2:** The Non-Examined Assessment (NEA) Task 2: Food Preparation Task — 269
- **Topic 3:** The Food Preparation and Nutrition written examination — 283

Glossary — 294
Picture credits — 299
Index — 300

Foreword

Congratulations on choosing to do the GCSE in Food Preparation and Nutrition – which has got to be one of the best courses on the curriculum. Now you might say, "Well, he's a chef, he would say that, wouldn't he," but it seems to me studying food and cooking has a lot going for it, including a lot of stuff you won't find on many other courses.

For a start, food is something that everybody has in common. We all need to eat it to stay alive. We all have strong feelings about it – the things we love; the things that make us go, "Yeuch" – and strong memories of it. So you're learning about something that's right at the heart of life, and very relevant to it.

What's more, it covers lots of different areas – art and design, visual presentation, technical dexterity, organisational skills, logic and analytical thinking, technology, philosophy, history, biology, chemistry, psychology. (Not to mention chopping, filleting, emulsifying and pasta-making.) You'll get to know a lot about a lot – and not just for its own sake. I've certainly found that, the more I research food and cooking, the more it all fits together, the more it offers up new avenues to explore, and the more exciting it becomes.

But it's not just theoretical, it's creative and practical too. There'll be plenty of opportunities to roll up your sleeves, get in the kitchen and actually do something. The kitchen is a wonderful environment to work in – part production line, part alchemist's lab, and full of amazing sights, sounds, smells, tastes and textures (the squidge of bread as you knead it, the sizzle and smell of bacon frying). A real sensory wonderland that it's great to be a part of.

Sadly, the number of people who don't know how to cook is growing. For them, the whole thing is a mystery, and those who can take a handful of ingredients and turn them into a plate of something tasty are seen almost as magicians. If you work hard on this course (and "Push on", as my chefs would say), you too will be one of those magicians. There's almost no pleasure greater than serving up a lovely dish and seeing people's faces light up. (Unless it's the pleasure of having achieved it in the first place.)

So this course is a great opportunity. Seize it with both hands (but make sure you've put your knife away first). There'll be plenty of information to process at first, but never lose sight of the fact that cooking is about emotion and inspiration. Follow your instincts, take some risks and don't be afraid to fail. Creativity comes out of questioning and exploring everything and not worrying too much about getting it right first time.

And, above all, have fun in the kitchen.

Heston Blumenthal

Introduction to OCR GCSE Food Preparation and Nutrition

This book has been written to help you master the skills, knowledge and understanding you need for the OCR GCSE (9–1) in Food Preparation and Nutrition.

This GCSE course will help you to make connections between theory and practice so you are able to apply your understanding of food and nutrition, food science and healthy eating to practical cooking. The content of the course is divided into four sections:

- **A. Nutrition:** this section will develop your knowledge and understanding of the nutritional content, functional properties and chemical processes of food and drinks. You will learn about the relationship between diet, nutrition and health, as well as the effects of poor diet and health.
- **B. Food (food provenance and food choice):** this section will help you to understand the economic, environmental, ethical, and socio-cultural influences on food availability, production processes and diet and health choices.
- **C. Cooking and food preparation:** in this section of the course you will demonstrate your knowledge and understanding of functional and nutritional properties, sensory qualities and food safety considerations when preparing, processing, storing, cooking and serving food.
- **D. Skill requirements (preparation and cooking techniques):** in this section you will demonstrate effective and safe cooking skills when planning, preparing and cooking using a variety of food commodities, cooking techniques and equipment. You will explore a range of ingredients and processes from different culinary traditions, including traditional British cuisine and other international cuisines.

Each of these areas will be assessed in the Food Preparation and Nutrition written examination you will complete at the end of the course. (You will find information to help you prepare for the written exam at the end of this book on pages 269–279.)

You will also complete two Non-Examination Assessments (NEAs): the Food Investigation Task and the Food Preparation Task. (You will find information to help you prepare for these tasks at the end of this book on pages 250–268.)

Summary of assessment

Component	Assessment type	Time and marks	% of qualification
Food Preparation and Nutrition	Written examination paper	100 marks 1 hour 30 minutes	50%
Food Investigation Task	Non-examined assessment (NEA)	45 marks	15%
Food Preparation Task	Non-examined assessment (NEA)	105 marks	35%

How to use this book

The book is divided into five sections.

Sections A–D cover the four areas of subject content you will be tested on in the Food Preparation and Nutrition written exam.

The final section of the book is divided into three topics:

- **Topics 1 and 2** cover the two non-examination assessments: The Food Investigation Task and the Food Preparation Task. They explain the format each assessment will take, how many marks are available for the different aspects of each assessment, and include example work for assessment tasks similar to those you will need to complete.
- **Topic 3** is designed to help you to prepare for the Food Preparation and Nutrition written exam. It includes details on the format of the exam paper, tips on how to revise, information on the types of questions you will encounter and advice on answering exam questions. It also includes practice questions with some sample answers and commentary.

Throughout the book, you will find the following features:

KEY WORDS

Key words are provided throughout each topic and define all of the important terms you will need to know and understand.

→ WHAT WILL I LEARN?

This box appears at the start of each topic and will tell you what you should know and understand by the end of the topic.

✔ KEY POINTS

Key points are provided throughout each section and summarise all of the important knowledge you will need about that topic.

Topic links

These will help you to make connections between different topics and tell you where you can find more information on a particular aspect of the course. They also help you to understand how different skills and topics will be relevant when you complete your Non-Examined Assessment (NEA) tasks.

PRACTICAL ACTIVITY

Practical activities are food preparation and cooking tasks that will provide you with opportunities to demonstrate the different food preparation skills and techniques, as well as allowing you to apply your subject knowledge and understanding in a practical context and see how it is relevant to practical food preparation and cooking.

RESEARCH ACTIVITY

Research activity boxes include short activities your teacher may ask you to complete either in class or at home to help you develop your knowledge and understanding of a topic.

Stretch and challenge

Stretch and challenge activities are extension tasks that will help you to develop your knowledge and understanding of a topic further. They may ask you to complete further research into a topic, or consider some of the more challenging aspects of the course.

TEST YOURSELF

These are short questions that appear at the end of each topic. They will help you to test your knowledge and understanding of the content covered within the topic.

Practice questions

These appear at the end of each section. They will help you to prepare for the written exam.

Section A: Nutrition

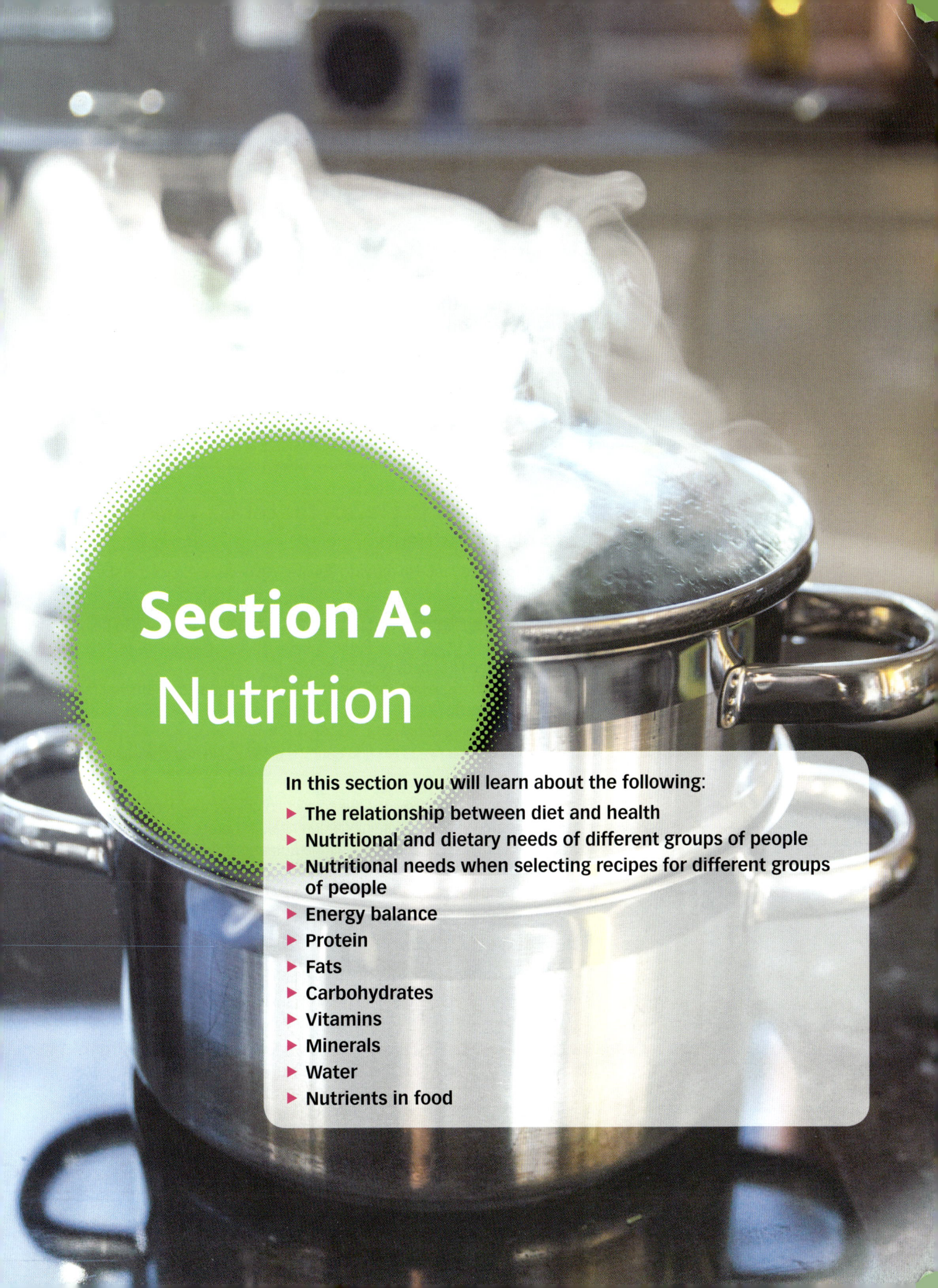

In this section you will learn about the following:
- The relationship between diet and health
- Nutritional and dietary needs of different groups of people
- Nutritional needs when selecting recipes for different groups of people
- Energy balance
- Protein
- Fats
- Carbohydrates
- Vitamins
- Minerals
- Water
- Nutrients in food

Topic 1
The relationship between diet and health

→ **WHAT WILL I LEARN?**

By the end of this topic you should have developed a knowledge and understanding of:

→ what a **balanced diet** is and how to provide the correct combination of food and nutrients for good health
→ the government's guidelines for a healthy diet
→ major diet-related health issues caused by poor diet and lifestyle.

A balanced diet to provide the correct combination of food and nutrients

All living things need food in order to survive. We need to eat food in the correct balance for:

- providing the energy we need to survive, to keep us healthy and to help fight disease
- growth and repair of body tissue
- all bodily functions, which depend on the energy and trace elements found in the food we eat
- stopping us feeling hungry
- health and well-being, as we find eating a pleasurable and enjoyable experience.

A healthy balanced diet provides the correct combination of food and nutrients for growth and maintaining good health. There is not one single food that will provide the body with all the nutrients it needs. To have a **balanced diet** you need to eat a mixture of foods from each of the main food groups and the correct amount of energy to carry out daily activities.

KEY WORD

Balanced diet – a diet that provides adequate amounts of nutrients and energy

The Eatwell Guide

The **Eatwell Guide** is a pictorial food guide showing the proportions and types of foods that are needed to make up a healthy balanced diet. The Guide is produced by Public Health England.

The Eatwell Guide can be followed by most people with the exception of children under 2 years who have special dietary needs. Children between the ages of 2 and 5 should start to follow the Eatwell Guide. If you have special dietary needs you should always check with a dietician or doctor how to adapt the Eatwell Guide to meet your specific needs. The Eatwell Guide is all about balance and figure 1.1 shows the proportions of the different groups of foods you should eat.

Topic 1 The relationship between diet and health

▲ Figure 1.1 The Eatwell Guide

KEY WORD

Eatwell Guide – a healthy eating model, to encourage people to eat the correct proportions of food to achieve a balanced diet.

The **Eatwell Guide** is based on the five food groups (shown in Figure 1.1) and supports advice to reduce fat, salt, sugar and alcohol in the diet, and to increase fibre.

The Eatwell Guide is all about balance. Figure 1.1 shows the proportions of the different groups of foods you should eat. There are no good or bad foods – all foods can be included in a healthy diet as long as the overall balance of foods is right. All foods supply energy and nutrients – it is achieving the correct intake of those nutrients that is important for health.

Topic links: You will learn about the functions of different nutrients in Section A: Nutrition, Topics 3 and Topics 5-9.

Table 1.1

	Fruits and vegetables
	• Many people do not eat sufficient fruits and vegetables • Fruits and vegetables should be just over a third of the food eaten in a day • We should eat at least five portions of a variety of fruit and vegetables each day • Fruit and vegetables are a good source of vitamins, minerals and fibre • Evidence shows that people who eat a lot of fruit and vegetables are less likely to develop diseases such as coronary heart disease and some types of cancer. **What is included:** • Choose from fresh, frozen, tinned, dried or juice • All fruit and vegetables, including: apples, pears, oranges, bananas, grapes, strawberries, mango, pineapple, raisins, broccoli, courgettes, cabbage, peas, sweetcorn, lettuce, tomatoes, carrots, peas, beans, lentils. **Remember:** • that a portion of dried fruit is 30 g and can only count as 1 of your 5-a-day • a portion of fruit juice or smoothie is 150 ml and also only counts as 1 of your 5-a-day • limit fruit juice and smoothies to a combined total of 150 ml per day • potatoes are not part of this group they belong in the Potatoes, bread, rice, pasta or other starchy carbohydrates.
	Potatoes, bread, rice, pasta or other starchy carbohydrates
	• Choose to eat wholegrain cereal products or higher fibre where possible, such as wholewheat pasta and brown rice • Starchy food should make up just over a third of the food we eat • Starchy foods are a good source of energy and provide use with other nutrients. **What is included:** • Bread, including: soda bread, rye bread, pitta, flour tortilla, baguettes, chapatti, bagels • rice • potatoes • breakfast cereals, oats • pasta, noodles • maize, cornmeal, polenta • millet, spelt • couscous, bulgur wheat • wheat, pearl barley • yams and plantains. **Remember:** • Starchy foods are often combined with other ingredients, e.g. in breakfast cereals. Check the labels and choose the products lowest in fat, salt and sugar • Consider the way you are cooking starchy foods, e.g. have oven chips rather than deep fried ones, try to avoid adding too much fat or creamy sauces as these contain lots of calories.
	Dairy and dairy alternatives
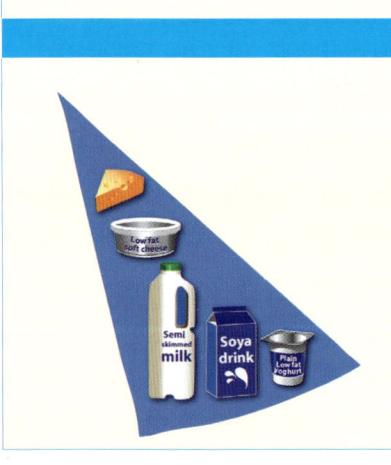	• Milk, cheese, yogurt and fromage frais are good sources of protein and some vitamins, and they are also good source of calcium, this helps to keep our bones strong • You should eat some dairy or dairy alternatives every day • There are many lower-fat and lower-sugar products which can replace those with a higher fat and sugar content for example, 1% fat milk, reduced-fat cheese or plain low-fat or fat-free yoghurt. **What is included:** • Milk • cheese • yogurt • fromage frais • quark, cream cheese. • This also includes non-dairy alternatives to these foods.

Section A: Nutrition

Topic 1 The relationship between diet and health

Remember:
- Butters and creams are not included in this group as they are high in saturated fat and so they fit into the 'foods to eat less often and in small amounts'.
- Check the labels on food products as some are high in saturated fats. There are alternatives, e.g. reduced-fat cheese, yogurt and milk. Yogurts may be high in sugar, choose low-fat and sugar natural ones.

Beans, pulses, fish, eggs, meat and other proteins

- These foods are a good sources of protein and other nutrients
- Beans, peas and lentils are low in fat and are good alternatives to meat
- It is recommended that we eat fish at least twice a week and that one of these is oily fish, such as mackerel
- Try to reduce red and processed meat to 70 g per day
- Some meat is high in fat (saturated)
- Choose lower-fat meat products, leaner cuts of meat, and trim off any visible fat and skin
- Use cooking methods that do not use any fat, and drain away fat. Grill, poach, steam, bake or microwave.

What is included:
- Meat, poultry and game, including: lamb, beef, pork, chicken, bacon, sausages, burgers
- White fish including: haddock, plaice, pollock, coley, cod
- Oily fish including: mackerel, sardines, trout, salmon, whitebait
- Shellfish including: prawns, mussels, crab, squid, oysters
- Eggs
- Nuts
- Beans and other pulses, including: lentils, chickpeas, baked beans, kidney beans, butter beans.

Oils and spreads

- Some fat is needed in the diet but most people need to reduce their intake of saturated fat
- We should not use a lot of these products because they are often high in fat
- Chose low-fat spreads when possible
- These foods are often high in calories so reducing the amount eaten can also help to control weight.

What is included:
- Unsaturated oil, e.g. vegetable oil, rapeseed oil, olive oil, sunflower oil
- Soft spreads made from unsaturated fats.

Remember:
- Butter is not included in this section it is in the section 'foods to eat less often and in small amounts'
- Check the labels on foods and choose fats and oils high in unsaturated fats and low in saturated fat.

The Eatwell Guide also gives additional information on:

- Foods high in fat and sugars
- Hydration
- Food labelling

Foods high in fat and sugars

▲ **Figure 1.2** Foods high in fat, salt and sugar

These foods are not needed in the diet and therefore should not be eaten very often. If you eat these foods and drinks you should eat them in very small quantities. Foods and drinks which contain a lot of fat and sugar are high in energy. You should check the food labels and choose foods which are low in fats, sugars and salt.

Hydration

Water, coffee, tea, lower fat milk, and sugar free drinks all contribute to meeting your needs of 6-8 glasses of fluid every day. Fruit juice and smoothies do count but they are also counted as free sugars. You should not have more than 150 ml of these a day.

Sugary drinks should be avoided and these should be swapped for sugar free and no added sugar varieties.

Alcohol also contains a lot of calories and adults should not consume more than 14 units a week.

Food labelling

A lot of foods have nutritional labelling on them. It often shows the nutritional information per serving. It also shows the contribution it makes to the daily amounts required.

6-8 a day

Water, lower fat milk, sugar-free drinks including tea and coffee all count.

Limit fruit juice and/or smoothies to a total of 150ml a day.

Energy	Fat	Saturates	Sugars	Salt
622kJ 146kcal	1.2g	0.2g	5.6g	1.7g
7%	2%	1%	6%	28%

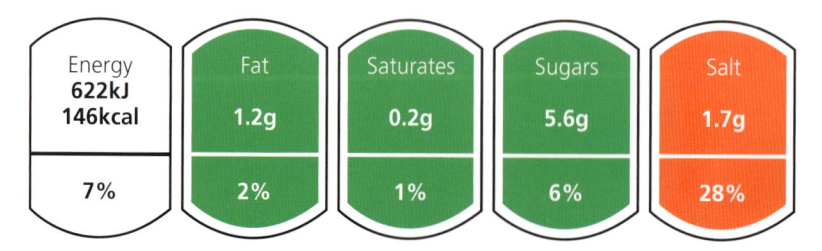

of an adult's Reference Intake.
Typical values per 100g: Energy 311kJ/73kcal

▲ **Figure 1.3** Food label showing contribution to daily required amount

Topic 1 The relationship between diet and health

The use of colour helps you to easily see whether they are high in saturated fat, sugar and salt.

Red = high

Amber = medium

Green = low

Cutting down on saturated fat

Reducing the amount of saturated fat eaten can:

- reduce the risk of heart disease
- lower blood cholesterol.

Men should have no more than 30 g saturated fat a day and women should have no more than 20 g per day.

Children need less than this. Children under five years of age should not have a low fat diet.

Cutting down on sugar

Reducing the amount of sugar can reduce the risk of:

- obesity
- tooth decay.

No more than 5% of the sugar we eat should come from free sugars. The chart below shows the amount of sugars recommended:

Table 1.2 How much sugar should we eat

Age	Recommended maximum free sugars intake	Sugar cubes
4-6 years	No more than 19 g/day	5 cubes
7-10 years	No more than 24 g/day	6 cubes
From 11 years, including adults	No more than 30 g/day	7 cubes

Source: Public Health England The Eatwell Guide March 2016

> **KEY WORDS**
>
> **Free sugars** – added to foods and drinks by manufacturers, cooks or consumers and found naturally in honey, syrups and fruit juice
>
> **Not free sugars** – found naturally in products, e.g. in milk

Many foods that contain sugar include **free sugars**, which can be high in energy but contain very few other nutrients. This can cause weight gain, obesity and increase the risk of tooth decay.

Manufacturers, chefs and consumers add sugars to products and dishes to make them taste sweeter and more palatable. These are called free sugars. Sugars found naturally in honey, syrups and fruit juice are also known as free sugars.

Sugars which are found naturally in foods are not counted, for example:

- in fresh, dried or frozen fruits and vegetables
- in milk, cheese and natural yoghurt.

Although ingredients lists are required by law on food products it is sometimes difficult to spot the difference between a free sugar and an ingredient that is not free sugar.

The following is a list of some of the common free sugars:

- cane sugar
- honey
- brown sugar
- dextrose
- fructose
- sucrose
- maltose
- fruit juice concentrate
- corn syrup
- mollases

On the nutritional labelling on the cereal bar packet the amount of sugar in the product will include free sugars and not free sugars (see Figure 1.4). Look at the label on the food to see whether there are free sugars in the product and how high up the food label list they appear.

An ingredients list on a food label always starts with the highest quantity and finishes with the smallest.

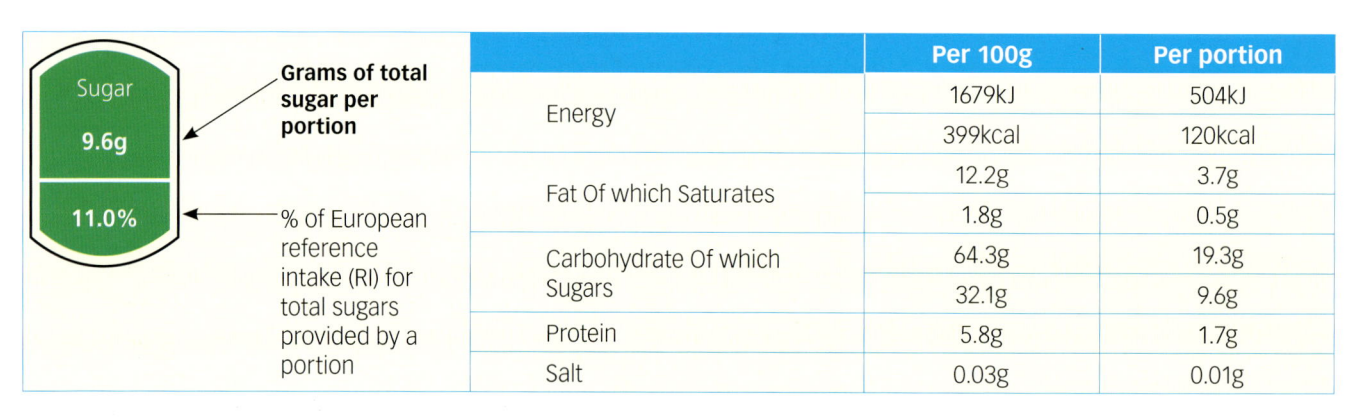

Sugar
9.6g ← **Grams of total sugar per portion**

11.0% ← % of European reference intake (RI) for total sugars provided by a portion

	Per 100g	Per portion
Energy	1679kJ	504kJ
	399kcal	120kcal
Fat Of which Saturates	12.2g	3.7g
	1.8g	0.5g
Carbohydrate Of which Sugars	64.3g	19.3g
	32.1g	9.6g
Protein	5.8g	1.7g
Salt	0.03g	0.01g

▲ Figure 1.4 Ingredients and nutritional information from a cereal bar

Figure 1.4 shows the ingredients in a cereal bar: can you spot the free sugars on the label?

Some of the sugars will be from:

- dried fruits and raisins – **not free sugars**
- glucose syrup, sugar, honey – **free sugars.**

Remember sugary drinks are not needed in and we should change these to water, low fat milk or sugar free drinks.

Cutting down on salt

Reducing the amount of salt can:

- reduce blood pressure
- reduce the risk of heart disease
- reduce the risk of a stroke.

Adults should have no more than 6 g salt per day and children should have less.

Remember salt is added to many foods that you buy so you need to check the labels carefully.

Topic 1 The relationship between diet and health

Topic link: Section A Topic 3

How much food do I need

Topic link: Section A Topic 4 Energy Balance

Everyone needs different amounts of energy to maintain a healthy body weight. The amount of energy we need depends on many different factors. One of the main ones is how active we are. If we do not use all the energy we consume it will be stored as fat.

Table 1.3 shows the daily energy requirements.

Table 1.3 Daily Energy requirements

Age	Daily energy requirements			
	Males		Females	
	Kcals	KJ	Kcals	KJ
1	765	3201	717	3000
2	1004	4201	932	3899
3	1171	4899	1076	4502
4	1386	5799	1291	5402
5	1482	6201	1362	5699
6	1577	6598	1482	6201
7	1649	6899	1530	6402
8	1745	7301	1625	6799
9	1840	7699	1721	7201
10	2032	8502	1936	8100
11 and over	2500	10,460	2000	8368

Source: Public Health England The Eatwell Guide March 2016

> ✔ **KEY POINTS**
>
> ✔ No more than 35 per cent of our food energy should come from fat.
> ✔ No more than 11 per cent of food energy should come from saturates.
> ✔ Carbohydrates should supply 50 per cent of our food energy.
> ✔ No more than 5 per cent of food energy should come from free sugars.
>
> (British Nutrition Foundation. 2015)

> **TEST YOURSELF**
>
> 1 Explain why the green and yellow sections of the Eatwell Guide are the largest.
> 2 Explain why the purple section of the Eatwell Guide is the smallest.
> 3 Why is it important that we do not call the section 'Bread, rice, potatoes, pasta and other starchy foods' the carbohydrate section?

Stretch and challenge

1. Use one or more of the following websites to find out further information about the Eatwell Guide.

   - www.nhs.uk/livewell/healthy-eating
   - www.foodafactoflife.org.uk
   - www.nutrition.org.uk

2. Investigate why there are concerns about the amount of free sugars eaten.

PRACTICAL ACTIVITY

Teenagers often eat snack meals.
Prepare, cook and serve a snack meal for a teenager.
Explain how you have adapted your ingredients so that it fits the Eatwell Guide.

The government's guidelines for a healthy diet

The government's recommendation is to use the Eatwell Guide as a model for healthy eating. The plate shows visually how different foods contribute to a healthy balanced diet. The size of the segment is linked to the government's recommendations for a diet that would provide children over five and healthy adults all their recommended nutrients.

The government has also produced other guidance linked to healthy eating, including the Department for Health's **eight tips for healthy eating** and the **five-a-day campaign**.

The eight tips for healthy eating

The eight tips for healthy eating are clearly linked to the Eatwell Guide.

1. Base your meals on starchy foods.
2. Eat lots of fruit and vegetables.
3. Eat more fish – aim for two portions a week; one of these should be oily.
4. Cut down on saturated fat and sugar.
5. Eat less salt – adults should eat no more than 6 g per day.
6. Get active and try to maintain a healthy weight.
7. Don't get thirsty - drink plenty of water.
8. Don't skip breakfast.

Five-a-day

To encourage us to eat more fruit and vegetables, the UK government introduced the 'five-a-day' campaign. This is to ensure that you get a variety of vitamins, minerals, trace elements and fibre in your diet. This will include the antioxidants and plant chemicals you need for good health.

Topic 1 The relationship between diet and health

▲ Figure 1.5 Fruits and vegetables can be eaten in a variety of ways

One adult portion is made up of 80 g of fruit or vegetables. Eating them fresh, frozen, canned or dried are all excellent ways of achieving your five-a-day. However, recent research has suggested that we now need to eat much more than five portions of fruit and vegetables a day.

Table 1.4 Guidelines on one portion of a 'five-a-day' source

Fruit or vegetable	One portion
Small-sized fresh fruit	Two or more small fruit (e.g. two plums, two satsumas, two kiwi fruit, three apricots, six lychees, seven strawberries or 14 cherries).
Medium-sized fresh fruit	One piece of fruit (e.g. apple, banana, pear, orange or nectarine).
Large fresh fruit	Half a grapefruit, one slice of papaya, one slice of melon (5 cm slice), one large slice of pineapple or two slices of mango (5 cm slices).
Dried fruit	A portion of dried fruit is around 30 g. **Remember** – dried fruit is high in sugar. Try to swap dried fruit for fresh fruit.
Tinned fruit in natural juice	One portion is roughly the same quantity of fruit that you would eat for a fresh portion.
Green vegetables	Two broccoli spears or four heaped tablespoons of cooked kale, spinach, spring greens or green beans.
Cooked vegetables	Three heaped tablespoons of cooked vegetables, such as carrots, peas or sweetcorn, or eight cauliflower florets.
Salad vegetables	Three sticks of celery, a 5 cm piece of cucumber, one medium tomato or seven cherry tomatoes.
Tinned and frozen vegetables	Roughly the same quantity as you would eat for a fresh portion.
Pulses and beans	Three heaped tablespoons of baked beans, haricot beans, kidney beans, cannellini beans, butter beans or chickpeas. **Remember**, however much you eat, beans and pulses count as a maximum of one portion a day.
Juices and smoothies	One 150 ml glass of unsweetened 100% fruit or vegetable juice can count as a portion. But only one glass counts.
Ready-made foods	Fruit and vegetables contained in shop-bought ready-made foods can also count toward your 'five-a-day'. Always read the label.

(Source http://www.nhs.uk/Livewell/5ADAY/Pages/Portionsizes.aspx)

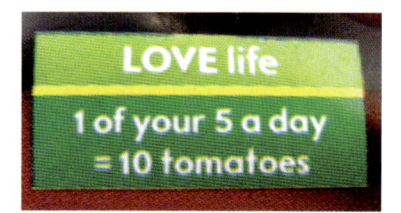

▲ **Figure 1.6** Labels used on food packaging showing the contribution the food makes to the 'five-a-day'

Some food products are labelled to show how many contributions they make to your 'five-a-day'. Figure 1.6 shows examples of labels.

PRACTICAL ACTIVITY

1 Prepare a savoury dish which would contain at least two of your 'five-a-day' portions of fruit and vegetables.
2 Explain how this dish would also contribute to meeting your other dietary needs.

RESEARCH ACTIVITY

Using a nutritional program investigate the amount of fibre found in a range of fruit and vegetables.

✔ KEY POINTS

- ✔ Base your diet on the eight tips for healthy eating.
- ✔ Include at least five portions of fruit and vegetables a day in your diet.
- ✔ Remember fruit juice and dried fruit can only count as one portion of fruit and vegetables.

TEST YOURSELF

1 State eight guidelines we should follow for healthy eating.
2 Why is it important that we have at least five portions of fruit and vegetables a day?
3 Which vegetable does not count as one of your five-a-day?

Topic 1 The relationship between diet and health

Major diet-related health issues caused by a poor diet and lifestyle

There are a number of diseases and conditions caused by having a poor diet and lifestyle.

Obesity

The number of people who are overweight or **obese** in the UK is increasing. Table 1.2 shows the changes in the numbers of people who were overweight and obese in 1993 and 2013.

> **KEY WORD**
>
> **Obese** – excessive fatness, measured as ratio of weight to height.

Table 1.2 Increase in the number of overweight and obese adults between 1993 and 2013

		1993	2013
Overweight	Men	41%	46%
	Women	32%	32%
Obese	Men	13.2%	26%
	Women	16.4%	23.8%
Overweight and obese	Men	57.6%	67.1%
	Women	48.6%	57.2%

(Source: Statistics on Obesity, Physical Activity and Diet England 2015, page 12)

People are now taking less exercise than in previous years, but are still eating the same amount of food. This means that their weight gradually increases and the ratio of their weight in relation to their height is high.

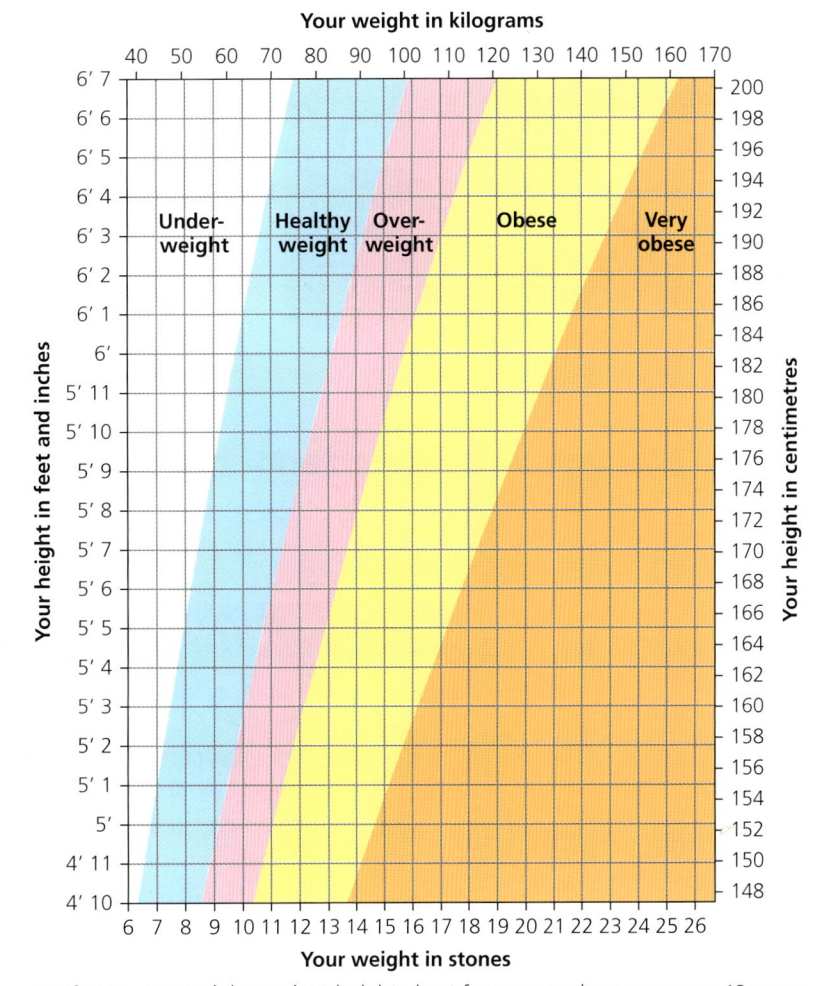

▲ Figure 1.7 Weight against height chart for men and women over 18 years

> **KEY WORD**
> **Diabetes** – a metabolic disorder caused by the poor absorption of glucose. This can be due to the failure to produce insulin (in type 1 insulin-dependent diabetes) or the poor response of tissues to insulin (in type 2 non-insulin-dependent diabetes). Type 1 (diabetes mellitus) develops in childhood. The onset of type 2 is usually from middle age onwards.

Being overweight is unhealthy because it puts a strain on the organs of the body. It can cause heart disease, high blood pressure, **diabetes**, osteoarthritis, varicose veins, breathlessness and chest infections. It also causes unhappiness, low self-esteem and may lead to depression.

The main cause of being overweight is eating more food than the body requires so that excess energy is stored as fat.

Topic link: *You will learn more about how the body stores excess energy as fat in Section A: Topic 4 Energy balance.*

Weight gain and weight loss

The number of people who are overweight or obese in the UK is increasing. People are now taking less exercise than in previous years, but are still eating the same amount of food.

The only way to lose weight is to reduce the number of calories consumed and combine this with increased physical exercise. Many people try to lose weight and the 'slimming industry' is a big part of the food market. There are clubs to help and support people by group therapy, slimming magazines and crash diets in the media, but they all rely on people controlling their intake of calories.

Meals for people who are trying to lose weight should include a variety of foods and follow the Eatwell Guide, reducing their intake of fat and sugar. We can buy reduced-fat, margarine-type spreads, salad dressings, low-sugar drinks, desserts, biscuits and yogurts. A calorie-controlled diet should consist of foods naturally low in fat, for example fruit and vegetables, white fish, poultry, skimmed milk and cheese, cereal, nuts and pulses.

People trying to lose weight should use low-fat methods of cooking, such as grilling, steaming, boiling and stir-frying.

Most foods have the amount of energy per 100 g printed on their nutritional label, so it is possible to count the calories. From December 2016 it will be the law to display nutritional information on the back of all pre-packed foods.

▲ Figure 1.8 A range of reduced-fat products

Stretch and challenge
Explain why there has been an increase in the number of overweight people between 1993 and 2013.

> **RESEARCH ACTIVITY**
> Visit a supermarket or look on a supermarket shopping website and investigate products aimed at adults on slimming diets.
> Using the information from the labels, compare the calories and nutritional values with similar 'non-diet' products.
> Collate the information in a chart.

Topic 1 The relationship between diet and health

> **INVESTIGATION ACTIVITY**
>
> Basic recipes can be adapted to reduce sugar content.
> Cakes made by the creaming method contain sugar.
> 1 Use the ingredients and method in the table to investigate whether you can successfully reduce the sugar content.
>
> | 100% sugar | 75% sugar | 50% sugar | 25% sugar |
> |---|---|---|---|
> | 50 g self raising flour
50 g sugar
50 g fat
1 egg | 50 g self raising flour
37 g sugar
50 g fat
1 egg | 50 g self raising flour
25 g sugar
50 g fat
1 egg | 50 g self raising flour
12.5 g sugar
50 g fat
1 egg |
>
> Method
> 1 Put oven on 180 ºC / gas mark 5.
> 2 Put the sugar and fat into a mixing bowl and beat until light and fluffy.
> 3 Crack the egg into a small basin and beat with a fork.
> 4 Gradually beat the egg into the fat and sugar mixture.
> 5 Fold in the flour.
> 6 Divide mixture evenly between eight cake cases.
> 7 Bake for 10–15 minutes until golden brown and springs back when touched.
>
> 2 Compare the different cakes for size, texture, colour and flavour. Produce a chart to record your findings.
> 3 What advice would you give to people about reducing the amount of sugar in a creamed cake mixture?

> **PRACTICAL ACTIVITY**
>
> Adapt a cake recipe to reduce the sugar and include more fruit and vegetables.

Cardiovascular disease

Cardiovascular disease is a term used to describe different types of diseases of the heart and circulatory system. Blood flow to the heart, brain or body is reduced because of a blood clot or narrowing of the arteries. Coronary heart disease is one of the main types of cardiovascular disease.

Topic link: Section A: Topic 3 Nutritional needs when selecting recipes for different groups of people.

Coronary heart disease

In the UK, coronary heart disease (CHD) is a major health problem and one of the main causes of death.

Causes of Coronary heart disease (CHD)

CHD is related to the amount of fat in the diet.

A diet high in saturated fats is also likely to be high in cholesterol. Cholesterol is a substance made in the liver and carried in the bloodstream. The cholesterol can build up and be deposited with other material as 'plaque' on the walls of the arteries, causing them to narrow. If the arteries then become blocked by a blood clot or more plaque, the person has a heart attack which, if severe, can cause death.

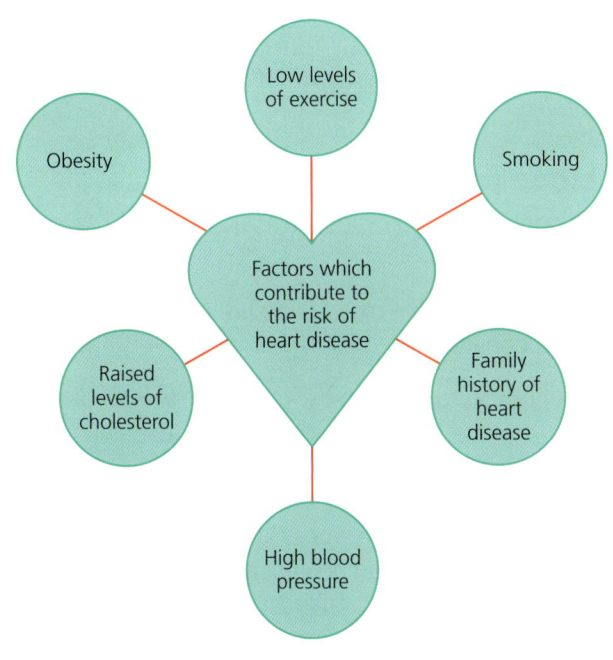

▲ Figure 1.9 Factors which influence the risk of heart disease

Factors which contribute to the risk of heart disease:
- Low levels of exercise
- Smoking
- Family history of heart disease
- High blood pressure
- Raised levels of cholesterol
- Obesity

The level of cholesterol in the blood depends on the amount of fatty acids in the diet. Saturated fatty acids can be replaced with polyunsaturated fats as alternatives to animal fat-based products. (Note that some low-fat spreads contain animal fat.) Soluble fibre is thought to remove cholesterol from arteries. This is discussed on page 55.

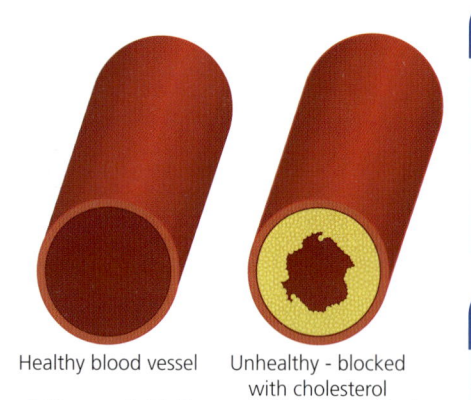

Healthy blood vessel   Unhealthy - blocked with cholesterol
▲ Figure 1.10 Plaque build-up in arteries

RESEARCH ACTIVITY

Your local health centre has asked for contributions to create a display on 'How to reduce your risk of heart disease'.

Produce suitable materials on one of the following:
- changes to your diet
- recipe book ideas
- foods to avoid
- changes to your lifestyle.

PRACTICAL ACTIVITY

Design and make a lower-fat luxury dessert suitable for someone who has CHD. Explain how you have modified your recipe.

Stretch and challenge

Using a nutrition programme calculate the nutritional value of your dessert and explain how it contributes to the recommended daily intake of an adult who has CHD.

Figure 1.11 below shows the general advice on how to reduce the risk of heart disease.

Stretch and challenge

Discuss why coronary heart disease is a major cause of death in the western world.

High blood pressure

In the UK, coronary heart disease (CHD) is a major health problem.

To reduce the risk of high blood pressure (and heart disease), the general advice is to:

- eat more fruits and vegetables – at least five portions a day
- eat a varied diet
- cut back on the fat in your diet and cooking
- eat more starchy carbohydrate
- use monounsaturated and polyunsaturated fats
- have fish instead of meat – at least twice a week.
- A diet high in salt can also be linked to high blood pressure.

Does this sound familiar? It is the Eatwell Guide again!

Topic link: *Section A Topic 3 nutritional needs when selecting for differnt groups of people, lowering the salt.*

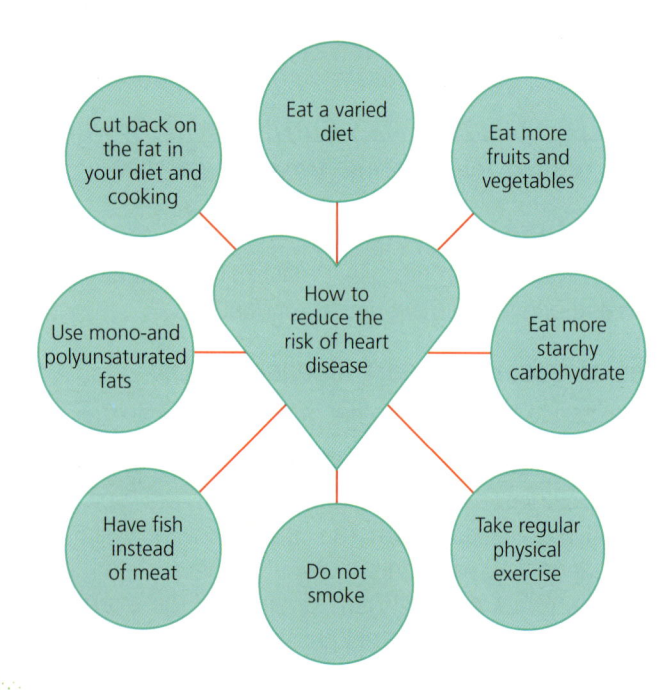

▲ Figure 1.11 How to reduce the risk of heart disease

Section A: Nutrition

Topic 1 The relationship between diet and health

> ✓ **KEY POINTS**
> ✓ CHD and high blood pressure is increasing.
> ✓ Obesity rates rising.
> ✓ Need to adapt diets to reduce the amount of fats and sugars.
> ✓ Use monounsaturated fats.

Diabetes

Diabetes is a medical condition where the glucose in the bloodstream is not balanced correctly. Glucose is carried in the blood to all body cells to supply them with energy. Insulin, a hormone produced by the pancreas, controls the amount of glucose in the bloodstream and stops it getting too high.

There are two types of diabetes:

- Type 1 – this is usually diagnosed in children and is caused by the pancreas not producing enough insulin. Type 1 diabetics have insulin injections daily and need to have a carefully balanced diet.
- **Type 2 diabetes** is usually diagnosed in older people, though there are more younger people being diagnosed with this due to a poor diet. Diets high in sugar can lead to type 2 diabetes. Type 2 diabetes is treated with a healthy diet and increased physical activity. Once diagnosed, diabetics may also have to take medication or have insulin injections.

Meals for those with diabetes should follow the guidance in the Eatwell Guide, which includes high-fibre starchy carbohydrate foods such as potatoes, rice and pasta, but should be low in sugar and sweet foods. Sorbitol (artificial sweetener) can be used instead of sucrose and glucose.

An increasing number of people have diabetes, particularly Type 2 diabetes. People with diabetes should maintain a healthy body weight. They should have a healthy diet that is low in saturated fat and salt and contains at least five portions of fruit and vegetables a day, and starchy foods such as bread, rice and potatoes.

▶ Figure 1.12 Those with diabetes must control their intake of sugar

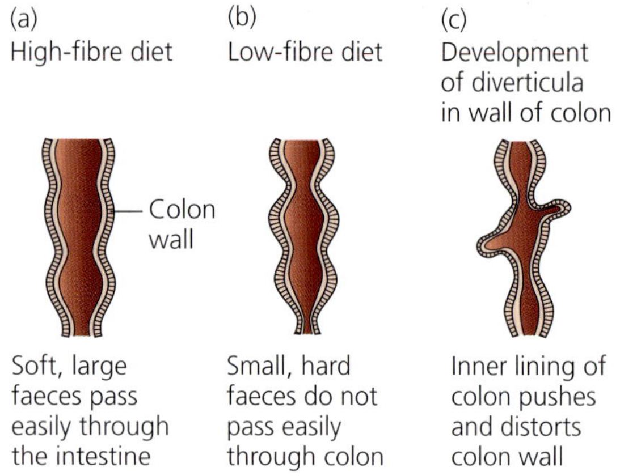

(a) High-fibre diet

Colon wall

Soft, large faeces pass easily through the intestine

(b) Low-fibre diet

Small, hard faeces do not pass easily through colon

(c) Development of diverticula in wall of colon

Inner lining of colon pushes and distorts colon wall

▲ Figure 1.13 Waste passing through the digestive system

KEY WORDS

Diverticular disease – caused by lack of fibre in the diet

Diverticulitis – a condition which affects the large intestine

Non starch polysaccharide (fibre) – the part of food that is not digested by the body

Osteoporosis – the bones start to lose minerals and their strength and break easily

Diverticulitis

Diverticulitis is a condition which affects the large intestine. It is often linked to having a diet which is low in fibre (**non-starch polysaccharide** [NSP]). The lining of the bowel becomes inflamed, infected and damaged.

Symptoms of **diverticular disease** include pain and discomfort in the abdomen and feeling bloated. Figure 1.13 shows what happens to your colon if you do not have a high-fibre diet.

✔ KEY POINT

✔ Increase the amount of high fibre foods to prevent diverticulitis.

Topic link: You will learn more about the effects of a deficiency in fibre in Section A: Topic 7 Carbohydrates.

Bone health (osteoporosis)

Healthy bones do not break easily. Calcium and other vitamins (vitamin D and phosphorus) and minerals are gradually added to children's, adolescents' and young adults' bones to strengthen them. Our bones are at their strongest between the ages of 20 and 35 when our peak bone mass is reached.

If we do not achieve peak bone mass then we are more likely to get **osteoporosis**. The bones start to lose minerals and their strength. If we lose too many minerals the bones become brittle and break.

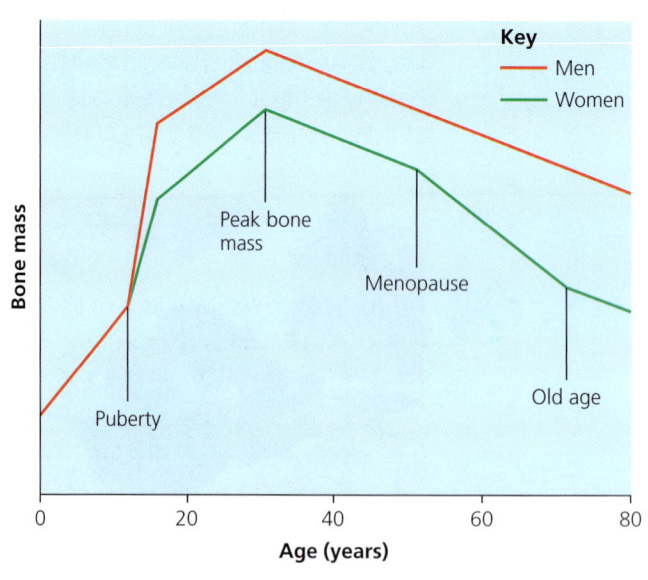

Source: Adapted with permission from Medical Research Council Human Nutrition Research

▲ Figure 1.14 Changes in bone mass with age

The following will increase your likelihood of suffering from osteoporosis:

- your genes – if other people in your family suffer from broken bones
- age – as you get older your bones become weaker

Section A: Nutrition

Topic 1 The relationship between diet and health

- race – Afro-Caribbean people suffer less from osteoporosis
- gender – women suffer more than men
- smoking
- low body weight
- if you have had previous fractures
- some medicines
- high alcohol consumption.

Dental health

To maintain healthy teeth you need to have a balanced diet based on the Eatwell Guide. Tooth decay is caused when:

- the bacteria in your mouth (plaque) feed on the sucrose found in the food you eat to produce an acid
- the acid then causes small holes in your teeth (dental caries).
- Sugars found naturally in fruits and vegetables are not as harmful as they are less likely to lead to tooth decay and are easier for the body to absorb. However, juice removed from fruit contains sugars that can cause tooth decay, so you are advised to drink only one glass of fruit juice (150 ml) a day.

▶ **Figure 1.15** Tooth decay can be caused by a poor diet

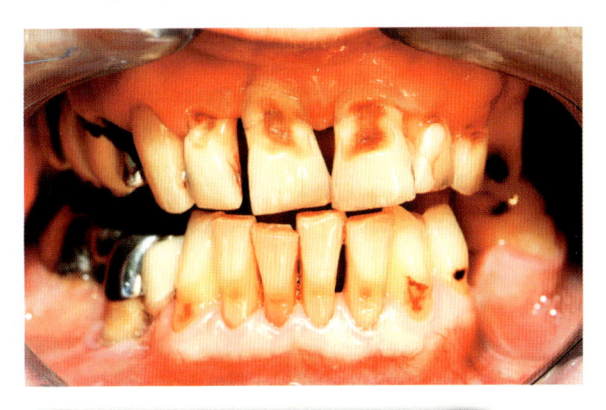

✓ **KEY POINT**

✓ Reduce sugar content of diet to reduce tooth decay.

Anaemia

KEY WORD

Anaemia – caused by lack of iron in the diet

Anaemia, caused by a lack of iron in the diet, is one of the most common nutritional problems worldwide. We need iron as it forms haemoglobin, which gives blood its red colour and carries oxygen round the body to the cells.

Women and children are the most at risk of developing anaemia. Teenage girls and women must make sure they have enough iron in their diet to cope with the loss of blood during menstruation. Pregnant women also need to have enough iron to support the baby's blood supply. Symptoms are tiredness and lack of energy.

Our bodies can store iron in the liver. The best sources of iron are:

- liver and kidney
- red meat
- oily fish
- leafy green vegetables.

In the UK, breakfast cereals and bread are fortified with iron. Iron obtained from red meat, known as haem iron, is more easily absorbed than that from vegetables. Vegetarians need to ensure that they get an adequate supply of iron from bread, pulses and vegetables. Iron absorption is reduced by the presence of tannins found in tea and coffee, and phytates found in unrefined cereals such as bran. Iron absorption is increased by eating non-haem, iron-rich foods with foods and drinks containing vitamin C.

Topic link: You will learn more about iron in Section A: Topic 9 Minerals.

✔ KEY POINTS

- ✔ Anaemia caused by lack of iron.
- ✔ Women more likely to suffer from anaemia than men.

TEST YOURSELF

1. Describe what the term obesity means.
2. State **three** causes of heart disease.
3. State **four** changes that a person with heart disease should make to their diet.
4. Explain why it is better to eat unsaturated fats than saturated fats.
5. Explain the difference between Type 1 and Type 2 diabetes.
6. What are the symptoms of diverticulitis?
7. State **three** factors which could increase your risk of osteoporosis.
8. Lack of which mineral causes anaemia?

Topic 2

Nutritional and dietary needs of different groups of people

→ **WHAT WILL I LEARN?**

By the end of this topic you should have developed a knowledge and understanding of:

→ the dietary needs for the different stages of lives
→ the lifestyle choices people make with reference to their diet
→ the dietary needs of people with specific medical conditions
→ how food allergies and intolerances affect what people eat
→ the dietary reference values
→ calculation of nutritional values.

Dietary needs for different stages of life

Most people make a choice about what type of food to eat at least two or three times a day. The availability of a wide range of foods makes it easier to choose foods that are nutritionally good for us, but we are all influenced by a variety of other factors and we all have differing nutritional needs. A range of different factors affects our choice of food.

During the different stages of life, people require different foods and quantities of nutrients to keep healthy. In this topic you are going to learn about the specific needs of different groups of people.

Topic links: You will learn more about the different nutrients in other Topics in Section A:

- Topic 4 Energy balance
- Topic 5 Protein
- Topic 6 Fat
- Topic 7 Carbohydrates
- Topic 8 Vitamins
- Topic 9 Minerals
- Topic 10 Water.

Babies

Babies are totally reliant on their parents to provide food. A baby needs essential nutrients for growth and development. Babies need energy-dense,

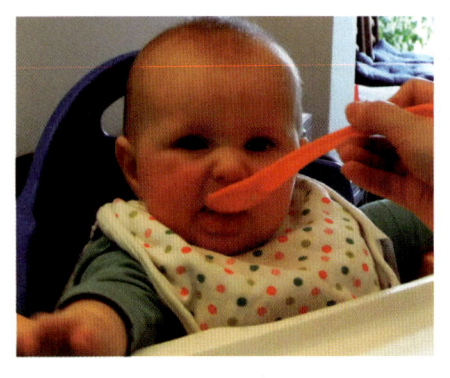

▲ Figure 2.1 At six months babies are weaned on to solid food

filling food that is easy to swallow. Food must be hygienic and safe. Babies initially drink only milk, but as they grow they require more energy, so they are weaned on to solid food.

Parents will want the food to be nutritious, appetising, easy to prepare, without additives, low in sugar and hygienic.

RESEARCH ACTIVITY

Design some promotional material to give a new parent some ideas for weaning foods for a six-month-old baby.

Stretch and challenge

Many women choose to breastfeed their babies.

Produce an information sheet for women on the benefits of breastfeeding their babies and provide them with some tips for healthy eating whilst breastfeeding.

Toddlers/pre-school children

Toddlers are growing fast, so they require a lot of energy from their food. They need a balanced diet that contains a high proportion of **complex carbohydrates** to provide this energy. If the Eatwell Guide is used as a model then toddlers and pre-school children should have the following portions:

- 5 portions – starchy foods
- 5 portions – fruit and vegetables
- 3 portions – dairy foods
- 2–3 portions – protein foods.

The food must be easy to hold, available in suitably sized portions, with interesting shapes, colours, textures and flavours.

KEY WORD

Complex carbohydrate – found in foods such as whole grains, vegetable like peas and beans.

RESEARCH ACTIVITY

Investigate what the portion size should be for a variety of foods from the different sections of the Eatwell Guide.

PRACTICAL ACTIVITY

Toddlers and young children sometimes do not like eating vegetables.
1. Prepare an interesting main course dish for a young child.
2. Explain clearly how you have introduced the vegetables to the dish and the contributions the dish will make to a child's daily nutritional needs.

School-aged children

School-aged children are still reliant on their parents, but they are influenced by the media and their peer group. They need products that meet current dietary guidelines on health while providing filling food, particularly for packed lunches.

Topic 2 Nutritional and dietary needs of different groups of people

School-aged children should eat a varied balanced diet which is based on the Eatwell Guide. They should regularly take part in physical activity so that they have a healthy body weight.

Adolescents

Adolescents are becoming aware of environmental, moral, economic and health issues. They also become more aware of peer group pressure and body image.

Body growth is rapid, so adolescents still require a lot of energy from their food, particularly boys during their growth spurts. Girls have a greater need for the mineral iron to replace that lost during menstruation.

Puberty is also the time when bones stop growing, and without sufficient calcium and phosphorus in the diet at this crucial time, there will be a weakening of the bones, leading to rickets and osteoporosis in later life.

Food must be affordable, fashionable, quick and easy to prepare, and suited to a busy and energetic lifestyle.

RESEARCH ACTIVITY

Many teenagers do not understand what is meant by a balanced diet.

Produce either a poster, storyboard or blog explaining what is meant by a balanced diet and give some healthy eating tips which could easily be followed by teenagers.

PRACTICAL ACTIVITY

Teenagers often cook their own meals when they get in from school.

1. Prepare a dish which they could eat as a main meal which is based on the proportions in the Eatwell Guide.
2. Explain how the dish helps to meet the nutritional needs of a teenager.

Stretch and challenge

1. Using a nutritional program, calculate the nutritional content of one portion of your meal from the practical activity above. Explain how it meets a teenager's needs.
2. Evaluate whether it could be improved further to meet their needs.

Adults

Adults' needs vary the most, depending on their lifestyle and occupation. The energy requirements of adults are lower than those of teenagers. The requirements for protein and most of the vitamins and minerals are similar or stay the same.

Many adults face the problem of consuming too much energy from food, leading to weight gain. They often look to buy products to help with weight loss. Some want foods that are lower in fat, salt or sugar and are eager to follow current healthy eating guidelines. They may also want luxury products as meals become more of a social occasion. Adults should base their diet on the Eatwell Guide.

Older people

Older people are growing in number, and many live on a limited income. They still require a balanced diet supplying a good range of nutrients, but they often suffer from loss of appetite.

They need appetising products in smaller quantities. They want easy-to-prepare, nutritional meals with easy-to-open packaging.

▲ Figure 2.2 Older adults enjoy cooking a meal together

RESEARCH ACTIVITY

What advice would you give to a catering company that wants to start a meals service for housebound older people?

Pregnant and lactating women

Pregnant and breastfeeding mothers must adapt their diet to provide adequate nutrients for themselves and their baby. A new mother does not need special food products, but must ensure that she has a varied, balanced diet. She must pay particular attention to ensuring that she has the following:

- an adequate supply of protein for the growth of the baby
- calcium and vitamin D for both her and the baby's bone and tooth development – if the mother does not have sufficient calcium in her diet for the baby's needs, it will be taken from the mother's bones and teeth
- folic acid supplements before and during the early stages of pregnancy to reduce the risk of spina bifida in the baby
- iron for the developing baby's blood supply; it also needs a store of iron in the liver as there is no iron in milk. If the mother does not get sufficient iron she will become anaemic
- a good supply of fruit and vegetables to provide vitamin C and fibre
- a diet that does not include too many fats and sugary foods as it is essential that she does not put on more than 10–12 kg in weight.

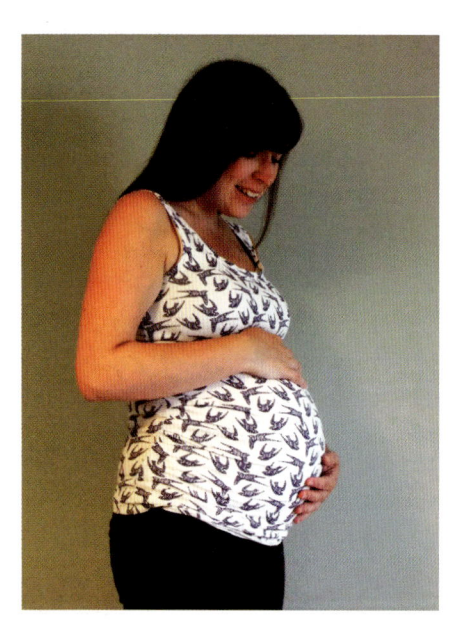

▲ Figure 2.3 A pregnant woman

Recent research has shown that mothers who follow a poor diet or who 'undereat' both before and during pregnancy may give birth to low-birthweight babies.

Topic 2 Nutritional and dietary needs of different groups of people

RESEARCH ACTIVITY

Produce a leaflet for pregnant mothers – 'A guide to healthy eating in pregnancy'.

PRACTICAL ACTIVITY

1. Produce a savoury main course dish that is high in iron and suitable for a pregnant mother.
2. Highlight which ingredients are high in iron.
3. Calculate the iron content per portion using a nutritional program.

Stretch and challenge

Investigate what foods a pregnant woman should avoid during pregnancy and explain the reasons why they should be avoided.

✔ KEY POINTS

- **During the different stages of life, people require different foods and quantities of nutrients.**
- **Babies need essential nutrients for growth and development, and energy-dense, filling foods.**
- **Toddlers need a balanced diet with a high proportion of complex carbohydrates.**
- **School-aged children should eat a varied balanced diet which is based on the Eatwell Guide.**
- **Adolescents require a lot of energy from their food, particularly boys during their growth spurts.**
- **Girls need the mineral iron to replace that lost during menstruation.**
- **Adults' needs vary depending on their lifestyle and occupation but should base their diet on the Eatwell Guide.**
- **Older people often suffer from loss of appetite so need appetising meals in smaller quantities.**
- **Pregnant women should ensure that they have good sources of energy and nutrients. They should maintain levels of calcium and iron.**

TEST YOURSELF

1. Explain why it is important for teenagers to eat a healthy, balanced diet.
2. Explain why breakfast is an important meal for everyone.
3. List **four** nutrients that are particularly important during pregnancy.
4. Give **one** reason why each of the nutrients you have listed is important.

KEY WORDS

Food intolerance – sensitivity to a food

Food allergy – when you have a severe reaction to a food

Anaphylactic reaction – an extreme reaction to a substance, needing immediate medical treatment

Coeliac disease – a medical condition caused by an allergy to the protein gluten present in the cereals wheat, barley and rye

Lactose intolerance – not able to digest milk sugar lactose

Food allergies and intolerances

Some people cannot eat certain types of food without becoming ill. This may be because of a medical condition or a reaction to food. This is known as **food intolerance** or **allergy**.

Our bodies have an immune system to protect us from harmful substances, but sometimes a person's body reacts too strongly to a particular substance. This is what happens when a person becomes allergic to a substance. Allergies to eggs, soya and certain artificial food flavours, colours or preservatives can also cause reactions.

Topic link: *Section C: Topic 3 Food safety principles – labelling and date marks.*

Nut allergy

Some allergies are very serious, for example, the allergic reaction to nuts. Some people have an **anaphylactic reaction** to even a minute quantity of an allergen in nuts. Their whole body reacts immediately and severely – blood vessels start to leak and they have difficulty breathing. They must be treated immediately with an injection of adrenalin, otherwise their reaction could result in death. In some cases even touching or breathing in particles of the allergen can cause a reaction. Consequently, even the smallest amount of nuts or nut contact must be included on food labelling.

Coeliac disease

Coeliac disease is an autoimmune disease triggered by the protein gluten, which is found in the grains wheat, rye and barley. Gluten damages the lining of the intestine and prevents nutrients from being absorbed. Adults with coeliac disease often have:

- anaemia
- weight loss and/or
- abdominal pain
- bloating
- diarrhoea.

The medical treatment for coeliac disease is a gluten-free diet. Gluten is commonly used in bread, pasta, biscuits, cakes and pizza. Food manufacturers may also use derivatives of these grains as thickeners. People with coeliac disease should check the labels on food products carefully to ensure they are safe for them to eat. Food products that have been certified gluten-free will have the Crossed Grain symbol on them.

▲ **Figure 2.4** Crossed Grain certification symbol for gluten-free foods found in food packaging

Those who are intolerant to certain foods

Some people develop sensitivity to certain foods, which gives them symptoms such as:

- diarrhoea,
- nausea,
- tiredness,
- weakness or
- stomach pains.

These reactions are not necessarily allergies, and it is often difficult to discover which foods the people are sensitive to.

Topic 2 Nutritional and dietary needs of different groups of people

> ✓ **KEY POINTS**
>
> ✓ People with allergies or food intolerances must read food labels carefully.
> ✓ There is a wide range of products available for people with special dietary needs.

An example of this is **lactose intolerance**, where a person cannot digest the milk sugar lactose. They become bloated, suffer abdominal pain and diarrhoea, so they have to avoid milk and milk products. Supermarkets now produce a range of food products which are lactose free, such as yoghurts and milk products.

Some people are intolerant to wheat, even though they do not have full coeliac disease. The list of food intolerances is getting longer and products now have to list their ingredients on their packaging by law.

▲ Figure 2.5 Alternatives to animal sources of milk

PRACTICAL ACTIVITY

Make a tray-bake product suitable for someone with coeliac disease.

Stretch and challenge

Suggest ways that someone with a lactose intolerance could ensure that they have sufficient calcium in their diet.

TEST YOURSELF

1 Why do people who have a nut allergy need to read food labels carefully?
2 What is coeliac disease?
3 If you suffer from coeliac disease what foods are you not able to eat?
4 If you are lactose intolerant which foods are you not able to eat?

Dietary Reference Values and calculating nutritional values

Different people need different amounts of nutrients depending on their age, lifestyle and stage of life.

Dietary Reference Values (DRVs)

In the UK, most of the estimated dietary requirements for particular groups of the population are based on advice that was published by the Committee on Medical Aspects of Food and Nutrition Policy (COMA) in the 1991 report Dietary Reference Values for Food Energy and Nutrients for the United Kingdom. These are known as the **Dietary Reference Values (DRVs)**.

Since this time, COMA has been superseded by the Scientific Advisory Committee on Nutrition (SACN). From time to time, SACN has reviewed the evidence for particular nutrients but in most cases has not identified a need to change the DRVs.

Nutrients

Nutrients are substances found in foods. They are divided into two types:

- **macronutrients** (fats, proteins and carbohydrates) – these are needed by the body in relatively large quantities and form the bulk of our diet.
- **micronutrients** (vitamins and minerals) – these are found in food and are vital to health, but are required in very small quantities.

Topic link: *In Topics 5–10 you will be learning about the different macro- and micronutrients.*

Nutrient requirements

DRVs are estimates of the requirements for groups of people. They are *not* recommendations or goals for individual people.

There are three types of estimates:

- **Estimated Average Requirements (EARs)** – An estimate of the average energy or nutrient needed by a group of people.
- **Reference Nutrient Intakes (RNIs)** – RNI is the amount of a nutrient that is enough to ensure that the needs of nearly all the group (97.5%) are being met. The RNI is used for recommendations on protein, vitamins and minerals.
- **Lower Reference Nutrient Intakes (LRNIs)** – LRNI is the amount that is enough for a group who only need small amounts. It is a useful measure of nutritional inadequacy.

Today, nutritionists have a wide knowledge of the role of nutrients in health and disease. We know that people need many different nutrients if they are to maintain health and reduce the risk of diet-related diseases. The amount of each nutrient needed is called the nutritional requirement. These are different for each nutrient and also vary between individuals and life stages (for example, women of childbearing age need more iron than men).

Tables 2.3a and b show the estimated average requirements for children and adults. The energy requirements for adults are based on the average amount of energy required for adults who are of a healthy weight and are moderately active.

KEY WORD

Dietary Reference Values (DRVs) – estimates of the amounts of nutrients needed for good health

KEY WORDS

Macronutrient – nutrients needed by the body in large amounts

Micronutrient – nutrients needed by the body in small amounts

Estimated Average Requirements (EARs) – the average amount of a nutrient needed

Reference Nutrient Intakes (RNIs) – the amount of a nutrient that is enough for most people in a group

Topic 2 Nutritional and dietary needs of different groups of people

Table 2.1a and 2.1b Estimated average requirement for energy for children and adults

	Males		Females	
Age (yrs)	MJ/d	kcal	MJ/d	kcal
4	5.8	1386	5.4	1291
5	6.2	1482	5.7	1362
6	6.6	1577	6.2	1482
7	6.9	1649	6.4	1530
8	7.3	1745	6.8	1625
9	7.7	1840	7.2	1721
10	8.5	2032	8.1	1936
11	8.9	2127	8.5	2032
12	9.4	2247	8.8	2103
13	10.1	2414	9.3	2223
14	11.0	2629	9.8	2342
15	11.8	2820	10.0	2390
16	12.4	2964	10.1	2414
17	12.9	3083	10.3	2462
18	13.2	3155	10.3	2462

	Males		Females	
Age (yrs)	MJ/d	kcal	MJ/d	kcal
19–24	11.6	2772	9.1	2175
25–34	11.5	2749	9.1	2175
35–44	11.0	2629	8.8	2103
45–54	10.8	2581	8.8	2103
55–64	10.8	2581	8.7	2079
65–74	9.8	2342	7.7	1912
75+	9.6	2294	8.7	1840

(Source: British Nutrition Foundation 2015)

KEY WORDS

Total carbohydrates – all starches, sugars and dietary fibre

Free sugars – sugars added to foods during manufacture plus honey, syrups and fruit juice

Total fat – includes all fats including saturated, mono and polyunsaturated fats

The dietary reference values for total fat, saturated fat, total carbohydrates and sugars are given as a percentage of the daily energy intake.

Table 2.2 shows the recommendations.

Table 2.2 DRVs for carbohydrate and fat as a percentage of energy intake

DRVs for carbohydrate and fat as a percentage of energy intake	
	% Daily Food Energy
Total Carbohydrate*	50%
of which free sugars*	Not more than 5%
Total Fat‡	Not more than 35%
of which Saturated Fat‡	Not more than 11%

*based on SACN 2015 recommendations for population aged 2 years and above
‡based on COMA 1991 recommendations for population aged 5 years and above

New recommendations were made for the amount of dietary fibre we should consume in 2015.

Table 2.3 below shows the recommended amounts.

Table 2.3 Daily recommended amounts of fibre

Age group	Recommended intake per day (g)
2–5 years	15g / day
5–11 years	20g / day
11–16 years	25g / day
17 years and over	30g / day

Table 2.4 shows the recommended target levels for salt.

Table 2.4 Target salt intake for children and adults

Age group	Maximum salt intake per day (g)
0–6 months	<1g / day
6–12 months	1g / day
1–3 years	2g / day
4–6 years	3g / day
7–10 years	5g / day
11 years and above	6g / day

(Source: British Nutrition Foundation 2015)

Table 2.5 Nutritional requirements of different groups of people

Age	Vitamin A µg/day	Thiamin mg/day	Riboflavin mg/day	Niacin mg/day	Vitamin B12 µg/day	Folate µg/day	Vitamin C mg/day	Vitamin D µg/day
Children								
0–3 months	350	0.2	0.4	3	0.3	50	25	8.5
4–6 months	350	0.2	0.4	3	0.3	50	25	8.5
7–9 months	350	0.2	0.4	4	0.4	50	25	7
10–12 months	350	0.3	0.4	5	0.4	50	25	7
1–3 years	400	0.5	0.6	8	0.5	70	30	7
4–6 years	500	0.7	0.8	11	0.8	100	30	–
7–10 years	500	0.7	1.0	12	1.0	150	30	–
Males								
11–14 years	600	0.9	1.2	15	1.2	200	35	–
15–18 years	700	1.1	1.3	18	1.5	200	40	–
19–50 years	700	1.0	1.3	17	1.5	200	40	–
50+ years	700	0.9	1.3	16	1.5	200	40	**
Females								
11–14 years	600	0.7	1.1	12	1.2	200	35	–
15–18 years	600	0.8	1.1	14	1.5	200	40	–
19–50 years	600	0.8	1.1	13	1.5	200	40	–
50+ years	600	0.8	1.1	12	1.5	200	40	–
Pregnancy	+10	+0.1***	+0.3	*	*	+100	+10	+10
Lactation	+350	+0.2	+0.5	+2	+0.5	+60	+30	+10

*No increment
** After age of 65 RNI is 10 µg/day
*** For last trimester only

(Source: http://www.nutrition.org.uk/attachments/053_Micronutrient%20DRVs.pdf)

Topic 2 Nutritional and dietary needs of different groups of people

Table 2.6 Mineral requirements for children and adults

Age	Calcium mg/day	Iron mg/day	Sodium mg/day	Iodine µg/day	Phosphorus mg/day
Children					
0–3 months	525	1.7	210	50	400
4–6 months	525	4.3	280	60	400
7–9 months	525	7.8	320	60	400
10–12 months	525	7.8	350	60	400
1–3 years	350	6.9	500	70	270
4–6 years	450	6.1	700	100	350
7–10 years	550	8.7	1200	110	450
Males					
11–14 years	1000	11.3	1600	130	775
15–18 years	1000	11.3	1600	140	775
19–50 years	700	8.7	1600	140	550
50+ years	700	8.7	1600	140	550
Females					
11–14 years	800	14.8	1600	130	625
15–18 years	800	14.8	1600	140	625
19–50 years	700	14.8	1600	140	550
50+ years	700	8.7	1600	140	550
Pregnancy	*	*	*	*	*
Lactation	550	*	*	*	+440

*No increment
** After age of 65 RNI is 10 µg/day
*** For last trimester only

Topic 3

Nutritional needs when selecting recipes for different groups of people

> ### → WHAT WILL I LEARN?
>
> By the end of this topic you should have developed a knowledge and understanding of:
> - → how to modify recipes and meals to follow current dietary guidelines
> - → how to modify dishes to promote health through altering or changing ingredients
> - → how to modify dishes to promote health through changing the method of cooking
> - → how to modify dishes to promote health through changing the portion size.

Modifying recipes and meals to follow current dietary guidelines

Everyone can use the Eatwell Guide as a model for planning and making balanced main course meals such as pasta dishes, curries and casseroles.

Topic link: *You will have learnt about using the Eatwell Guide to make balanced food choices in Topic 1 The relationship between diet and health.*

You need to think more carefully when you are adapting snacks, cakes and pastry products, as changing the proportion of some ingredients may mean the product does not work.

There is a variety of reasons we may want to modify recipes.

We usually modify recipes in order to improve the nutritional qualities of the product. The main point to remember when you are modifying the nutritional profile of recipes is that you are aiming to:

- lower the fat
- lower the sugar
- lower the salt
- increase the fibre.

When you are modifying a recipe you must also consider any other needs of the person you are cooking for.

Topic 3 Nutritional needs when selecting recipes for different groups of people

When modifying a recipe you may need to
- Change it to meet a specific dietary need
- Adapt it to meet cultural needs
- Change the method of cooking
- Change its appearance
- Improve the nutritional content
- Change its shape
- Improve its flavour
- Modify the ingredients used
- Change how it is assembled
- Improve its texture
- Improve its colour
- Reduce the cost

▲ **Figure 3.1** Why we modify recipes

Topic link: You will have learnt about the nutritional and dietary needs of different people in Topic 2 Nutritional and dietary needs of different groups of people.

When choosing ingredients to use in your cooking, the following advice from the NHS website gives you a guideline to whether the food is high or low in fats, sugars and salt.

Table 3.1 How do I know if a food is high in fat, saturated fat, sugar or salt?

There are guidelines to tell you if a food is high in fat, saturated fat, salt or sugar, or not. These are:

Total fat
High: more than 17.5 g of fat per 100 g
Low: 3 g of fat or less per 100 g

Saturated fat
High: more than 5 g of saturated fat per 100 g
Low: 1.5 g of saturated fat or less per 100 g

Sugars
High: more than 22.5 g of total sugars per 100 g
Low: 5 g of total sugars or less per 100 g

Salt
High: more than 1.5 g of salt per 100 g (or 0.6 g sodium)
Low: 0.3 g of salt or less per 100 g (or 0.1 g sodium)

(Source: http://www.nhs.uk/Livewell/Goodfood/Pages/food-labelling.aspx#Nutrition)

Figure 3.2 Lower-fat food alternatives

KEY WORDS

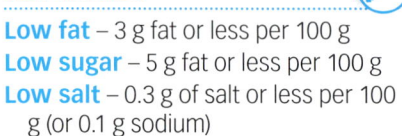

Low fat – 3 g fat or less per 100 g

Low sugar – 5 g fat or less per 100 g

Low salt – 0.3 g of salt or less per 100 g (or 0.1 g sodium)

Dietary guidelines – advice from the Government on recommended food intake in order to achieve dietary goals

You can modify recipes in many ways. Below are suggestions for how this can be achieved.

Altering or substituting ingredients

Lowering the fat

- Change to lower-fat or reduced-fat dairy products such as skimmed and semi-skimmed milk and zero per cent fat yoghurts.
- Use fromage frais, quark, or plain yogurt in place of cream.
- Use smaller amounts of stronger tasting cheese, such as mature Cheddar cheese or Parmesan instead of mild cheese.
- Use reduced-fat cheese when possible.
- Choose lean cuts of meat or cut visible fat off meat.
- Check the label on meat products and purchase ones with a lower fat content.
- Reduce the amount of butter on bread or change to a **low-fat** spread. Remember, you do not get low-fat butter.
- Choose canned fish such as tuna in water or brine rather than oil.
- Swap ice cream for sorbet.

Food manufacturers are continuing to develop reduced- and low-fat products. At the moment it is not possible to buy low-fat butter or low-fat hard cheeses. There are reduced-fat products on the market, some of which can be used in cooking but not all of them. You therefore have to read the labels carefully. Remember reduced-fat or low-fat products may be high in another nutrient which you are trying to reduce – for example a fruit yoghurt may be low in fat but contain a high amount of sugar.

RESEARCH ACTIVITY

Using food packaging or online supermarket websites investigate the information available on different butter, margarine and spreads, including low-fat spreads. Which ones are suitable for cooking with? Which ones are not recommended for baking and frying with?

Stretch and challenge

Having carried out the investigation above, explain the link with the fat and water content to their suitability for use in cooking.

INVESTIGATION ACTIVITY

Are all fats suitable for baking with?

Cakes made by the creaming method contain fat.

Use the recipe on the next page to make cakes using each of the following fats:

- hard butter
- soft butter
- hard yellow fat (for example, Stork)
- soft spread
- a low-fat spread (less than 5 per cent fat)

Topic 3 Nutritional needs when selecting recipes for different groups of people

RECIPE

Ingredients	Method
50 g self-raising flour 50 g sugar 50 g fat 1 egg	1 Put oven on 180° C / gas mark 5. 2 Put the sugar and fat into a mixing bowl and beat till light and fluffy. 3 Crack the egg into a small basin and beat with a fork. 4 Gradually beat the egg into the fat and sugar mixture. 5 Fold in the flour. 6 Divide mixture evenly between eight cake cases. 7 Bake for 10–15 minutes until golden brown and springs back when touched.

RESEARCH ACTIVITY

1 Compare different buns for size, texture, colour and flavour. Produce a chart to record your findings.
2 What advice would you give to people about the best fat to make a cake?

Stretch and challenge

Using a nutritional program enter the ingredients used for each of the cakes made. How does the nutritional value vary? Can you explain any links with the total fat content and the success of the cakes?

Lowering the sugar

- Reduce the quantity of sugar in recipes. In many recipes they will still work with a smaller amount. You would have to try some recipes out, though, for example creamed caked mixtures and whisked sponges.
- Replace sugar with dried or fresh fruit, for example banana in muffins adds both sweetness and moisture.
- Use sweeteners which add flavour.

Remember many artificial sweeteners will not work in all recipes.

▲ Figure 3.3 Alternative sweeteners

Lowering the salt

- Make use of herbs and spices instead of salt.
- Read the labels on food products and purchase ones with a lower salt content, for example baked beans which are low in salt.
- Reduce the amount of processed foods you eat, for example ready meals, processed meats and snacks.
- Reduce the amount of savoury snacks you eat, for example crisps.
- Read labels and check that sodium has not been added to the ingredients. (You will sometimes see this added to bread products and cereals.)
- Read the labels on food and avoid foods which have a lot of salt added to them (for example, if you look at some stock cubes salt is the highest ingredient in the stock cube). Table 3.2 shows foods which are high in salt.

▲ Figure 3.4 Ingredients which can be used to replace salt.

Table 3.2 Foods which are high in salt

Foods that are almost always high in salt	Foods that can be high in salt
Bacon, ham and smoked meats Cheese Pickles Salami Salted and dry roasted nuts Salt fish and smoked fish Soy sauce Gravy granules, stock cubes and yeast extract	Bread, bread products like wraps, crumpets, scones and sandwiches Pasta sauces Savoury snacks like crisps and salted nuts Pizza Ready meals Soup Sausages Tomato ketchup, mayonnaise and other sauces Breakfast cereals

(Source: http://www.nhs.uk/change4life/Pages/high-salt-foods.aspx)

Increasing the amount of fibre

- Incorporate extra vegetables into casseroles, soups, pasta dishes, meat sauces and stir-fries.
- Use wholegrain cereal products, such as wholemeal pasta, wholemeal bread, brown rice.
- Substitute all or half and half wholemeal flour for white flour.
- Choose breakfast cereals which are wholegrain.
- Add fresh or dried fruit to puddings, cakes and biscuit recipes.
- Have dried fruit, nuts and seeds as snacks.
- Add seeds such as sunflower and flax seeds to crumble toppings, bread, breakfast cereals, biscuit and cake mixtures.

▲ Figure 3.5 Foods containing fibre which can be added to many recipes

Changing the cooking method

As well as changing the ingredients used you can also modify the method of cooking to reduce the amount of fat in food.

Topic link: *You will learn about how cooking methods affect the nutritional value of foods in Section C: Topic 2 Sensory and nutritional properties.*

Some traditional methods of cooking use a lot of added fat, so try to avoid roasting, shallow-and deep-frying.

Table 3.3 shows the comparison of cooking potatoes in three different ways.

Table 3.3 Nutritional value per 100 g of potatoes cooked by different methods

Nutrient	Homemade chips fried in blended oil	Boiled potatoes	Baked potatoes	Roast potatoes in blended oil
Energy kJ/Kcal	796 kJ 189 kcal	306 kJ 72 kcal	581 kJ 138 kcal	630 kJ 149 kcal
Fat	6.7 g	0.1 g	0.2 g	4.5 g
Carbohydrate	30.1 g	17.0 g	31.7 g	25.9 g
Protein	3.9 g	1.8 g	3.9 g	2.9 g
Fibre	2.2 g	1.2 g	2.7 g	1.8 g

▲ Figure 3.6 Change your method of cooking: try using a steamer

(Source http://explorefood.foodafactoflife.org.uk)

Topic 3 Nutritional needs when selecting recipes for different groups of people

- Grill or oven-bake foods (instead of frying), which will remove some of the fat from them.
- Steam fish instead of frying.
- Poach, bake or boil foods so that no fat is added.
- Dry-fry meat in a non-stick pan.
- Use fats and oils sparingly. Try to spray oil as this just puts a thin film on the pan.
- When stir-frying, if the pan is getting dry add a small amount of water so steam is created to complete the cooking.
- When frying ensure the fat is at the correct temperature so that less fat is absorbed by the food. When it is cooked put the food on to a kitchen towel to absorb any excess fat on the outside of the food.

PRACTICAL ACTIVITY

Find either a basic spaghetti bolognaise recipe or a fruit crumble recipe. Modify the recipe to produce an innovative, healthier product that will appeal to teenagers.

Changing the portion size

As well as looking at the proportion of food we eat in comparison to our energy expenditure, we need to be aware of our portion sizes of different foods. The Eatwell Guide shows the proportion of different foods we should eat each day. When we cook food we should look at what the recommended portion size is, and use that alongside the Eatwell Guide when planning meals.

RESEARCH ACTIVITY

Investigate what the correct portion size is per person for the following foods:

- bread
- jacket potatoes
- rice
- pasta
- green vegetables
- baked beans
- apple
- dried fruit
- cheese
- sausages
- fruit juice
- strawberries

✔ KEY POINTS

- ✔ **Include a high proportion of starchy foods and fruit and vegetables in comparison to protein, dairy foods, fats and sugars.**
- ✔ **Adapt recipes by replacing high-fat, sugar and salt ingredients.**
- ✔ **Change the cooking method to one which does not need fat.**
- ✔ **Check portion sizes carefully.**

TEST YOURSELF

1. State the **four** areas of our diet which we should be changing.
2. State **three** methods of cooking which do not need fat adding to them.
3. State **two** different flavourings which could be used instead of salt.
4. Explain why it is important that you know what the recommended portion size is for different foods.

Topic 4   Energy balance

> **→ WHAT WILL I LEARN?**
>
> By the end of this topic you should have developed a knowledge and understanding of:
> → the relationship between food intake and physical activity
> → how to maintain a healthy body weight throughout life
> → how to calculate energy and the main sources of energy in our diet
> → the main factors that influence an individual's energy requirements.

The relationship between food intake and physical activity

We need energy to stay alive, move around and to keep warm. We get energy from the food we eat.

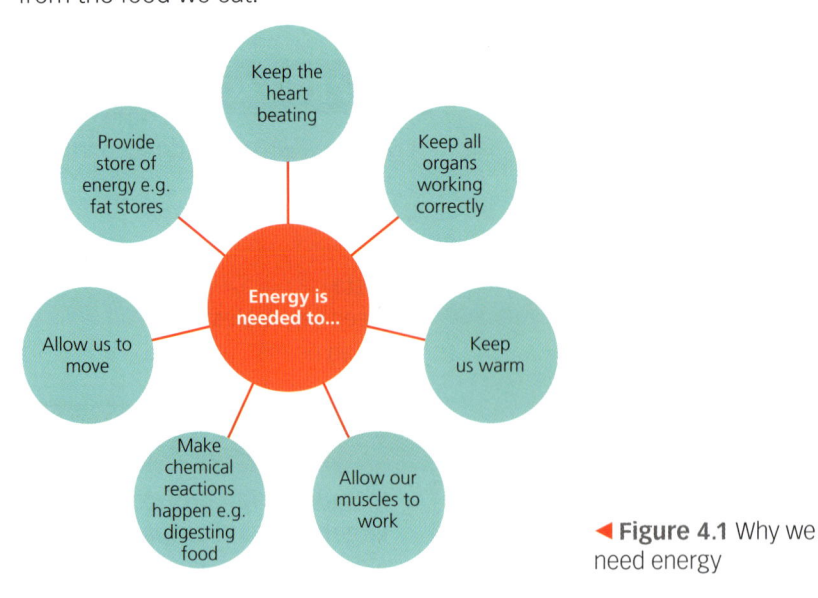

Energy is needed to...
- Keep the heart beating
- Keep all organs working correctly
- Keep us warm
- Allow our muscles to work
- Make chemical reactions happen e.g. digesting food
- Allow us to move
- Provide store of energy e.g. fat stores

◀ **Figure 4.1** Why we need energy

The relationship between the energy input and the energy we use is known as **energy balance**.

Energy is measured in **kilocalories (kcal)** or **kilojoules (kJ)**. Our bodies obtain energy from the foods we eat.

- Our body prefers to get energy from carbohydrate foods.
- Fats also supply our bodies with energy.
- We can also get energy from protein foods, but if it is used for energy it cannot be used for its main function which is growth and repair.

To be used for energy all foods have to be broken down through digestion into glucose units.

▲ **Figure 4.2** Older adults have a lower BMI

Topic 4 Energy balance

Basal metabolic rate

The amount of energy we need varies with age, gender and the amount of activity we carry out. Of the energy we consume, 70 per cent is used for all bodily functions (breathing, warmth, nerves, brain cells, digestion). This is called our **basal metabolic rate (BMR)**. The rest of our energy is used for all other activities.

- Infants and young children tend to have a higher BMR because they are growing rapidly.
- Men often have a higher BMR than women.
- Older adults have a lower BMR because they have less muscle mass than younger people.

To calculate your body mass you use the following calculation:

$$\frac{\text{weight in kg}}{(\text{height in m})^2} = \text{BMI}$$

For example, if you weigh 70 kg and you are 1.75 m tall, your BMI would be 22.9.

The BMI weight ranges, as set out by the World Health Organization (WHO), are outlined below.

- If your BMI is less than **18.4**, you are underweight for your height.
- If your BMI is between **18.5 and 24.9**, you are an ideal weight for your height.
- If your BMI is between **25 and 29.9**, you are over the ideal weight for your height.
- If your BMI is between **30 and 39.9**, you are obese.
- If your BMI is over **40**, you are clinically obese.

> **KEY WORDS**
>
> **Body mass index (BMI)** – a measurement which compares weight to height and is used to measure obesity
>
> **Basal metabolic rate (BMR)** – amount of energy we need for all bodily functions
>
> **Energy balance** – the relationship between energy input and energy used by the body
>
> **Kilocalories (kcal)** and **kilojoules (kJ)** – measurements of energy in foods
>
> **Physical activity level (PAL)** – the energy used for all types of movement

Stretch and challenge

What are the consequences for adults if they do not fall in the correct BMI band?

Physical activity level (PAL)

As well as having a BMR, people use energy for all other types of movement. This is called our **physical activity level (PAL)**. The amount of energy a person uses to complete different activities will vary depending on their weight. Table 4.1 shows what different PAL levels mean.

Table 4.1 What different PAL levels mean

Physical activity level (PAL)	Explanation
1.4	A low level of physical activity at work and/or during leisure time. This applies to a large proportion of the UK population.
1.6 (women) 1.7 (men)	Represents a moderate-intensity activity.
1.8 (women) 1.9 (men)	Represents a high level of physical activity.

How to calculate the main sources of energy in our diet

Different foods provide us with different amounts of energy. Table 4.2 shows you the amount of energy gained from the three main sources of energy in the diet.

Table 4.2 Amount of energy obtained from the main nutrients

1 g carbohydrate	1 g fat	1 g protein
3.75 kcal/16kJ	9 kcal/37kJ	4 kcal/17kJ

To calculate the amount of energy obtained from different foods you multiply the number of grams of the nutrient by the kcals/kJ. The higher the number, the more energy dense is the food.

It is recommended that we get the following percentage of energy from the different nutrients:

- 15 per cent protein
- 35 per cent or less from fat
- 50 per cent from carbohydrates with a maximum of 11 per cent energy from free sugar
- Alcohol also supplies the body with energy.

RESEARCH ACTIVITY

1 Using a nutritional program investigate the energy content per 100 g of the following foods. Put them in rank order, with the energy-dense ones at the top.

- potato crisps
- roast chicken
- green salad
- chicken curry
- boiled spaghetti
- eating apple
- fried chips
- muesli
- watermelon
- boiled potatoes

2 Explain what the link is between the energy density and the number of calories per 100 g.

KEY WORD

Calorie – a unit of energy that is used to give the energy yield of foods and the energy expenditure by the body

Table 4.3 shows the amount of energy different groups of people require. This is based on the lifestyle and activity levels of the UK population.

Table 4.3 Estimated average requirements for energy

Age	Males		Females	
	MJ/day	kcal/day	MJ/day	kcal/day
4	5.8	1386	5.4	1291
5	6.2	1482	5.7	1362
6	606	1577	6.2	1482
7	6.9	1649	6.4	1530
8	7.3	1745	6.8	1625
9	7.7	1840	7.2	1721
10	8.5	2032	8.1	1936
11	8.9	2127	8.5	2032
12	9.4	2247	8.8	2103
13	10.1	2414	9.3	2223
14	11.0	2629	9.8	2342
15	11.8	2820	10.0	2390
16	12.4	2964	10.1	2414
17	12.9	3083	10.3	2462
18	13.2	3155	10.3	2462
19–24	11.6	2772	9.1	2175
25–34	11.5	2749	9.1	2175
35–44	11.0	2629	8.8	2103
45–54	10.8	2581	8.8	2103
55–64	10.8	2581	8.7	2079
67–74	9.8	2342	7.7	1912
75+	9.6	2294	8.7	1840
Pregnant women require an additional 0.8MJ/200Kcal per day in final 3 months of pregnancy				

(Source: British Nutrition Foundation 2015)

Topic 4 Energy balance

The main factors that influence an individual's energy requirements

Different people require different amounts of energy depending on their stage in life.

If you eat and drink food higher in energy than your body needs, the energy is stored as fat and you gain weight and may eventually become obese. If you use more energy than the calories you consume you will lose weight.

Gender

Males need more energy than females. This is because they are usually larger and have more muscles.

Age

Babies and young children need more energy because they are very active; teenagers also need more energy as they are growing and may also be active. As people get older the amount of energy they need reduces.

Activity levels

The more active you are the more energy you need. If you work in an office you will not need as much energy to carry out your work as someone who has a very physical job (such as a builder). You also need more energy if you are doing a lot of physical activity, for example when climbing mountains or playing sport.

Health

If you are unwell your body may use more energy to fight off the disease; however, it may also reduce your appetite as you do not feel well. This means your body will use your energy reserves from fat stored in your body and you may then lose weight.

Pregnancy and lactating women

A woman will need additional energy in the last 3 months of pregnancy or when breastfeeding.

Size, body weight and genetics

If you have a lean body it is metabolically more active. People who have a leaner body are more likely to burn off excess energy than those who have a heavier body.

▲ Figure 4.3 Babies and young children require more energy

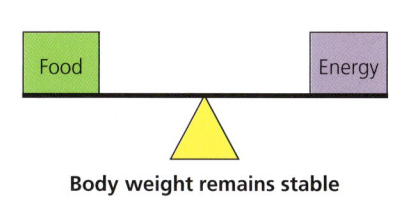

▲ Figure 4.4 It is a matter of choice

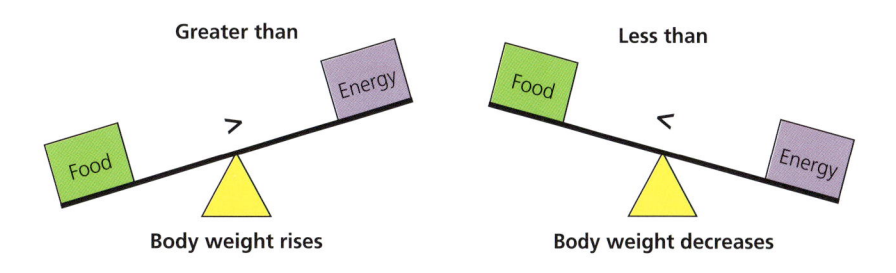

RESEARCH ACTIVITY

1 Use nutrition software to analyse the amount of energy that you should be consuming. Input everything that you consume in one day. Remember to include all of your drinks and snacks. Analyse your results and make a list of the ways that you could improve your diet.
2 Research how much energy you use doing each of the following activities for an hour:
   - playing tennis
   - walking slowly
   - playing a video game
   - dancing
   - cycling

✔ KEY POINTS

✔ Requirements for energy vary for different groups.
✔ We need to maintain a balance of energy input and energy output.
✔ If too much food is consumed it is stored as fat, resulting in weight gain.
✔ If food consumed equals the energy used, your weight stays the same.
✔ If food consumed is greater than the energy used, weight increases.
✔ If food consumed is less than the energy used, there is weight loss.

TEST YOURSELF

1 What units are used to measure energy?
2 Explain what is meant by basal metabolic rate.
3 Explain what is meant by physical activity level.
4 State four factors that affect how much energy a person needs.
5 State one group of people who might have a higher energy intake.
6 Which nutrient provides the most energy per gram?
7 What is meant by the term 'energy dense'?

Topic 5 — Protein

> **WHAT WILL I LEARN?**
>
> By the end of this topic you should have developed a knowledge and understanding of:
> - the structure of proteins, including the difference between high biological value and low biological value proteins
> - the functions of proteins in the diet
> - the main sources of protein in the diet
> - what happens if we have a deficiency or excess of protein in our diet.

Types and functions of protein in the diet

Protein is a macronutrient. **Macronutrients** are nutrients needed by the body in large amounts.

Protein is made up of complex chains of molecules called **amino acids**.

- There are 20 different types of amino acid, each with a specific function in the body.
- Some amino acids are essential for both adults and children (**essential amino acids**), but they cannot be made by the body, so they have to be provided through the food we eat.
- All the other amino acids can be made by the body from the protein eaten in other foods.

The foods that contain all the essential amino acids are said to have a **high biological value** (HBV). Most of these come from animal sources (meat, fish, poultry and dairy products) plus the vegetable source, soya. As the vegetarian market grows there is a large range of food products made from soya, such as soya mince, textured vegetable protein (known as TVP), and tofu. Another HBV protein is Quorn®, which is the brand name for a food product made from mycoprotein.

Foods that do not contain all the essential amino acids are said to have **low biological value** (LBV). Low biological value sources of protein include cereals, peas, beans, pulses, nuts and seeds.

Low biological value proteins can easily be combined in a meal or product to provide all the essential amino acids. This is called **food combining** or **complementary proteins**. Vegetarian, vegan or other limited diets rely on combining LBV proteins, for instance beans on toast, dhal and rice, hummus and pitta bread, to form proteins of higher value.

KEY WORDS

Macronutrients – nutrients needed by the body in large amounts.
Amino acids – the smallest units of a protein
Complementary proteins – mixing different low biological value proteins to supply all the essential amino acids
Essential amino acids – amino acids that cannot be made by the body (8 for adults, 10 for children)
Food combining – mixing different low biological value proteins to supply all the essential amino acids
High biological value (HBV) proteins – proteins that contain all the essential amino acids
Low biological value (LBV) proteins – proteins that do not contain all the essential amino acids

▲ **Figure 5.1** High biological value protein foods

▲ **Figure 5.2** Low biological value protein foods

PRACTICAL ACTIVITIES

1 Prepare a main course product that combines a range of LBV proteins.
2 Use nutritional software to find out how one portion of the product meets the needs of a teenager.

The functions of protein in the diet

We need to eat protein every day. The amount of protein required changes depending on our age and stage in life. Table 5.1 shows the amount of protein needed by different groups.

Table 5.1 Amount of protein required per day

Age group	RNI per day (g)
0–3 m	12.5
4–6 m	12.7
7–9 m	13.7
10–12 m	14.9
1–3 y	14.5
4–6 y	19.7
7–10 y	28.3

(Source: British Nutrition Foundation 2015)

The reference nutrient intake (RNI) is 0.75 g of protein per kilogram of bodyweight. If an adult weighs 62 kg they will need 62 × 0.75 g per day = 45.5 g protein per day. Pregnant women need an extra 6 g per day and breastfeeding women need an extra 11 g per day in the first six months and 8 g per day for the following 6 months.

Topic 5 Protein

Functions of protein

- Used for growth, especially in children and pregnant women.
- Used to repair body tissue after illness, accidents and surgery; renewal of cell proteins for people of all ages.
- Enzymes vital for metabolism are composed of proteins.
- Hormones, which regulate some important bodily functions, are also composed of protein.
- Proteins provide a secondary source of energy. When the body has used all the amino acids it needs for construction, the remainder are 'burnt' for energy.

Protein deficiency

Protein deficiency is rare in the developed world. However, not eating enough protein can cause various problems:

- In children, growth slows down or stops.
- Digestive upsets are caused as enzymes are not produced.
- The liver fails to function normally.
- Muscles become weak, so limbs are thin and the tummy is soft and may look distended.

Sources of protein in the diet

Animal sources include:

- all meats, such as poultry, offal and game
- fish
- cheese
- milk
- eggs
- gelatine.

Vegetable sources include:

- soya beans and soya products
- pulses and beans
- cereal grains and cereal products
- nuts
- Quorn®.

Stretch and challenge

Find out what is meant by indispensable and dispensable amino acids.

RESEARCH ACTIVITY

1. Using a nutritional program, compare the amount of protein available in different animal and vegetable sources of food.
2. Record your daily diet for a day. Use a nutrition program and calculate your protein intake for the day.
    a How does this compare to your daily requirement?
    b Do you need to make any changes to your diet?

✔ KEY POINTS

- ✔ **Protein is needed for growth and repair of body tissues.**
- ✔ **Protein is made up of amino acids.**
- ✔ **Good sources of high biological protein are animal meat, fish, eggs, milk, cheese and soya.**
- ✔ **Good sources of low biological protein include cereals, nuts and pulses.**

TEST YOURSELF

1. State **four** functions of protein in the diet.
2. State **four** sources of high biological value protein foods.
3. State **four** sources of low biological value protein foods.
4. Explain the difference between HBV and LBV proteins.
5. Explain why you would combine protein foods to complement each other.
6. Give **two** examples of complementary proteins.
7. Name **three** groups of people who need extra protein in their diet.

Topic 6 Fats

→ WHAT WILL I LEARN?

By the end of this topic you should have developed a knowledge and understanding of:

→ the types and structure of fats including the differences between saturated, unsaturated and polyunsaturated fats
→ the functions of fats in the diet
→ the main sources of fat in the diet
→ what happens if we have a deficiency or excess of fats in our diet.

Types and functions of fats

Fats are one of the macronutrients essential to health. **Lipids** is the general term to describe both fats and oils. All fats and oils have a similar chemical structure and functions. All fats are high in calories. 1 g of fat provides 9 kcal/37 kJ.

The structure and chemistry of fats

Fats are large molecules made up of the elements carbon, hydrogen and oxygen. They are composed of fatty acids and glycerol. Fatty acids may be **saturated** or unsaturated.

Saturated fats

In saturated fats, each carbon atom in the fatty acid is combined with two hydrogen atoms (see Figure 6.1).

Saturated fats are solid at room temperature and are mainly found in animal foods (see Figure 6.2).

KEY WORD

Lipids – another name for fats and oils

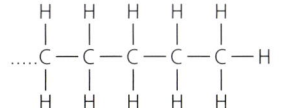

These are fully of hydrogen atoms and cannot accept any more.

▲ Figure 6.1 Structure of saturated fats

▲ Figure 6.2 Sources of saturated fat in the diet

47

Too much saturated fat in the diet has been linked to high blood cholesterol, leading to an increased risk of coronary heart disease, diabetes and obesity.

Cholesterol, a type of saturated fat, has the consistency of soft wax and is produced in the liver and transported round the body in the blood. It has been found that when too much cholesterol is in the blood it is deposited on the walls of the arteries, narrowing them and making them less efficient. Narrowed arteries are one of the major causes of coronary heart disease.

Topic link: You have already learnt about coronary heart disease in Section A: Topic 1 The relationship between diet and health, in the section on major diet-related health issues caused by a poor diet and lifestyle.

Unsaturated fats

There are two types of unsaturated fats: **monounsaturated** and **polyunsaturated**. Unsaturated fats are usually soft or liquid at room temperature and have a lower melting point.

Monounsaturated fats have one pair of carbon atoms, with only one hydrogen atom attached, so they are capable of taking one more hydrogen atom.

They are soft at room temperature but will go solid when placed in the coldest part of the refrigerator. They are found in both animal and vegetable fats. Monounsaturated fatty acids are considered healthier because they can help to lower blood cholesterol, reduce the risk of diabetes and are linked with a lower rate of cancer.

> **KEY WORDS**
>
> **Saturated fats** – each atom is combined with 2 hydrogen atoms.
> **Unsaturated fats** – have at least one carbon atom not surrounded by hydrogen
> **Polyunsaturated fats** – a fat molecule with more than one hydrogen space
> **Monounsaturated fats** – a fat molecule with one hydrogen space

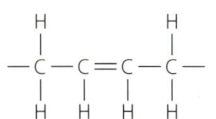

▲ Figure 6.3 Structure of monounsaturated fatty acids

▲ Figure 6.4 Sources of monounsaturated fat in the diet

Topic 6 Fats

▲ Figure 6.5 Structure of polyunsaturated fatty acids

▶ Figure 6.6 Sources of polyunsaturated fat in the diet

Polyunsaturated fats have two or more pairs of carbon atoms, which are capable of taking up more hydrogen atoms.

They are very soft or oily at room temperature. They will not go solid even in the refrigerator.

Trans-fatty acids are man-made molecules produced when hydrogen is added to vegetable oils. This is called **hydrogenation**. This process is used to make solid fats from oil and is used in a variety of manufactured foods. Trans-fatty acids behave like saturated fats, raising your level of cholesterol. Medical research has shown that trans-fatty acids are very bad for your cardiovascular system and may increase the risk of breast cancer.

> **KEY WORDS**
>
> **Essential fatty acids** – small unit of fat that must be supplied in the diet
>
> **Hydrogenation** – the process of adding hydrogen to oils to make them into solid fats

Stretch and challenge

Visit a supermarket or use a supermarket shopping website to investigate which foods contain hydrogenated fats. What else do you notice about the nutritional value of these foods?

Essential fatty acids (EFAs) cannot be made by the body but are important to the healthy and efficient functioning of the body. It is important to get the right balance of EFAs in our diet. They are essential for regulating body processes, including blood clotting and control of inflammation. Two important ones are:

- **Omega-3:** found in oily fish, seeds, walnut oil, and green leafy vegetables. It helps protect the heart.
- **Omega-6:** found in vegetables, fruits, grains, chicken and seeds. It helps lower cholesterol in the blood.

The functions of fat in the diet

- Fats are used by the body for energy.
- They form part of the structure of cells.
- Fats are stored under the skin and help insulate the body against the cold.
- Fat protects vital organs, such as kidneys.
- Fat is a source of the fat-soluble vitamins A, D, E and K.
- Fat in our diet helps to promote a feeling of **satiety** (we feel full).

▲ Figure 6.7 Food sources of Omega-3 and -6

> **KEY WORD**
>
> **Satiety** – feeling full after eating

Fat deficiency

In the UK it is very rare for anyone to have a lack of fat in their diet. However, some of the essential fatty acids (EFA) are essential for the correct growth and functioning of the body and must be obtained from food. In fact it is often the case that we consume too much fat. We are advised to reduce our fat intake so that it contributes no more than 35 per cent of our energy intake. If you look at the Eatwell Guide you will see that oils and spreads are the smallest section.

Excess fat

Consuming too much fat in our diet can lead to a variety of health problems including:

- obesity
- coronary heart disease
- high blood pressure
- diabetes
- strokes; and
- other health problems.

There are many different ways of reducing the fat content in our diet. These include:

- buying lean cuts of meat
- checking the fat content of products and choosing lower-in-fat varieties
- trimming fat from meat
- choosing methods of cooking which do not include adding fat.

Topic link: *You have already learnt about health issues caused by poor diet in Section A: Topic 1 The relationship between diet and health, in the section on major-diet related health issues caused by poor diet and lifestyles.*

RESEARCH ACTIVITY

1. Produce a poster or leaflet which could be displayed in a local health centre explaining the dangers of a diet which contains a lot of fat.

   Suggest ways the fat content of a person's diet could be reduced.

2. Using a supermarket website investigate the range of fats and oils available to consumers. Identify the source of fat, the amount of saturated and polyunsaturated fat, and whether it is suitable for cooking.

Stretch and challenge

Explain the difference between 'low fat' and 'lower in fat' or 'reduced fat' in a food product.

PRACTICAL ACTIVITY

It is possible to modify the total amount of fat content of some recipes. For either a sweet or savoury dish show how you can successfully reduce the fat content.

Topic 6 Fats

Sources of fat in the diet

Fats come from both plant and animal sources. Plant sources include:

- some fruits, for example, avocado, olives
- nuts and pulses, for example, peanuts, walnuts
- seeds, for example, sesame, sunflower and soya.

Animal sources include:

- meat and meat products, for example lard and suet
- dairy products, for example milk, butter, cheese and cream
- fish, particularly oily fish, for example tuna, salmon and sardines.

Visible and invisible fats

Some fats are **visible**, such as the fat on meat or solid fats such as butter. Other fats are **invisible** and form part of the food product and cannot be seen, for example in ready meals, chocolate, biscuits and burgers.

> **KEY WORDS**
> **Invisible fats** – foods containing fat which cannot be seen
> **Visible fats** – fats that can be seen

▲ Figure 6.8 Visible fats and oils

▲ Figure 6.9 Invisible fats

> ✔ **KEY POINTS**
>
> ✔ Fat is a concentrated source of energy.
> ✔ Excess fat in the diet is stored as body fat.
> ✔ We are advised to reduce our fat intake to no more than 35 per cent of our total energy intake.
> ✔ Saturated fats contribute to a high level of cholesterol in the blood.
> ✔ Monounsaturated fatty acids can help to lower blood cholesterol, reduce the risk of diabetes and are linked with a lower rate of cancer.
> ✔ Plant sources of fats include some fruits, nuts and pulses and seeds.
> ✔ Animal sources of fats include meat and meat products, dairy products and fish (particularly oily fish).

> **TEST YOURSELF**
>
> 1 State **three** functions of fat in the diet.
> 2 What percentage of our energy intake should come from fats?
> 3 Explain the difference between fats and oils.
> 4 State **four** animal sources of fat.
> 5 State **four** vegetable sources of fat.
> 6 Explain the difference between saturated and unsaturated fats.
> 7 What are essential fatty acids?
> 8 Why should we avoid a diet which is high in fats?

Topic 7 Carbohydrates

> **→ WHAT WILL I LEARN?**
>
> By the end of this topic you should have developed a knowledge and understanding of:
>
> → the structure of carbohydrates including the difference between sugars, starches and non-starch polysaccharide (NSP/fibre)
> → the functions of carbohydrates in the diet
> → the main sources of the different types of carbohydrates in the diet
> → what happens if we have a deficiency or excess of carbohydrates in our diet.

Types and functions of carbohydrates

Carbohydrates are important macronutrients formed from carbon, hydrogen and oxygen. There are two types of carbohydrate:

- sugar
- complex carbohydrates

The functions of carbohydrates in the diet are:

- They provide the body with energy for physical activity.
- They provide the body with energy to maintain bodily functions.
- They provide dietary fibre/non-starch polysaccharide (NSP) to help digestion.
- Sugars also sweeten and flavour foods.

Sugars

Sugars are the simple units all carbohydrates are made from.

There are two main types of simple sugars: **monosaccharides** and **disaccharides**.

Monosaccharides

Monosaccharides are simple sugars. The simpler the carbohydrate, the more quickly it can be absorbed in the body and the faster energy can be provided.

- **Glucose** is one of these simple sugars. Although found in some fruits and vegetables, it is often used by athletes in tablet or powder form to provide a fast energy boost.
- **Fructose** is similar in structure to glucose and is found naturally in the juices of some fruits and plants, but mainly in honey. As it is the sweetest of all sugars, manufacturers can use a low amount but still provide the same level of sweetness as sucrose.
- **Galactose** is formed during digestion of lactose (milk sugar).

KEY WORDS

Carbohydrate – the major source of energy in the body
Disaccharide – two monosaccharides combined
Monosaccharide – simple sugar

Topic 7 Carbohydrates

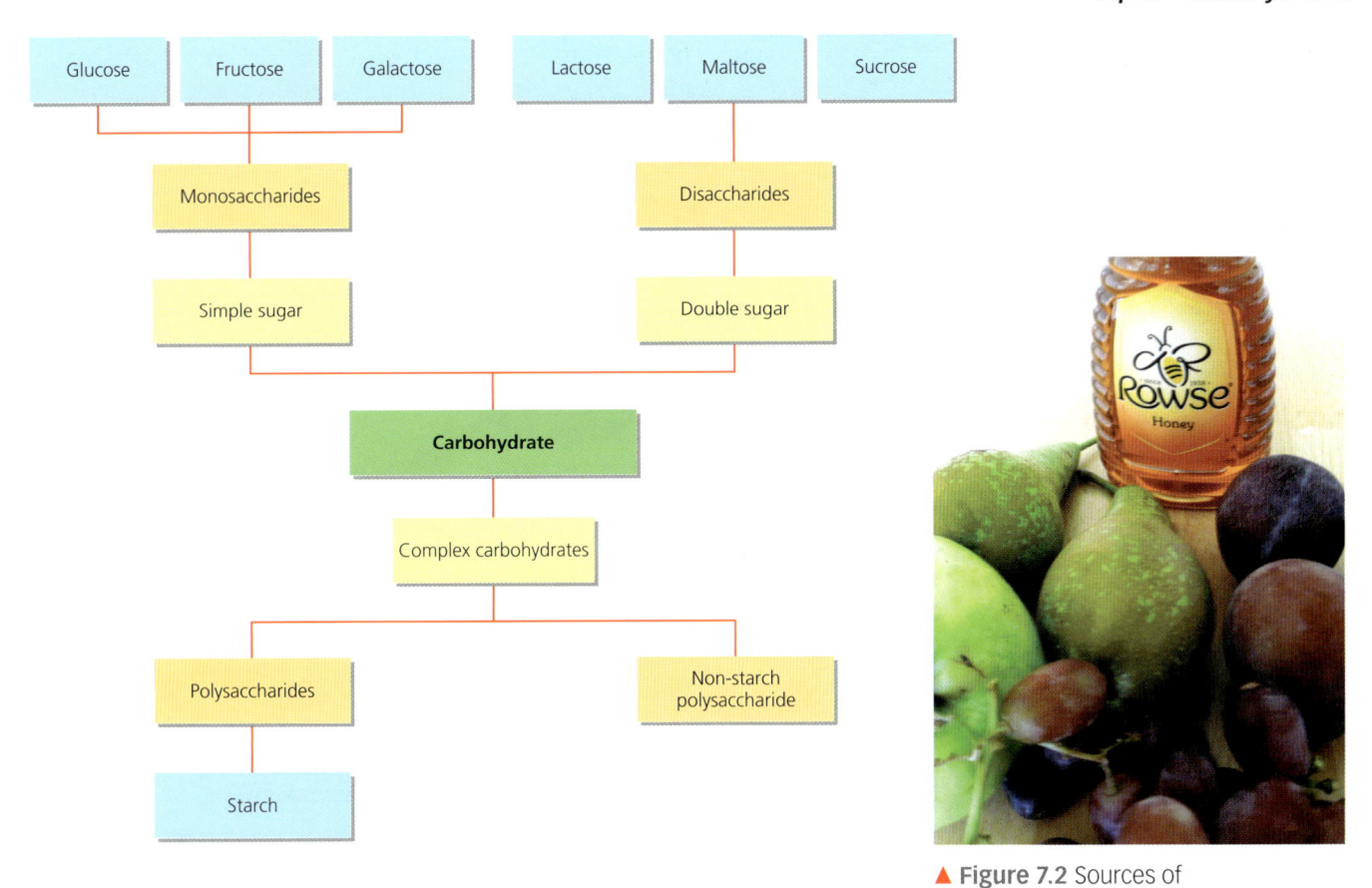

▲ Figure 7.1 Types of carbohydrate

▲ Figure 7.2 Sources of monosaccharides

▲ Figure 7.3 Sources of disaccharides

Disaccharides

Disaccharides are double sugars that are made up of two monosaccharides.

- **Lactose** is the disaccharide found in milk, which some people think gives milk its slightly sweet taste.
- **Maltose**, another of the disaccharides, results from the fermentation of cereal grains.
- **Sucrose** is the most common disaccharide. It is known as sugar.
  It provides the body with energy but has no other benefits in the diet.
  It contains no other nutrients. Sucrose comes from sugar beet or sugar cane. We buy it as granulated sugar, brown sugar, caster sugar, icing sugar, sugar syrup and treacle.

> ## Stretch and challenge
> Disaccharides are made up of two monosaccharides.
> Find out which monosaccharides make up the disaccharides.

Sources of sugar

We eat sugar in different forms:

- as non-free sugar – these are found naturally in the cells of fruits and vegetables; they are part of the cells
- as free sugar – sugar that you can see, such as cane sugar, syrup and those added to cakes, biscuits, desserts and sweets.

53

The most common problems relating to sucrose are obesity, tooth decay and Type 2 diabetes. Not free sugars are less harmful as they are less likely to lead to tooth decay and are easier for the body to absorb.

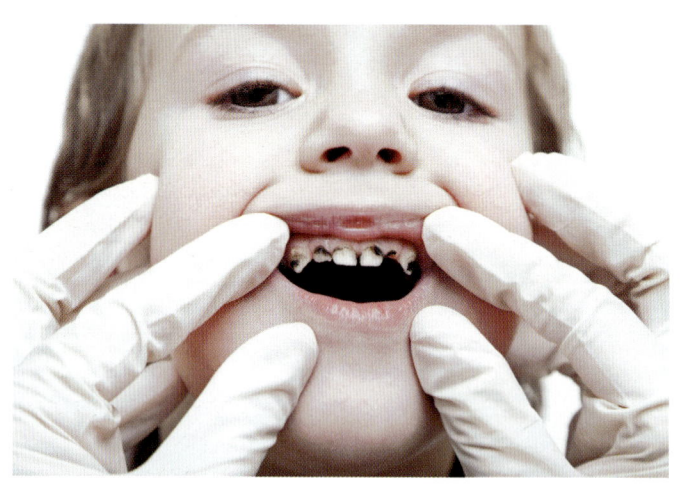

▲ Figure 7.4 Tooth decay

> **KEY WORD**
> **Polysaccharide** – complex carbohydrate, either starch or fibre

Polysaccharides

These are complex carbohydrates formed from hundreds of glucose molecules strung together. They provide the body with energy.

Starches

Starches take longer than sugars for the body to digest and so provide a feeling of fullness for longer, helping to avoid overeating and obesity. All starch comes from plant sources. Starchy foods should make up about one third of our daily food.

Functions of starch in the diet
- Starch is broken down slowly into simple sugars by the digestive system to provide energy.
- It adds bulk to our diet.
- It gives a feeling of fullness.
- Excess is converted to fat.

Sources of starch

Starches are found in grain products like bread, rice, cereals and pasta, and in some fruits and vegetables.

▲ Figure 7.5 Sources of starch

> **RESEARCH ACTIVITY**
>
> Make a list of starchy foods and show how they could be used in a variety of different products for packed lunches and the main meal of the day.

> **PRACTICAL ACTIVITY**
>
> 1 Prepare one of the dishes you have included for the research activity and use a nutritional program to calculate the amount of carbohydrate in this dish. Evaluate the dish to see if you could make further improvements.
> 2 Design and make a high-carbohydrate main course dish for an athlete. Use nutritional software to calculate the percentage of carbohydrate in your dish.

Topic 7 Carbohydrates

Deficiency of carbohydrates

The body needs to have a constant supply of energy. If it does not have enough from carbohydrate foods it will use protein foods for energy. In the UK having insufficient carbohydrate foods in the form of starch and sugar is rare. If we eat too much carbohydrate food it is stored as fat. It can also lead to other health-related problems such as cancer, cardiovascular disease (CSV), coronary heart disease (CHD), diabetes and dental problems.

Topic link: *You have learnt about some of these health-related problems in Section A: Topic 1 The relationship between diet and health, in the major diet-related health issues caused by poor diet and lifestyle section.*

Fibre/NSP

Fibre/NSP (non-starch polysaccharide) is the non-digestible cellulose found in plant foods. It cannot be digested so it passes straight through the digestive system, absorbing moisture and providing bulk. **Dietary fibre** helps to 'push' other food through the system and helps to 'clean' the walls of the intestine of bacteria. The efficient removal of waste products from the body is vital to health.

We should be eating more fibre in the diet. The recommended amounts are shown in the table below:

> **KEY WORDS**
>
> **Dietary fibre** – material from plants, which is not digested by humans but which absorbs water and binds other residues in the intestine, thus aiding the excretion of waste material from the body
>
> **Diverticular disease** – a disease caused by lack of fibre in the diet

Table 7.1 Recommended intake for fibre

Age group	Recommended intake per day (g)
2–5 years	15g / day
5–11 years	20g / day
11–16 years	25g / day
17 years and over	30g / day

(Source: British Nutrition Foundation 2015)

Functions of dietary fibre

- Holds water and keeps the faeces soft and bulky.
- Helps prevent various bowel disorders, including constipation, bowel cancer, **diverticular disease**, appendicitis and haemorrhoids (piles).
- Can help people to control their body weight because high-fibre foods are filling.
- High-fibre diets are linked to lower blood cholesterol whilst reducing the risk of diabetes.

Deficiency of fibre

Too little fibre in the diet can cause constipation and, in extreme cases, diverticular disease, where the lining of the intestine becomes distorted and inflamed.

Topic link: *You have learnt about some of these health-related problems in Section A: Topic 1 The relationship between diet and health, in the major diet-related health issues caused by poor diet and lifestyle section.*

Figure 7.6 Sources of fibre in the diet

KEY WORDS

Insoluble fibre – absorbs water and increases bulk

Soluble fibre – slows down digestion and absorption of carbohydrates

Sources of fibre in the diet

There are two types of dietary fibre: **insoluble** and **soluble**, which have different functions.

Insoluble fibre absorbs water and increases bulk, making the faeces very soft and bulky and easy to pass through the digestive system.

Good sources of insoluble fibre are:

- wholemeal flour
- wholegrain breakfast cereals and pasta
- brown rice
- some fruits and vegetables.

Soluble fibre slows down the digestion and absorption of carbohydrates and so helps to control blood sugar levels, which helps stop us feeling hungry. Soluble fibre may also reduce blood cholesterol levels and so may reduce our risk of heart disease.

Good sources of soluble fibre are:

- oats
- peas, beans and lentils
- most types of fruit and vegetables. Vegetables and fruits also provide more fibre if eaten with their skins on.

RESEARCH ACTIVITY

1. Look at the day's diet below. Suggest what changes could be made to increase the fibre content.

    Breakfast
    Sugar puff cereals with milk
    Glass of fruit juice
    Slice of toast with low-fat spread and jam

    Lunch
    White pasta with tuna and mayonnaise as a salad
    Fruit scone

    Evening meal
    Beef curry and plain white rice
    Low-fat fruit-flavoured yoghurt

    Snacks eaten during the day
    packet of crisps

2. Collect a range of different breakfast cereal packets or use a nutritional program and make a chart to show how much starch, sugar and fibre they contain.

    Using the information you have discovered, what advice would you give to teenagers about the breakfast cereals they should eat?

3. Look at the foods listed as good sources of fibre. Using a nutritional program investigate the fibre content of those foods.

PRACTICAL ACTIVITY

1 Many dishes we eat are low in fibre. Prepare either a sweet or savoury dish which shows how you can modify a traditional dish to include more fibre.
2 Using a nutritional program compare the fibre content of both recipes.

✔ KEY POINTS

- ✔ Sugars and starches release energy into the body.
- ✔ Starches are converted to energy more slowly than sugars.
- ✔ Sugars contain no other nutrients apart from energy.
- ✔ If we eat more carbohydrates than we need for energy, the excess is stored as fat.
- ✔ Dietary fibre is a very complex structure and cannot be digested.
- ✔ We should be increasing our fibre content.

TEST YOURSELF

1 What are the main functions of sugars and starches in the diet?
2 What happens to our body if too much carbohydrate is eaten?
3 Explain why it is important we eat 18 g of fibre per day.
4 State **three** foods which contain simple sugars.
5 State **three** foods which are a good source of starch.
6 State **three** foods which are a good source of fibre.
7 Explain the difference between simple and complex carbohydrates.
8 Why should we reduce our intake of extrinsic sugars?
9 Explain the difference between soluble and insoluble fibre.

Topic 8

Vitamins

> **→ WHAT WILL I LEARN?**
>
> By the end of this topic you should have developed a knowledge and understanding of:
> - the functions of vitamins in the diet
> - the different types of vitamins
> - the main sources of vitamins in the diet
> - what happens if we have a deficiency or excess of vitamins in our diet.

Types and functions of vitamins in the diet

Vitamins are micronutrients because they are needed only in very small quantities. They are natural substances found in foods and they do different jobs in the diet. Each vitamin has a chemical name, for example, vitamin C's chemical name is ascorbic acid. Each vitamin is also given a letter. It is useful to know the chemical names as well as the letter as either can be seen on food packaging.

The amount of vitamins we need changes depending on age and life stage.

Tables 8.1 and 8.2 show the functions of the different vitamins.

Vitamins are divided into two different groups:

- **fat-soluble vitamins**
- **water-soluble vitamins.**

Fat-soluble vitamins

There are four vitamins in this group:

- vitamin A
- vitamin D
- vitamin E
- vitamin K

Table 8.1 shows the functions of each of the different fat-soluble vitamins.

Sources

Fat-soluble vitamins A, D, and K are found in the fat in foods, for example, in the fat found in dairy foods. They can be stored in the liver and used by the body when needed. Figure 8.1 shows which foods are good sources of each vitamin.

KEY WORDS
Fat-soluble vitamins – dissolve in fat
Water-soluble vitamins – dissolve in water

Topic 8 Vitamins

Table 8.1 Fat-soluble vitamins

Fat-soluble vitamins and chemical name	Function (its job) in the body	Deficiency (what happens if we do not get enough)	Good sources	Examples of good sources
Vitamin A (retinol, beta carotene)	Growth and development. Keeps the lining of the throat, digestive system and lungs moist and free from infection. Keeps the eyes healthy and enables vision in dim light. Beta carotene – an anti-oxidant vitamin which might protect against cancer	Children do not grow properly. Difficult for the body to fight infection. Long-term deficiency may lead to night blindness. Excess may lead to liver and bone damage	Retinol: liver, oily fish, eggs, milk, cheese and butter, margarine. Beta carotene: is in red, green and orange vegetables and fruits, especially carrots	
Vitamin D (cholecalciferol)	Works with calcium to build and maintain strong bones and teeth	In children it can cause **rickets**, which is a softening of the bones. In adults it is called **osteomalacia** – softening of the bones in adults caused by lack of vitamin D. It can also cause **osteoporosis**.	Dairy products, oily fish, liver, cereals. Available by exposure to sunlight	
Vitamin E (tocopherol)	For healthy cell walls and blood. Thought to reduce the risk of developing some types of heart disease and cancer	A deficiency in vitamin E is rare	Vegetables, oils, lettuce, wheat grasses, seeds, peanuts, wheat germ oil	
Vitamin K	Helps the blood to clot	A deficiency in vitamin K is rare	Cheese, liver, leafy vegetables, asparagus, coffee, wheat germ oil	

KEY WORDS

Osteomalacia – caused by lack of vitamin D in adults

Rickets – caused by lack of vitamin D in children

Osteoporosis – a disease in which the bones start to lose minerals and their strength and break easily

Topic links: You will learn more about fat-soluble vitamins in the following topics:

- Section C: Topic 19 How cooking methods affect the nutritional value of foods
- Section B: Topic 14 Fortification.

Stretch and challenge

1. Find out why vitamins A and D are added to margarine by law.
2. Do manufacturers have to add vitamins A and D to other spreads and low-fat spreads?
3. Have a look at a range of spreads and low-fat spreads to see if they have added vitamins A and D. You will find this in the ingredients list. Why do you think some manufacturers add these vitamins?

Topic 8 Vitamins

> **PRACTICAL ACTIVITY**
>
> 1 Prepare a dish which would appeal to children which contains foods containing vitamin A.
> 2 Calculate the amount of vitamin A in the dish. How does this compare to the recommended daily intake for children?

Water-soluble vitamins

Water-soluble vitamins dissolve in water. They include the vitamin B group and vitamin C.

Table 8.2 shows the functions of these different vitamins.

Vitamin B is a group of vitamins that all have similar functions.

Sources

Sources of the water-soluble vitamins include a wide range of different foods. See Table 8.2 for examples for each specific vitamin.

Table 8.2 Water-soluble vitamins

Water-soluble vitamins and chemical name	Function (its job) in the body	Deficiency (what happens if we do not get enough)	Good sources	Examples of good sources
B1 (thiamine)	Helps the release of energy from carbohydrates Helps the body to grow Functioning and normal nervous system	Slows growth and development Severe deficiency causes beri beri	**Fortified** breakfast cereals, whole grains, wheat germ, meat, eggs, milk and dairy foods, seeds, nuts, beans	
B2 (riboflavin)	Helps the release of energy from carbohydrates, fats and proteins Involved in the transport and metabolism of iron Required for the normal structure and function of mucous membranes Normal growth Healthy skin	Poor growth rate Skin and eye problems	Liver, kidneys, meat, milk, eggs and green vegetables fortified breakfast cereals, mushrooms and green vegetables	
B3 (niacin)	Metabolism growth and energy release Essential for healthy skin, mucous membranes and nerves	Deficiency is very rare in the UK Pellagra, rough sore skin, weakness and depression	Meat, eggs, wheat and maize flour, dairy products, yeast	

Section A: Nutrition

60

Topic 8 Vitamins

Water-soluble vitamins and chemical name	Function (its job) in the body	Deficiency (what happens if we do not get enough)	Good sources	Examples of good sources
B9 (Folate or folic acid)	Essential for the formation of red blood cells Foetal development	Tiredness and anaemia Depression Forgetfulness Irritability	Liver, wholegrain cereals, pulses, dark green vegetables, peas, oranges, bananas, fortified breakfast cereals	
B12 (cobalamin)	Normal functioning of the nervous system The formation of red blood cells Involved in energy production	Nerves not working correctly may lead to paralysis, memory loss and confusion Pernicious anaemia	Only found in animal products (meat, dairy products, liver)	
Vitamin C (ascorbic acid)	Formation of connective tissue Helps wound healing and calcium absorption Blood and blood vessel formation Helps absorb iron	Spotty skin, swollen gums, loose teeth In severe cases scurvy develops	Citrus and soft fruits, oranges, blackcurrants, strawberries, green vegetables, cabbage, new potatoes, peppers	

KEY WORDS

Folate or folic acid – important in the diet of pregnant women for the development of the foetus

Fortification – adding nutrients to a food product to improve its nutritional content

Topic links: You will learn more about the water-soluble vitamins in the following topics:

- Section C: Topic 2 Sensory and Nutritional Properties, How cooking methods affect the nutritional value of foods.
- Section A: Topic 2 Nutritional and dietary needs of different groups of people, Dietary needs for different stages of life.

RESEARCH ACTIVITY

Write a short article for a magazine to explain to a pregnant woman why folic acid is important in the diet.

Topic 8 Vitamins

RESEARCH ACTIVITY

1 Analyse a range of orange drinks to determine the amount of vitamin C in each one. Compare the amount of vitamin C, sugar and the cost of each.
2 Explain which drink you would recommend for the following people:
   - toddler
   - pregnant woman
   - older adult
   - teenager.

PRACTICAL ACTIVITY

1 Students often take packed lunches to college. Prepare an interesting salad which could be included as a packed lunch which contains a range of water-soluble vitamins. Calculate the nutritional value of the water-soluble vitamins per portion for a young adult.
2 Prepare a main course dish which would be suitable for a pregnant woman which contains a good source of folate. Calculate the nutritional content for the dish.

✔ KEY POINTS

✔ **Vitamins are required in very small amounts.**
✔ **Vitamins promote health and help prevent disease.**
✔ **They regulate the building and repair of the body.**
✔ **They help regulate the chemical reactions which release energy in body cells.**
✔ **Fortified food products have vitamins added to improve their nutritional value.**

TEST YOURSELF

1 What are the chemical names for the **four** fat-soluble vitamins?
2 Give **two** animal and **two** vegetable sources of vitamin A.
3 Name **two** deficiency diseases caused by lack of vitamin D in the diet.
4 Name **one** deficiency disease caused by lack of vitamin A.
5 State **one** function of vitamin E in the diet.
6 Name the **four** water-soluble vitamins.
7 Name the deficiency disease caused by lack of vitamin C.
8 Name **three** good sources of vitamin C.
9 Name **three** sources of food which will provide you with all the B vitamins.
10 Why is Vitamin B9 important for pregnant women?

Topic 9   Minerals

> ### → WHAT WILL I LEARN?
>
> By the end of this topic you should have developed a knowledge and understanding of:
> - → the functions of minerals in the diet
> - → the main sources of minerals in the diet
> - → what happens if we have a deficiency or excess of minerals in our diet.

Minerals are micronutrients and are required in very small amounts. Some minerals are needed in larger amounts than others, including calcium, iron, phosphorus and sodium. Some minerals are required in smaller amounts. These are sometimes called trace elements and include fluoride and iodine.

Types and functions of minerals in the diet

Minerals have four major functions:

- body building (bones and teeth)
- control of body processes, especially the nervous system
- they are an essential part of body fluids and cells
- Calcium and iron are the most important minerals needed by the body.

Table 9.1 The functions and sources of minerals in the diet

Minerals	Function in the body	Deficiency	Good sources	Example of food source
Iron	Production of haemoglobin in red blood cells to carry oxygen in the blood	Anaemia	Red meat, kidneys, liver, eggs, bread, green vegetables, dried apricots, lentils, cocoa,	
Calcium	Combines with phosphorus to harden bones and teeth Blood clotting Nerve and muscle function Heart regulation	Stunted growth Can cause rickets Osteomalacia	Dairy products, fortified white bread, tinned (oily) fish, green vegetables, seeds, nuts. lentils	
Phosphorus	Combines with calcium to harden bones and teeth Muscle function Energy production	People are rarely deficient in this mineral, but deficiency causes tiredness and depression	Dairy products, nuts, meat, fish and foods rich in calcium	
Sodium	Maintains water balance in the body Nerve transmission	Deficiency is highly unlikely	Cheese, bacon, smoked meats, fish, processed foods, table salt	

63

Minerals	Function in the body	Deficiency	Good sources	Example of food source
Trace elements				
Fluoride	Strengthens teeth against decay	Tooth decay	Fish, tea, drinking water, toothpaste	
Iodine	Needed to make thyroid hormones – to control the metabolic rate of the body	Leads to reduction in amount of thyroxine hormone produced, leading to tiredness and weight gain The thyroid gland (goitre) in the neck swells	Fish, milk and dairy foods	

> **KEY WORDS**
>
> **Anaemia** – deficiency disease caused by lack of iron
> **Calcium** – a mineral element that is essential for strong bones and teeth
> **Iron** – a mineral present in the blood and stored in the liver; prolonged lack of iron leads to anaemia

Calcium

Functions of calcium

- **Calcium** helps form teeth and bones and gives them strength. (An adult body contains more than 1 kg of calcium.)
- It is also needed for blood clotting after injury or surgery.
- It helps the muscles and nerves work properly.
- It is needed for normal growth in children.
- Vitamin D and phosphorus work together with calcium to help maintain strong bones and teeth.

People need differing amounts of calcium each day, depending on their age and gender.

- Pregnant women and those who are breastfeeding need an increased amount.
- Young children need a diet high in calcium because their bones are growing rapidly. By about the age of 18 years bones stop growing.
- We reach peak bone mass at about 30 years of age, when our bones are fully calcified.

Calcium is added to flour and bread by law and many foods we buy are fortified with calcium.

Topic link: You have learnt about calcium and bone health in Section A: Topic 1 The relationship between diet and health, in the section on bone health.

PRACTICAL ACTIVITY

Milk is a good source of calcium. However, many children do not like to drink milk.
1. Prepare a range of savoury dishes which contain calcium.
2. Clearly identify the foods which are a good source of calcium.
3. Calculate the calcium content per portion.

Topic 9 Minerals

▲ Figure 9.2 Osteoporosis is a common condition in older people

Calcium deficiency

Our body cannot make calcium and it must be provided from the food we eat. Our body will take calcium from our bones and unless it is replaced it will cause osteoporosis. **Osteoporosis** is a condition of weakening and thinning of the bones, most common in older adults, especially women. Vitamin D and phosphorus work together with calcium to help maintain strong bones and teeth. If we do not have enough calcium in our diet:

- Blood will not clot properly after injury.
- Muscles will not work properly.
- Children's growth will be slowed, as bones will not develop normally.

If children do not have sufficient calcium they may suffer from rickets which is the softening of the bones. The adult version of rickets is called osteomalacia.

Iron

Functions of iron

We need **iron** as it forms haemoglobin, which gives blood its red colour and carries oxygen round the body to the cells. Vitamin C is needed in the diet to help absorb iron.

Iron deficiency

Anaemia, caused by a lack of iron in the diet, is one of the most common nutritional problems worldwide. Women and children are the most at risk. Symptoms are tiredness and lack of energy.

Topic link: You have learnt about anaemia in Section A: Topic 1 The relationship between diet and health.

KEY POINTS

- ✓ Minerals are substances used by the body to control processes; they form an essential part of body fluids.
- ✓ Calcium and iron are the most important minerals needed by our body.

TEST YOURSELF

1. Name **four** minerals.
2. Name **two** trace elements.
3. Explain the difference between a mineral and a trace element.
4. State two functions of calcium in the diet.
5. What happens if we do not have sufficient calcium in our diet?
6. State **two** functions of iron in the diet.
7. Name **two** groups of people who have a greater need for iron in their diet.
8. State the function of fluoride in the diet.

RESEARCH ACTIVITY

1. A pregnant woman needs 14.8 mg iron per day. Plan a day's menu for a pregnant woman which will ensure that she meets her daily requirements for iron.

PRACTICAL ACTIVITY

Vegetarians often find it difficult to eat sufficient foods containing iron.
1. Make a list of interesting dishes containing iron which could be prepared for a vegetarian.
2. Choose one of your dishes to make.
3. Calculate the amount of iron per portion of the dish.

Stretch and challenge

Find out how much iron the following groups of people need per day:

- 2-year-olds
- 7-year-olds
- 15-year-old boys
- 15-year-old girls
- 45-year-olds
- pregnant women

Explain why the amounts vary for the different groups.

Topic 10 Water

> **→ WHAT WILL I LEARN?**
>
> **By the end of this topic you should have developed a knowledge and understanding of:**
> - the functions of water in the diet
> - what happens if we have a deficiency or excess of water in our diet
> - recommended guidelines for our daily intake of water
> - sources and foods that give us water.

Importance of water in the diet

Water is not usually called a nutrient, but it is essential for life. Nearly 65 per cent of the body is made up of water. We need a lot of water every day.

▲ **Figure 10.1** We need to replace the water lost in physical activity

Functions of water in the body

- It helps regulate the body's temperature (37° C). Sweat evaporates and cools us. Without this cooling system we would become ill from heatstroke.
- It helps the kidneys flush out harmful excess or foreign substances from our blood.
- The kidneys filter waste products and eliminate them from the body as urine.
- It transports nutrients, oxygen and carbon dioxide round the body.
- It is needed by nearly all body processes, for example digestion to remove waste products from the body as urine and faeces.
- Water is found in all cells and tissues in our body.
- It helps to prevent the skin drying out and ensures that the lining of the digestive system, mucus membranes and lungs are kept moist.

Lack of water

The body can protect itself to some extent against shortage of water by reducing its water output. It cannot stop losses due to breathing and sweating, but it can limit the production of urine. The medical condition known as **dehydration** occurs when more water is being lost from the body than is being replaced by drinking. This can lead to a variety of different symptoms including:

- headaches
- dark-coloured urine
- feeling weak
- feeling sick
- being confused
- quick heartbeat
- changes in blood pressure.

If someone becomes very short of water they can die within hours because the blood gets thicker and difficult to pump, so the heart stops. Lack of water to drink is therefore more harmful than shortage of food.

How much water do we need?

If we eat a lot of watery food we can drink less. Many foods contain water, especially fruits and vegetables. On average 1 to 2.5 litres of water pass out of the body each day as urine. Some water is also removed with faeces. At least 1 litre of water is lost from the body each day as breath and sweat. It is difficult to say exactly how much water we need. It can depend on all of the following:

- weather
- the physical activities we take part in
- the amount of salt we eat
- our age.

The recommended intake of water is 6–8 glasses a day.

This does not include the water you get from the food you eat. It does, however, include the drinks that you have such as fruit juices and milk.

What happens if you have too much water?

Drinking too much water is called **water intoxication**. If you have too much water in your diet the kidneys will not be able to work quickly enough to remove the water from the body. This can cause headaches, nausea, vomiting and in extreme circumstances can cause death.

Sources of water

Fruits and vegetables are good sources of water as well as the water we get from the drinks that we consume.

KEY WORDS

Dehydration – a medical condition resulting from insufficient water in the diet

Water intoxication – having too much water

▲ Figure 10.2 Foods which provide a good source of water

Stretch and challenge

Investigate whether some groups of people need more water than others.

Investigate the implications for the environment and food security in the increased sales of bottled water.

Topic link: Section B: Topic 3 Food security

✔ KEY POINTS

- ✔ **Water is essential for life.**
- ✔ **Water provides us with no energy.**
- ✔ **There must be a balance between input and output of water or dehydration will occur.**

TEST YOURSELF

1. Give **three** reasons why it is important that we have sufficient water in our diet.
2. State **three** factors which will influence the amount of water that is required in a day.
3. State **four** foods which are a good source of water.
4. Explain what is meant by the term dehydration. \

Topic 11 Nutrients in foods

> **→ WHAT WILL I LEARN?**
>
> By the end of this topic you should have developed a knowledge and understanding of:
>
> → nutrients found in and the structure of the following foods:
> - bread, rice, potatoes, pasta and other starchy foods
> - fruit and vegetables
> - milk and dairy foods
> - meat, fish, eggs, beans and other non-dairy sources of protein
> - foods and drinks high in fat and/or sugar.

Potatoes, Bread, rice, pasta and other starchy foods

The main nutrient in this group of foods is carbohydrate in the form of starch. However, it also contains other nutrients which can make a valuable contribution to a person's diet.

Wheat

wheat is used to make bread and pasta. Figure 11.1 shows the nutrients found in wheat. However, you must remember that when the wheat is processed some nutrients are removed. It is still mandatory to fortify all wheat flour except whole-meal with:

- iron
- niacin and all flours except whole meal
- thiamine (vitamin B1)
- calcium.

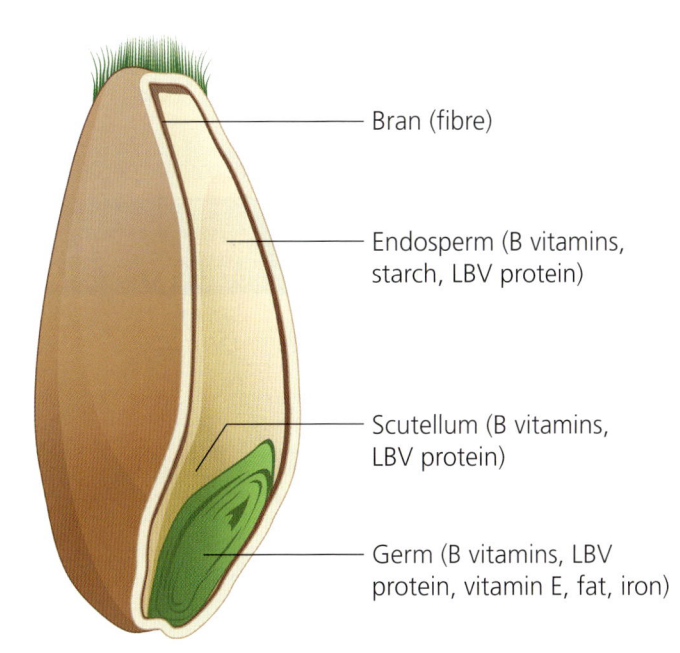

▲ Figure 11.1 The structure and nutrients found in wheat

- Bran (fibre)
- Endosperm (B vitamins, starch, LBV protein)
- Scutellum (B vitamins, LBV protein)
- Germ (B vitamins, LBV protein, vitamin E, fat, iron)

69

Table 11.1 shows how the nutritional values of flours vary.

Table 11.1 Comparison of nutrients in different flour (per 100 g)

Nutrient	Wholemeal	Brown	White
Energy	1318 kJ 310 kcal	1384 kJ 324 kcal	1450 kJ 341 kcal
Fat	2.2 g	2.0 g	1.3 g
Saturated fat	0.3 g	0.3 g	0.2 g
Polyunsaturated fat	1.0 g	0.9 g	0.6 g
Carbohydrate	63.9 g	68.5 g	77.7 g
Sugar	2.1 g	1.7 g	1.5 g
Dietary fibre	9.0 g	6.4 g	3.1 g
Protein	12.7 g	12.6 g	9.4 g
Iron	3.9 mg	3.2 mg	2.0 mg
Thiamine	0.47 mg	0.39 mg	0.31 mg
Niacin	5.7 mg	4.0 mg	1.7 mg
Calcium	38.0 mg	130.0 mg	140.0 mg

Topic link: Section B: Topic 2 Processing of wheat

Other starchy foods contain similar nutrients to wheat.

Table 11.2 Main nutrients found in other grains

Rice	Maize	Oats
• carbohydrate – starch and fibre (if brown rice) • B vitamins (thiamin and niacin) • protein (**LBV**).	• nutrient content of maize is similar to other cereals • good source of vitamin A.	• carbohydrates (starch and fibre) • B vitamins (thiamin, riboflavin and B6) • calcium • iron • small amounts of folic acid • soluble fibre

Potatoes

Potatoes are classed as a starchy food; however, the nutritional content of potatoes will vary depending on the season and how they are cooked. Table 11.3 shows the differences for some types of potatoes and the changes that occur when they are cooked.

Table 11.3 Nutrient content per 100 g of potatoes

	New potatoes, raw	Old potatoes, raw	Baked potatoes	Old potatoes, boiled	Old potatoes, roast in vegetable oil	Chips fried in sunflower oil
Energy	298 kJ 70 kcal	318 kJ 75 kcal	581 kJ 136 kcal	306 kJ 72 kcal	630 kJ 149 kcal	796 kJ 189 kcal
Fat (g) of which saturates (g) polyunsaturates (g)	0.3 0.1 0.1	0.2 trace 0.1	0.2 trace 0.1	0.1 trace 0.1	4.5 0.4 1.6	6.7 0.8 4.2
Carbohydrate (g)	16.1	17.2	31.7	17	25.9	30.1
Protein (g)	1.7	2.1	3.9	1.8	2.9	3.9
Fibre (g)	1	1.3	2.7	1.2	1.8	2.2
Vitamin C (mg)	16	11	14	6	8	9

KEY WORD

LBV – low biological value protein

Stretch and challenge

Explain why the carbohydrate content of 100 g of baked potato is higher than in any of the other potatoes shown in Table 11.3:

RESEARCH ACTIVITY

1 Using a nutritional program investigate further how different methods of cooking affect the nutritional content of potatoes.
   Give reasons for the differences
2 Using a nutritional program investigate the nutritional content of different types of bread. Explain which type of bread you would give to the following groups of people:
   - young people
   - older adults
   - teenagers.

PRACTICAL ACTIVITY

1 Oats and other cereals provide long-term energy. Prepare and cook an interesting dish which illustrates the use of oats.
2 Potatoes are a staple food. Prepare, cook and serve a main course dish which illustrates the use of potatoes.
3 Many children do not like wholemeal bread. Take a traditional recipe and modify it to:
   - contain wholemeal flour
   - be attractive to primary school age children.
   Explain how you have modified the recipe to make it appealing to children.

✔ KEY POINTS

- ✔ Cereals are an important source of nutrients in the diet, particularly carbohydrates (starch).
- ✔ There are a wide range of cereal products from which to choose.
- ✔ Cereals are used in a wide range of different food products.
- ✔ Cereals are often the staple food of the countries they are grown in.

TEST YOURSELF

1 Name the main nutrient found in starchy foods.
2 Explain why we should eat more wholegrain cereal products.

Fruit and vegetables

Fruit

The nutritional content of fruit varies depending on the type of fruit it is. In general, fruits are high in vitamins, carbohydrates (**sucrose**, **fructose** and fibre) and minerals. They are low in protein and fat.

KEY WORDS
Sucrose – simple sugar
Fructose – simple sugar

Table 11.4 Nutrients found in fruit

Nutrient	Sources
Vitamin C	• rich sources – blackcurrants, rosehips • good sources – citrus fruits, strawberries, gooseberries, raspberries (Remember, vitamin C is destroyed by heat.)
Vitamin A	• apricots
Carbohydrate	• found in the form of sucrose and fructose in ripe fruit • fibre is found in the skin and fibrous parts of the fruit

Vegetables

Vegetables are eaten mostly as part of main meals, though we are encouraged to eat them as snacks instead of high-calorie foods. It is recommended that we eat a minimum of five portions of fruit and vegetables a day.

The nutrient content of vegetables varies depending on their type and how they are cooked. Many vitamins are water soluble and destroyed by heat.

Topic links:

- Topic 8 Vitamins
- Topic 9 Minerals
- Section C: Topic 1 Food Science — how cooking methods affect the nutritional value

KEY WORD
HBV – high biological value protein

Table 11.5 Nutrients found in vegetables

Nutrients	Sources
Protein	• only found in pulses and beans • is of a low biological value except in soya beans, which are high biological value (**HBV**)
Carbohydrate	• root vegetables and tubers are the best sources, in the form of starch • vegetables are a good source of fibre
Vitamin C	• rich sources – sprouts, cabbage, green peppers, spinach, watercress • reasonable sources – peas, beansprouts, potatoes (because we consume them in quite large quantities)
B vitamins	• pulses provide a good source of thiamine • most vegetables contain some of the B group
Vitamin A	• carrots and dark green vegetables
Calcium and iron	• found in some vegetables such as watercress, cabbage and spinach, but it is not always available to the body

✔ KEY POINTS

✔ Fruit and vegetables are good sources of vitamins, carbohydrates and fibre.
✔ Many of the vitamins are water soluble, therefore we need to cook them carefully to reduce the loss of nutritional value.

Section A: Nutrition

Topic 11 Nutrients in foods

KEY WORDS
Casein – protein found in milk
Lactose – sugar found in milk

RESEARCH ACTIVITY

Compare the nutritional value of a variety of different fruits and vegetables which are preserved in different ways; for example:
- fresh, frozen and canned raspberries
- fresh, canned and sundried tomatoes.

Explain how the preservation process affects the nutritional content of the fruit.

PRACTICAL ACTIVITY

1 We are being encouraged to eat more fruit and vegetables.
   - Prepare a dish that would be interesting and appealing to young children who claim they do not like to eat fruit and vegetables.
   - Calculate the nutritional value of your dish and explain its contribution to a child's diet.
   - Explain any modifications you could make to improve the nutritional content.
2 Some fruits and vegetables can be eaten raw. Prepare, cook and serve an interesting dish which includes raw fruit and or vegetables.
   Calculate the cost and the nutritional value of the dish.

Small and large fat globules in milk which rise to the top of milk that has not been homogenised

Small fat globules evenly dispersed through the milk

▲ Figure 11.2 Comparison of milk and homogenised milk

TEST YOURSELF

1 Explain why fruits and vegetables are important in our diet.
2 Explain how you can preserve the vitamin C content when cooking vegetables.

Dairy and dairy alternatives

Milk

Milk is mainly water. It is an emulsion and has tiny drops of fat suspended in it. As oil and water do not mix, the fat will rise to the top of the milk. This is seen as the cream line in the milk. Today, much of the milk we buy is homogenised so that the fat is distributed evenly throughout the milk. This means that this fat line is not visible.

Milk contains the following nutrients:
- water
- protein – approximately 82 per cent of milk protein is **casein**
- fat
- carbohydrate – **lactose** is a milk sugar
- vitamins and minerals.

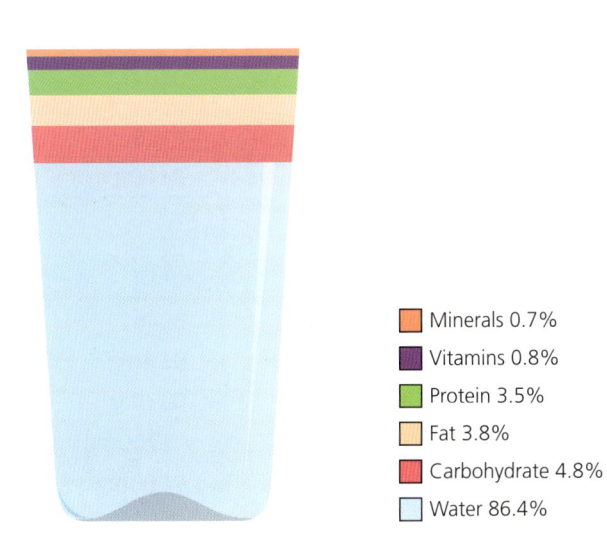

Minerals 0.7%
Vitamins 0.8%
Protein 3.5%
Fat 3.8%
Carbohydrate 4.8%
Water 86.4%

▲ Figure 11.3 Average nutrient content of milk

Milk provides you with energy. It is often described as a perfect food because it is designed to feed the young of the animals it is produced by.

73

KEY WORDS
Retinol – vitamin A
Carotene – vitamin A

There are many varieties of milk we can buy. These vary according to how they have been produced and in their fat content (see Section B: Topic 2 Food processing and production).

The fat content of milk varies depending on how it is processed. Table 11.7 shows the main nutrients found in milk.

Table 11.6 Nutrients found in milk

Nutrients	Information
Protein	• high biological value protein – contains all the essential amino acids
Fat	• amount of fat depends of the type of milk • standardised whole milk has a fat content of 3.5 per cent • contains both saturated and unsaturated fats • sales of reduced-fat milks have increased as we are encouraged to consume less fat (semi-skimmed milk is the most popular milk in the UK)
Carbohydrate	• in the form of lactose • does not taste sweet • can now purchase lactose-free milk for those people who have intolerance
Vitamins	• vitamin A (retinol and carotene) – the amount varies – more in summer • skimmed milk contains fewer vitamins as the fat is removed and vitamin A is fat soluble • vitamin D – it contains more in summer • water-soluble vitamins riboflavin (B2), thiamine (B1) and nicotinic acid (B3)
Minerals	• calcium and phosphorus • approximately 43 per cent of the calcium intake of adults is provided from milk and milk products

Table 11.7 Nutritional value of different types of milk (per 100 g)

Nutritional content	Channel Island	Whole, pasteurised, winter	Semi-skimmed	Skimmed
Energy	327.00 kJ 78.00 kcal	275.00 kJ 66.00 kcal	195.00 kJ 46.00 kcal	140.00 kJ 33.00 kcal
Protein	3.60 g	3.20 g	3.30 g	3.30 g
Carbohydrate of which: sugars starch	 4.80 g 0.00 g	 4.80 g 0.00 g	 5.00 g 0.00 g	 5.00 g 0.00 g
	4.80 g	4.80 g	5.00 g	5.00 g
Fat of which: saturates unsaturates polyunsaturates	5.10 g 3.30 g 1.30 g 0.10 g	3.90 g 2.50 g 1.10 g 0.10 g	1.70 g 1.00 g 0.50 g trace	0.10 g 0.10 g trace trace
Sodium	54.00 mg	55.00 mg	55.00 mg	54.00 mg
Vitamin A Retinol Carotene	 46.00 µg 71.00 µg	 41.00 µg 11.00 µg	 21.00 µg 9.00 µg	 µg trace
Vitamin D	0.03 µg	0.03 µg	0.01 µg	trace
Thiamin	0.04 mg	0.04 mg	0.04 mg	0.04 mg
Riboflavin	0.19 mg	0.17 mg	0.18 mg	0.17 mg
Calcium	130.00 mg	115.00 mg	120.00 mg	120.00 mg
Phosphorus	100.00 mg	92.00 mg	95.00 mg	94.00 mg

(kJ = kilojoules; kcal = kilocalories; g = grams; mg = milligrams; µg = micrograms)

Milk can be processed to produce other milk products such as dried milk powder, evaporated and condensed milk. The nutritional value of these products will be different to the types of milk shown in Table 11.7.

Topic 11 Nutrients in foods

Some people are allergic to cow's milk or are lactose intolerant. This means they may want to buy alternative products which contain similar nutrients.

Table 11.8 Alternatives to milk

Alternative to milk	Nutrients
Rice milk	<ul><li>low in fat and calories</li><li>easily digested source of carbohydrate</li><li>has less protein and essential fatty acids than cow's milk</li></ul>
Oat milk	<ul><li>research shows that oats can help to reduce cholesterol</li><li>rich in folic acid and vitamin E</li><li>low in saturated fat</li><li>good source of fibre and soluble fibre</li></ul>
Soya milk	<ul><li>lower fat content than full-fat cow's milk</li><li>low in carbohydrates</li><li>provides high biological value protein</li></ul>

✔ **KEY POINTS**

- ✔ **Milk is a good source of protein, calcium, vitamin B12 and riboflavin (B2).**
- ✔ **Vitamins A and D content are reduced in skimmed and semi-skimmed milk.**

RESEARCH ACTIVITY

1 Investigate the nutritional value of milk products available and produce a chart or mind map to show their main characteristics and nutritional values.
2 Many people choose to use alternatives to cow's milk such as sheep's milk, goat's milk, rice or almond milk. Investigate how the nutritional values of these milks compare to the milk shown in Table 11.7.

PRACTICAL ACTIVITY

Milk is a versatile food product. Prepare, cook and serve a main course dish which includes milk. Calculate the nutritional value of this dish and explain the contribution it would make to your nutritional requirements.

Cheese

Cheese is made from milk solids and therefore contains similar nutrients. However, their amounts depend on the type of cheese. A hard cheese will contain more fat and protein as more of the liquid has been pressed out during the processing.

Cheese is a concentrated source of protein and also a good source of calcium, vitamin A and riboflavin. However, some types – the harder varieties and cream cheeses – have a high fat content. There are many reduced-fat varieties available today.

Table 11.9 Nutritional content of cheese per 100g

Nutritional content	Cheddar (hard)	Cheddar – reduced fat	Brie (soft)	Cream cheese	Cottage cheese – reduced fat
Energy	1725.00 kJ 416.00 kcal	1141 kJ 273 kcal	1422.00 kJ 343 kcal	1807.00 kJ 439.00 kcal	334.00 kJ 74.00 kcal
Protein	25.40 g	32.7 g	20.30 g	3.10 g	13.30 g
Fat of which saturates	34.90 g 21.68 g	15.8 g 9.9 g	29.1 g 18.20 g	47.40 g 29.70 g	1.50 g 0.96 g
Vitamin A	388 µg	388 µg	329 µg	422 µg	17 µg
Vitamin D	0.3 µg	0.03 µg	0.2 µg	0.3 µg	0 µg
Thiamin	0.03 mg	0.03 mg	0.03 mg	0.03 mg	0.05 mg
Riboflavin	0.39 mg	0.53 mg	0.33 mg	0.13 mg	0.24 mg
Calcium	739 mg	840 mg	256 mg	98 mg	127 mg
Phosphorus	505 mg	620 mg	232 mg	100 mg	171 mg
Sodium	723 mg	670 mg	556 mg	300 mg	300 mg

Yoghurt

There are many different kinds of yoghurt products available to buy. The nutrients present in plain yoghurt are the same as in milk. However, there are many different yoghurts available to purchase and consumers need to read the nutritional labels carefully as some yoghurts are advertised as fat free but have added sugar to them and therefore have a high energy value.

Stretch and challenge

1 Explain why the amount of vitamin A found in milk is reduced in skimmed and semi-skimmed milk.
2 Which type of milk would you recommend for children under the age of five? Give reasons for your decision.

RESEARCH ACTIVITY

There is a wide range of yoghurts available. Investigate the nutritional values of different yoghurt products and produce a report giving advice to parents on which yoghurts to buy for children.

PRACTICAL ACTIVITY

Cheese can be included as an ingredient in both sweet and savoury products.
Prepare a suitable dish for a lacto vegetarian which includes cheese as a main ingredient.

TEST YOURSELF

1 Name the main nutrients found in milk and their functions in the diet.
2 Explain why the fat content of different milks varies.
3 There is a wide range of reduced-fat dairy products available.
   Explain why there has been an increase in the sales of reduced-fat products.

Topic 11 Nutrients in foods

Beans, pulses, fish, eggs, meat and other proteins

Meat

Meat is the muscle tissue of animals.

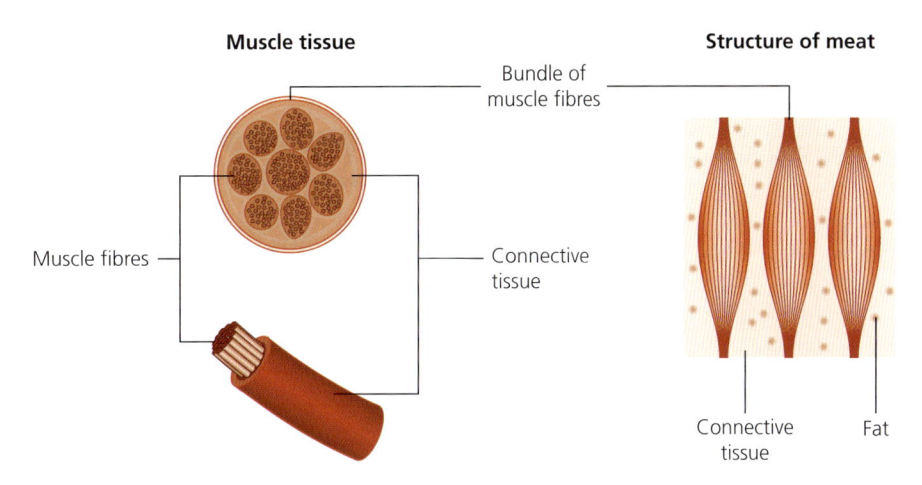

▲ Figure 11.4 Structure of meat

The muscles are fibres bundled together and surrounded by **connective tissue**. Connective tissue is made up of two proteins called **collagen** and **elastin**. **Myoglobin** is a protein which gives meat its red colour, along with some of the haemoglobin which is in the muscles.

Fat is found between the bundles of tissues. The fat helps to keep the meat moist when cooked and it adds flavour.

Different meats contain different amounts of nutrients, particularly fat. The main nutrients found in meat are:

- protein – high biological value
- fat – the amount varies depending on the cut of meat; many farmers are now producing meat that has a lot less fat than in the past
- vitamins – fat-soluble vitamins (vitamins A and D) are found in meat (the amount depends on the amount of fat present as these are fat-soluble vitamins); meat is also a good source of B vitamins but they may leach into cooking liquid as they are water soluble
- iron – red meat is a good source of iron, as is offal (liver, kidney)
- water – makes up approximately 74 per cent of meat.

Poultry is similar to meat in nutritional value, except that it generally contains less fat (apart from goose and duck). Poultry also contains less iron than meat.

We can also eat the internal organs of animals. This is called offal and includes:

- kidneys
- liver
- heart
- tongue
- tripe.

Offal contains similar nutrients to meat but:

- it is usually lower in fat than meat
- liver is a good source of vitamins
- liver is a good source of iron.

> **KEY WORDS**
>
> **Connective tissue** – surrounds the muscle fibres
> **Collagen** – protein found in meat
> **Elastin** – protein found in meat
> **Myoglobin** – the colour pigment that gives red meat its red colour

▲ Figure 11.5 Meat display

✔ KEY POINTS

- ✔ Meat is a good source of protein.
- ✔ Red meat is a good source of iron.
- ✔ Poultry is a good source of protein and contains less fat than meat.

RESEARCH ACTIVITY

Using nutritional software investigate the nutritional content of the following meat and poultry:

- minced beef
- belly pork
- leg of lamb
- chicken breast
- chicken leg.

Explain how you will use this information when you are choosing meat.

PRACTICAL ACTIVITY

Meat is expensive.

Prepare cook, and serve an interesting, filling and nutritious dish for your family using a cheaper cut of meat.

Calculate the nutritional value of the dish and explain what you would serve with it to make it into a balanced meal.

Calculate the cost of the dish per portion.

Fish

The nutritional value of fish depends on its type.

Fish is a good source of:

- protein – fish contains high biological value protein
- fat – white fish and shellfish contain very little fat; oily fish are a good source of essential fatty acids that the body cannot make (omega 3)
- minerals – calcium is a good source in fish where the bones are eaten (for example, in sprats and tinned fish when the bones are softened in processing)
- vitamins A and D – oily fish are good sources.

We are recommended to eat at least two portions of fish a week and one of these should be oily fish.

Topic 11 Nutrients in foods

Table 11.10 Nutrients in fish (per 100 g)

Nutrient	White (cod)	Oily (mackerel)	Shell (prawns)
Energy (kJ)	322.00 kJ	926.00 kJ	321.00 kJ
Energy (kcal)	76.00 kcal	223.00 kcal	76.00 kcal
Protein	17.40 g	19.00 g	17.60 g
Carbohydrate	0 g	0 g	0 g
Fat: of which saturates	0.70 g 0.10 g	16.30 g 3.30 g	0.60 g 0.10 g
Water	82.10 g	64.00 g	79.20 g

✔ KEY POINTS

- ✔ The government recommends that we should eat at least two portions of fish a week.
- ✔ Fish is a good source of protein and iodine.
- ✔ White fish and shellfish are low in fat.

PRACTICAL ACTIVITY

Many children say they do not like fish.
Prepare cook and serve a dish which would encourage children to eat fish.

Eggs

Most of the eggs we use come from hens. However, we can also use duck, goose and quail eggs. Eggs are a very versatile food and can be used in a wide variety of ways in food preparation.

Structure of eggs

Eggs are made up of three parts:

- shell (10 per cent) – the colour of the shell does not affect the nutritional value of the egg
- egg white (60 per cent) – there are two parts to the egg white, the thick and thin
- egg yolk (30 per cent) – the colour of the yolk is related to what the hens are fed on; the yolk also contains **lecithin**, which is an emulsifier. This is useful when combining ingredients that would normally separate (for instance, when it is used in mayonnaise to prevent the oil and water separating).

KEY WORD

Lecithin – found in egg yolk, it is an emulsifier

79

Table 11.11 Structure and nutritional content of an egg

Structure of an egg	Nutrients in eggs (per 100 g)			
		Whole egg	Egg white	Egg yolk
	Energy	627 kJ 151 kcal	153 kJ 36 kcal	1402 kJ 339 kcal
	Fat	11.2 g	trace	30.5 g
	Saturates	3.15 g	trace	8.7 g
	Protein	12.5 g	9 g	16.1 g
	Riboflavin	0.47 mg	0.43 mg	0.54 mg
	Vitamin A	190 µg	0 µg	535 µg
	Iron	1.9 mg	0.1 mg	6.1 mg

Structure of an egg labels: Shell, Inner membrane, Thin white, Yolk, Nucleus of yolk, Cuticle, Air space, Chalaza (plural chalazae), Yolk membrane, Thick white.

KEY WORD

Albumin – protein found in egg white

Eggs are a very useful food in preparing other dishes. They are particularly useful for setting, combining, aerating and thickening mixtures. **Albumin** is the name of the protein in egg white.

Topic links:

- Section C: Topic 1 Food Science
- Section D: Topics 5 and 6

> ✔ **KEY POINTS**
>
> **Eggs are a good source of protein and fat-soluble vitamins.**

PRACTICAL ACTIVITY

Prepare, cook and serve a main course dish using eggs as a main ingredient.

Beans and non-dairy sources of protein

These foods provide protein from sources other than animals. There is a variety of meat-like products available in supermarkets. They have been developed to resemble meat products.

Types of non-dairy protein foods

Soya beans are made into a variety of products, including milk, soy sauce and tofu. Soya beans contain high biological value protein. Textured vegetable protein (TVP) is made from soya beans. The soya beans are made into a flour-like substance and then mixed with water so that the starch can be removed. The mixture is then made into a variety of shapes. It can be bought as a dried or frozen product. It is very bland and needs ingredients with strong flavours to be added to it to make it into an interesting product.

Topic 11 Nutrients in foods

> **KEY WORDS**
> **Tofu** – is made from ground soya beans
> **Mycoprotein** – is produced from micro-organisms

Tofu is made from ground soya beans. It resembles a soft cheese in texture. As it is soft it absorbs flavours easily.

Mycoprotein (Quorn®) is produced from micro-organisms. When it is made into a food product it has egg white added to it to bind it together. The mycoprotein is then shaped into a variety of shapes, such as mince, slices and fillets. It is also used to make ready-to-use products such as sausages. Recently, Quorn™ products have been developed that are suitable for vegans.

Table 11.12 Beans and non-dairy sources of protein

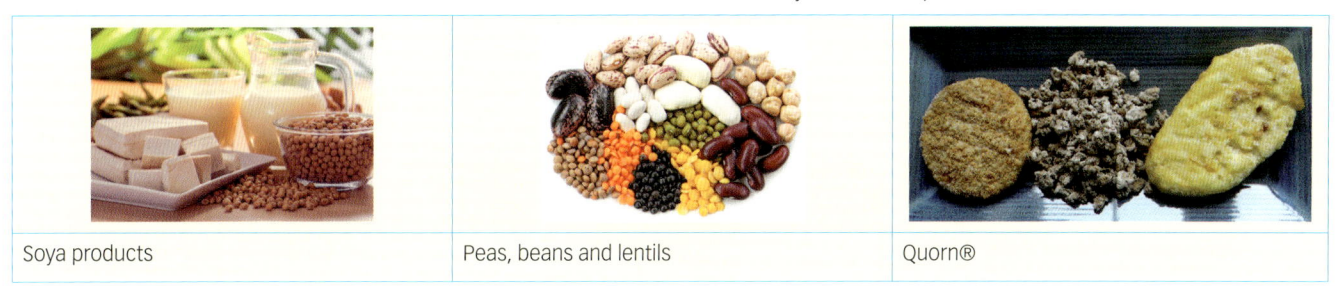

Soya products	Peas, beans and lentils	Quorn®

Peas, beans and lentils are also a source of protein. They are low biological value protein foods.

Nutrients found in alternative protein foods

Alternative protein foods contain the following nutrients:

- protein – soya beans are a high biological value protein
- vitamins and minerals – often they have been enriched with these (for example, soya fortified with vitamin B12 – vitamin B12 is found mainly in animal foods and therefore this helps to meet the needs of vegans)
- fibre – often found in soya mince and Quorn®
- they are low in fat.

Table 11.13 Nutrients found in a range of non-dairy protein foods (per 100 g)

Nutrients	Quorn®	Tofu	Soya mince (frozen)
Energy	433 kJ/103 kcal	438 kJ/105 kcal	727 kJ/175 kcal
Protein	14 g	12.1 g	18.0 g
Carbohydrate of which sugars	5.8 g 1.3 g	0.6 g 0.5 g	3.0 g 2.0 g
Fat of which saturates	2.6 g 0.6 g	6.0 g 1.0 g	10.0 g 1.0 g
Fibre	5.5 g	0.5 g	3.0 g
Sodium	0.4 g	trace	0.12 g

> ✔ **KEY POINTS**
> ✔ Soya and mycoprotein (Quorn®) foods provide protein and are low in fat.
> ✔ They are a valuable source of protein for vegetarians.

> **RESEARCH ACTIVITY**
>
> Using a nutritional program investigate the nutritional value of a range of peas, beans and lentils.
>
> Explain how you could use these ingredients in making balanced meals for different types of vegetarians.

> **PRACTICAL ACTIVITY**
>
> Prepare, cook and serve a main course dish which shows the use of a non-dairy protein food.
>
> Give reasons for your choice of ingredients.
>
> Calculate the nutritional value of the dish.

> **TEST YOURSELF**
>
> 1 Which non-dairy protein food contains all the essential amino acids?
> 2 What are the main nutrients found in non-dairy protein foods?

Foods high in fats and/or sugar

Fats and oils

Fats and oils have lots of different uses in food preparation. There is a great variety of fats and oils that we can purchase, and the market is continuing to expand.

Many foods which can be purchased are high in fat (for example, cheddar cheese is 33 per cent fat). Many processed foods are high in fat, therefore you should look at the nutritional information on the labels.

> **KEY WORDS**
>
> **Oils** – are liquid
> **Fats** – are solid

Structure of fats and oils

- Animal fats contain more saturated fats than vegetable and fish oils.
- Fats and oils can come from both animal and vegetable sources.
- **Oils** are a liquid and **fats** are solid at room temperature.
- Oils come from vegetable sources such as olives, corn, rape, nuts, soya, ground nuts and fish.
- Fats come from animal sources.
- The more saturated fatty acids a product has, the more solid the fat will be.

Nutrients found in fats

The main nutrient in fats is fat. However, the amount of different types of fat they contain varies.

Fats also contain fat-soluble vitamins.

Topic link: You can find more information about fats in Section A: Topic 6 Fats

Topic 11 Nutrients in foods

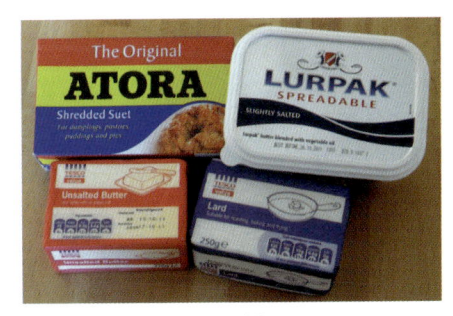

▲ Figure 11.6 Animal fats

▲ Figure 11.7 White fat

▲ Figure 11.8 Low-fat spread

▲ Figure 11.9 Oils

Animal fats

The following foods are made from animal fats:

- butter – from milk
- animal suet – from cows
- lard – from pigs.

They are traditionally high in saturated fats. Today manufacturers make lighter varieties by adding ingredients such as water and vegetable oil.

White fats

White fats are made from oils and can be used to replace lard. They can be used in products such as pastry and for frying. The consistency of the products can vary. Some have air added, making them softer and easier to combine into other ingredients, for instance when rubbing into pastry. As they are made from oils they contain less saturated fat.

Margarine

Margarine has the same total amount of fat as butter but with less saturated fat. Margarine can contain both animal and vegetable fats and is between 80 per cent and 90 per cent fat. By law it must be fortified with vitamins A and D.

Spreads and low-fat spreads

Spreads are similar to margarine but are often lower in fat. There are many low-fat spreads available to buy. These contain a lower fat content than butter, or margarine. The percentage of water in these products is higher. Often they cannot be used for cooking, so the labels on these products need to be read carefully. These are often fortified with vitamins A and D but this is not required by law.

Topic link: Section B: Topic 4 Fortification

Oils

Oils contain 100 per cent fat. They mostly contain unsaturated fats from vegetable sources.

RESEARCH ACTIVITY

Investigate the nutritional content of the following types of fats:

- olive oil
- corn oil
- block butter
- Stork original baking block
- spreadable butter
- low-fat spread
- lard.

Explain how your findings will influence your choice of fats.

83

Sugar

Many foods we buy have additional sugar added to them which increases the energy content of the food. Therefore we need to read the label carefully on all foods. Some foods which we assume to be healthy can have a lot of sugar added to them (for example, yoghurts).

Pure sugar, such as granulated sugar, has very little nutritional value other than providing us with energy. Table 11.14 shows the nutrient content of some sugars and honey.

Table 11.14 Nutrients in sugar, honey and syrup

	Sugar	Honey	Golden syrup
Energy	1700 kJ 400 kcal	1398 kJ 329 kcal	1396kJ 328 kcal
Fat **of which saturates**	0 g 0g	<0.5 g 0.2g	0 g 0 g
Carbohydrate **of which sugars**	99.9 5g 99.95 g	81.5 g 80.8 g	82.0 g 82.0 g

✔ KEY POINTS

- ✔ Sugars only contain calories which supply us with energy.
- ✔ Many foods contain hidden sugars.

RESEARCH ACTIVITY

Investigate the nutritional value of the following drinks:
- fresh orange juice, unsweetened
- orange juice made from concentrate
- fruit smoothie
- orange squash.

Explain what advice you would give to consumers when purchasing fruit drinks.

TEST YOURSELF

1. State the main vitamins found in fats.
2. Margarine is fortified by law. Name the vitamins.
3. Explain why low-fat spreads are not always suitable for cooking.
4. Name the main nutrient found in sugars.

Practice questions

1. Explain why the Eatwell Guide is a good model to use when modifying recipes. (4 marks)

2. State **one** other method of cooking which would lower the fat content of the following dishes:
   - fried beefburger
   - fried egg
   - roast potatoes (3 marks)

3. The recipe below is for a beef lasagne. Explain in detail how this recipe could be modified to meet the requirements of the Eatwell Guide. (6 marks)

   8 sheets white lasagne

   Meat sauce
   200 g minced beef
   1 onion
   400 g tinned tomatoes
   1 bay leaf
   Salt and pepper
   1/4 teaspoon mixed herbs

   Cheese sauce
   40 g butter
   40 g plain flour
   375 ml full fat milk
   50 g mild Cheddar cheese

   Topping
   50 g mild Cheddar cheese–grated

4. State **two** functions of protein in the diet. (2 marks)

5. a State **two** functions of fat in the diet. (2 marks)

   b Give **four** reasons why we should reduce the amount of fat we eat. (4 marks)

   c Explain what is meant by visible and invisible fat. (2 marks)

   d Explain the difference between saturated and polyunsaturated fatty acids. (4 marks)

6. Explain the importance of fibre in the diet. (4 marks)

7. This is a recipe for a chicken curry served with white basmati rice.
   - Chicken breast
   - Double cream
   - Fresh ginger
   - Garlic
   - Chilli powder
   - Fresh coriander
   - Lime juice
   - Butter

- Onion
- Red chilli
- White basmati rice

Explain how you could amend the recipe to reduce the fat content and increase the fibre content. (4 marks)

8 Explain what is meant by the term energy balance. (2 marks)

The quality of written communication will be assessed in the following questions.

9 The following is a primary school child's breakfast:
- Orange squash
- Sugared breakfast cereal with whole milk
- Jam sandwich (white bread).

Explain how this breakfast could be changed to meet current dietary advice. (10 marks)

10 More people are becoming overweight and obese. Discuss how consumers can modify their diet so that they do not become overweight. (12 marks)

Section B: Food

In this section you will learn about the following:
- Food provenance: food source and supply
- Food provenance: food processing and production
- Food security
- Technological developments to support better health and food production
- Development of culinary traditions
- Factors influencing food choice

Topic 1

Food provenance: food source and supply

> **→ WHAT WILL I LEARN?**
>
> **By the end of this topic you should have developed a knowledge and understanding of food sources and types and how:**
>
> → cereals, sugars, fruits and vegetables are grown
> → meat and poultry are reared
> → fish is caught.

How cereals, sugars, fruits and vegetables are grown

Cereals

Cereals are an important food around the world. They are often the **staple food** within a country because they are cheap to produce in comparison to protein foods. The main types of cereal foods are:

- wheat
- rice
- maize
- oats
- barley
- rye.

KEY WORDS

Staple food – food that forms the basis of a traditional diet (for example, wheat, barley, rice, maize)

Table 1.1 Types of cereals

Cereal type	Where grown	What they are used for
Wheat	Europe China India Russia USA Canada Australia	• In many baked products. • Some wheat contains more gluten and is used for specific products like bread, pastry, flaky and rough puff pastry. • Made into other products such as pasta, semolina, couscous. • Used to make breakfast cereals, e.g. Shreddies, Weetabix, Shredded Wheat.

Topic 1 Food provenance: food source and supply

Cereal type	Where grown	What they are used for
Rice	China India Indonesia Bangladesh Vietnam Thailand	There are many different types; they are grouped as long or short (round) grains. • Long-grain rice is usually served with savoury dishes (e.g. a curry, in paella). • Short-grain rice is usually used in puddings (e.g. rice pudding, Indian rice pudding [kheer]) or risotto where the grains tend to clump together when they are cooked. • Rice can be made into flour and is used in biscuits (e.g. shortbread). • Rice can also be made into breakfast cereals (e.g. Rice Krispies).
Maize	USA China Brazil Mexico Indonesia India France	• Made into a variety of food products including breakfast cereals, polenta, cornflour. • Made into corn oil. • Can be eaten as a vegetable – corn on the cob – or can be frozen or canned.
Oats	Russia Canada Finland Poland Australia UK	• Oats are usually rolled rather than crushed when processed. They are then sold by grade – coarse, medium and fine. • Oats can be used as an ingredient in many products (e.g. flapjack, crumbles, porridge). • It can be bought as oatmeal, jumbo oats, porridge oats, oat flakes. • They are often used in breakfast cereals (e.g., muesli). • Can be used to make Oatly, a milk alternative.
Barley	Russia France Germany UK Australia Canada	• Used as an alternative to rice. • Can be made into malt extract and used as a sweetener. • Used in soups and stews. • Often used as animal feed.
Rye	Europe Russia Canada USA	• Usually ground into flour and used to make a dark bread and crispbread.
Spelt	UK Russia Spain Eastern Europe	• Used in a similar way to wheat in baked foods.

All the cereal products are similar to each other in structure. Wheat is one of the main cereals grown around the world. It therefore makes a valuable contribution to our diets.

Topic links:

- Section A: Topic 1 The relationship between diet and health
- Section A: Topic 4 Energy balance
- Section A: Topic 7 Carbohydrates
- Section B: Topic 5 Culinary traditions

Sugars

Sugars are natural sweeteners made from plants. We get sugar from two types of plants: sugar beet and sugar cane.

Sugar cane

Sugar cane is a tall, bamboo-like grass that can grow up to six metres tall. It is mainly grown in tropical countries. Approximately 80 per cent of the world's sugar comes from sugar cane. The cost of producing sugar is generally cheaper from sugar cane than sugar beet.

Sugar beet

Sugar beet is a root crop and looks like a large turnip. It is grown in the northern hemisphere. About 20 per cent of the world's sugar supply comes from sugar beet.

Honey

Honey is also a natural sweetener and is produced by bees from the nectar of plants. The flavour of the honey varies depending on the flowers from which the bees have collected their nectar.

Maple syrup

Maple syrup is made from the plant juices (sap) of the maple tree. It has a very distinct flavour and is very sweet.

Topic links:

- Section A: Topic 1 The relationship between diet and health
- Section A: Topic 4 Energy balance
- Section A: Topic 7 Carbohydrates

▲ Figure 1.1 Sugar cane plantation

▲ Figure 1.2 Sugar beet

▲ Figure 1.3 Honeycomb and honey

RESEARCH ACTIVITY

Either visit a supermarket or use a supermarket website to investigate different types of sugars and syrups that are available.

Display your results in a table with the following headings:

Type of sugar	Description	Uses in cooking

Topic links:

- Section B: Topic 1 page 90

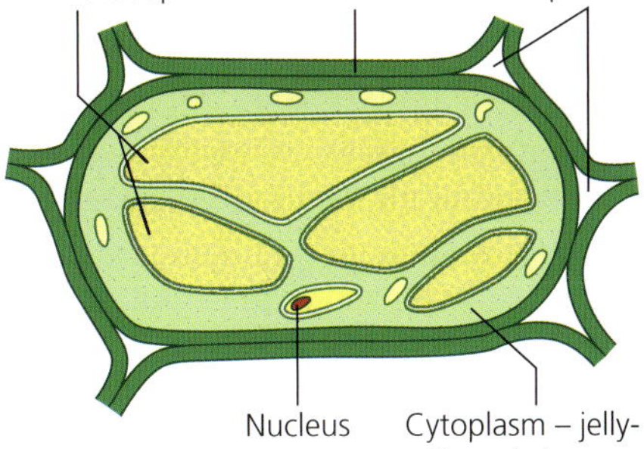

Topic 1 Food provenance: food source and supply

Fruits and vegetables

Fruits

There is a large range of fruits which come in a variety of flavours, colours, sizes and textures. They are mostly eaten raw, but on some occasions are cooked.

Fruits are made up of cells, which in turn are made up of:

- cell wall – mainly cellulose
- cytoplasm – jelly-like substance that contains the colour pigments and fat droplets
- vacuole – the largest part of the cell, which contains sugar, pigments and salts.

Fruits can be categorised by their type. The four main types are shown in Table 1.2.

▲ Figure 1.4 Structure of a fruit cell

Table 1.2 Categories of fruit

Type	Examples	
Citrus		Lemons Limes Oranges Grapefruit Tangerines
Soft or berry fruits		Raspberries Strawberries Blueberries Blackcurrants
Hard fruit		Apples Pears
Some fruits do not fit any category		Kiwi Pomegranate Melon Banana

91

▲ **Figure 1.5** Many vegetables are brightly coloured

▶ **Figure 1.6** We eat different parts of the vegetable plants and this is how they are classified

RESEARCH ACTIVITY

Investigate where each of the fruits in Figure 1.6 are grown.

Vegetables

Vegetables are similar to fruit in structure. However, they do vary depending on the type. For example, the cellulose which makes up the cell walls is thin and delicate in leaf products like spinach and lettuce. The cells also contain a lot of water; if the water is lost, the leaves become limp.

Vegetables also come in a variety of colours. The colour depends on:

- chlorophyll – provides the green colour, for example in cabbage, sprouts, lettuce
- carotenoids – yellow and orange, for example in carrots
- anthocyanins – red and blue, for example in beetroot, red cabbage.

The nutrient content of vegetables varies depending on their type and how they are cooked.

For both fruits and vegetables the many water-soluble vitamins are destroyed when they are processed, especially when canning. Some vegetables are harvested in the field and then frozen in less than three hours.

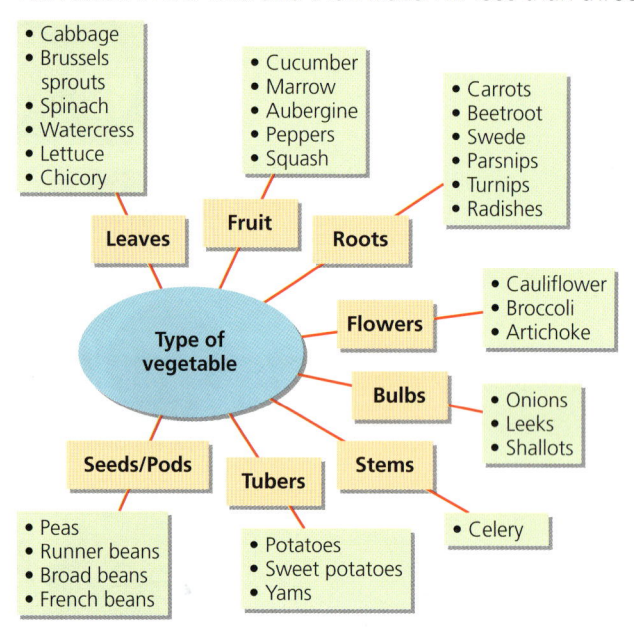

Type of vegetable

- **Leaves**: Cabbage, Brussels sprouts, Spinach, Watercress, Lettuce, Chicory
- **Fruit**: Cucumber, Marrow, Aubergine, Peppers, Squash
- **Roots**: Carrots, Beetroot, Swede, Parsnips, Turnips, Radishes
- **Flowers**: Cauliflower, Broccoli, Artichoke
- **Bulbs**: Onions, Leeks, Shallots
- **Stems**: Celery
- **Tubers**: Potatoes, Sweet potatoes, Yams
- **Seeds/Pods**: Peas, Runner beans, Broad beans, French beans

Topic links:

- Section A: Topic 1 The relationship between diet and health
- Section A: Topic 8 Vitamins
- Section C: Topic 1 Food science
- Section A: Topic 11 Nutrients in food

The advantages of locally produced and seasonal foods

There are large amounts of fruit and vegetables available in the shops. Many are grown in the UK. There are many advantages and disadvantages of buying **locally produced** fruit and vegetables.

KEY WORDS

Locally produced – grown or reared close to where it is purchased

Section B: Food

92

Topic 1 Food provenance: food source and supply

Table 1.3 Advantages and disadvantages of buying locally produced fruit and vegetables

Advantages	Disadvantages
- Fresher - Fewer food miles - Reduced carbon footprint - Less energy used in transporting - Supports local farmers/UK farmers	- May not be as much choice - Some people do not like the food being different sizes - Is sometimes more expensive

We also **import** a lot of fruit and vegetables from around the world. This gives us greater variety in the diet. Table 1.4 shows a range of fruits and vegetables which were imported to the UK in April.

Table 1.4 Fruit and vegetables imported to the UK

Butternut squash South Africa	Aubergine Canary Islands		Banana Columbia	Pineapple Costa Rica
Pak choi Spain				Mango South Africa
Sweet potato USA				Strawberries Spain
Tomatoes Morocco				Blackberries Mexico
Baby sweetcorn Mozambique				Raspberries Portugal
New Potatoes Jersey	Red pepper Holland	Watercress Spain	Lime Brazil	Plums South Africa

Table 1.5 Fruit and vegetables in season in the UK

January	February	March	April
Cabbage Kale Parsnips Swede	Artichokes Spring greens Watercress	Cauliflower Purple sprouting broccoli	Greenhouse lettuce Spring greens Salad onions Rhubarb
May	**June**	**July**	**August**
Asparagus Tomatoes Spring cabbage Strawberries	Carrots Broad beans Lettuce Spinach Strawberries Blackcurrants Gooseberries	Cauliflower Mange tout/peas Salad potatoes Blueberries Cherries Raspberries	Charlotte potatoes Courgettes French beans Romaine lettuce Discovery apples
September	**October**	**November**	**December**
Beetroot Runner beans Plums Pears Apples	Celery Pumpkin Turnips Squash Damsons Pears	Chinese leaves Green cabbage Brussels sprouts Pumpkin	Brussels sprouts on a stalk Leeks Savoy cabbage Red cabbage Chantenay carrots

With the development of technology the seasons of fruit and vegetable availability are getting longer in the UK. For example, you can now buy strawberries grown in England in December. They are being grown in glasshouses and growers are developing new plants with longer growing seasons.

> **RESEARCH ACTIVITY**
>
> Either visit a supermarket or look at a supermarket website and make a list of the products they stock that are produced in the UK and imported. Produce a chart which compares:
> - Price per 100 g
> - Food miles from the country of origin

Some vegetable products are grown in artificial environments to increase productivity (for instance, growing lettuces in glasshouses). The benefits of these methods are that the growing conditions can be monitored and controlled to improve **productivity**.

The method that is used to grow some products (like lettuce) in glasshouses is hydroponics. This means that the soil is replaced with a mineral solution which is pumped around the plant's roots. Not having soil means there is less risk of disease in the plants.

> **KEY WORDS**
>
> **Carbon footprint** – a measure of the impact human activities have on the environment in terms of greenhouse gases produced through the outlet of carbon dioxide
>
> **Imported** – food that is grown in a different country and brought to the UK
>
> **Productivity** – amount of food produced

▲ Figure 1.7 Lettuce grown on a hydroponic farm

Using local products means you are getting quality products with a low **carbon footprint**. Carbon footprint is a measure of the impact human activities have on the environment in terms of greenhouse gases produced through the outlet of carbon dioxide.

Stretch and challenge

Investigate which crops are being produced using hydroponic systems.

Topic 1 Food provenance: food source and supply

> **RESEARCH ACTIVITY**
>
> Research which foods are grown locally.

> **PRACTICAL ACTIVITY**
>
> Prepare a dish to show how local ingredients can be used to make creative dishes.

> **✔ KEY POINTS**
>
> ✔ Cereals such as wheat, rice, maize, oats, barley and rye are staple foods in many countries around the world.
> ✔ Sugars are natural sweeteners made from plants. We get sugar from two types of plants: sugar beet and sugar cane.
> ✔ A wide variety of fruits and vegetables is grown in the UK.
> ✔ Locally produced fruit and vegetables have a lower carbon footprint.
> ✔ Fruits and vegetables can be classified into different groups.

> **TEST YOURSELF**
>
> 1 Name the **three** different groups of fruits. For each, give **two** examples of fruit.
> 2 Name the **eight** classifications for vegetables. For each, give **two** examples of vegetables.
> 3 State **two** advantages and two disadvantages of buying locally produced fruits and vegetables.

How meat and poultry are reared

There is a large range of meat and meat products available to purchase in the shops. The quality of the product will depend on how the animal has been kept, what it was fed, its age, and how it is processed and cooked.

Classification of meat, poultry and game

Classification of meat

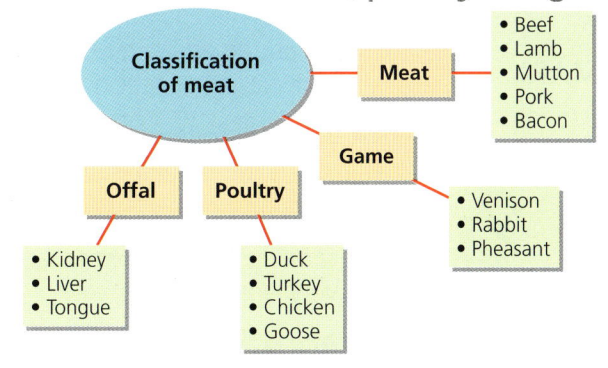

- Meat
  - Beef
  - Lamb
  - Mutton
  - Pork
  - Bacon
- Game
  - Venison
  - Rabbit
  - Pheasant
- Poultry
  - Duck
  - Turkey
  - Chicken
  - Goose
- Offal
  - Kidney
  - Liver
  - Tongue

▲ Figure 1.8 Classification of meat

Animal welfare in food production

There are many different farming methods for producing meat, poultry and dairy products.

Some of these have clear regulations, such as the production of chickens for meat and as laying hens. The different types of production include:

- laying cage systems – enriched colony cages
- barn egg
- free range
- **organic.**

Stretch and challenge

Investigate the requirements for:

- enriched colony cages
- barn egg production
- free-range chicken and egg production.

Many other claims are made on food products, such as outdoor reared, outdoor bred and free range for pigs. These terms can mean a variety of different things, depending on the farmer who has produced the product, because there is currently no legislation regarding the use of these terms. Consumers need to read and look carefully at the labels on food products or on the producer's website to see what they mean by the description they are using.

One of the best ways to know that food has been produced **sustainably** and taking into consideration animal welfare is when it has the Red Tractor or RSPCA Assured (previously known as Freedom Food) marks.

We all want quality food that is affordable and safe to eat. The Red Tractor is an independent mark of quality that guarantees that the food we are buying comes from farms and food companies that meet high standards of food safety and hygiene, animal welfare and environmental protection. Look for the Red Tractor Assurance logo.

Farming methods

Most agricultural farming relies heavily on chemical fertilisers and pesticides (this is often called **intensive farming**). These are often used to ensure that a large quantity is produced. Around 350 pesticides are permitted in the UK, and it is estimated that 4.5 billion litres of them are used annually. Many people are concerned about the long term effect the fertilisers and pesticides can have on us; the effect these have on the environment, for example on wildlife; chemicals and pesticides can leach into rivers and pollute the waters.

Intensive farming is often called 'factory farming'. Intensive farming means that a large amount of food is produced from a relatively small amount of land. Intensive methods are used to increase the amount of food produced.

Intensive farming also includes growing high-yield crops which are often grown in very large fields.

Many vegetables crops are grown intensively in greenhouses, e.g. tomatoes. More recent developments have included using hydroponic systems where food is grown in a nutrient solution rather than soil.

In intensive farming animals are often kept indoors so that their diet, breeding and disease control can be managed. Some animals can be kept indoors for the whole of their lives.

▲ **Figure 1.9** Red Tractor and RSPCA Assured logos

KEY WORDS

Intensive farming – large amount of produce is generated from a relatively Small area of land

Organic – grown or reared without the use of artificial aids, fertilisers, pesticides and antibiotics

Sustainable – the resource will not run out

Topic 1 Food provenance: food source and supply

Organic farming

certifies over 80 per cent of organic farming and food processing in the UK. For more information see www.soilassociation.org.

Organic farming strictly limits the use of artificial chemical fertilisers or pesticides. Antibiotics for animals are kept to an absolute minimum. Genetically modified crops are forbidden. Organic bodies also demand more space for animals and higher welfare standards.

What does organic mean?

- All food sold as organic must be approved by organic certification bodies and produced according to stringent EC laws.
- It is produced by farmers who grow, handle and process crops without synthetic fertilisers, pesticides and herbicides or any other artificial ingredient.
- It will not contain any genetically engineered ingredients.
- Organic meat, poultry, eggs and dairy products come from animals that are given no antibiotics or growth hormones.
- Organic producers can only use natural fertilisers, not synthetic ones.
- Organic foods are considered to taste nicer, avoid the risk of a combination of chemicals and respect soil structure and wildlife.

Most large supermarkets sell organic foods and you can often buy them at farmers' markets and organic farm shops. There has also been an increase in the number of organic box schemes. This means that you get organic, often locally produced, seasonal foods delivered to your home. Some people will choose to buy organic foods for the following reasons:

- They believe that it tastes better.
- They are concerned about the use of chemical pesticides on crops and that they could harm their health.
- They are concerned about the effect the use of chemicals can have on the environment (for example, chemicals getting into rivers, destroying wildlife).

▲ Figure 1.10 The Soil Association organic logo

▲ Figure 1.11 Able and Cole organic vegetable box

RESEARCH ACTIVITY

Investigate the range of organic products in the supermarket. Compare prices with non-organic products.

✔ KEY POINTS

- The quality of meat and meat products will depend on how the animal has been kept, what it was fed, its age, and how it is processed and cooked.
- Meat includes beef, lamb, mutton, pork and bacon.
- Poultry includes duck, turkey, chicken and goose.
- Game includes venison, rabbit and pheasant.
- Different farming systems can be used for rearing meat and poultry.
- Organic farming limits the use of artificial chemical fertilisers or pesticides and demands more space and higher welfare standards for animals. Antibiotics for animals are kept to an absolute minimum. Genetically modified crops are forbidden.

▲ **Figure 1.12** Rope-grown mussels

TEST YOURSELF

1. Why do some people choose to buy meat products displaying the Red Tractor logo?
2. Give **three** reasons why some people choose to buy organic food.
3. State **three** methods of egg production.
4. How is meat classified? Draw a table and give examples of meat for each group.

How fish are caught

There are many varieties of fish available. Fish can be bought in many different forms, for instance fresh, frozen and canned.

Classification of fish

Table 1.6 Types of fish

Type of fish	Examples	Description
White, round	Cod, haddock, coley, whiting	• Has firm white flesh • Very low in fat
White, flat	Plaice, turbot, halibut, Dover sole	
Oily	Tuna, salmon, sardines, trout, herring, mackerel, whitebait, pilchards	• Flesh is quite dark due to the oil • Contains omega-3 fatty acids, which may help prevent heart disease.
Shellfish, molluscs	Oysters, scallops, cockles, mussels, clams	• Have an outer shell which needs to be removed to get the flesh out of the fish • Low in fat.
Shellfish, crustaceans	Crab, lobster, prawns, shrimps	• Have a tougher outer shell than molluscs • Have flexible joints that allow for quick movement • Low in fat.

▲ **Figure 1.13** White fish (cod)

▲ **Figure 1.14** Oily fish (herring)

▲ **Figure 1.15** Shellfish

Topic 1 Food provenance: food source and supply

Fishing methods

There are a number of different methods used to catch fish, including:

- **Trawling:** this is the most common method; it uses nets, which are pulled along the sea floor to catch the fish.
- **Dredging:** metal cages or baskets are towed across the sea floor to catch shellfish.
- **Gill netting:** this method uses curtains of netting which are suspended in the sea into which fish swim.
- **Harpooning:** a long metal or wooden pole is lunged into the fish.
- **Jigging:** uses a grappling hook attached to a line and targets fish.
- **Long lining:** uses long lines that run for miles, which are strung with baited hooks to attract the fish.
- **Pole and line fishing:** uses a fishing pole and bait to target fish.
- **Purse seining:** drawing a large net around a school of fish.
- **Traps and pots:** wire or wood cages with bait to attract fish are placed on the sea floor.
- **Cyanide fishing:** uses explosives to stun or kill fish, making them easier to catch. This method of fishing is prohibited in many parts of the world.

However, some of these fishing methods are seen as harmful to the environment:

- Trawler nets and dredging baskets damage the seabed.
- Dredging is noisy and can disturb whales and dolphins.
- Some fishing methods such as purse seining, trawling, and dredging can result in a **bycatch**. These fish are often returned to the sea and may be either dead or dying.
- Other marine life such as sharks and turtles can be trapped in nets.

Sustainable fish supply

Overfishing and use of intensive fishing methods has caused a decline in wild fish stocks.

In order for wild fish stocks to recover, we need to fish more responsibly and ensure the fish we eat only comes from sustainably managed stocks where they are farmed and caught using methods that have minimal damage to the marine environment and other wildlife.

When you buy fish with the Marine Stewardship Council logo it is clear that the fish comes from a sustainable source. The Marine Stewardship Council sets standards for sustainable fishing and seafood traceability.

Harpooning and jigging are seen as more environmentally responsible than some of the other fishing methods, as they only target the fish to be killed. Other measures used to reduce the environmental impact of fishing include:

- sinking long lines deeper, or using different hooks to reduce bycatch
- releasing unwanted species if caught when pole or line fishing
- using larger holes in nets so younger fish are not caught and have chance to grow
- setting up marine reserves (areas where fishing is banned) to allow stocks to recover.

KEY WORD

By catch – all types of fish which are caught unintentionally when catching other fish

▲ Figure 1.18 Marine Stewardship Council logo

Fish farming

Fish farming is seen as one way of ensuring future fish supplies. Fish are reared in tanks or enclosures either using an indoor or outdoor cage system.

Fish farming can be divided into three groups:

1 **Farming** – the whole process takes place in captivity. This is from the breeding of the eggs through to the catching of the fish.
2 **Sea rearing** – young fish are caught in the wild and then grown in a controlled environment, such as rope grown mussels.
3 **Sea ranching** – young fish are bred in captivity and then released into the wild. This helps to increase the fish stocks.

Fish farming is one of the world's fastest expanding food production industries. For many years prawns, scallops, lobster, salmon, sea bass, trout and tilapia have been farmed. Recently there has been the development of some deep sea farmed fish in the UK (cod and halibut).

While intensive farming of some animals is viewed negatively due to concerns over animal welfare, intensive fish farming is seen more positively as it allows wild fish stocks to recover and eliminates bycatch. There are strict standards of hygiene and welfare for fish farms and they are regularly checked to ensure that high standards are maintained.

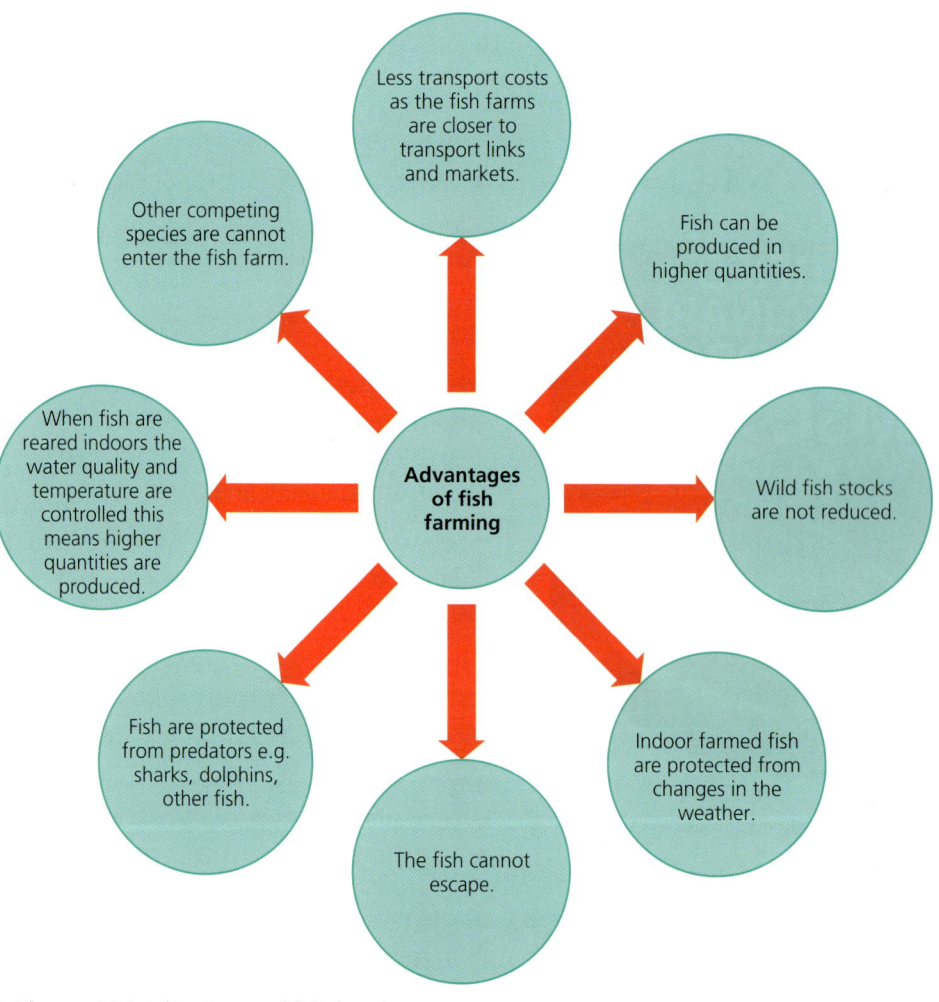

Advantages of fish farming:
- Less transport costs as the fish farms are closer to transport links and markets.
- Fish can be produced in higher quantities.
- Wild fish stocks are not reduced.
- Indoor farmed fish are protected from changes in the weather.
- The fish cannot escape.
- Fish are protected from predators e.g. sharks, dolphins, other fish.
- When fish are reared indoors the water quality and temperature are controlled this means higher quantities are produced.
- Other competing species are cannot enter the fish farm.

▲ Figure 1.16 Advantages of fish farming

Topic 1 Food provenance: food source and supply

Disadvantages of fish farming

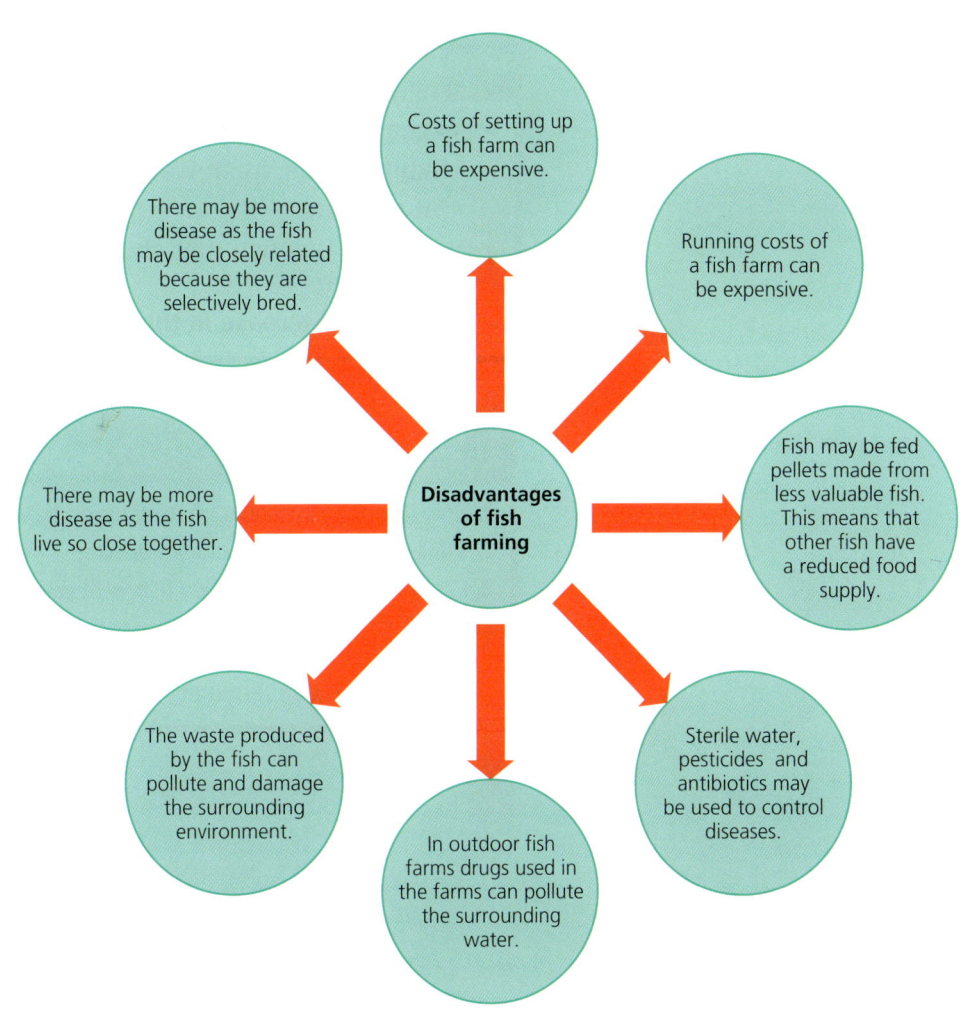

- Costs of setting up a fish farm can be expensive.
- Running costs of a fish farm can be expensive.
- Fish may be fed pellets made from less valuable fish. This means that other fish have a reduced food supply.
- Sterile water, pesticides and antibiotics may be used to control diseases.
- In outdoor fish farms drugs used in the farms can pollute the surrounding water.
- The waste produced by the fish can pollute and damage the surrounding environment.
- There may be more disease as the fish live so close together.
- There may be more disease as the fish may be closely related because they are selectively bred.

▲ Figure 1.17 Disadvantages of fish farming

Stretch and challenge

The European Union sets fishing quotas which dictate the amounts and types of fish which can be caught. Investigate the different campaigns which support fish being caught and reared in a sustainable way.

Stretch and challenge

Explain why responsible sourcing of fish is important.

Investigate the disadvantages of fish farming.

Sustainable fish supply

When you buy fish with the Marine Stewardship Council logo it is clear that the fish comes from a sustainable source. The Marine Stewardship Council sets standards for sustainable fishing and seafood **traceability**.

> **KEY WORD**
>
> **Traceability** – can track the product back through all stages of production
>
> **By catch** – all types of fish which are caught unintentionally when catching other fish

✔ KEY POINTS

✔ **Fish can be classified by:**
  - habitat – sea, fresh water
  - fat content.
✔ **We should buy fish that shows the Marine Stewardship Council logo.**
✔ **There is an increase in the numbers and types of fish farms.**

TEST YOURSELF

1. How are fish classified? Draw a table and give examples of fish for each group.
2. State the **three** types of fish farming.
3. Explain why we should buy fish with the Marine Stewardship Council logo on the packaging.
4. Give **three** advantages and disadvantages of fish farming.
5. Describe **five** different methods of catching fish.

Topic 2
Food provenance: food processing and production

> ### → WHAT WILL I LEARN?
> By the end of this topic you should have developed a knowledge and understanding of:
> → primary processing of wheat and milk
> → secondary processing of:
>   - milk into butter, cream, yoghurt and cheese
>   - flour into bread and pasta
> → industrial and domestic food processing and preserving methods.

Introduction

Different foods are grown in different countries depending on the suitability of the climate. After the food has been grown it is processed. There are two types of processing: **primary** and **secondary**.

Primary processing

This is changing a basic food to preserve it or to prepare it for sale or cooking. Examples of primary food processing include:

- milling wheat into flour
- heat-treating milk
- extracting oil from crops, such as maize for corn oil, rape for rapeseed oil, olives for olive oil
- peeling, stoning and slicing fruit for canning or freezing.

Secondary processing

This is when the primary processed foods are made into other products. Examples of this include:

- making flour into pasta, bread, biscuits and other flour-based products
- making milk into cheese, butter and yoghurt.

Primary stages of food processing

Primary processing of wheat

Grains of wheat are made into flour through the process of **milling**. Figure 2.1 shows the stages of milling wheat.

> **KEY WORDS**
> **Primary processing** – changing a basic food to preserve it or prepare it for sale or cooking
> **Secondary processing** – using a primary processed food to make it into another product

103

Cleaned wheat	Magnets, metal detectors and other machines extract metal objects, stones and other grains, such as barley, oats and small seeds from the wheat grain. Throughout the cleaning process, air currents lift off dust and chaff.
Conditioned wheat	Water softens the outer pericarp (bran) layer of the wheat and makes it easier to remove the floury endosperm during milling.
Gristing	The cleaned and conditioned wheat is blended with other types of wheat in a process called gristing to make different kinds of flour. Wheat gluten is sometimes added to increase the protein content of milled flours.
Break Rolls / Sieves	**Stage 1:** The grist is passed through a series of fluted break rolls rotating at different speeds. These rolls are set so that they do not crush the wheat but shear it open, separating the white, inner portion from the outer skins.
Reduction Rolls	**Stage 2:** The fragments of wheat grain are separated by a complex arrangement of sieves. White endosperm particles are channelled to a series of sieves of smooth reduction rolls for final milling into white flour.
Wheat germ / Wheat flour / Bran	Coarser pieces of bran with endosperm still attached go to a second break roll, and stages 1 and 2 are repeated until the flour bran and wheat germ are completely separated. The result is a number of flour streams containing white flour bran and wheat germ.

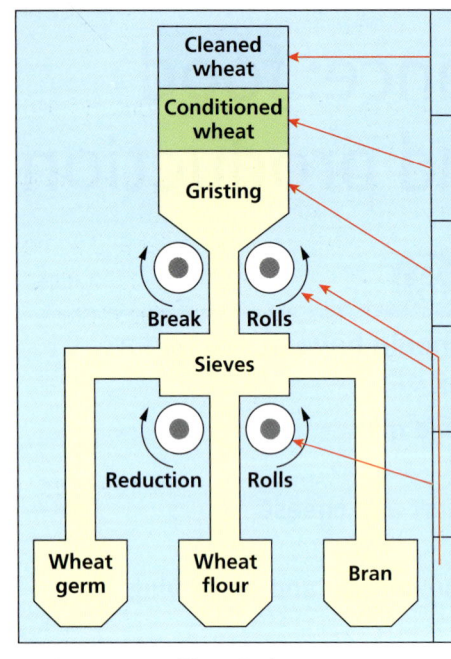

▲ Figure 2.1 Milling of wheat

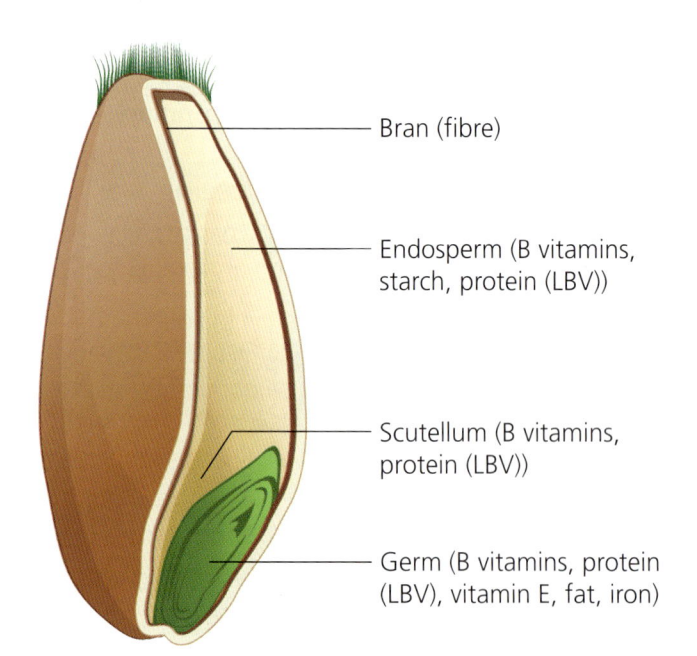

- Bran (fibre)
- Endosperm (B vitamins, starch, protein (LBV))
- Scutellum (B vitamins, protein (LBV))
- Germ (B vitamins, protein (LBV), vitamin E, fat, iron)

▲ Figure 2.2 Structure of wheat

There is a large variety of flours available and they are used for making many different products. Figure 2.2 shows the structure of wheat. From this diagram you can see which parts of the wheat grain are used to make different types of flour.

Topic 2 Food provenance: food processing and production

Flours can be described by their **extraction rate**; that is how much of the whole grain is used:

- Wholemeal flour – extraction rate of 100 per cent means that nothing has been removed from it. It is light brown in colour.
- Brown flour – extraction rate of 85–90 per cent (10–15 per cent of the grain is removed as bran). It is also light brown in colour.
- White flour – extraction rate of 70–75 per cent (the bran, germ, fat and some of the minerals have been removed). In the UK white flour has to be fortified by law with iron, calcium, thiamine and niacin. This is replacing the iron and B vitamins that have been lost in processing. It is white in appearance.

All flours apart from wholemeal and some self-raising flours are **fortified** by law.

There is a large range of different flours that can be bought in supermarkets. Table 2.1 shows the most common ones.

Table 2.1 Types of flour and their uses

Type of flour	Uses
Strong flour	This has a higher **gluten** content, which is needed in bread making and in flaky and choux pastry. The gluten is able to stretch after it is mixed with water and developed, for example, by kneading or rolling and folding, and helps to produce an elastic mixture.
Soft flour	This is used for cake and pastry making and has a lower gluten content.
Self-raising flour	This has a **chemical raising agent** added to it.
Gluten-free flour	Made from flours which do not contain gluten i.e. rice, tapioca, potato flour. It is made for people who have **coeliac disease**.

KEY WORDS

Chemical raising agent – baking powder or bicarbonate of soda are examples of chemical raising agents

Coeliac disease – a medical condition caused by an allergy to the protein gluten, present in cereals – wheat, barley and rye

Extraction rate – how much of the whole grain is used

Fortified – when a nutrient is added to a product to improve its nutritional value

Gluten – protein in flour

RESEARCH ACTIVITY

Table 2.1 shows the main types of flour available. Investigate what other flours are available and what they are used for.

Topic links:

- Section B: Topic 4 Technological developments to support better health and food production — Fortification
- Section D: Topic 3 Food security

Primary processing of milk

There is a wide variety of milk available. Cow's milk is the most popular milk consumed in the UK. Other sources of milk come from goats and sheep. Cows are milked twice a day and the average UK dairy farm produces 2,000 litres of milk. Once the cows have been milked it is stored in tanks at 4°C until it is collected and taken to a dairy for processing.

Milk is mainly water. It is an **emulsion** and has tiny drops of fat suspended in it. As oil and water do not mix, the fat will rise to the top of the milk. This is seen as the cream line in the milk. Today, much of the milk we buy is homogenised so that the fat is distributed evenly throughout the milk, which means that the fat line is not visible. **Homogenisation** involves forcing the milk at high pressure through small holes. This breaks up the fat globules in order to spread them evenly throughout the milk.

KEY WORDS

Emulsion – a mixture of two liquids

Homogenisation – involves forcing the milk at high pressure through small holes. This breaks up the fat globules in order to spread them evenly throughout the milk and prevent separation of a cream layer

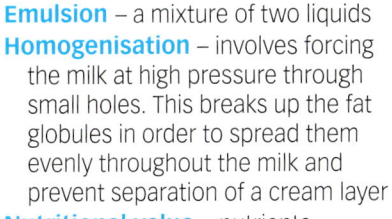

Nutritional value – nutrients contained in product

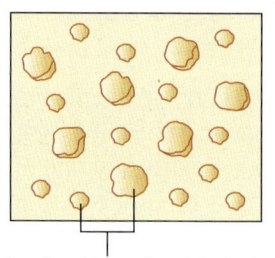

Small and large fat globules in milk which rise to the top of milk that has not been homogenised

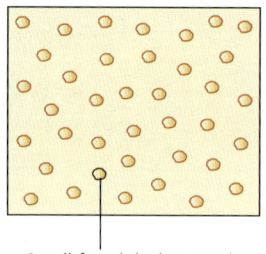

Small fat globules evenly dispersed through the milk

▲ Figure 2.3 Comparison of milk and homogenised milk

KEY WORD

Pasteurised – a method of heat-treating milk to kill harmful bacteria

Sterlisation – a method of heat treatment which kills all micro ogranisisms

Most of the milk consumed in England has been **pasteurised**. This means that any harmful micro-organisms have been destroyed. Table 2.2 shows three methods of heat-treating milk which are used in the UK.

Table 2.2 Heat treatment of milk

Method of heat treatment	Treatment	Effect of the treatment
Pasteurised milk	Heated to a temperature of at least 72°C for a minimum of 15 seconds and maximum of 25 seconds Milk is cooled quickly to below 6°C	Kills harmful bacteria Little effect on the nutritional value of the milk Extends the shelf life of the milk
Sterilised milk	Heated to a temperature of 113–130°C for approximately 10–30 minutes Then cooled quickly	Destroys nearly all the bacteria Changes the taste and colour Destroys some vitamins Unopened bottles or cartons can be kept for several months without being in a fridge Once opened it must be treated as fresh
UHT milk (ultra heat-treated)	Heated to a temperature of at least 135°C for 1 second Put into sterile, sealed containers	Unopened packs have a long shelf life Once opened it must be treated as fresh Little effect on flavour or nutritional value

Varieties of milk

There are many different types of milk available for us to buy. These vary according to how they have been produced and their fat content.

- Whole milk:
  - has had nothing added or removed
  - has a minimum content of 3.5 per cent fat.
- Semi-skimmed milk:
  - is the most popular type of milk in the UK
  - has a fat content of 1.7 per cent.
- Skimmed milk:
  - has a fat content of 0–0.5 per cent
  - contains slightly more calcium than whole milk
  - has lower levels of fat-soluble vitamins
  - is not recommended for children under the age of five.

Topic 2 Food provenance: food processing and production

- Channel Island milk:
  - is higher in calories and fat than whole milk
  - has a higher content of fat-soluble vitamins
  - has a visible cream line and is commonly sold in supermarkets as Channel Island or Jersey milk. There are also products sold as breakfast milk – this is Channel Island milk which has been homogenised so that the cream is evenly distributed throughout the milk. The milk has a very creamy flavour throughout.
- Organic milk:
  - comes from cows grazed in fields where there are no added chemical fertilisers or chemicals
  - it is heat-treated in the same way as other milk
  - can be purchased as whole, semi-skimmed or skimmed.

RESEARCH ACTIVITY

1 Milk can be purchased in other ways (for example, evaporated, condensed, dried). Investigate how milk is treated to produced these different types.
2 Using a nutritional program investigate how the nutritional value of milk changes depending on the fat content. Explain the differences.
3 Using a nutritional program investigate how the heat treatment of milk affects the nutritional content of milk. Explain the differences

Stretch and challenge

1 Investigate what is meant by 'untreated' milk.
2 Investigate how the nutritional content of goat's and sheep's milk compares with that of cow's milk.

✔ KEY POINTS

- ✔ **Primary processing is changing a basic food to preserve it or to prepare it for sale or cooking.**
- ✔ **The grains of wheat are made into flour through the process of milling.**
- ✔ **Flours can be described by their extraction rates.**
- ✔ **The three main methods of heat-treating milk are pasteurisation, sterilisation, ultra heat-treated (UHT).**
- ✔ **The fat content of milk can vary.**

TEST YOURSELF

1 Explain what is meant by the 'extraction rate' of wheat.
2 Which type of flour contains the most gluten?
3 State **three** different methods of heat-treating milk.
4 Explain what is meant by 'homogenisation'.

Secondary stages of food processing and production

How flour is made into bread

When flour is made into bread this is secondary processing. All white bread is made with flour which has been fortified with calcium, iron and B vitamins. The same ingredients are used in bread when it is made in industry and in the home. The main ingredients are:

- flour – strong plain flour as the gluten content is higher
- **yeast** – to make the bread rise
- salt – to add taste and aid proving
- vegetable fat – to make the loaf lighter and airier and extend its shelf life
- water.

Table 2.3 shows how bread is made in industry.

> **KEY WORDS**
> **Prove** – when the yeast fills the dough with gas, causing it to rise and aerate
> **Yeast** – raising agent used in bread

Table 2.3 Bread made in industry

Delivery and storage Flour and other ingredients are delivered to the bakery.	
Mixing, dividing and first proving The ingredients are mixed at high speed, in under 5 minutes. The dough mixture is removed and divided into individual pieces by machine. It passes along a conveyor belt and is left to '**prove**' (when the yeast fills the dough with gas, causing it to rise and aerate).	

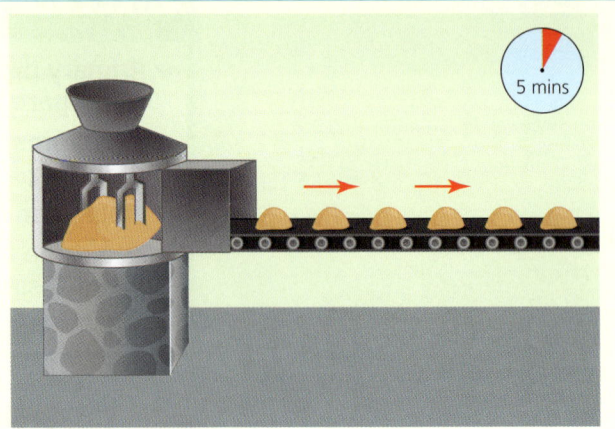

Topic 2 Food provenance: food processing and production

Kneading and preparation
The dough is continuously kneaded for about 2 minutes, as it circles through a spiral-shaped machine. The kneaded dough passes along a conveyor belt until it is dropped into pre-greased baking tins.

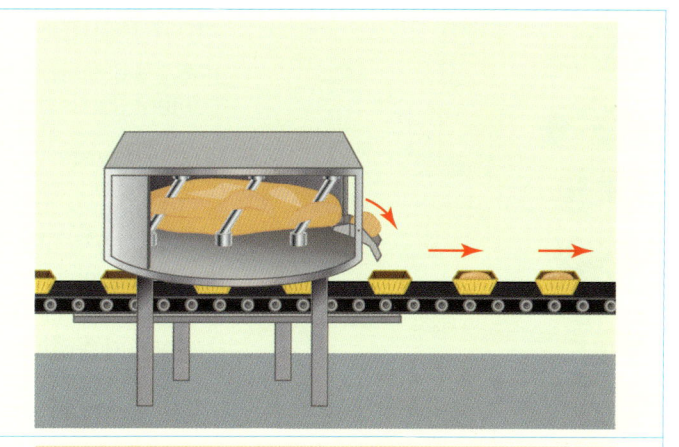

Second proving
The tins pass along the conveyor belt into a warm area. Here the second proving stage takes place, lasting around 50 minutes.

Baking
The loaves pass on a conveyor belt slowly through a huge oven for about 20 minutes. Basic bread doughs are usually baked at 230° C (450° F, gas mark 8).

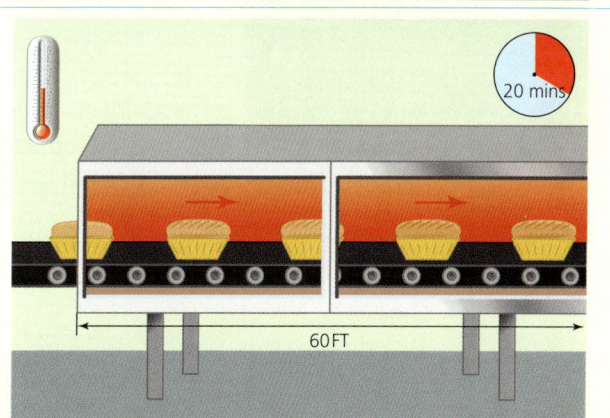

Depanning and cooling
The baked loaves come out of the oven into the cooling area. The bread is sucked out of the tins and left to cool for up to 1.5 hours. Once cooled, it passes down the conveyor belt to be sliced (if needed) and bagged.

▲ Figure 2.4 Different-shaped pasta

How flour is made into pasta

Pasta is usually made from durum wheat. It has a higher gluten (protein) content and is more golden in colour than white plain flour.

To make pasta:

- The flour is mixed with liquid – usually water and sometimes egg.
- A lumpy dough is formed.
- The dough is put into an extruder where the gluten is developed.
- The dough is then forced through different shaped dies to make different-shaped pasta or rolled to make pasta sheets which are then cut into shapes (for example, lasagne). Sometimes the other machines help fold the pasta into flat shapes such as bows.
- The pasta is then dried; this can take several hours.
- It is then packaged to be sold dried in shops.

Pasta can be flavoured with different ingredients (for example, spinach or tomatoes). You can also buy whole wheat pasta as well as fresh pasta from the chilled sections of supermarkets.

How milk is processed to make butter, cream, yoghurt and cheese

Butter

Butter is made by churning cream to remove even more liquid. There is a variety of different types of butter available:

- Unsalted butter – no additional ingredients added
- Salted butter – salt is added for additional flavour
- Clarified butter – butter is melted and the fat that rises to the top is separated and used for cooking
- Ghee – a form of clarified butter used in Indian cooking, usually packaged in a tin
- Spreadable butter – butter that has had vegetable oil added, which means that it is spreadable straight from the refrigerator

Butter, by law, has to have a fat content of between 80 and 90 per cent. There is no such thing as a **low-fat butter** or a **reduced-fat butter** (these are categorised as spreads). Some spreads are still marketed under the brand name, which can be confusing (see the label in Figure 2.6).

▲ Figure 2.5 Ghee

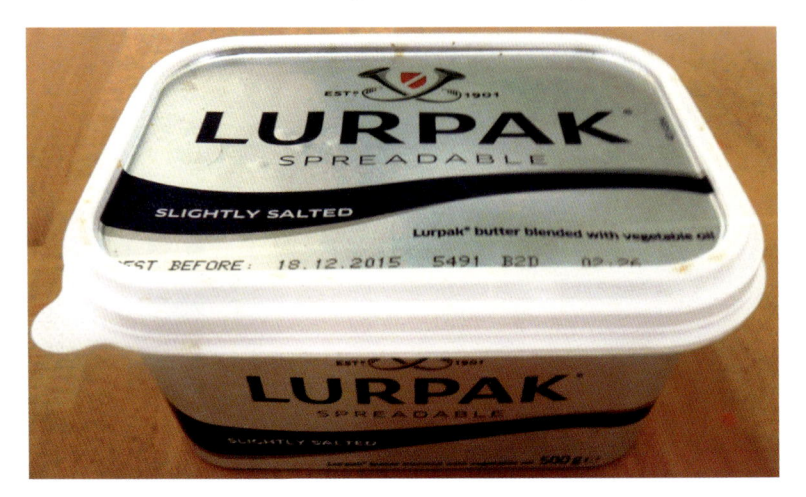

▲ Figure 2.6 Spreadable fat

Topic 2 Food provenance: food processing and production

Cream

Cream is the fat found in milk. It is separated from the milk by rotating it at a fast speed. The cream is then pasteurised to kill any harmful bacteria and destroy **enzymes** that can affect the flavour and shorten the shelf life of the cream. In the UK types of cream are defined by the amount of fat they contain.

Table 2.4 Types of cream

Type of cream	Minimum fat content	Use
Half cream	Contains no less than 12% milk fat (not sterilised)	In coffee, pouring on fruit and desserts
Single cream	Contains no less than 18% milk fat (not sterilised)	In coffee, pouring on fruit and desserts, adding to soups and savoury recipes
Double cream	Contains no less than 48% milk fat	Pouring/spooning cream for desserts, can be whipped for piping onto cakes and pastries
Whipping cream	Contains no less than 35% milk fat	Aeration for applications including desserts, cakes and pastry fillings
Whipped cream	Contains no less than 35% milk fat (cream has been whipped)	For desserts, cakes and pastry fillings
Clotted cream	Contains no less than 55% milk fat (cream is clotted)	Used in the classic English cream tea and as a dessert cream. Virtually unique to Cornwall, Devon and Somerset.
Sterilised cream	Contains no less than 23% milk fat (cream is sterilised)	On or in desserts

Source http://www.milk.co.uk/page.aspx?intPageID=370

KEY WORDS

Enzymes – can affect the flavour and shorten the shelf life of products
Yoghurt – made from fermented milk

Yoghurt

Yoghurt is made by fermenting milk with harmless bacteria. In the UK most yoghurt is made from cow's milk, but you can also buy goat's yogurt and yoghurt made from milk alternatives such as soya.

Process	Reason
Milk is pasteurised.	To remove harmful bacteria
The milk is homogenised.	To distribute the fat particles evenly throughout the milk (this helps to make the yogurt thick and creamy)
The milk is incubated and the harmless bacteria are added.	To change the natural sugar in milk (lactose) into lactic acid; the lactic acid causes the milk to coagulate/thicken and to give the yogurt a tangy taste
The yogurt is left to set until it reaches the correct acidity level.	
Fruit or flavourings are then added.	

▲ Figure 2.7 Making yoghurt

> **RESEARCH ACTIVITY**
>
> There is a wide range of yoghurts available to buy.
>
> Visit a supermarket or online supermarket website and investigate the following:
> - the different types of yoghurt
> - nutritional value of the yoghurts
> - compare the calorie content of different yoghurts
> - the additional ingredients added to the yoghurts.

Cheese

There are many different varieties of cheese you can buy, some traditionally produced in the UK and others from around the world. Cheese can be made with different types of milk such as cow's, sheep's, buffalo's and goat's milk. Slight variations in the methods of making cheese mean that the flavours are all different.

Process	Reason
The milk is usually pasteurised and is cooled to 30°C.	To destroy harmful bacteria
A starter culture of bacteria is added.	So that the lactic acid bacteria change the lactose (milk sugar) in the milk into lactic acid; the lactic acid helps to coagulate (set) the protein in the milk, to preserve the cheese, and to help develop the flavour
Rennet is added and the mixture is left to set.	So that the enzyme in rennet will coagulate the milk and turn it into solids (curds and whey)
The curd is cut so the whey is released.	For hard cheese the curd is cut finely so more whey is released; for soft cheese the whey is lightly cut
For soft cheese the whey is left to drain away naturally. For hard cheese the curds are heated and piled on top of each other to release more whey.	
The cheese is then milled, and for many cheeses salt is added and the curd is pressed into moulds.	
The cheese is left to ripen.	The temperature and humidity are controlled to produce different types of cheese. As the cheese ripens the colour, flavour and rind of the cheese develops

▲ Figure 2.8 How cheese is made

Topic 2 Food provenance: food processing and production

▲ Figure 2.9 Cutting curd

There are many different ways of grouping cheese. Table 2.5 shows one way of categorising cheese.

Table 2.5 Categories of cheese

Cheese	Example
Hard	Cheddar, Double Gloucester, Parmesan, Ricotta Salata
Semi-hard	Cheshire, Wensleydale, Edam
Soft ripened or bloomy rind	Brie, Camembert
Blue	Blue Stilton, Shropshire Blue, Roquefort, Gorgonzola
Washed rind	Stinking Bishop
Fresh	Mozzarella, Cottage Cheese

RESEARCH ACTIVITY

Investigate which types of cheese can now be purchased with reduced-fat options.

PRACTICAL ACTIVITY

Taste a range of different cheeses. Produce a chart to describe their taste, texture and appearance and origin.

✔ KEY POINTS

- ✔ Flour with a high gluten content is used to make pasta and bread.
- ✔ The fat content of cheese, yoghurt and cream varies.
- ✔ Pasteurised milk is usually used to make cream, butter, cheese and yoghurt.

TEST YOURSELF

1 Why is milk pasteurised before making it into cream, yoghurt and cheese?
2 Name **three** types of butter and give an example of their use in cooking for each.
3 List the different categories of cheese in the UK and give an example of a cheese for each category.

Food processing and preserving methods including those used in industry and in the domestic setting

Bacteria, yeasts and mould cause changes in food, which can be harmful. Micro-organisms need food, warmth, moisture and time to multiply. If one of these conditions is removed, the food is preserved and will keep for a longer time. If micro-organisms and enzymes are destroyed or a chemical is added (**preservative**) this also allows food to last longer.

There are benefits and limitations of preserving food.

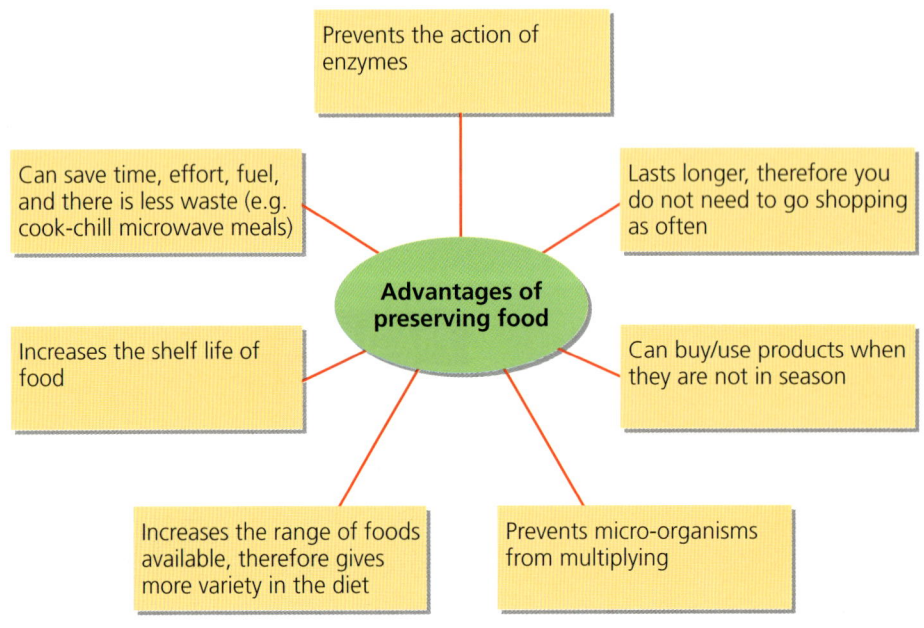

Advantages of preserving food
- Prevents the action of enzymes
- Lasts longer, therefore you do not need to go shopping as often
- Can save time, effort, fuel, and there is less waste (e.g. cook-chill microwave meals)
- Increases the shelf life of food
- Can buy/use products when they are not in season
- Increases the range of foods available, therefore gives more variety in the diet
- Prevents micro-organisms from multiplying

▲ **Figure 2.10** Advantages of preserving food

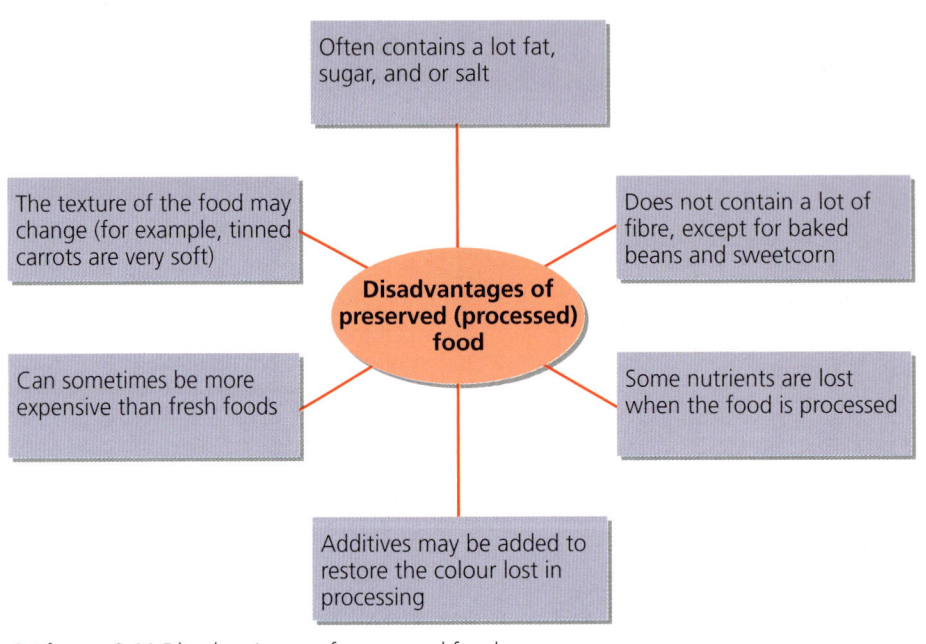

Disadvantages of preserved (processed) food
- Often contains a lot fat, sugar, and or salt
- The texture of the food may change (for example, tinned carrots are very soft)
- Does not contain a lot of fibre, except for baked beans and sweetcorn
- Can sometimes be more expensive than fresh foods
- Some nutrients are lost when the food is processed
- Additives may be added to restore the colour lost in processing

▲ **Figure 2.11** Disadvantages of preserved food

Topic 2 Food provenance: food processing and production

Topic links:
- Section C: Topic 3 Food safety — Conditions and control for bacterial growth
- Section C: Topic 3 Food safety — Growth conditions for mould growth and yeast production
- Section B: Topic 4 — The use of additives

High-temperature methods

High temperature methods of preservation are mostly carried out in the food industry. High temperature methods include **pasteurisation** and **sterilisation**.

Pasteurisation

- Pathogenic micro-organisms are destroyed. The food is heated to 72°C for 15 seconds.
- Storage of food is extended for a limited time – days not months.
- Examples of food preserved by pasteurisation: milk, some soups, liquid egg and ice cream, fruit juices.

Sterilisation

- Food is heated for a long period of time at higher temperatures. The food is heated to 104°C for 40 minutes.
- Destroys nearly all micro-organisms and enzymes.
- Extends storage period.
- Used for milk and fruit juices.
- Milk is changed to a creamy colour, with a slight caramelisation of the milk sugar content, giving a 'cooked' flavour.
- Examples of foods preserved by sterilisation: milk, low acid canned food.

Sterilisation methods include ultra heat treatment (UHT) and canning.

Ultra heat treatment (UHT):

- Uses very high temperatures, up to 130°C for 1–5 seconds. Destroys all bacteria.
- Extends storage period of milk, up to 6 months unopened.
- Little colour change.
- Only slight change in taste.
- Little loss of nutrient content.
- Sold in airtight cartons made from layers of plastic and aluminium coated paperboard. When sealed they can be kept at room temperature. Once opened they need to be stored as fresh products would be.
- Examples of foods preserved by UHT: milk, soups, prepared sauces, such as chilli.

Canning is a form of sterilisation. Food can be:

- packed in cans and then sterilised
- sterilised and then packed into **aseptic** (sterilised) cans.

The cans are then sealed with a double seam (or hermetic seal) to prevent leakage and to prevent **contamination**.

Temperature and time vary depending on the food type, but it is crucial to ensure that the sterilisation process is complete and that the food retains its

▲ Figure 2.12 Pasteurised milk

▲ Figure 2.13 Examples of food preserved by UHT

KEY WORDS

Aseptic – filling sterilised pouch or can

Contamination – when food is affected with micro organisms

Pasteurisation – the process of prolonging the keeping quality of products such as milk by heating to destroy harmful bacteria

Preservative – allows food to be kept for longer

Sterilisation – a method of heat treatment used to kill harmful bacteria. Used when canning food

Ultra heat treatment (UHT) – high-temperature, short-time sterilisation of products such as milk – known as long-life milk

structure and texture. After sterilisation the cans are sprayed with water to prevent the contents overcooking.

- The texture of some foods may change, for example, strawberries become soft.
- There is some loss of nutrients, especially vitamins B and C.
- Acid foods, for example, grapefruit, are canned in plastic-lined cans to prevent corrosion.
- Examples of food preserved by canning include: soup, vegetables, fruit, meat and fish, to give a long shelf life.

Stretch and challenge

The shelf life of milk can be extended by pasteurisation, sterilisation and UHT treatment.

Using a nutritional program investigate how the nutritional values differ.

Explain the differences.

Low-temperature methods

Cold temperatures slow down the speed at which bacteria reproduce but do not destroy bacteria. The very low temperatures of freezing (−18° C) cause the bacteria to be dormant.

Chilling

- Refrigerators should be set at a temperature of 0°–5° C.
- Placing food in a refrigerator will not extend its shelf life for long as bacterial growth is only slowed down.

Topic link: Section C: Topic 3 Storing food

Blast chilling

All foods must be cooled as quickly as possible. This means that whenever food is chilled, it must be in the danger zone between 5°C and 63°C, for as little time as possible. Blast chilling food reduces the temperature of foods to below 3°C whithin 90 minutes.

Cook-chill

This is a short-term way of preserving fresh food. Cook-chill products are often thought to be of a better quality than frozen products. They have a short shelf life, usually 4–5 days.

It is critical that the correct temperature controls are followed at all stages of manufacture, storage and distribution. This is in order to:

- have records of temperature control which can be shown to the Environmental Health Officer
- prevent waste
- avoid bacterial growth
- avoid complaints
- meet the requirements of the Food Safety Regulations
- keep the food at its best (texture/colour/taste/appearance).

There are many advantages of cook-chill foods for the consumer. Figure 2.15 shows some examples.

▲ **Figure 2.14** Examples of food preserved by canning

Topic 2 Food provenance: food processing and production

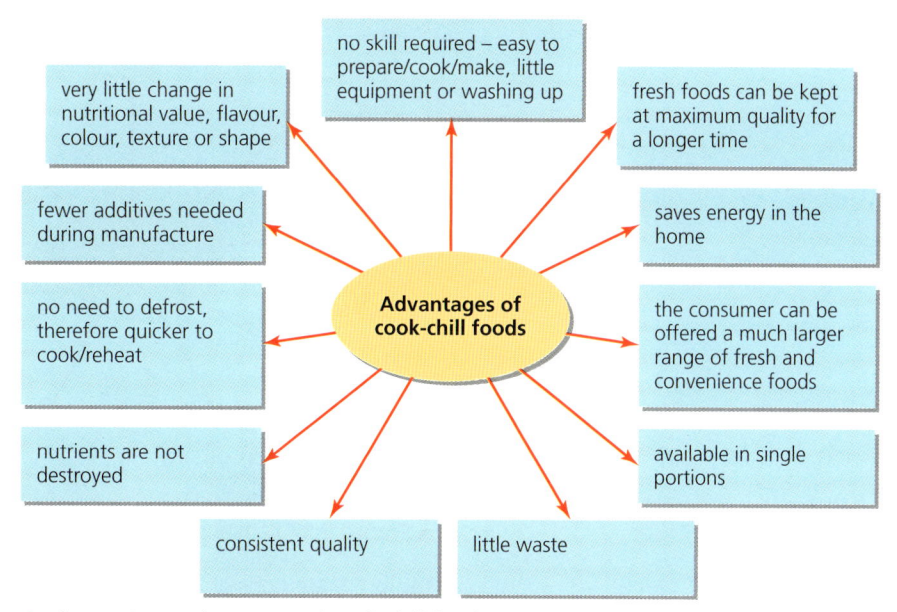

Advantages of cook-chill foods:
- no skill required – easy to prepare/cook/make, little equipment or washing up
- very little change in nutritional value, flavour, colour, texture or shape
- fresh foods can be kept at maximum quality for a longer time
- fewer additives needed during manufacture
- saves energy in the home
- no need to defrost, therefore quicker to cook/reheat
- the consumer can be offered a much larger range of fresh and convenience foods
- nutrients are not destroyed
- available in single portions
- consistent quality
- little waste

▲ Figure 2.15 Advantages of cook-chill foods

Examples of food preserved by cook-chilling are:

- those made from cooked ingredients, for example soup, and recipe meals such as lasagne
- mixtures of both raw and cooked foods, for example potato salad.

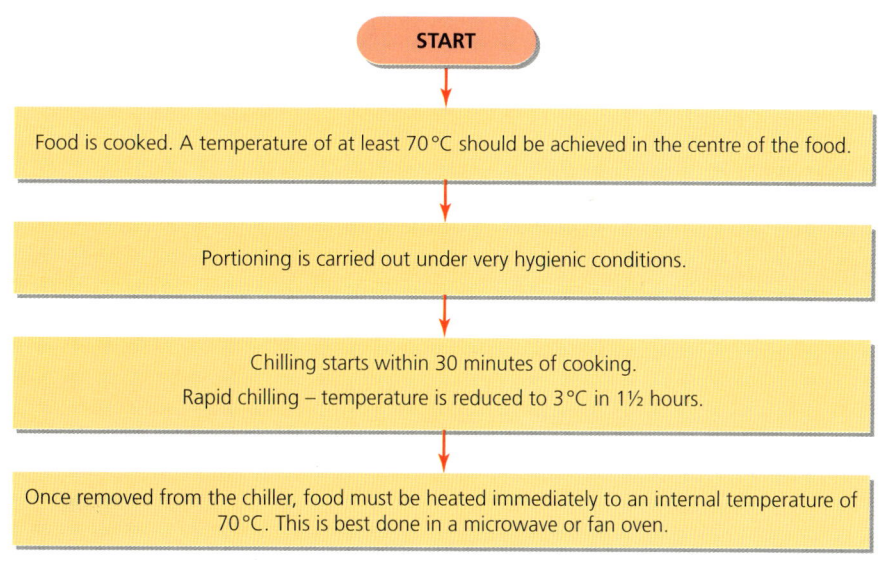

START

↓

Food is cooked. A temperature of at least 70 °C should be achieved in the centre of the food.

↓

Portioning is carried out under very hygienic conditions.

↓

Chilling starts within 30 minutes of cooking.
Rapid chilling – temperature is reduced to 3 °C in 1½ hours.

↓

Once removed from the chiller, food must be heated immediately to an internal temperature of 70 °C. This is best done in a microwave or fan oven.

▲ Figure 2.16 The cook-chill process

Freezing

There are several different methods of industrial freezing. The principle of freezing is the same as doing it in the home – to reduce the temperature as quickly as possible so that you have small ice crystals in the food. The temperature of a domestic freezer should be −18 °C. Many frozen products can be purchased. Figure 2.17 shows some reasons why sales have increased.

▲ Figure 2.17 Reasons for increase in frozen food products

Reasons for the increase in frozen food products:
- Gives the consumer more choice
- Saves time
- Handy in emergencies
- Consumer demands
- Boosts sales
- Extends shelf life
- Keeps up with competitors
- Lack of cooking skills
- Better results

Table 2.6 Methods of freezing used in industry

Freezing method	What this means	Diagram	Example of foods
Blast	Food is frozen at −30°C to −40°C. Cold air is circulated around the food. Food must then be kept in storage units between −20°C and −30°C.	Vanes to ensure laminar air flow; Return air to fan; Fan; Product on shelves; Evaporator coils	Fish, ready meals, meat joints, chicken, pizza, cakes, desserts
Fluidised bed	Used to freeze small fruit and vegetables so they do not stick together. The air causes the food to float above the conveyor belt.	Fluidised product; Conveyor; Evaporator coil; Fan	Peas, beans, raspberries
Plate	Food is placed between two cold plates. It is not suitable for freezing irregular-shaped foods.	Hydraulic ram; Hollow freezer plate; Packed food	Fish, ready meals

Section B: Food

118

Topic 2 Food provenance: food processing and production

Table 2.6 continued

Freezing method	What this means	Diagram	Example of foods
Cryogenic freezing	Liquid nitrogen is used to freeze the food. Liquid nitrogen has a temperature of –190°C.	*Diagram showing liquid nitrogen spray freezing on a conveyor with a fan, product in and frozen product out*	Expensive foods such as raspberries, prawns, strawberries. Some chefs also use this to produce interesting dishes

> **KEY WORDS**
>
> **Blast freezing** – a quick freezing method; small ice crystals form and there is less damage to the food than in slow freezing
>
> **Cryogenic freezing** – food is immersed or sprayed with liquid nitrogen
>
> **Dehydrating** – removing water

Cook-freeze

Meals are blast-frozen and stored at –20°C until required. Dishes must be prepared with strict attention to hygiene. Many large catering operators find it convenient to use cook-freeze systems today. Meals are prepared and frozen rapidly. The food can be distributed to branch outlets in the frozen state and heated by microwave or micro-ovens when required for service. (Micro-ovens cook using both microwaves and convected heat.)

Dehydration (drying)

There are various methods of **dehydrating** food, as shown in Figure 2.18. Dried foods are cheaper and easy to transport and store. They have a relatively long shelf life if stored in protective packaging. The flavour, colour, texture and nutritional value of dried foods are affected.

Drying is mostly completed in industry; however, it is now possible to buy a dehydrator to use in the home.

▲ Figure 2.19 Dehydrator that can be used in the home

▲ Figure 2.20 Different dehydrated foods

▲ Figure 2.18 Methods of dehydration

Sunlight
- Drying in direct sunlight, e.g. raisins and tomatoes
- Moisture evaporates slowly, which may allow the food to become contaminated

Fluidised bed drying
- Used to clump-dry particles into granules which dissolve more easily in water, e.g. potato and coffee

- All micro-organisms need moisture. By removing moisture in food, micro-organisms cannot grow.
- Sometimes drying is referred to as dehydration.
- Hot or warm temperatures remove the moisture.
- Rehydration is when a liquid is added to reconstitute the food.
- Storage, Dried foods must be stored in a cool dry place.
- Colour, texture, flavour and nutritional content of foods may be affected.

Oven-drying
- Warm ovens are used
- Suitable for herbs, tea and vegetables

Spray drying
- Suitable for foods that may be damaged by excessive heating, e.g. milk, coffee

Roller drying
- Used for instant breakfast cereal, mashed potato and baby foods

Accelerated freeze-drying (AFD)
- AFD is a combination of freezing and drying. Food is quick-frozen, then placed in a vacuum under reduced pressure.
- The heat vaporises the ice, which turns to steam and leaves the food dry.
- There is little change to the colour, flavour, texture and nutritive value.
- AFD food is light to carry and easy to hydrate. More costly than simply drying food.

119

▲ Figure 2.21 Smoking fish

Chemical preservation

Chemical preservation destroys bacteria or prevents them reproducing. The chemicals work by affecting the growth of micro-organisms. Chemicals and chemical methods used for preserving food include the following.

Smoking

This involves smoking the food over wood. It is the chemicals in the wood smoke that give the food flavour and also help to preserve the food. The food being smoked has often been dipped in either salt or an acid solution first.

Examples of food preserved by smoking include meat and fish.

Using acids, salt and sugar

Using acids, salt and sugar destroys bacteria or prevents them reproducing.

Vinegar is:

- An acetic acid with a low pH of 3.5 (bacteria cannot survive below 4.5).
- Used for foods such as pickled onions, cabbage and eggs.

Salt:

- Is used to coat foods such as ham, bacon and fish, or used in a brine solution (salt and water), for tuna and vegetables.
- Reduces moisture content by osmosis.

Sugar:

- In high concentrations (60 per cent of final product) it prevents bacteria from growing because it makes water unavailable.
- Used in jams, marmalades and jellies.
- Strong sugar solutions can also be used for coating candied and crystallised fruit.

▲ Figure 2.22 Preservation using sugar

Modified atmosphere packaging (MAP)/controlled atmosphere packaging (CAP)

Modified atmosphere packaging is sometimes called **controlled atmosphere packaging**.

MAP involves changing the atmosphere around the food inside the packaging so that growth of micro-organisms is slowed down. Altering the gas in the packet prevents bacteria being able to use the oxygen for growth, which means the product has an increased shelf life. The advantage is that, because clear plastic is used in this process, you can see the product. MAP is used for chilled meats, vegetables and fruits.

The process involves:

- packaging fresh foods in peak condition; the colour of the food remains the same until the pack is opened, and once opened the food has a normal shelf life
- replacing the air by 'gas-flushing' a combination of gases around the food; gases used are oxygen, nitrogen and carbon dioxide
- sealing the plastic bag or plastic lid to a food tray by means of a **hermetic** sealing process.

▲ Figure 2.23 Using MAP to package apples

Topic 2 Food provenance: food processing and production

KEY WORDS

Accelerated freeze-drying (AFD) – a technique where food is frozen and then dried
Hermetic – airtight
Modified atmosphere packaging (MAP) – packaging containing a mixture of gasses which helps to preserve food

Vacuum packing

- This is done by removing air and sealing the package. It also prevents bacteria growing. Once opened it has a normal shelf life.
- The food is kept in anaerobic conditions (that is, there is no oxygen).
- Foods maintain colour and texture.
- Coffee, once **accelerated freeze-dried (AFD)** is vacuum packed so that it does not lose taste or flavour.

RESEARCH ACTIVITY

Using a nutritional program compare the nutritional value of:
- fresh and dried apricots
- fresh, frozen and tinned peas.

Explain why the nutritional value of the foods has changed

PRACTICAL ACTIVITY

Fruits and vegetables are often preserved when there is a surplus of them.
Using a surplus of fruit and/or vegetables, make a preserve which could be used at a later date.

✔ KEY POINTS

- ✔ **Preservation is used to prolong the shelf life of food.**
- ✔ **Foods can be processed in a variety of ways to extend their shelf life.**
- ✔ **The nutritional value of foods changes when they are processed.**

TEST YOURSELF

1. State **three** methods of freezing used in industry. Give **one** example of a food that could be frozen by this method.
2. Give **three** reasons why freezing is a popular method of preserving foods.
3. State **three** high-temperature methods of preservation.
4. State **two** low-temperature methods of extending the shelf life of foods.
5. What does MAP stand for?
6. What does AFD stand for?
7. What does 'anaerobic conditions' mean?

Topic 3

Food security

→ WHAT WILL I LEARN?

By the end of this topic you should have developed a knowledge and understanding of:

→ the impact of food security on consumers, producers and the environment
→ moral, ethical and environmental issues which affect food production.

The availability of food, the access to food and an individual's ability to utilise food

Food security has been defined by the United Nations Food and Agriculture Organization as: 'when all people, at all times, have physical and economic access to sufficient, safe and nutritious food to meet their dietary needs and food preferences for an active and healthy life.'

This includes all of the following:

- Availability – is there a sufficient amount of food available all the time?
- Access – can it be reached efficiently? This includes if it can be bought at a fair price (affordability) and is of a high quality.
- Utilisation – is the food part of a balanced diet?

Therefore, food security is about having access to affordable, safe and nutritious food, today and tomorrow.

Food availability

This includes how much food is available as well as the reliability of the supply. In the UK we are, in 2016, food secure. In 2013, 23 countries supplied 90 per cent of the UK's food; 54 per cent of this was grown and produced in the UK.

KEY WORD

Food security – considers availability, accesses and utilization of food

▶ **Figure 3.1** Countries which supplied the UK with food in 2014

- Australasia 1%
- Rest of Europe 2%
- South America 4%
- North America 4%
- Asia 4%
- Africa 4%
- EU 27%
- UK (a) 54%

(a) Consumption of UK origin consists of UK domestic production minus UK exports.

Source: *Food Statistics Pocket Book (2014)*, Department for Environment, Food and Rural Affairs, p. 24

Topic 3 Food security

Not all countries are as food secure as the UK, because they either cannot grow sufficient food or do not have the money to import the necessary foods. It is often smaller, poor countries who suffer the most. You will have seen many examples of when crops fail in a country and the people are hungry.

Food accessibility

Not everyone is able to have access to a wide range of foods because they do not have enough money to buy the food they need. Poorer people spend more of their money on food than wealthy people. There is sufficient food being produced in the world, but not everyone has access to it.

Physical factors can affect the amount of food which is produced and what is produced. In some countries there are no effective trading policies or good transport systems to help to distribute food. Organisations such as Fairtrade are helping many communities overcome some of these problems in some parts of the world.

As populations of some countries increase there is a need for more housing, and therefore the amount of land available for farming is reduced.

In some countries the population is becoming wealthier (for example, in parts of India and China.) This has meant they have the income to buy more expensive meat and dairy foods, which takes more land to produce meat than cereals.

Nourishment and utilisation

These include the following:

- the way the body makes use of the different nutrients in food
- that a person has sufficient nutrients, a healthy and varied diet.

▲ Figure 3.2 Crop failure in Africa

When people are **malnourished** it means they have a diet that is unbalanced and health begins to suffer. Malnutrition can be caused when there is not enough food or too much of a particular nutrient is consumed.

Topic link: Section A: Nutrition

TEST YOURSELF

1 State the **three** elements of food security.
2 Explain what is meant by food accessibility.

KEY WORDS

Malnourished – an unbalanced diet when health suffers
Fairtrade – guarantees that producers get a fair deal
Organic – grown or reared without the use of artificial aids/fertilisers/pesticides/antibiotics

Moral issues which affect food production

How Fairtrade affects food producers and workers

Fairtrade requires companies to pay farmers sustainable prices for their products (these must not fall below the market prices). Fairtrade addresses the injustices of conventional trade, which traditionally discriminates against the poorest, weakest producers:

- Farmers and communities have a more secure income and are less likely to live in poverty.
- It is helping communities to establish cooperatives.
- It is improving the farmers' access to training (for example, **organic** farming).
- Workers who work on Fairtrade certified farms and plantations can be involved in deciding how to spend the Fairtrade Premium money (for example, to improve education, training, medical facilities).
- When food has the Fairtrade logo on it the producers have had to consider the care of the environment, which includes reducing carbon emissions, ensuring good soil, pest and water management and avoiding the use of harmful chemicals.

The Fairtrade Foundation has licensed over 4,500 Fairtrade certified products for sale through retail and catering outlets in the UK. Fairtrade food products include:

- bananas
- dried fruit
- nuts/oil seeds
- sugar
- cocoa
- fresh fruit and fresh vegetables
- rice
- tea
- coffee
- honey
- spices

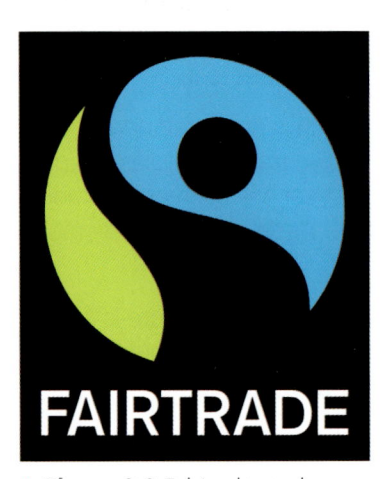

▲ Figure 3.3 Fairtrade mark

Many consumers will choose to buy Fairtrade products because they see it as an ethical choice.

They know that when they buy these foods that:

- producers get paid a fair price for the product and this should help to reduce poverty
- by purchasing these foods they can be supporting health and education programmes in the countries involved
- the workers in those countries have improved working conditions
- there is also a wide range of products available and their flavour and taste are usually comparable to other products.

Organisations such as Traidcraft use only ethically produced materials and ingredients, which helps both the producers and the manufacturers in developing countries.

The Fairtrade premium sales of sugar mean the two villages near Kasinthula Cane Growers Ltd already have a borehole, so now they don't have to rely on water from the crocodile-infested Shire River.

▲ Figure 3.4 Borehole provided because of Fairtrade payments

Topic 3 Food security

▲ Figure 3.5 Genetically modified crops

Ethical issues which affect food production

Genetically modified foods

The use of new technology in the food industry is controversial, especially products made by modifying or engineering the genetic make-up of food. This is undertaken by copying a gene with its code and inserting it into another living organism. That gene will then be able to produce that characteristic in the food. It might improve the quality of the food (for instance, blackcurrants can be modified to make them higher in vitamin C; tomatoes can be modified to improve their flavour or keeping qualities).

The advantages of **genetically modified** (GM) foods to the producers are:

- improvements to quantity and quality of food
- it can grow in adverse conditions (for example, drought)
- they can be herbicide- and insect-resistant, therefore thrive better
- higher in nutritional quality
- cheaper to produce.

Many people do not want to buy genetically modified foods because:

- long-term safety is unknown
- environmental concerns, as the pollen does not stop in one place and can spread
- ethics – we need adequate labelling; from January 2000 if a product has over 1 per cent of GM food it must be stated on the label (under 1 per cent does not need to be stated)
- there is a lack of communication between provider and consumer.

Some people would argue that it is difficult to work out if a food has been affected by genetic modification because of the lack of labelling requirements. Examples of this are meat, milk and eggs from animals fed on GM animal feed, which do not need to be labelled as GM foods.

> **KEY WORD**
> **Genetically modified** – describes crops where the genetic structure of the crops has been changed

Stretch and challenge

Carry out research to find out what common foods contain GM ingredients.

Environmental issues which affect food production

Many food producers consider environmental issues when they are producing food. Over time the focus of these has changed.

Food waste

In the UK we throw away over 7 million tonnes of food and drink a year, worth over £120.5 billion. This equals the average family wasting £700 per year. Much of the food waste from consumers ends up in landfill sites. Here the food rots down and produces harmful greenhouse gases, for example methane and carbon dioxide. The increase in the amount of greenhouse gases we are producing has been linked to global warming and climate change.

The main reasons we throw food away are:

- too much food is prepared and cooked
- we do not use the food in time.

The food which is wasted the most is:

- fresh vegetables
- salad
- drink
- fresh fruit
- bakery items (for example, bread, cakes).

▲ Figure 3.6 Landfill site

RESEARCH ACTIVITY

Prepare either a leaflet, blog, poster or presentation which could be used to inform families how to reduce their food waste.

PRACTICAL ACTIVITY

The following is a list of ingredients which are about to be thrown away:
- sliced white bread
- cooked pasta shells
- grated carrot
- grated cheese
- $\frac{1}{2}$ onion
- strawberries
- $\frac{1}{2}$ tub crème fraiche

1. Make a list of dishes which could be made using these ingredients.
2. What additional ingredients would need to be added?
3. Prepare one of your ideas.

Carbon footprint

The **carbon footprint** of a product is the amount of carbon emissions produced in the growing, processing, production and disposal of food. It is not just the food miles – you need to consider all the processes the food has gone through from being grown to it been eaten or disposed of.

More people, including food manufacturers, are stopping to consider the impact that our food has on the environment. **Eco footprint** is the term used to refer to the measurement of our actions on the environment. To achieve sustainable food production the food industry must reduce waste, water and energy inefficiency by using **sustainable resources**.

▲ Figure 3.7 Carbon footprint logo

To reduce your carbon footprint you can:

- buy fresh local produce
- cook fresh meals
- use seasonal UK ingredients
- reduce your consumption of meat – more energy is used to raise animals than to grow cereals
- consider the methods of cooking you use to reduce the amount of energy used.

> ## Stretch and challenge
> Explain how you can reduce your energy consumption when preparing meals.

Food miles

The distance food travels from field to plate is one way of indicating the environmental impact of the food we eat. Approximately 54 per cent of vegetables and 90 per cent of the fruit eaten in the UK is imported. Food is transported across the world because we want to buy foods out of season. For instance, asparagus is only in season for May and June in the UK, but we want to buy it all year. Out of season it comes from Italy or Spain for a few months and the rest of the year it comes from Peru.

Planes are powered by fossil fuel oil. When the oil is burnt it gives off carbon dioxide gas emissions, which contribute hugely to global warming. You can offset this by planting trees to absorb the carbon dioxide given off. This is called **carbon offsetting**.

If we reduced the amount of packaging used in products, it might reduce costs and save energy in terms of fuel and transportation.

To reduce food miles, some food manufacturers are sourcing their ingredients from the UK. However, these ingredients are often transported round the country to distribution centres before being sent to the shops.

▲ Figure 3.8 Transportation by aeroplane

KEY WORDS
Carbon footprint – the amount of carbon emissions produced in the growing, processing, production and disposal of food
Carbon offsetting – planting trees to absorb carbon dioxide
Eco footprint – measurement of our actions on the environment
Food miles – distance food travels from farm to plate
Sustainable resources – resources which will not run out

Food sustainability

When choosing foods we do need to think about whether they are sustainable and have been produced sustainably. This list below shows some of the factors you can consider:

- Where has the food come from, has it been produced locally, if it was imported could a Fairtrade product have been purchased?
- How was it produced? For example, were organic and sustainable methods of farming used?
- Is the food sustainable? For example, have you chosen fish from a sustainable source? Have you considered reducing the amount of meat you eat and do you check that the meat was produced with high welfare standards?

- How much energy was used in its production?
- Were the energy sources used sustainable?
- What impact has the production of the food had on the environment? For example, pollution and carbon emissions.

PRACTICAL ACTIVITY

1. Design and make a dish using locally produced foods.
2. Calculate the food miles for the ingredients you have used.

RESEARCH ACTIVITY

Investigate the different symbols that may be found on food packaging to show a product's eco footprint.

✔ KEY POINTS

- ✔ **Food security is when all people, at all times, have physical and economic access to sufficient, safe and nutritious food to meet their dietary needs and food preferences for an active and healthy life.**
- ✔ **The Fairtrade logo is an independent consumer label that appears on products as a guarantee that disadvantaged producers are getting a better deal. It guarantees that farmers in developing countries get a fair price for their products, which covers their costs.**
- ✔ **Carbon footprint is the amount of carbon dioxide produced in growing, processing, distributing and disposing of food.**

TEST YOURSELF

1. What are the advantages to a banana producer of being part of the Fairtrade organisation?
2. Give **three** reasons why people choose to buy Fairtrade products.
3. Give **two** reasons why a farmer may want to produce genetically modified crops.
4. Give **two** reasons why we should try to reduce our food waste.
5. Explain what is meant by 'food miles'.
6. Give **three** reasons why people choose to buy locally produced foods.
7. Explain what is meant by 'eco footprint'.

Topic 4

Technological developments to support better health and food production

→ **WHAT WILL I LEARN?**

By the end of this topic you should have developed a knowledge and understanding of:
→ fortification
→ the use of additives
→ new and emerging foods.

Fortification of foods

In the UK there is a wide range of **fortified** foods available. Some are fortified by law, such as all wheat flour except wholemeal which is fortified with iron, niacin and thiamine. All flours except wholemeal and some self-raising flours are fortified with calcium. There are also many foods that are voluntarily fortified, as food manufacturers seek to promote foods that are linked to healthy lifestyles (for instance, fruit juices and the majority of breakfast cereals have added vitamins and other nutrients).

KEY WORD

Fortification – the addition of nutrients to a food product to improve its nutritional value

▲ Figure 4.1 Examples of foods that have been fortified

Advantages of fortification

- To increase the nutrient content, especially when added to staple foods such as bread. When wheat is processed, iron, thiamine and niacin are removed with the bran. These nutrients have to be replaced in white and brown flour by law in the UK.
- Where there is nutrient deficiency in a country, fortification can help to reduce the deficiency.
- Manufacturers may see it as an advantage in helping them to sell more of their product, as it can be marketed as containing the nutrient or having added nutrients.
- The addition of some nutrients may help with other aspects of the product. Vitamin C is an antioxidant; it will therefore reduce the rate of spoilage in some products.
- Can replace the nutrients lost during the processing of the food. This is very important if the food was a good source of the nutrient before it was processed.
- To produce a product that is similar to another. By law, margarine has to have vitamins A and D added to similar levels as they exist in butter. Manufacturers of some soya-based drinks add calcium, as the drinks are sold as a substitute for milk.

Sometimes manufacturers choose to voluntarily fortify foods. Some examples of voluntary fortification are given below:

- Fruit juices made from concentrate are often fortified with vitamin C so that they have the same nutritional profile as freshly squeezed fruit juice.
- Textured vegetable protein, when used for savoury products, is fortified with iron and the vitamin B complex so that its nutritional profile is similar to that of meat.
- Low-fat spreads often have vitamins A and D added to them so they are similar to margarine and butter.
- Many breakfast cereal products are fortified. These are clearly labelled on the packet.

RESEARCH ACTIVITY

Look at a variety of fortified food ingredient labels and complete the table below to show how they have been fortified and the function of the nutrient added.

Product	Nutrient added	Function of the nutrient in the diet

Topic links:

- Section A: Topic 8 Vitamins
- Section A: Topic 9 Minerals

Topic 4 Technological developments to support better health and food production

> **Stretch and challenge**
> Investigate how fortified foods can make a contribution to the nutritional intake of consumers in the UK.

✔ KEY POINTS

- ✔ Some foods are fortified by law.
- ✔ Safety and technical considerations are taken into account when deciding which foods to fortify and to what level.
- ✔ Fortified foods make an important contribution to diets in the UK.

TEST YOURSELF

1 Give **two** advantages of fortifying food.
2 Give **two** disadvantages of fortifying food.
3 Explain why flour is fortified.
4 Manufacturers sometimes choose to fortify foods. Give **three** reasons why manufacturers may choose to fortify their foods.

The use of additives

Additives are substances that are added to foods during manufacturing or processing to improve their:

- keeping properties
- flavour
- colour
- texture
- appearance
- stability.

Additives are used in a large range of food products today. The main groups of food additives are:

- preservatives
- antioxidants
- colours
- flavourings and flavour enhancers
- sweeteners
- emulsifiers and stabilisers.

Over 300 additives are allowed by law in the UK (flavourings are not included in this figure). More than 3,000 flavourings are used in many different combinations. All additives have to be checked for safety before they can be used in any foods. Additives that manufacturers are allowed to use are given a number. Many are also given an 'E' if they have been accepted as safe for use within the European Union. All additives also have a chemical name.

KEY WORDS

Additives – substances added to food in small amounts to improve colour, flavour, texture or to make the food stay safe for longer

E number – a number given to an additive to indicate that it has been approved for use in the EU

Why are additives used?

Additives are used for the following reasons:

- They can help make food safe for longer.
- They can make food more attractive or taste better.
- They can help to keep the price of food competitive.
- They can give food an improved nutritional profile (higher in vitamins or lower in fat).

Additives may be:

- **natural** – obtained from natural sources (for instance, red colouring made from beetroot juice [E162] is used in making ice cream, sweets and liquorice)
- **nature identical (synthetic)** – made in a laboratory to be chemically the same as certain natural materials, such as vanillin, which is found naturally in vanilla pods
- **artificial** – synthetic compounds that do not occur in nature, such as saccharin (E954), a low-calorie sweetener.

Many consumers prefer food products to contain additives obtained from natural sources. Many manufacturers now try to use fewer synthetic additives. For example, a cake manufacturer may use additives from natural sources and will then advertise the range of cakes as 'homestyle baking'.

Artificial additives are used frequently by the food manufacturing industry. Their use is controlled by government departments. The long-term effects of additives are not known.

The additives must be listed on the label by their:

- type
- chemical name or number.

They must appear on the label in descending order of quantity (greatest amount first).

▲ **Figure 4.2** Colourings used in sweets

Advantages of using additives for the manufacturer

- used in a wide range of food products to meet consumer needs (for example, quick, easy, convenient meals, such as Pot Noodles, instant whipped desserts and instant mash)
- to improve a specific characteristic of a food (for example, vanilla-flavoured ice cream, orange-flavoured soft centres in chocolates, coffee liqueur-flavoured hot chocolate drinks)
- to produce the expected qualities in foods, such as colour and flavour (for example, soft-centred chocolates with pink colouring and strawberry flavouring)
- to produce a product range by using different additives in the basic food (for example, potato crisps flavoured with salt and vinegar, cheese and onion, smoky bacon, etc.)
- to help maintain product consistency in large-scale production (for example, the use of emulsifiers to prevent salad cream separating)

Topic 4 Technological developments to support better health and food production

- to restore original characteristics of a food after processing (for example, adding colour to processed vegetables such as canned peas)
- to prevent food spoilage, to preserve foods and give them a longer shelf life (for example, bread, cakes and biscuits)
- to disguise inferior ingredients; this can help to reduce the cost of food products.

Disadvantages of using additives for the manufacturer

Some people may have an allergy to additives and therefore may choose not to purchase a product containing them. It is often difficult to find out which additive is causing the allergic reaction. Examples of allergies caused by food additives include asthma attacks, skin rashes and hyperactivity in children. The long-term effects of additives on the body are unknown.

Types of food additives and their functions

Preservatives

Preservatives help to keep food safe for longer. They are added to foods to:

- extend shelf life, which means that consumers do not need to go shopping too often
- prevent the growth of micro-organisms, which can cause food spoilage and lead to poisoning.

Preservatives are found in:

- many processed foods with a long shelf life
- cured meats, such as bacon, ham, corned beef
- dried fruit, such as sultanas, raisins.

Sugar, salt and vinegar are still used to preserve some foods, but most people tend to think of preservatives as chemicals. Some additives used for preservation have been used for a long time, for instance:

- sugar to make jam and marmalade
- vinegar to make pickles (for example, pickled cabbage, eggs and onions)
- salt in meat and fish
- alcohol (for example, peaches in brandy).

Topic link: Section B: Topic 2 Food Processing and preserving

> **KEY WORDS**
>
> **Preservatives** – substances that extend the shelf life of a product
> **Antioxidants** – substances that stop fat from going rancid; stops enzymic brawning

Antioxidants

Most foods containing fats and oils, such as pies, cakes, biscuits, dried soups, preserved meat and fish products and cheese spreads, are likely to contain **antioxidants**. Some antioxidants are natural, such as vitamins C and E.

These are used to:

- help prevent fat-soluble vitamins (A and D), oils and fats from combining with oxygen and making the product rancid; rancid fats have an unpleasant smell and taste
- prevent some foods from going brown, for example apples and pears when they are exposed to air.

Colourings

Colourings are added to make foods look more attractive. They are used in manufacturing to:

- replace colour lost during heat treatment (for example, in canned peas)
- boost colours already in foods (for example, strawberry yoghurt)
- maintain consistency between different batch productions as they are added in precise quantities (for example, yellow colouring in tinned custard)
- make foods that are normally colourless look attractive (for example, carbonated drinks).

Manufacturers are not allowed to add colours to baby foods.

▲ Figure 4.3 Natural colourings added to yoghurt to make it more appealing to the consumer

Stretch and challenge

1 Food colourings are either natural, nature identical or artificial.
  a Produce a chart to show examples of:
   - natural
   - nature identical
   - artificial colours.
  b Use a supermarket website and find examples of foods which use each category of colouring.
2 Some consumers believe that the use of colour additives is not necessary for foods to taste good. What are the arguments for and against using artificial colours from the consumer's and the manufacturer's perspective?

Flavourings and flavour enhancers

- Flavourings and flavour enhancers must meet the requirements of the Food Safety Act 1990 and all other flavouring regulations.
- They are used widely in savoury foods to make the existing flavour in the food stronger. Monosodium glutamate (MSG) is an example of a flavour enhancer. It is often used in Chinese foods. Some consumers may be allergic to MSG, causing them to suffer sickness and dizziness.
- They replace flavours lost during the processing of the food.
- Flavourings can also be natural flavourings (for example, vanilla, and herbs and spices).

PRACTICAL ACTIVITY

Prepare a dish that showcases the use of herbs and spices.

Topic 4 Technological developments to support better health and food production

Sweeteners

There are two types of sweeteners, **intense sweeteners** and **bulk sweeteners**.

> **KEY WORDS**
> **Intense sweeteners** – examples are saccharin and aspartame
> **Bulk sweeteners** – have a similar level of sweetness to sugar

Intense sweeteners

Intense sweeteners are aspartame and saccharin. They are:

- approximately 300 times sweeter than sugar and only used in very small amounts
- very low in energy
- used in low-calorie drinks and reduced-sugar products, and are also available as sweetening tablets often added to coffee and tea
- useful for consumers who want to reduce the amount of sugar in their diet.

However, they:

- lack the bulk that is needed in recipes that normally use sugar cane or beet
- do not have the same characteristics as sugar for cooking
- may leave a bitter aftertaste.

Bulk sweeteners

Examples of bulk sweeteners include hydrogenated glucose syrup, sorbital (E420) and sucralose. They are:

- similar to sugar in levels of sweetness
- used in similar amounts to sugar
- used in sugar-free confectionery and preserves for diabetics.

There have been developments recently in half-sugar products. This is where ordinary sugar has a small amount of aspartame added, which makes it twice as sweet, which means that half the amount of sugar is needed, and therefore half the amount of calories are consumed.

> **INVESTIGATION ACTIVITY**
>
> 1 Investigate how successfully half-sugar can be used in traditional, sweet, baked products such as Victoria sandwich cake, scones or biscuits.
> 2 Produce a chart to show how the products differ when cooked with half-sugar rather than normal sugar.

Stretch and challenge

For the activity above compare the nutritional value of the products.

Emulsifiers and stabilisers

These help to improve the consistency of food during processing and storage. **Emulsifiers** and **stabilisers** help mix together ingredients like oil and water that would normally separate (for instance, when a salad dressing is left to stand the oil rises to the top). Lecithin is a natural emulsifier found in eggs, and is used to make mayonnaise, low-fat spreads and salad dressings.

> **KEY WORDS**
> **Emulsifiers** – help to prevent mixtures separating
> **Stabilisers** – help to prevent mixtures separating
> **Thickeners** – modified starches are often used as thickeners in food products

▲ Figure 4.4 Oil and water do not mix

Thickeners and gelling agents

In Section C: Topic 1 Food science we looked at the function of starches in food. Manufacturers often use modified starches in food products to improve the quality of foods. The most common types of foods that include modified starches are:

- frozen foods
- ready-made meals
- microwave meals
- sauces
- dressings
- soups
- thick and creamy desserts
- snacks
- low-fat products which have a high percentage of water.

Our ingredients: Haricot Beans (52%), Tomato Purée (32%), Water, Sugar, Modified Maize Starch, Salt, Seasoning (Onion Powder, Salt, Maltodextrin, Paprika Powder, Rapeseed Oil, Clove Extract, Paprika Extract, Capsicum Extract, Cinnamon Extract, Flavouring: Chilli, Garlic Oil), Antioxidant: Ascorbic Acid; Citric Acid.

▲ Figure 4.5 Food label showing modified starch

Modified starches are available in many forms, such as maize, wheat, potato, oat and tapioca starches.

They undergo a range of processes to alter them structurally in order to give specific properties. Examples of when modified starches are used:

- in ready meals – to prevent sauces separating, so that the desired sauce thickness is maintained
- in instant soups/Pot Noodles – to produce a thick sauce as soon as hot liquid is added (no further heating is required)
- in cold, gelling desserts – a cold liquid is added and the mixture thickens
- to stabilise emulsions so that they do not separate (for example, low-fat spreads, salad dressings).

There are occasions in food preparation when a product needs the assistance of a gelling agent in order to produce the correct consistency. Some gelling agents are used:

- to create a smooth, set texture (for example, in a cheesecake)
- for setting meat and fish in savoury jelly
- as a stabiliser to stop separation (for example, yogurt)
- as a stabiliser to ensure smooth texture
- to give set liquid a pliable texture (for example, marshmallows).

Gelling agents are often extracted from foods such as beans, seaweed and plants.

Topic 4 Technological developments to support better health and food production

▲ Figure 4.6 Examples of foods containing modified starches

▲ Figure 4.7 Functional foods

✔ KEY POINTS

- ✔ Additives are substances that are added to foods during manufacturing or processing to improve their keeping properties, flavour, colour, texture, appearance or stability.
- ✔ Additives can be natural or synthetic.
- ✔ There are six groups of E numbers – preservatives, antioxidants, colourings, and emulsifiers and stabilisers, sweeteners and thickeners/gelling agents.

TEST YOURSELF

1 State **two** advantages of using additives.
2 State **two** concerns about additives being used in food products.
3 Give **three** examples of foods which might have an emulsifier or stabiliser added.
4 Explain why preservatives are added to some foods.

New and emerging foods

Functional foods

Functional foods are foods that have health-promoting benefits over and above their basic nutritional value. Many foods are promoted in the supermarket as 'functional foods' because they contribute to good health. The number is likely to increase as scientists carry out more investigations into the benefits of eating certain foods.

Figure 4.7 shows some examples of functional foods.

KEY WORD

Functional foods – have extra health benefits

137

Probiotic foods

These include food ranges such as Yakult, Actimel™ and Müller®, and Petit Filous® yoghurts and drinks. These foods contain large numbers of naturally occurring live bacteria. These bacteria are often known as 'good' or 'friendly' bacteria. It is thought that they help to:

- maintain a healthy digestive system
- strengthen the immune system.

Prebiotic foods

These contain a carbohydrate which the digestive system cannot break down. They occur naturally in some foods (for example, leeks, onions and asparagus). Prebiotics help feed the good bacteria in the digestive system. They can improve the health of the digestive system.

Plant sterols and stanols

These help to reduce the absorption of cholesterol from the gut, therefore lowering cholesterol levels. Plant sterols are found in small amounts in fruits, vegetables, vegetable oils, grains, nuts and seeds. Foods containing sterols and stanols include Benecol®, Danone and Flora pro.activ® products.

Phytochemicals or other antioxidants

Phytochemicals can be found in a whole range of foods including:

- onions, garlic, leeks
- brightly coloured fruit and vegetables
- green leafy vegetables
- soya and soya products
- berries (e.g. blueberries, strawberries, blackcurrants)
- nuts and seeds
- fresh herbs
- wholegrain cereals.

▲ **Figure 4.8** Example of yoghurt containing stanols

There are many other foods that are considered functional foods because of their health benefits.

TEST YOURSELF

1 Explain what functional foods are.
2 Give **three** examples of probiotic foods.

Topic 5

Development of culinary traditions

→ **WHAT WILL I LEARN?**

By the end of this topic you should have developed a knowledge and understanding of:

→ **the features and characteristics of British cuisine**
→ **the factors that influence other international cuisines**.

Features and characteristics of British cuisine

British cuisine is influenced by many factors, which include:

- we are an island surrounded by seawater
- there is plenty of land to grow and rear food
- we have sufficient energy to allow us to cook food
- our climate
- our history.

Historically we have been influenced by:

- Romans – who brought many fruits, herbs and spices (for example, mustard). They introduced cheese making, and also pheasants, rabbits, geese and guinea fowl.
- Anglo Saxons – the poorer people ate a lot of bread and a porridge-style food. Pigs were used for meat and this was preserved by salting. Fruits such as blackberries and raspberries were starting to be eaten.
- Norman and medieval – exotic spices were brought into the country and used on special occasions and often to disguise the flavour of poor food. Sugar was also introduced to the UK.
- Sixteenth to eighteenth century – improved farming methods brought better ingredients for people to use. The cooking methods were simple. Meat started to be eaten more than fish. Roast beef became a dish associated with Britain. More imported foods were being introduced – for the wealthier sections of the population. Potatoes were introduced to England (in the sixteenth century).
- Nineteenth century – many foods were imported from the British Empire and we were influenced by their ingredients (for example curry was introduced from India). Industrialisation also had an influence on the foods which were eaten (for example fish and chips in northern industrial towns became a popular dish).
- Twentieth century onwards – through the wars there were food shortages and rationing. However, now we have a very wide variety of foods to eat which are influenced by the **multicultural** society in which we live and our access to food from all over the world. Meat and two vegetables was often thought of as the traditional British meal.

KEY WORD

Multicultural – several cultures or ethnic groups within society

139

There has been a trend in recent years to use British grown and seasonal foods, which support local farmers.

If you asked people today what traditional British food is, you would get a wide variety of responses including the following:

- roast beef
- trifle
- fish and chips
- apple pie and custard.
- curry

There is a wide variety of traditional foods produced all around the country. For example, we do not just produce one type of cheese; there are many different types.

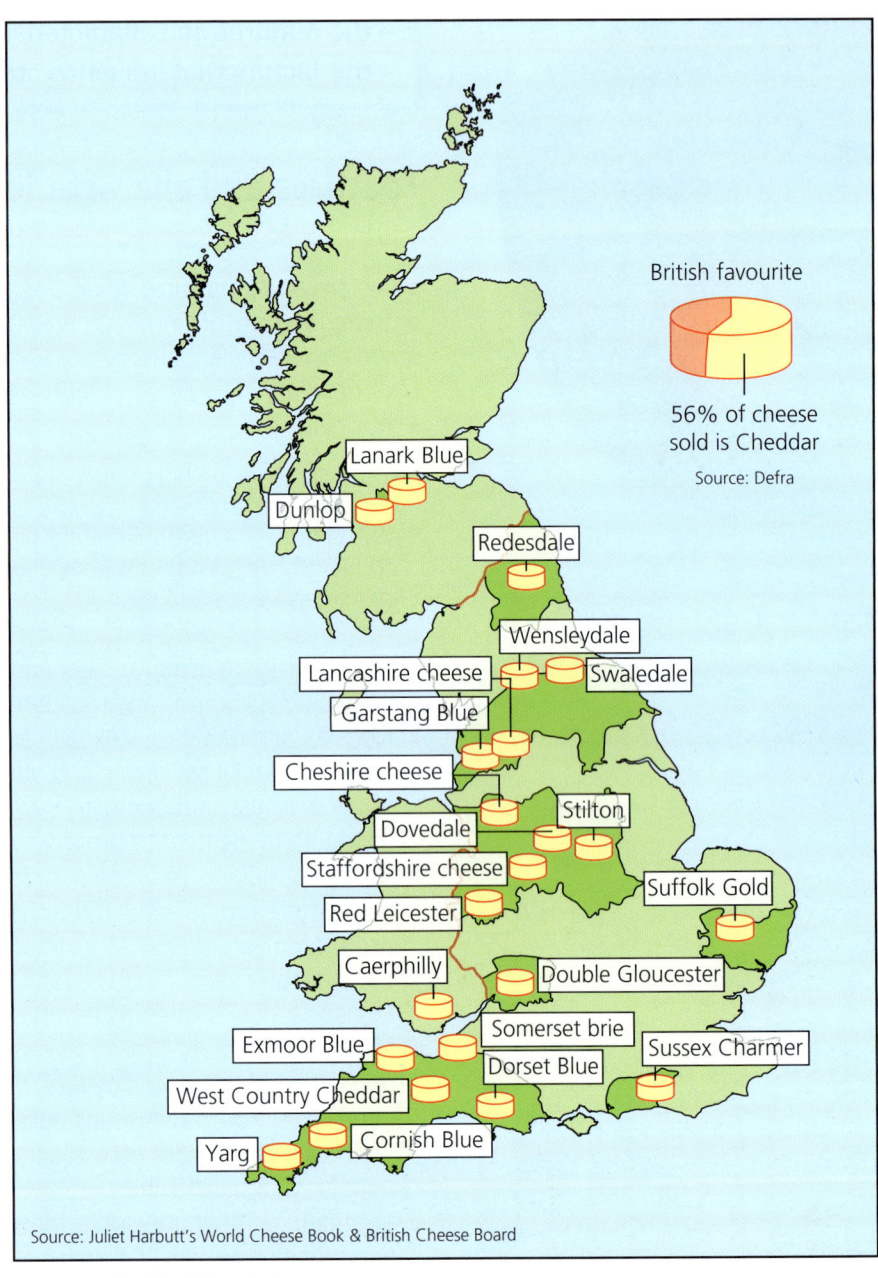

British favourite

56% of cheese sold is Cheddar

Source: Defra

Lanark Blue
Dunlop
Redesdale
Wensleydale
Lancashire cheese
Swaledale
Garstang Blue
Cheshire cheese
Dovedale
Stilton
Staffordshire cheese
Suffolk Gold
Red Leicester
Caerphilly
Double Gloucester
Exmoor Blue
Somerset brie
Dorset Blue
Sussex Charmer
West Country Cheddar
Yarg
Cornish Blue

Source: Juliet Harbutt's World Cheese Book & British Cheese Board

▲ Figure 5.1 Traditional cheeses

Topic 5 Development of culinary traditions

There is also a variety of dishes associated with different parts of the country; for example:

- Cornish pasties
- Lancashire hotpot
- Yorkshire pudding
- Welsh cakes
- Lincolnshire sausage
- Bakewell tart

to name but a few.

RESEARCH ACTIVITY

Investigate what traditional food products are produced in your locality.
- When are they served?
- What are dishes the ingredients traditionally used for?

Present the information as either a poster or information leaflet.

Stretch and challenge

Some foods are covered by the protected food names scheme.

1 Explain what is meant by the protected food names scheme.
2 Investigate which foods are covered by this scheme.

Traditional ingredients

The traditional ingredients used in different countries are usually linked to the main crops they produce or animals which are reared.

Topic link: *Section B: Topic 1 for the cereals which are traditionally grown in different countries*

In England we grow a lot of wheat for bread which is considered a **staple food** as it is consumed by most households on a daily basis. In addition we also eat a lot of potatoes; however, the consumption of these has reduced and we are now eating more pasta and rice. There may be a variety of reasons for this:

- no preparation is required
- they are quicker to cook than potatoes
- more interesting and reflect the multicultural society we live in
- we have travelled abroad and tasted these foods or visited restaurants that serve them.

Wheat is a staple crop in many parts of the world as you will see from the many different types of bread product throughout the world.

In China and in India a lot of rice is grown and this forms the basis of many of their dishes and meals. However, the spices and other ingredients which are served with the rice may vary depending on which part of the country you are in.

KEY WORDS

Staple food – a food that forms the basis of a traditional diet, such as rice, maize, wheat

▲ Figure 5.2 Different types of bread from around the world

Table 5.1 Traditional ingredients and dishes in international cuisines

Cuisine	Traditional ingredients	Examples of traditional dishes
Chinese	Rice Wheat Noodles – rice or wheat Vegetables e.g. bok choy, eggplant, chinese cabbage, bean sprouts, white radish Meat – chicken, duck, pork Tofu or bean curd Sesame oil Soy sauce	Soups Dumplings Stir fried dishes including meat and vegetables Peking duck Chop suey – prawn, beef, pork Fried rice Sweet and sour dishes e.g. pork Wantons Chow Mein – chicken, fish or pork
Indian	Rice – southern India Wheat – northern India Maize Vegetables – wide variety including okra, cabbage, bean, peppers, chillies Chicken, lamb Fish – in southern India	Flat bread – naan, roti, parathe Dhal Samosa Tandori meat e.g. chicken, beef Allo gobi Rogan josh Biriyani Tikkas Jeera Masala Lassi – yoghurt-based drink
Italian	Arboria rice Cured meat – e.g. salami, pancetta, Parma ham Fruit and vegetables e.g. lemons, oranges, peppers, potato Garlic Olives – eaten fresh or made into oil Pasta Sea food e.g. tuna, squid, Tomatoes	Bread – e.g. focaccia, ciabatta Pizza Gnocchi Risotto Pasta dishes for example - lasagne, ravioli. spaghetti bolognaise, spaghetti carbonara Arancini Minestrone soup Tiramisu Ice cream Biscotti
Mexican	Avocado Wheat Corn Beans e.g. black and pinto beans Oaxaca cheese Tomatoes Corn, Wheat, Chili peppers, Fruit e.g. bananas, limes, oranges, lemons, limes, mangos	Chilaquiles Tacos as pastor Enchiladas Pozole – corn, meat and vegetable stew Tostadas often served with refried beans, cooked meat, seafood Mole Guacamole Tamales – corn dough stuffed with a sweet or savoury filling
Spanish	Fish – e.g. anchovies, shell fish, squid, calamari Fruits e.g., figs, melons, dates, Seville oranges Meat – chicken, pork Olives – eaten fresh or made into oil Preserved meats e.g. chorizo, Serrano ham, Vegetables for example tomatoes, peppers, chillies	Spanish bread e.g. Pan Rustico Paella Frittata Gazpacho Tortilla Churros Clam, chorizo & white bean stew Chorizo and chicken stew Pestiños (sweet fritters) Empanada de manzana (Spanish Apple pie)

Topic 5 Development of culinary traditions

Cuisine	Traditional ingredients	Examples of traditional dishes
Jamaican	Ackee Breadfruit Coconut Citrus fruit – lemon, lime, oranges, Cashew Banana Rice Root crops e.g. Cassava, weet Potato Yams - Yellow, White, Negro Chillies Okra Tomatoes Goat Fish – e.g. snapper, jack fish	Jerk chicken Jamaican patti Rice and peas Pumpkin soup Red pea soup Ackee and salt fish Curried goat Escovitch fish Plantain tart Banana fritters Toto (coconut cake)

Table 5.1 shows foods grown in some countries and examples of the dishes eaten. It must be remembered that what is eaten in a country can vary in different for example:

- spicier foods are eaten more in northern India and milder and more sea food is eaten in southern regions
- in China wheat is grown in the northern part of the country and is often made into noodles and rice is grown in southern china and can be eaten on its own or made into rice noodles.

Herbs and spices are used in many countries cuisines see tables 5.2 and 5.3.

RESEARCH ACTIVITY

For the countries you are studying make a list of the ingredients often used in their recipes.

PRACTICAL ACTIVITY

Prepare a range of dishes which are traditionally cooked in the countries you are studying.

▲ Figure 5.3 Traditional Mexican chicken fajita

▲ Figure 5.4 Jamaican jerk chicken

In some countries the use of herbs and spices is very important in their cooking. Tables 5.2 and 5.3 show some of the popular herbs and spices used in cooking.

Table 5.2 Spices used in cooking

Name	Description
Allspice	• It is a dark-brown, pea-size berry. • It is used widely in West Indian recipes and in some Indian and Middle Eastern rice and meat dishes.
Cayenne pepper	• It is made from chilli peppers. • It is used in many Asian dishes as well as with shellfish.
Chilli powder	• This is a mixture of dried chillies and other spices. It varies in strength from mild to hot. • Used in hot pickles, spicy dishes.
Cinnamon	• Cinnamon sticks are added to dishes during the cooking process to add flavour. • It can also be bought as a powder. • Used in mulled wine, with apples, in cakes and biscuits, with meat and poultry dishes.
Clove	• These are used in Chinese five-spice mixtures and Asian curry mixtures or can be used on their own. • They give a strong flavour to foods when used on their own. • Used with poultry and ham, fruits, in biscuits, cakes and bread.
Coriander	• Used in a lot of Middle Eastern and Asian cooking. • Used in meat and chicken dishes, chutneys and as an ingredient of the garam masala curry spice.
Cumin	• This is often used with coriander in recipes. • Used in Middle Eastern, Indian, Moroccan, Mexican and Mediterranean dishes.
Ginger	• Can be bought fresh, dried or preserved in syrup. • It is used in a wide variety of cuisines (e.g. Indian, Chinese, Jamaican savoury dishes) as well as a spice in cakes and biscuits.
Mustard seed	• Comes in white, yellow, and brown seeds. • Used to flavour meat, poultry and fish. • Powdered mustard (finely ground) is used in sauces.
Nutmeg and mace	• Oval seeds from the nutmeg tree. Dark grey colour. Mace is the spice obtained from the membrane of the seeds. • Nutty, warm, spicy. • Used in cakes, cookies, white sauces, as well as tomato and fish dishes.
Paprika	• This is made from dried red peppers. • It is used as the main spice in Hungarian goulash, is used in Austrian cooking and as smoked paprika in Spain.
Peppercorn	• Available as black, white and green peppercorns. • Used to flavour meats, eggs and poultry in most countries' cuisines.
Poppy seeds	• Very small black seeds from the poppy plant. • Used in Jewish cookery and in some Indian curries. They are also used in pastries, breads, cakes, salad dressings.
Saffron	• Dried yellow-orange stigmas from the crocus plant. • Used in French, Italian and Spanish cooking.
Star anise	• Used in Chinese cooking. • Used in dishes containing meat, poultry and with fruits.
Turmeric	• Used to flavour and to colour food. • Used in curries, East Indian cuisine, chutneys and pickles.

◀ Figure 5.5 Different spices

Topic 5 Development of culinary traditions

Table 5.3 Herbs used in cooking

Name	Description
Basil	• Member of the mint family. • Mostly used in Italian and Mediterranean dishes.
Bay leaf	• Leaves from the evergreen bay laurel tree. • Used to make stocks, in pickles, sauces, soups, stews, vegetables.
Chives	• Belongs to the onion and leek family. • Used in salads, omelettes and soups.
Marjoram	• Member of the mint and oregano family. • Used with fish, meat, poultry, sausages, stuffing, vegetables.
Mint	There are many different varieties of mint available and it is used in many different countries' traditional dishes: • UK – served with roast lamb • Middle East – tabbouleh • India – in raita, often served with a curry.
Oregano	• Member of the mint family. • Often used with fish, meat, poultry, tomatoes. • Used a lot in Greek, Italian and Mexican recipes.
Parsley	• There is a variety of different parsleys available (e.g. flat leaf and curly leaf). • Slightly peppery. • Sprigs used as garnish, herb mixtures, sauces, soups, stews. • Used a lot in French and Italian cooking.
Rosemary	Used in lamb and poultry dishes, in stuffing.
Sage	• Used in stuffing (e.g. sage and onion stuffing). • Used a lot in Italian cooking.
Thyme	Used in Mediterranean cooking, often with tomatoes, poultry and in stuffing and pateés.

▲ Figure 5.6 Herbs

RESEARCH INVESTIGATION

Investigate the range of herbs and spices sold in supermarkets which are linked to the countries you are studying.

▲ Figure 5.7 Panforte

▲ Figure 5.8 Dhal

▲ Figure 5.9 Challah bread

▲ Figure 5.10 Chicken biryani

How religious or cultural factors affect cuisine

A person's religious beliefs can influence their choice of foods they eat; for example:

- Hindus do not eat beef.
- Muslims do not eat pork.
- Jews do not eat pork.

Topic link: *Further details on how religion can influence what a person eats can be found in Section B: Topic 6.*

The celebrations linked to a religion or culture can also influence food traditions. For example, Christmas is often associated with eating turkey and Christmas pudding in the UK.

Pancakes are traditionally eaten on Shrove Tuesday, the day before Lent when all rich foods are avoided. Many people still say they are going to give something up for Lent, but it is far more usual now that they give up chocolate or another luxury food that they eat or drink. Then, after Lent, on Easter Day rich foods are eaten again (for example, panforte in Italy and gâteau de Pâques in France).

Other cultures and religions have different celebrations. For example:

- Diwali is the festival of light; it is a Hindu festival and there is a range of traditional foods served. These can include different dhal, curries, pakora and samosa. The dishes vary depending on where in the country people come from.
- Jewish festivals include Shabbat, Pesach, Rosh Hashanah and Purim.
- Purim is a celebration which remembers one of the stories in the book of Esther. The traditional food served is Hamantaschen or Hamen's pockets. Challah is a special bread made for the Sabbath.

Muslims celebrate the end of Ramadan with the festival of Eid Al-Fitr. The type of dishes which will be eaten will be different in different countries and will reflect the foods typical to that country. For example:

- Asia – sheer khurma, a sweet dish made with milk and vermicelli and biryani (steamed rice with meat and spices)
- Bosnia Herzegovina – stuffed vegetables
- Java – brongkos made from oxtail meat, tofu and red beans which is eaten with rice.

RESEARCH ACTIVITY

Investigate which foods are traditionally eaten during different religious or cultural festivals around the world.

PRACTICAL ACTIVITY

For one of the festivals you have investigated prepare a dish which is traditionally served.

Topic 5 Development of culinary traditions

Traditional cooking methods and equipment

There are some cooking methods which are linked to certain countries and are reflected in the foods they produce. Table 5.4 below shows some traditional cooking methods used in some countries and foods that are cooked by these methods.

Table 5.4 Traditional cooking equipment

Country	Traditional cooking equipment
Morocco	A tagine – used to cook meat dishes
China	Dim sum being cooked in a steamer
	Stir-frying meat and vegetables in a wok
India	Tawa – used for cooking chapatti
	Chokla belma – a circular wooden board and rolling pin used to make chapattis (an ordinary rolling pin and board can also be used)
	Kadhee – this is a deep cast-iron bowl with handles used for frying (a saucepan or wok could also be used)
Italy	Used for making pasta

> **RESEARCH ACTIVITY**
>
> 1 For the cuisines you are studying, identify:
>   - the cooking methods often used
>   - equipment that is used.
> 2 For each of the cooking methods and pieces of equipment identified suggest a dish which would use that method or piece of equipment.

Presentation styles and eating patterns

Different countries and cuisines often have different ways of presenting food and their eating patterns vary.

The traditional British eating pattern is to have three meals a day: breakfast, lunch and an evening meal. Sometimes, afternoon tea (which includes tea, sandwiches, small cakes and scones with clotted cream and jam) is served mid- to late afternoon. For most people weekday lunches are light, quick meals such as sandwiches, soups or salads. The evening meal is often more substantial and usually served between 6 p.m. and 9 p.m.

In other European countries, such as Italy and Spain, mealtimes are social occasions and tend to last much longer. Evening meals in particular are enjoyed over several hours and usually include three or more courses, followed by coffee. The evening meal is often eaten much later in the evening.

In other countries, such as in China and India, several dishes are often placed on the table at the same time and everyone shares the food, rather than courses being served separately to each person.

How traditional recipes have been adapted to suit today's society

Many people want to try different foods from around the world. There has been an increase in shops selling specialist ingredients to enable us to have a more varied diet. Large supermarkets also sell ingredients from around the world so that we can make a wide variety of dishes. However, this can be expensive for some dishes as they require many different ingredients including a range of spices. Food manufacturers have produced a wide range of ready-prepared ingredients which help us access these different countries' traditional dishes by:

- selling frozen, cook-chill ready meals
- selling dried ingredients ready to use (for example, pasta and noodles)
- providing jars of ready-made sauces, such as Patak's Medium Balti Sauce.

▲ Figure 5.11 Dried noodles

Topic 5 Development of culinary traditions

▲ Figure 5.12 Jar of curry sauce

▲ Figure 5.13 Ready-made meals

✔ KEY POINTS

- ✔ British food is influenced by many different countries.
- ✔ We have access to a wide variety of ingredients from around the world.
- ✔ Staple foods of a country often influence the foods eaten.
- ✔ A person's religion and the celebrations of that religion may influence food choices.
- ✔ Different methods of cooking and different equipment are used by different cultures and culinary traditions.

TEST YOURSELF

1 Explain **three** factors that have influenced food in the UK.
2 For the cuisines you are studying state **three** herbs and spices that are often used. For each one, give an example of a dish in which it is used.
3 Give **three** examples of festivals where foods are served. For each festival list some of the dishes which are traditionally eaten.
4 State **five** traditionally British dishes and where they come from in the UK.
5 Explain how supermarkets are helping to meet our needs for a culturally wide range of ingredients and food products.
6 For the cuisines you are studying complete the following chart.

Cuisine	Traditional ingredients	Typical traditional ingredients
British		

149

Topic 6
Factors influencing food choice

> **→ WHAT WILL I LEARN?**
>
> **By the end of this topic you should have developed a knowledge and understanding of how the following affect food choice:**
>
> → personal, social and economic factors
> → medical factors
> → religious and cultural beliefs
> → ethical and moral beliefs.

There is a wide range of foods available for people to choose from. During the day people make many decisions about the food they eat. The availability of a wide range of foods makes it easier to choose ones that are nutritionally good for us, but we are all influenced by a variety of other factors.

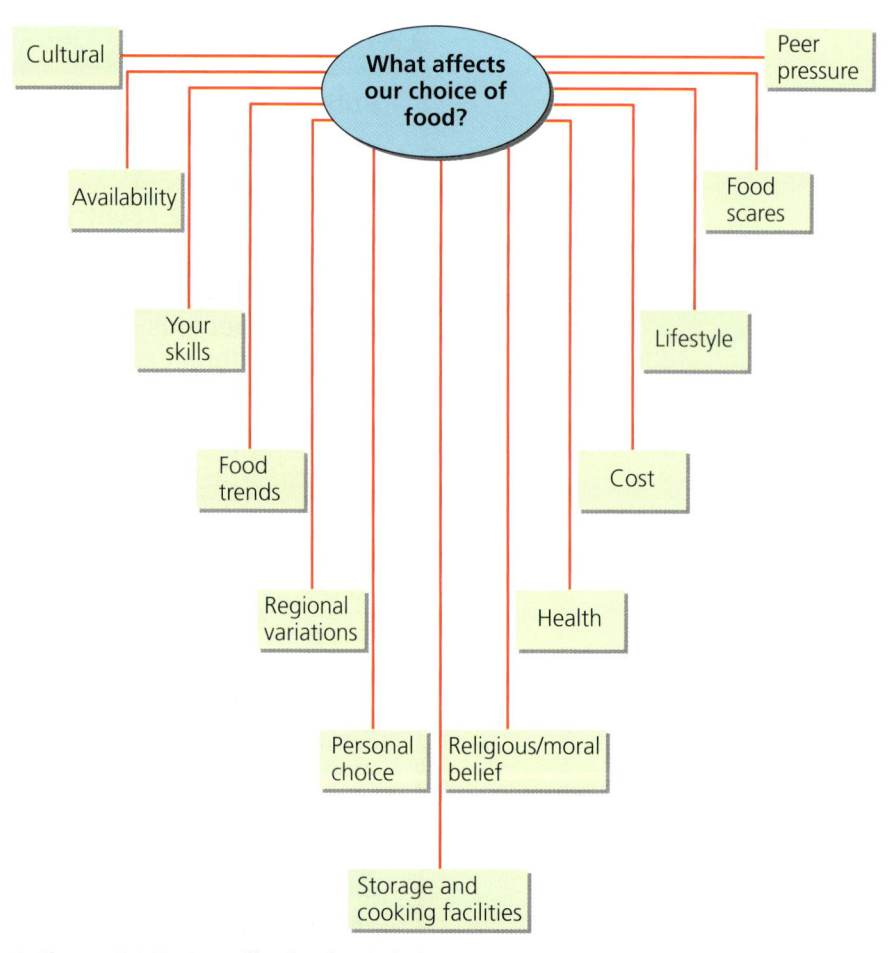

What affects our choice of food?
- Cultural
- Peer pressure
- Availability
- Food scares
- Your skills
- Lifestyle
- Food trends
- Cost
- Regional variations
- Health
- Personal choice
- Religious/moral belief
- Storage and cooking facilities

▲ Figure 6.1 Factors affecting food choice

150

Topic 6 Factors influencing food choice

Figure 6.2 shows the statistics for 2015 on the factors which influence our choices.

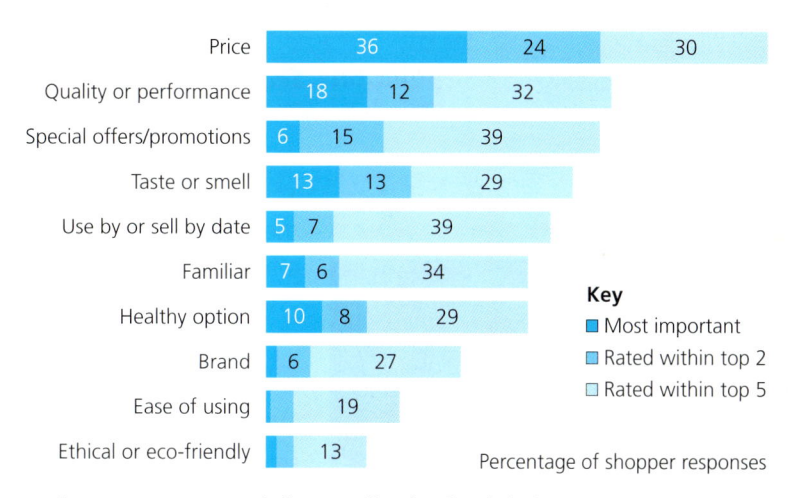

Factor	Most important	Rated within top 2	Rated within top 5
Price	36	24	30
Quality or performance	18	12	32
Special offers/promotions	6	15	39
Taste or smell	13	13	29
Use by or sell by date	5	7	39
Familiar	7	6	34
Healthy option	10	8	29
Brand		6	27
Ease of using			19
Ethical or eco-friendly			13

Percentage of shopper responses

▲ Figure 6.2 2014 Statistics on affecting food choice

Source Food Statistics pocket book 2015 Page 21

Personal, social and economic factors

Cost

One of the most important influences on food choice is how much people can afford to spend. They may have to think of ways they can save money on their food bill; for example:

- using cheaper protein foods (for example, eggs, cheese and pulses)
- buying locally grown vegetables or even growing your own
- buying special offers, such as 'buy one get one free'
- using a variety of supermarkets and planning meals around their special offers
- buying foods with a short shelf life that have been reduced in price
- not wasting foods – the average family in the UK throws away £600 worth of food in a year
- following the advice of the Eatwell Guide and using more starchy carbohydrates (which are cheaper) in meals
- adapting recipes by swapping expensive ingredients for cheaper ones (for example, yoghurt instead of cream)
- planning meals and shopping carefully
- using 'own-brand' economy-range products
- buying loose produce, which is often cheaper than the pre-packaged varieties
- using economical methods of cooking.

Better-off people often buy more protein foods, so their starch and fibre intake tends to decrease, while those on lower incomes tend to buy less fruit and vegetables, thus having a lower intake of vitamins and minerals. Foods that are advertised as 'on offer' are not always cheaper.

Enjoyment

We will always tend to choose the foods we enjoy and like. However, with young children you may have to introduce them to foods more than once before they like them. Also remember your tastes may change as you get older.

> **KEY WORDS**
>
> **Globalisation** – process by which different parts of the globe become interconnected by economic, social, cultural and political means
>
> **Carbon footprint** – the amount of carbon emissions produced in the growing, processing and distribution of our food

Preference

We all have our personal likes and dislikes and are influenced by our senses. We use all of our five senses when we eat.

Topic link: Section C: Topic 2 Sensory properties

Seasonality

This relates to the availability and use of products when they are in season. We have become accustomed to going into supermarkets and buying anything at any time, but the production of crops in the UK is limited to short seasons during the year. (See Section B: Topic 1, Table 1.5 for the seasons for fruits and vegetables in the UK.)

The wide range of products and ingredients available for us to buy is a result of **globalisation**. This has been made possible by improved storage, preservation and transportation of foods. Many of our food products travel many miles to reach our table. Think about the effect on the environment of the miles that food travels. This is called the **carbon footprint** of the product, or 'food miles'.

Topic link: Section B: Topic 1 Food source and Supply

▲ **Figure 6.3** Autumn fruit

Availability

Choice depends on the type of food available in the country and place where you live. In developing countries, such as in parts of Africa, there is very little choice and often insufficient food available. They may not be able to grow produce because of climate, or because they cannot afford expensive agricultural equipment.

In the UK there is a wide variety of food because of technological developments and improvements in the growth, transport, preservation and storage of food. Food technologists have also created many new foods, such as Quorn®. We can import foods that we cannot grow ourselves. In the UK we can go to the supermarket at any time of the year and buy whatever food we want, as long as we are prepared to pay for it.

▲ **Figure 6.4** Imported vegetables

Storage and cooking facilities

Most households have a microwave to reheat convenience foods. A refrigerator is considered an essential item of equipment to ensure food safety – if you do not have a refrigerator, your choice is restricted to canned and dried foods, or preparing and eating fresh food as soon as you have purchased it. Most households have a freezer, which means that they can shop weekly. Research shows that in 2011, 99 per cent of households owned a refrigerator (either as a separate unit or combined with a freezer) and 93 per cent of households owned some kind of freezer.

If you do not have the skills to prepare ingredients, you can buy them ready-prepared, such as frozen vegetables. Students at university and older people, for instance, often have limited cooking facilities.

▲ **Figure 6.5** Modern transportation has improved consumer choice

Topic 6 Factors influencing food choice

There is a wide range of equipment available for consumers to purchase to help with the preparation of food and these are continually being developed. They will perform different tasks, including low-fat grilling machines, electric woks, soup makers and slow cookers.

▲ **Figure 6.6** Range of electrical cooking equipment

Time of day

In some homes, because different members of the family eat at different times, some of the traditional mealtimes of breakfast, lunch and dinner are being replaced by snack meals, takeaway dinners and TV tray meals. People who work shifts often find it difficult to eat meals with other members of the household and to eat traditional meals.

Activity and lifestyle

Our food choice may depend on the activities we are participating in.

For example, if you are going to be taking part in a strenuous sporting activity (e.g. a football or hockey match), you may choose to eat some starchy carbohydrate foods before the game so you have sufficient energy.

▲ **Figure 6.7** Taking part in sporting activity

Topic link: Section A: Topic 4 The main factors that influence an individual's energy requirements

Eating habits have been affected by social changes within households during the past 30 years. Changes in lifestyle due to both parents working and the consequent increase in income (two wages) have resulted in people spending less time in the kitchen preparing food from raw ingredients. Therefore, more people are choosing to buy more foods that are ready to eat or just need reheating, and there has been an increase in eating out.

Lifestyle factors that affect eating habits include:

- More women are employed outside the home.
- More people live alone.
- People travel greater distances to work.
- People have social activities outside the home.

▲ **Figure 6.8** Shopping has become a family occasion, with everyone choosing food

- The use of convenience foods and ready meals, and the availability of takeaways allow people to have more flexible lifestyles.
- There has been an increase in snack foods available.
- There is a wide variety of foods available to choose from.
- There are many types of restaurants in most cities.
- There is less emphasis on the family meal, and family members eat when they want to (grazing).

Health and medical reasons

The nutritional needs of individuals and groups of people are affected by their health. Eating for health means making small changes to the meals that we already eat.

We should all choose foods carefully.

- Overweight people should choose low-calorie, low-fat foods.
- People recovering from an injury or illness should choose high-protein foods.
- Someone recovering from a heart attack should choose products lower in fat.
- Anyone suffering from high blood pressure is usually advised to have a diet lower in salt.

Many people are in hospital because of diet-related conditions. We do not have deficiency diseases in the UK, but there is a problem because of people eating the wrong foods.

▲ **Figure 6.9** The NHS is spending valuable resources on helping people with diet-related disorders

Topic link: Section A: Topic 1 The relationship between diet and health, Major diet-related health issues

Celebration or occasion

Certain foods have become an important part of celebrations in many cultures, such as:

- special events in the year (for example, Christmas, Divali, Barmitzva, Chinese New Year, Eid, Purim)
- birthdays
- weddings
- retirements
- special achievements
- celebrating someone's life.

There are many more.

Topic link: Section B: Topic 5

Marketing, advertising and promotions

We are strongly influenced by our peer group and the media. Manufacturers spend millions of pounds every year on advertising, especially on chocolate, crisps, snacks and sweets. They may also promote the product by special offers, free gifts and competitions.

Section B: Food

Topic 6 Factors influencing food choice

Ways of advertising and promoting food products include:

- advertisements on the television and the internet, in cinemas, newspapers and magazines, on posters and flyers, sides of buses, trains, 'pop ups' on digital media (e.g. phone, iPad, etc.)
- celebrity endorsements by sports or pop stars
- competitions
- displays in supermarkets and shop windows
- eye-catching, attractive packaging
- free gifts
- free samples or tasting in supermarkets
- special money offers, such as 'buy one get one free' (bogof) or money-off coupons.

▲ Figure 6.10 Special offers in a supermarket

We watch chefs on the television and see advertising all around us. This influences our choice of food. Advertising must be legal, decent, honest and truthful, and this is monitored by the Office of Fair Trading. In recent years there has been a lot of discussion about the types of food advertising which appear on television and the impact these have on healthy food choices.

Consumers need to look carefully at special offers and read the small print – what is advertised as a special offer is not always that special if you look at the price per 100 g. If you buy vegetables pre-wrapped in a supermarket you will often pay more than selecting the vegetables yourself. Look at the difference in the price of the carrots below. The pre-prepared ones are more expensive and also have a much shorter shelf life.

Table 6.1 Different prices for carrot

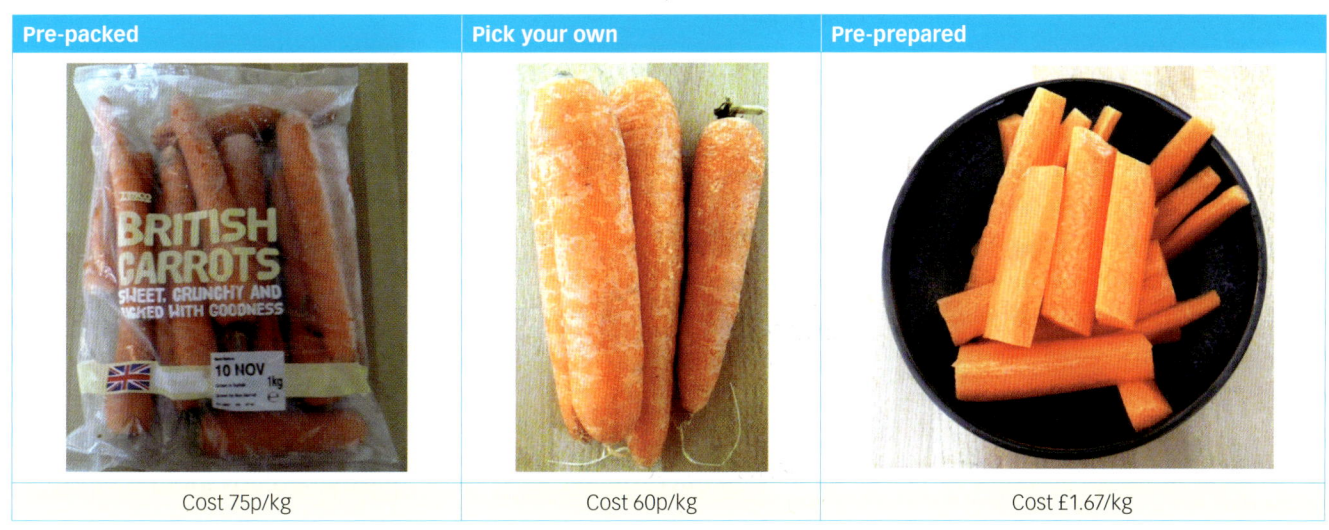

Pre-packed	Pick your own	Pre-prepared
Cost 75p/kg	Cost 60p/kg	Cost £1.67/kg

Food labelling

There is a lot of information on food labelling which can help you make choices about which food to choose. If you are on a special diet or have a medical condition you will need to look at the nutritional information. If you have an allergy you will need to look at the ingredients. You may want to be able to freeze the food – the label will tell if you can.

Topic link: Section C: Topic 3 Food safety, Food labelling

155

> **RESEARCH ACTIVITY**
>
> Look at a piece of food packaging.
>
> List the parts of the packaging which would influence your choosing to purchase or not purchase the product. Give reasons for what you say.

Food scares

Food scares in the media have a dramatic influence on food choice and sometimes result in product sales dropping so sharply that the company involved ceases to exist. Recent food scares include:

- salmonella in eggs
- hazelnut yoghurts
- listeria in chilled foods
- E. coli in meat products
- food contamination during production (for example, metals, insects, glass, fabric)
- BSE
- health standards in chicken factories
- horsemeat sold as beef.

> **RESEARCH ACTIVITY**
>
> Look at the list of ways food manufacturers promote foods (see 'Marketing, advertising and promotions').
>
> For each method on the list, find a current example. Put your information into a chart to display.

> **PRACTICAL ACTIVITY**
>
> 1 Select a savoury dish which you could make for your family. Work out how much it would cost to make the dish.
> 2 Modify the recipe to reduce the cost. Show the new cost.
> 3 Carry out a sensory analysis test for the new dish. Evaluate the success of your modification.

Topic link: As part of your food preparation NEA task you will need to be able to cost recipes, carry out sensory analysis and evaluate dishes.

Stretch and challenge

Look at the food promotions in a supermarket.

Write a report on whether they provide good value for money.

Topic 6 Factors influencing food choice

> ✓ **KEY POINTS**
>
> ✓ There are many personal, social and economic factors that affect the foods we choose to eat, including:
> ✓ Medical and health reasons can also affect the foods we choose to eat.

TEST YOURSELF

List the factors that can affect food choice.

Religious and cultural beliefs

Cultural beliefs

The word **culture** is used to describe our way of life. A cultural group is a group of people who share the same norms, beliefs and values.

We adopt the eating patterns of our parents from infancy; we learn to like the foods that our families prefer. Styles of eating and cooking tend to be determined by the availability of cheap, locally grown food products. Rice is the staple crop in India, China and Japan; the potato in Britain and yams in parts of Africa.

Wheat is grown in many countries, but is used in a variety of ways. Look at Figure 6.11. Can you name the wheat products and their country of origin?

Religious beliefs

Religious beliefs influence eating habits, as religions often have laws related to foods. In some cultures and religions certain foods are not permitted because they are considered 'dirty', 'unclean' or sacred.

Buddhism
- Most Buddhists are vegetarian.

Christianity
There are very few eating traditions associated with Christianity.

- During Lent many Christians will give up rich food and will then celebrate Easter when rich foods are eaten again. On Good Friday many avoid eating meat.
- Different countries celebrate Christian festivals with traditional dishes (e.g. hot cross buns on Good Friday).
- Christmas day is a feast day and is celebrated with traditional foods such as turkey and mince pies in the UK. In other countries they celebrate with different foods.
- Harvest festival is celebrated in many churches in order to celebrate getting the harvest in. In some parts of the country there are traditional foods eaten at this time such as fidget pie and harvest cakes.

Hinduism
- The cow is sacred to Hindus, so they will not eat beef or any product from slaughtered cows.
- They avoid foods that may have caused an animal pain, so are usually vegetarians and have many days of fasting.

KEY WORD

Culture – the way of life, customs and beliefs of a particular group of people at a particular time.

▲ **Figure 6.11** Wheat is the basis for staple foods across the world

Sikhism
- Sikhs have similar eating habits to Hindus.
- Again, many are vegetarian.
- Some do not drink alcohol, tea or coffee.

Islam
- Muslims have a set of dietary rules.
- The pig is considered unclean, so Muslims do not eat pork or any pork products.
- Other meats and poultry must be slaughtered in a particular way so that no blood remains.
- This is called halal meat.
- Unlawful foods are called 'haram' and include alcohol and caffeine.

Judaism
- Food is an important part of the Jewish religion.
- Kosher food is food that Jews are allowed to eat.
- Meat must be specially slaughtered, soaked and then treated with kosher salt. Jews do not eat pork. Meat and dairy produce must not be eaten at the same meal.

Rastafarianism
- Rastafarians eat food that is natural and clean.
- They do not eat pork and only eat fish that is longer than 30 cm.
- They cook with coconut oil and do not drink alcohol, milk or coffee.

KEY WORDS
Buddhism – a religion; most Buddhists are vegetarian
Halal meat – meat and poultry slaughtered in a particular way so that no blood remains
Hinduism - Hindus will not eat any meat from cows
Islam – a religion where people do not eat any pork or pork products; they only eat halal meat
Judaism – a religion where people eat kosher food and do not eat any pork; meat and dairy products are not eaten in the same meal
Rastafarianism – a religion where people only eat clean food
Sikhism – Sikhs have similar eating patterns to Hindus

RESEARCH ACTIVITY
Make a list of religious and cultural celebrations which take place.
Which ones do the supermarkets sell foods for?
For each celebration name traditional foods served.

TEST YOURSELF
1. What is meant by 'halal' meat?
2. What foods to Jews not eat in the same meal?
3. What foods are not allowed by Hindus?
4. What meat is not eaten by Muslims?

✔ KEY POINTS
- The foods we choose to eat are often influenced by our culture. We often learn to like the foods that our families prefer or the foods that are available in the country in which we live.
- Food choice is also affected by our religious beliefs.
- Most Buddhists are vegetarian.
- Christianity has many traditional foods associated with different festivals, celebrations or occasions.
- Hindus believe the cow is sacred and will not eat beef or products from slaughtered cows. They are often vegetarian.
- Many Sikhs are vegetarian and do not drink alcohol, tea or coffee.
- Muslims do not eat pork or any pork products. They eat halal meat. Unlawful foods are called 'haram' and include alcohol and caffeine.
- Jews also have special methods for slaughtering meat. Food they are allowed to eat is called kosher. Jews do not eat pork.
- Rastafarians eat food that is natural and clean. They do not eat pork, or drink alcohol, milk or coffee. They only eat fish that is longer than 30 cm.

Topic 6 Factors influencing food choice

Ethical and moral beliefs

Vegetarians

Some people may make ethical and moral decisions (for example, vegetarians who decide that it is wrong to kill animals to eat their flesh). Vegans will not eat or wear anything that has come from an animal. This limits their choices of food. Other types of vegetarians have a much wider choice of foods as they will eat animal products.

Other reasons why a person might become a vegetarian are because of their religious beliefs, or for medical reasons.

There are two main types of vegetarian:

- lacto-ovo vegetarians
- vegans.

Lacto-ovo vegetarians

Lacto-ovo vegetarians will not eat meat, meat products, fish, poultry, lard, suet, fish oils or gelatine because they involve killing an animal. They will, however, eat food products from animals, such as eggs, milk, cheese, butter, cream and yoghurt.

One concern for this type of vegetarian is that cheese is made using rennin, an enzyme from a calf's stomach, but vegetarian cheese is made using a vegetable rennet (chymosin).

Lacto-ovo vegetarians can choose from a wide range of food products and recipes, and they have no difficulties in obtaining the essential amino acids for proteins or a wide range of vitamins and minerals. Quorn®, a commercially made mycoprotein, is an excellent meat substitute for lacto-ovo vegetarians; however, vegans cannot eat it as it contains egg white. Cheese, eggs, nuts, beans, lentils, tofu and textured vegetable protein can all be used to make an exciting range of products.

Lacto vegetarians

Lacto vegetarians are similar to lacto-ovo vegetarians except they will not eat eggs.

Ovo vegetarians

Ovo vegetarians will eat eggs, but not dairy foods, meat, poultry or seafood.

Vegans

Vegans are strict vegetarians who avoid eating all animal products, including meat, fish, eggs, cheese, dairy milk and cream. Vegans must ensure that they have an adequate nutritional balance in their diet. They have particular difficulties getting an adequate supply of:

- a range of proteins to ensure that they get all the essential amino acids
- vitamins A and D, which are plentiful in animal fats
- mineral elements calcium, phosphorus and iron, found in dairy products and meat
- vitamin B12, as there is no B12 in cereals or vegetables.

KEY WORD

Lacto-ovo vegetarians – eat dairy foods and eggs

▲ Figure 6.12 Vegetarian Society trademark

KEY WORDS

Lacto vegetarians – does not eat eggs, meat or fish

Ovo vegetarians – does not eat dairy products, meat or fish

Vegans – strict vegetarians who will not eat any animal products

▲ Figure 6.13 The combination of pulses, nuts and cereals in this chickpea salad will give a vegan the essential amino acids

There are many types of nuts, pulses and cereals for vegans to use, particularly products made from soya, which is high in biological value. They need to make sure that they use herbs, spices and a variety of vegetables to avoid their diet being monotonous.

A further concern is that vegan diets are sometimes very bulky, and excessive amounts of fibre can cause digestive upsets. A vegan diet can include bean and vegetable stews, salads with nuts, nut roasts, pasta and rice dishes, and soya milk instead of cow's milk. You can buy Quorn® products suitable for vegans. These do not contain egg white.

Topic link: You will learn more about how ethical and moral beliefs affect food choice in Section B: Topic 6 Factors influencing food choice.

KEY WORD

Intensive farming – practices used to produce high volumes of food

PRACTICAL ACTIVITY

1 Modify a main course meat recipe to meet the needs of a vegan. Explain the reasons for your adaptation.
2 Cook the product and evaluate it against the needs of a vegan.

Stretch and challenge

Suggest two nutrients that a vegan may have missing from their diet and explain foods that they could eat to supply these nutrients.

Animal welfare

Some people will look at how food is produced before deciding whether to buy it. For example, many people are concerned about food that been produced using **intensive farming** methods or factory farming methods. They are concerned these methods mean that the animals have cramped living conditions, with limited lighting and space to move or exercise in. Instead, people may choose to purchase foods where animals have been allowed to live and grow in natural surroundings. Products from these animals may cost the consumer more because the farmer will not produce in larger quantities.

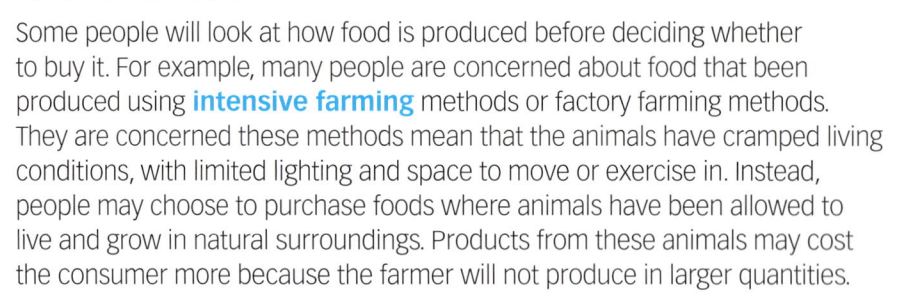

Many foods today carry the Red Tractor mark, which shows that the foods have been safely produced with high animal welfare standards. Some food products also have information on the packet about the producer.

▲ Figure 6.14 Indoor-reared chickens

▲ Figure 6.15 Free-range chickens

"We are very proud of the quality of our bacon. All Wicks Manor bacon is dry cured by hand and allowed to mature. The results speak for themselves the bacon does not leak in the pan and tastes the way bacon should. Our pigs are born and bred on the farm at Wicks Manor and live in large open straw yards with plenty of space to express natural behaviour. We have been farming pigs at Wicks Manor for nearly 50 years growing the wheat and barley we feed to our pigs. Pigs are reared on the home farm and sourced from East Anglian farms with similar high standards. As we say a happy pig is a growing pig."

Fergus & Hamish Howie
– we grow the crops to feed our pigs at Wicks Manor.

▲ Figure 6.16 Information on a food packet about how the meat is produced

Topic 6 Factors influencing food choice

Topic link: Section B: Topic 1 Food source and supply

Locally produced foods

Some people will choose to purchase locally produced food. They do this for many reasons including:

- supporting local farmers and industry
- it may have a lower carbon footprint as less energy is used in transport
- reduced food miles
- may be fresher.

Topic link:
- Section B: Topic1 Food provenance: Food Souce and Supply
- Section B: Topic 3 Food Security

✔ KEY POINTS

- ✔ Lacto-ovo vegetarians eat eggs and dairy foods but not poultry, meat or fish or seafood.
- ✔ Lacto vegetarians eat dairy products but not eggs, poultry, meat or fish or seafood.
- ✔ Ovo vegetarians eat eggs but not dairy products, poultry, meat or fish or seafood.
- ✔ Vegans do not eat any products of animal origin.
- ✔ Some people consider animal welfare when deciding which foods to buy and will only buy foods where animals have been allowed to live and grow in natural surroundings with high standards of animal welfare.
- ✔ Some people will choose to purchase locally produced food.
- ✔ Some people will choose to buy organic foods because they believe it tastes better and they are concerned about the use of chemical pesticides.

TEST YOURSELF

1. List **six** reasons why a person may become a vegetarian.
2. Explain the differences between a lacto-ovo vegetarian and a vegan.
3. List **six** sources of protein suitable for a lacto-ovo vegetarian.
4. List **six** sources of protein suitable for a vegan.
5. Which vitamins and minerals may be difficult for a vegan to obtain from food sources?
6. State **three** reasons why a family might choose to buy organic foods.
7. Give **three** reasons why people choose to buy locally produced foods.

Practice questions

1. Complete the table below to show one example of each type of meat. (4 marks)

Classification	Example
Meat	
Poultry	
Offal	
Game	

2. Explain what is meant by primary and secondary processing of food. Give **one** example of primary and secondary processing. (4 marks)

3. Explain how wheat is milled into flour. (6 marks)

4. Give **one** function in foods of:

   a preservatives

   b colourings

   c antioxidants

   d emulsifiers. (4 marks)

5. Explain how a person's religious and cultural beliefs can affect their choice of food. (6 marks)

The quality of written communication will be assessed in the following questions.

6. Evaluate how Fairtrade affects food producers and workers. (8 marks)

7. Discuss the nutritional factors that should be considered when planning meals for different types of vegetarians. (10 marks)

8. Over 7 million tonnes of food waste is thrown away every year in the UK. Discuss how consumers could reduce their amount of food waste. (8 marks)

Section C: Cooking and food preparation

In this section you will learn about the following:
- Topic 1 Food science
- Topic 2 Sensory properties
- Topic 3 Food safety

Topic 1 Food science

→ WHAT WILL I LEARN?

By the end of this topic you should have developed a knowledge and understanding of:

→ why food is cooked
→ how heat is transferred through different cooking methods
→ how cooking methods/processing affect the nutritional value of foods
→ how cooking methods/processing improve the sensory properties
→ the working characteristics and the functional and chemical properties of ingredients.

Why food is cooked

When preparing foods to eat, there are many different processes and skills involved. It is essential that preparation is carried out correctly so that food is safe to eat and is presented in a way that is appetising and appealing.

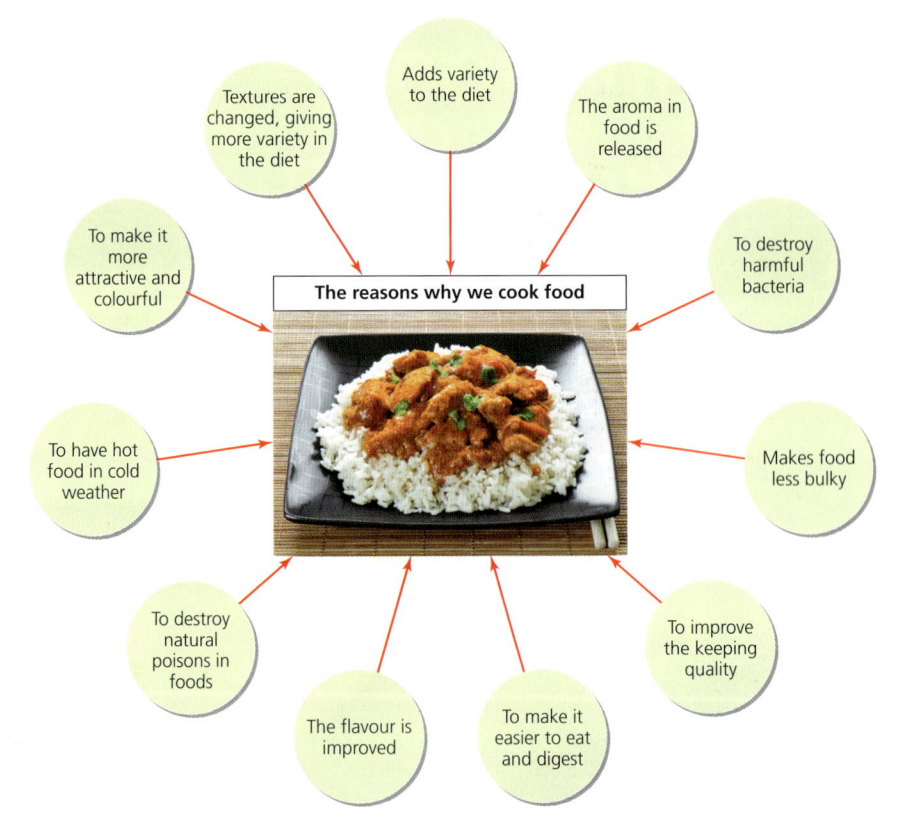

▲ Figure 1.1 The reasons why we cook food

Topic 1 Food science

To destroy harmful bacteria
This includes yeasts, moulds and bacteria.

Topic link: *See Section C: Topic 3 Food safety for more information on yeasts, moulds and bacteria.*

To make food less bulky
The volume of some food is reduced when it is cooked. For example, when you cook cooking apples or spinach the volume you have when it is cooked is much less than the volume you start with.

▲ Figure 1.2 500 g cooking apples before cooking and after cooking

To improve the keeping quality of food
Foods can be preserved to make them last longer.

Topic link: *See Section B: Topic 2 Food processing and production for more information on preservation methods.*

To make food easier to digest
When we cook food we change its structure. For example, when we cook vegetables the fibres in them are softened; or in meat the connective tissue softens.

Topic link: *See Section C: Topic 1 Working characteristics and the functional and chemical properties of ingredients for more information on how the structure of food changes.*

To improve flavour
When cooking meat and vegetables in a casserole, for example, the flavours develop as the ingredients cook together. We dry-fry herbs and spices to extract their flavour before putting them in a curry.

To destroy natural poisons in food
Some foods contain natural poisons that need to be destroyed to make food safe to eat. For instance, red kidney beans contain a poison which needs to be destroyed.

▲ Figure 1.3 Red kidney beans contain a natural poison

Stretch and challenge
Investigate which foods contain natural poisons. What advice would you give to consumers about cooking these foods?

To have hot food in cold weather
In cold weather we need hot food to provide a 'feel good' factor and to maintain our body temperature.

To make food more colourful and attractive
Many foods change colour when they are cooked. For example, bread will brown when grilled. The method of cooking affects the colour of the food: steaming and boiling do not add colour to food but baking does add colour.

Topic link: *See Section C: Topic 1 Working characteristics and the functional and chemical properties of ingredients for more information on how the colour of food changes.*

To change the texture, giving more variety in the diet
Cooking foods by different methods changes the texture. For example, protein foods become firmer and fruits become softer. This also means some foods become more **palatable** (pleasant to taste).

To provide variety in the diet
We can cook foods in different ways, therefore giving us more variety. Consider a food you use frequently in cooking, such as tomatoes – they can be eaten raw in a salad, baked, grilled, or added to a curry or a casserole.

To release the aroma in food
This helps to get your digestive juices working. Consider what happens when you smell bread baking or onions cooking.

Topic 1 Food science

> ✔ **KEY POINTS**
>
> Food is cooked for many reasons, including in order to:
>
> ✔ destroy harmful bacteria or natural poisons and make it safe to eat
> ✔ make it less bulky
> ✔ improve the keeping quality
> ✔ make it easier to digest
> ✔ improve the flavour
> ✔ provide warmth in cold weather
> ✔ make it more colourful and attractive
> ✔ change the texture and therefore provide variety in the diet
> ✔ release an aroma.

> **KEY WORD**
>
> **Conduction** – where heat is transferred from one molecule to another
> **Convection** – where warm molecules rise and the cooler molecules fall closer to the source of heat
> **Radiation** – where heat is passed by electromagnetic waves from one place to another

Heat transfer through cooking methods

Heat is a type of energy. When it is applied to foods, they will change. The most noticeable changes in foods are:

- changes in colour
- changes in texture.

The nutritional content of the food may also change and this needs to be considered when deciding on the method of cooking.

There are three basic methods of transferring heat:

- **conduction**
- **convection**
- **radiation**.

The different methods of cooking available use at least one of these methods.

Table 1.1 shows the different methods of transferring heat for the most common methods of cooking foods.

Table 1.1 Different methods of heat transfer

Method of heat transfer	Method of cooking	How heat is transferred
Conduction	Boiling, simmering, blanching, poaching, baking, frying, microwaving, roasting, braising, casserole	Heat is transferred by contact with heat.

167

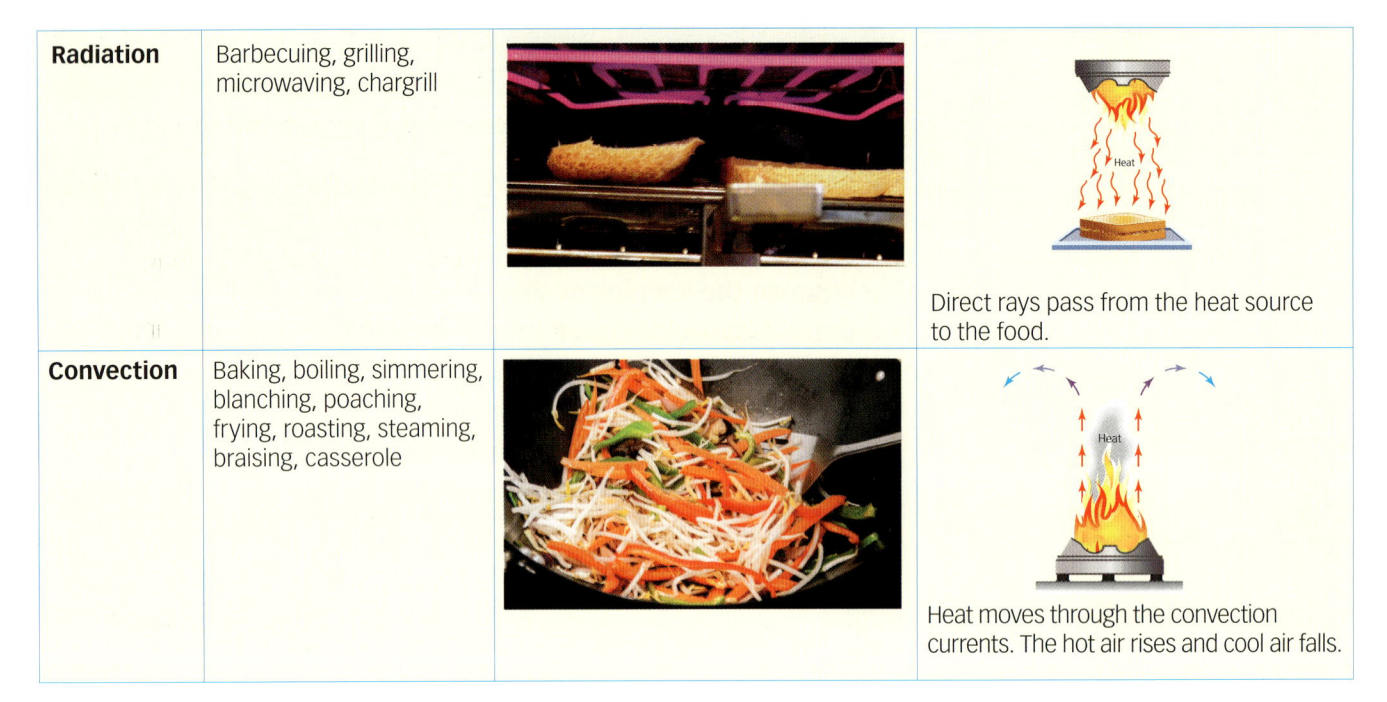

Radiation	Barbecuing, grilling, microwaving, chargrill		Direct rays pass from the heat source to the food.
Convection	Baking, boiling, simmering, blanching, poaching, frying, roasting, steaming, braising, casserole		Heat moves through the convection currents. The hot air rises and cool air falls.

Topic links:

- Section C: Topic 1 How cooking methods affect the nutritional value of foods for more information on the different cooking methods
- Section: C Topic 3 Food safety principles

> ✔ **KEY POINTS**
>
> ✔ **Conduction is when heat is transferred by direct contact.**
> ✔ **Radiation is when direct rays pass from heat source to the food.**
> ✔ **Convection is when hot air and cool air falls.**

Cooking methods

The method of cooking used will depend on many factors, including those shown in Figure 1.4.

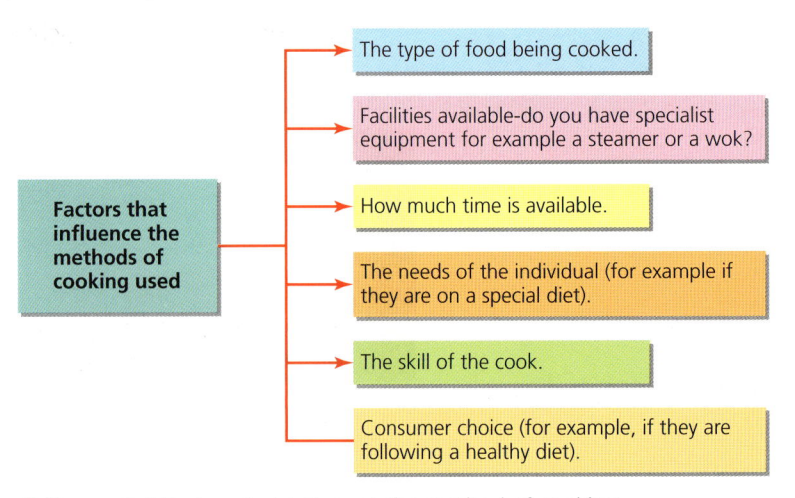

Factors that influence the methods of cooking used:
- The type of food being cooked.
- Facilities available-do you have specialist equipment for example a steamer or a wok?
- How much time is available.
- The needs of the individual (for example if they are on a special diet).
- The skill of the cook.
- Consumer choice (for example, if they are following a healthy diet).

▲ Figure 1.4 Factors that influence the method of cooking

Section C: Cooking and food preparation

168

Topic 1 Food science

When you choose a method of cooking you need to ensure that you cook the food thoroughly so that it is safe to eat.

Topic link: *Section C: Topic 3 Food safety, cooking and serving food*

Cooking methods are classified as either dry or moist, depending on whether water is involved.

- Moist-heat cooking methods include boiling, simmering, poaching, and steaming.
- Dry-heat cooking methods include baking, roasting, frying, sautéing and stir-frying.

Moist methods of cooking (using the hob)

These use fairly low temperatures (45–100° C) to cook foods. The liquid used to cook the food can vary, for example fruit juice, milk, water and stock.

Boiling

Boiling is probably the most popular of the moist-heat cooking methods. Boiling uses large amounts of rapidly bubbling liquid (100° C) to cook foods. Heat is transferred through both conduction and convection.

Types of food suitable for boiling include:

- rice
- pasta
- potatoes
- vegetables.

▲ Figure 1.5 Boiling vegetables

Simmering

Simmering is one of the most widely used moist-heat cooking methods. Food simmered correctly should be moist and tender. The foods are cooked in hot liquid (85–99° C), but require gentler treatment than boiling, to prevent food such as fish or meat from toughening or vegetables from disintegrating.

▲ Figure 1.6 Poaching fish

Poaching

For poaching, the temperature of the liquid should be just below simmering (85° C). These foods do not need a long cooking time.

The types of food suitable for poaching include:

- eggs
- fish
- fruit.

Blanching

Food is cooked and is then cooled quickly to stop the cooking process. This is achieved by putting the food into iced water. Vegetables are also blanched before they are frozen to stop the enzymic action, which continues to cause decay even when they are frozen.

▲ Figure 1.7 Rapidly cooling vegetables after blanching

Steaming

With this method, the food does not come into contact with the boiling water, but is cooked by the steam that is rising from the boiling water. It is the convection currents that transfer the heat to the food. Steaming can be carried out in a variety of ways, as shown in Figures 1.8 to 1.11.

▲ Figure 1.8 Plate method

▲ Figure 1.9 Saucepan method

▲ Figure 1.10 Tiered steamer

▲ Figure 1.11 Electric steamer

In a tiered steamer it is also possible to cook several foods at once, such as potatoes in the base and various vegetables in the different layers of the steamer. This can help to reduce energy costs.

The types of foods suitable for steaming include:

- puddings – suet, sponge
- fish
- vegetables.

Using the oven – dry methods of cooking

Higher temperatures are used in dry methods of cooking, compared with moist methods.

Baking

When food is baked it mainly uses dry heat.

The temperature used varies depending on the type of food product being cooked – a very low temperature is used to cook meringues so that they will dry out and have a crisp texture; while Yorkshire puddings are cooked at a high temperature so that steam is produced in the mixture to cause the batter to rise.

Topic 1 Food science

On some occasions moisture may be added to help develop certain textures in a food, for instance placing egg custards in a bath of water (bain-marie) to prevent them from curdling.

In gas ovens the top of the oven is usually the hottest because the warm air rises to the top of the oven by convection. Therefore, it is important that food is put on the correct shelf. Most electric ovens have a fan which circulates the air round the oven meaning that the temperature is the same throughout the oven.

Types of food suitable for baking include:

- cakes and biscuits
- some vegetables (for example, potatoes)
- pastry products.

▲ Figure 1.12 Egg custard being cooked in a water bath (bain-marie)

Roasting

Food is cooked by dry heat. A small amount of fat is also used to prevent the food from drying out and to develop the flavour. Heat is transferred to the meat by conduction (as the meat or vegetables are in contact with the metal roasting tin, and also by any bones which are in the meat) as well as by convection currents from the oven.

Types of food suitable for roasting include:

- vegetables
- meat and poultry.

Using the oven – moist methods of cooking

Braising

This method is used to cook meat. The meat is first browned in a pan using a small amount of fat. It is then put in a container with some liquid and covered with a lid.

Types of food suitable for braising:

- meat
- vegetables; for example onions, leeks, carrots, celery.

Casserole

Using this method, food is cooked in a small amount of liquid that simmers. A casserole is cooked in a container with a tight-fitting lid so the liquid does not evaporate. The liquid is served with the food.

Types of food suitable for casseroling:

- meat – usually tougher cuts are used
- vegetables.

RESEARCH ACTIVITY

Investigate which cuts of meat are suitable for braising and casseroling.

Dry heat – fat based

Frying

This is still a popular method of cooking, although we are being encouraged to reduce the amount of fried food we consume. There are four different types of frying:

- dry-frying
- shallow-frying /pan-frying
- stir-frying
- deep-frying.

Heat is transferred to the food by conduction through the pan and by convection from the hot fat.

When frying food it is important that you do not leave the pan unattended as fat can easily catch fire.

The correct type of fat should always be used when frying. A low-fat spread is unsuitable for frying due to its high water content. The water causes the fat to split and separate when it is heated. The fat used must be suitable to heat to a temperature of 200° C without it burning or changing in taste. The most common type of fat for frying is vegetable oil, although in the past lard was often used.

▲ Figure 1.13 Dry-frying

INVESTIGATION ACTIVITY

1 Melt 25 g of the following fats over a low heat:
   - butter
   - soft spread/margarine
   - block margarine
   - block white fat
2 Allow each to cool.
3 Explain which fats are suitable for frying.

RESEARCH ACTIVITY

Using either a website or food packaging, look at a variety of different fats (for example, butter, soft spread, block margarine, block white fat).

Make a list of what methods of cooking they can be used for.

Dry-frying

Some foods can be fried without any fat being added to the pan. Non-stick frying pans are the best as they help to prevent the food from sticking.

It is possible to purchase fat sprays which can be used to put a very thin layer of oil onto a frying pan.

Foods suitable for dry-frying usually have a high fat content. Types of food suitable for dry-frying include:

- sausages
- bacon.

▲ Figure 1.14 Example of a spray which can be used when frying

Topic 1 Food science

▲ Figure 1.15 Shallow-frying

▲ Figure 1.16 Stir-frying

▲ Figure 1.17 An electric deep-fat fryer

Shallow-frying

This is when foods are cooked in a shallow layer of hot fat or oil. The fat comes about half-way up the food. As this is a very quick method of cooking it is not suitable for tough cuts of meat and poultry. Types of food suitable for Shallow-frying include:

- eggs – omelettes, fried eggs, pancakes, crêpes
- fish (fresh/frozen) – various cuts, fillets, small whole fish
- meat and poultry – prime cuts, for example fillet steak, chicken breast.

Stir-frying

This method of frying originated in East Asia. Small pieces of finely chopped food are cooked in a wok. The temperature of the oil is high and the food is constantly moved around the pan. This is becoming a popular method of cooking foods as:

- it is a quick method of cooking
- it is an energy-saving method of cooking
- only a small amount of fat is used.

Types of food suitable for stir-frying include:

- meat
- fish
- vegetables.

Deep-frying

It is recommended that we reduce the amount of deep-fried foods we consume. When food is deep-fried it is totally covered in fat during the frying process.

Types of foods suitable for deep-fat frying include:

- chips
- small poultry joints
- fish.

RESEARCH ACTIVITY

Make a list of the types of foods that are commonly fried. Suggest an alternative way each food could be cooked to reduce the amount of fat in the product.

Grilling

This is a quick method of cooking, where heat is conducted through radiation. The source of heat can come from above and/or below the food. When the foods are cooked, the surface is quickly sealed due to the dry heat. The food must be turned often to ensure even cooking. It is recommended that foods which are to be grilled are no more than 3.5 cm thick.

With the trend to reduce the amount of fat used in cooking foods, manufacturers have also developed electric griddles, which cook food from both the top and the bottom and have ridges on the heat plates so that the fat drains away from the food.

▲ Figure 1.18 An electric griddle

Types of food suitable for grilling include:

- tender cuts of meat, such as chops and chicken breast,
- sausages
- beefburgers
- mushrooms
- bread.

Microwaving

Over 93 per cent of households had a microwave in 2012. They are also widely used in catering kitchens, shops, offices and work canteens.

Microwave ovens work by:

- the microwaves penetrating into the food and causing the molecules in the food to vibrate – this is by radiation.
- the molecules causing friction when they vibrate against each other, which produces heat – this is conduction.
- the water molecules continuing to vibrate when food comes out of the oven, which generates heat, allowing the cooking process to be completed. During this time the centre of the food will gain rather than lose temperature.

Microwaves are popular because foods can be defrosted, cooked and reheated quickly. Standing times given on food labels should always be followed as this is part of the cooking process.

Microwaves are continually being developed to include extra features, such as:

- child locks
- weight sensors
- different cooking modes (for example, cooking vegetables, meat, fish, pasta)
- defrost modes
- turbo reheat
- auto-sensor cooking.

There are many different types of microwaves available today. These allow us to combine other methods of cooking with microwaving.

Table 1.2 Different types of microwave

Type of microwave	Standard	Standard with grill	Combination
Example			
Uses	To defrost, reheat and cook foods.	All the features of a standard microwave oven, plus an internal grill; this can be used as a stand-alone grill or for browning or crisping food, in conjunction with the microwave.	A combined microwave, grill and convection (hot-air) oven, gives more flexibility; the functions can be used independently or together: some combination ovens also offer a steaming function.

Topic 1 Food science

When deciding which method of cooking to use there are always advantages and disadvantages to each method. Table 1.3 shows some of these.

Table 1.3 Advantages and disadvantages of the different methods of cooking

Method of cooking	Advantages	Disadvantages
Boiling	<ul><li>A quick method of cooking as the transfer of heat is rapid</li><li>Food is not likely to burn</li><li>A simple method of cooking</li></ul>	<ul><li>Food may disintegrate if it is not carefully timed</li><li>Some flavour from the foods will leach into the water</li><li>Water-soluble vitamins (B and C) may be lost</li></ul>
Steaming	<ul><li>Food cooked by this method is usually light in texture and therefore easy to digest</li><li>Different foods can be cooked in the different tiers of a steamer, therefore reducing energy costs</li><li>Steaming retains the natural vitamins found in each food.</li></ul>	<ul><li>Depending on the product being cooked, it can take a long time (for example, a steamed pudding)</li><li>Care with timings must be taken so that delicate foods such as fish are not overcooked</li></ul>
Grilling	<ul><li>A quick method of cooking food, therefore reduces the energy costs</li><li>It is possible to trim excess fat off some meats, for example, bacon, before grilling</li></ul>	<ul><li>Not suitable for tough cuts of meat</li><li>Careful timing of cooking is needed so that foods are not overcooked or undercooked</li></ul>
Frying	<ul><li>A quick method of cooking food</li><li>Food is usually attractive in colour – golden brown</li></ul>	<ul><li>Fats need straining and changing regularly</li><li>Fried food is more difficult to digest</li><li>Great care has to be taken from a safety perspective when frying food</li><li>Heat-sensitive vitamins are destroyed</li><li>We are being encouraged to eat less fat – this method of cooking does not assist this</li></ul>
Microwave	<ul><li>Food is cooked very quickly – saves energy</li><li>Useful for people who have busy lifestyles</li><li>The bright colour of vegetables is retained as cooking time is short</li><li>Very useful for defrosting frozen foods</li><li>Less destruction of heat-sensitive vitamins as the cooking time is short</li><li>Less loss of water-soluble vitamins when cooking vegetables</li></ul>	<ul><li>Careful timing is required as foods can easily be overcooked</li><li>As the food is cooked so quickly the flavours may not develop in the food</li><li>The colour of the food may be pale if it is cooked in a standard microwave</li></ul>

Stretch and challenge

What are the advantages and disadvantages of each of the following methods of cooking?

- simmering
- poaching
- chargrilling
- baking
- roasting
- casseroling
- braising

INVESTIGATION ACTIVITY

1 Cook a variety of different vegetables in different ways and compare the end results in terms of colour, flavour, texture and length of time taken to cook.

   Which method of cooking would you recommend for each vegetable you have cooked?

2 Microwaves can be used to cook a variety of foods.

   Compare cooking the following foods in a microwave with cooking them by a traditional method.
   - Victoria sandwich cake – baking
   - steamed pudding – steaming
   - jacket potato – baking

   a Produce a chart to compare the following:
   - length of cooking time
   - colour before and after cooking
   - texture
   - mouth feel
   - aroma

   for each of the foods cooked.

   b Explain your findings and which methods of cooking you would recommend for each product.

✔ KEY POINTS

- ✔ The different methods of cooking available use at least one of these methods of heat transfer. Some cooking methods use more than one type of heat transfer.
- ✔ Boiling, simmering, blanching, poaching, baking, frying, roasting, braising and casseroling use both conduction and convection to transfer heat to food.
- ✔ Steaming uses convection to transfer heat to food.
- ✔ Barbecuing, grilling and chargrilling use radiation to transfer heat to food.
- ✔ Microwaving uses both conduction and radiation to transfer heat to food.

TEST YOURSELF

1 State the **three** different methods of heat transfer.
2 Give **two** disadvantages of boiling as a method of cooking.
3 Give **two** advantages of steaming as a method of cooking.
4 What safety precautions should be taken when frying food?
5 State **four** foods which are suitable for grilling.
6 Why do some people use a bain-marie when cooking a baked custard?

How cooking methods/processing affect the nutritional value of foods

We cannot see how the different methods of cooking we use affect the nutritional value of foods. However, when we apply heat to foods it can affect the nutritional value.

How the nutritional content is affected depends on how we cook the food. For example:

- if we cook foods in fat, the fat content and calorie content will increase
- if we cook foods in liquid the nutritional content may decrease if the liquid is not consumed (for example, loss of vitamin C when we boil vegetables).

Table 1.4 shows how the different methods of cooking affect the nutritional value of foods.

Table 1.4 How nutrients are affected by heat

Nutrient	How it is affected by cooking processes
Protein	The amount of protein in the food is not affected by the method of cooking.
Carbohydrate	Fibre (NSP) is softened, particularly when cooked by moist methods of cooking. Starch may be reduced when food is cooked in water. This is because the starch dissolves into the liquid.
Fat	The fat content of some foods may be reduced when food is cooked. For example, grilling will allow the fat to drain out of the food. Cooking food in fat will increase the fat content and the calorie content.
Vitamin A – retinol, beta carotene	Not affected by cooking processes except for frying, where high temperatures are used.
Vitamin D – cholecalciferol	Not affected by normal cooking temperatures and does not dissolve in water.
Vitamin E – tocopherol	Not affected by most cooking processes.
Vitamin K	Not affected by most processes.
B1 – thiamine	Soluble in water, therefore the cooking liquid should be used (e.g. in a sauce or the gravy for meat dishes). Easily destroyed by heat.
B2 – riboflavin	Soluble in water. Destroyed by heat if heated in the presence of an alkali (e.g. bicarbonate of soda).
B3 – niacin	Soluble in water, therefore the cooking liquid should be used (e.g. in a sauce or the gravy for meat dishes). More resistant to heat than any of the other B vitamin group.
B9 – folate or folic acid	Less sensitive to heat than other vitamins, but is destroyed if food is reheated or kept warm for a long time.
B12 – cobalamin	Soluble in water.
Vitamin C – ascorbic acid	Destroyed by moist and dry heat. Dissolves in water so cooking methods which use the minimum amount of water should be chosen.
Minerals	The nutritional value of minerals is not affected by normal cooking processes.

Topic link: Section B: Topic 2 Food processing and production

> **RESEARCH ACTIVITY**
>
> Using a nutritional program investigate:
> 1. The different fibre content of vegetables which can be eaten raw and cooked.
> 2. How the different methods of cooking vegetables affect the water-soluble vitamin content.

> **✓ KEY POINTS**
>
> ✓ Water-soluble nutrients are lost when cooking food in liquid.
> ✓ Some vitamins are destroyed by heat.
> ✓ The calorie content of foods can increase by cooking them in fats and oils.

> **TEST YOURSELF**
>
> 1. Name **two** water-soluble vitamins.
> 2. Name **two** heat sensitive vitamins.
> 3. How does fibre change when it is cooked?
> 4. Which methods of cooking would you recommend for green vegetables?

▲ Figure 1.19 Beef casserole cooked for a long time to tenderise the meat

How cooking methods/processing improve the sensory properties of food

When cooking food, the choice of cooking method can determine the sensory qualities and palatability of the food. We need to consider the food we cook to make sure it is easier to chew, swallow and digest.

Not all methods of cooking are suitable for all foods. For example, some cuts of meat are not suitable for some methods of cooking.

- If you grilled a piece of shin beef it would be tough and very difficult to chew and swallow. This is because the fibres of the meat are long with a lot of connective tissue and therefore need long, slow cooking so that these become tender.
- Steaming foods will make them light in texture and people will find this type of food more palatable.

The method of cooking chosen can affect the look of a food and may affect your choice of food. For example, steaming does not add any colour to food, so white fish which is steamed lacks colour on its own. If the same fish was baked or grilled it would be golden in colour.

Some foods should not be eaten raw and therefore require cooking (for example, potatoes, rice, snails and prawns).

▲ Figure 1.20 Steamed fish

Section C: Cooking and food preparation

Topic 1 Food science

▲ **Figure 1.21** Grilled fish

Many foods are processed into ingredients which then need to be cooked. For example, you would never eat raw wheat grains; wheat is processed into flour and then it is combined with other ingredients to make a product which needs cooking. Figure 1.22 illustrates this.

▲ **Figure 1.22** Ingredients for making chapatti

Topic link: *You will have learnt more about food processing in Section B: Topic 2 Food processing and production.*

The flavour of food is often developed by the method of cooking chosen. For example, when beans are steamed this enhances the flavour. Putting a variety of different ingredients in a dish, such as meat, vegetables and spices in a curry, means the flavours of the individual ingredients are blended, which therefore makes more interesting and palatable foods.

> ✔ **KEY POINTS**
>
> ✔ We cook food to make it easier to chew, swallow and digest.
> ✔ Not all methods of cooking are suitable for all foods.
> ✔ The method of cooking chosen can affect the look of the food (for example, its colour).
> ✔ Some foods are not eaten raw and therefore require cooking.
> ✔ Many foods are processed into ingredients that need to be cooked.
> ✔ The flavour of food is often developed by the method of cooking chosen.

Working characteristics and the functional and chemical properties of ingredients groups

Every ingredient used in a recipe has a specific function, for example, to:

- thicken,
- aerate,
- coagulate,
- or add nutritional value. You need to understand the function of ingredients in order to choose the correct ingredients when making food products.

It will be important that you can explain these functions when making decisions about your choices when completing your NEA (Non-Examined Assessments). It is the way we prepare, combine and cook ingredients that gives us the vast range of food products that we can eat.

Skills link: *You will need to give your reasons for choice of ingredients (and return to the functions of ingredients) when completing your NEA Food Preparation Task.*

Most food products that we purchase and make contain more than one ingredient. The technical term **colloidal structure** is what is formed when at least two ingredients are mixed together. It is these structures that often give the texture to the food products.

Carbohydrates

Starch

Starch is mainly used to thicken mixtures.

KEY WORD

Coagulate – to set; the change in structure of protein brought about by heat, mechanical action or acids

Colloidal structure – when two substances are mixed together

Emulsion – a mixture of two liquids

Gelatinisation – this is what happens to starches and water when cooked together

Shortening – when fat coats the flour grains and prevents the gluten from developing and absorbing water, resulting in a crumbly mixture

Topic 1 Food science

Flour

There are many different types of flour available in the shops. Flour forms the main structure of many products, including cakes, bread, pastry and biscuits. The type of flour used will vary depending on the desired texture and product being made.

Wheat flour is one of the most common starchy foods used in cooking. It is often used to bulk out a recipe. The way it reacts to heat depends on the type of heat applied (dry or moist heat) and the ingredients it is mixed with.

When dry heat is applied to products, such as when baking bread, the crust of the product becomes brown – this process is called **dextrinisation**.

When flour is mixed with a liquid and heated, such as in a sauce, the mixture will thicken. This is known as **gelatinisation**. This occurs because:

- the starch grains cannot dissolve in the liquid, so they form a suspension
- as the liquid is heated the starch grains swell (at 60° C), and as more heat is applied the starch grains break open, causing the mixture to thicken (at 80° C).

The mixture must be stirred as it is being heated to prevent lumps forming.

Cornflour

Cornflour is often used as an alternative to flour in sauces. It is obtained from maize kernels. It is virtually tasteless. Unlike other flours, it blends to a smooth cream with liquid; it still needs to be stirred when it is being heated so lumps do not form.

Other starch sources

Other starch foods that thicken mixtures are:

- potatoes – potato flour is used to thicken sauces, soups and casseroles, as the starch is released from the potatoes into the cooking liquid
- other root vegetables, for example, swedes and sweet potatoes, will thicken soups and stews; tapioca is made from the cassava plant and is used in puddings, stews and soups
- rice – rice flour is used to thicken sauces, useful to those who are on a gluten-free or wheat-free diet; rice thickens milk puddings such as rice pudding and savoury dishes such as risotto
- arrowroot – made from the maranta plant, used to make clear glazes which are often used on fruit tarts.

KEY WORD

Gelatinisation – This is what happens to starches and a liquid when they are cooked together

▲ Figure 1.23 Different types of thickeners

PRACTICAL ACTIVITY

1 In groups, prepare a variety of dishes which show how carbohydrate foods can be used to thicken mixtures.
2 Make a savoury dish which illustrates the process of dextrinisation.

INVESTIGATION ACTIVITY

1 Make a variety of sauces using different types of starches (see Section D for proportions of ingredients).
2 Carry out a sensory analysis on the sauces.
3 Write a detailed evaluation, explaining your results and suggesting when consumers may choose to use the different sauces.

RESEARCH ACTIVITY

Food manufacturers use many different thickeners in food products. Produce a chart to show the range of thickeners used in different food products.

✔ KEY POINTS

- **Carbohydrate in the form of starch is mainly used to thicken mixtures. Flour is one of the most common starchy foods used in cooking.**
- **When dry heat is applied to carbohydrates (such as when baking bread) the product becomes brown. This is called dextrinisation.**
- **When flour is mixed with a liquid, such as in a sauce, the mixture will thicken. This is known as gelatinisation.**

Sugars

There are many different types of sugars used in food production. Sugars add flavour and bulk out ingredients.

▲ Figure 1.24 Different types of sugars (caster, demerara, granulated, soft brown, icing)

Adding flavour and colour

Most sugars taste sweet and are added to products for this purpose. Some savoury products also contain sugar (for example, baked beans). There are some sugars that do not taste sweet, such as lactose, which is the sugar found in milk.

Sugar helps with the browning of sweet foods.

Moist heat on sugars

When moist heat is applied to sugar, the following happens:

- The sugar melts and becomes syrup. It is sometimes used in this syrup state, for example in fruit salads, though most people today put fruit salads into fruit juices to reduce the sugar and calorie content of the product.
- At 154° C the sugar starts to change colour – this process is called **caramelisation**. The longer the sugar is heated, the deeper the colour of the caramel and the harder it will set when it is cooled.

Table 1.6 How sugar changes the appearance of foods

 Sugar which has been browned under a hot grill to create the hard caramel on top of a crème brûlée.	 Sugar which has changed to a syrup and caramelised in a crème caramel.	 Maillard reaction, which occurs in biscuits when they contain carbohydrate and protein.

Dry heat on sugars

Sugars will also caramelise when dry heat is applied to them. When sugars are mixed with other products, such as eggs and flour (which both contain protein) in baked products, browning occurs in these products. This is called a **Maillard reaction**.

Aerating

Aerating means adding air to mixtures. When sugar is beaten with a fat or with egg, air is added to the mixture. This helps to make cakes rise and gives them a light texture. Examples of this are whisked sponges, creamed or all-in-one cake mixtures.

Preserving

Sugars are also used to help preserve foods. In jams and chutneys the concentration of sugar is high and this prevents the growth of micro-organisms.

KEY WORD

Aeration – the process of trapping air in a mixture

Caramelisation – process of changing the colour of sugar from white to brown when heated

Dextrinisation – when dry heat is applied to flour and it browns as the starch is changed into a sugar

Maillard reaction – this happens when foods containing proteins and carbohydrates are cooked by dry methods

INVESTIGATION ACTIVITY

1 Use the recipe below to make buns using each of the following sugars:
   - caster
   - granulated
   - demerara
   - soft brown
   - icing

Recipe	Method
50 g self raising flour 50 g sugar 50 g fat 1 egg	1 Put oven on 180° C/Gas Mark 5. 2 Put the sugar and fat into a mixing bowl and beat till light and fluffy. 3 Crack the egg into a small basin and beat with a fork. 4 Gradually beat the egg into the fat and sugar mixture. 5 Fold in the flour. 6 Divide mixture evenly between eight bun cases. 7 Bake for 10–15 minutes until golden brown and springs back when touched.

2 Record the colour, texture and appearance before baking and after baking.

   a Photograph your results so that you can see the effect the sugars had on the colour, texture and appearance of your product.

   b Copy and complete the table below:

Sugar used	Before cooking			After cooking			
	Colour	Texture	Appearance	Colour	Texture	Appearance	Taste
Caster							
Granulated							
Demerara							
Soft brown							
Icing							

PRACTICAL ACTIVITY

1 Make a dish which illustrates the process of caramelisation.
2 Make a dish which illustrates the process of Maillard reaction.

KEY QUESTIONS

1 Explain what happens to sugar when heated.
2 Explain how sugar can act as a preservative.

✔ KEY POINTS

✔ When moist heat is applied to sugar, at 154° C the sugar starts to change colour – this process is called caramelisation.

✔ When sugars are mixed with other ingredients such as eggs and flour, and dry heat is applied to them in the baking process, browning occurs. This is called a Maillard reaction.

Topic 1 Food science

KEY WORD
Emulsifier – a substance that stops oil and water separating (for example, lecithin in egg yolk)
Plasticity – consistency of fats

▲ Figure 1.25 Fats which spread straight from the fridge

▲ Figure 1.26 Products made by the rubbing-in methods, which have a short crumbly texture

▲ Figure 1.27 Low-fat spread containing an emulsifier

Topic link: You will use these skills when completing your Food Investigation Task.

Fats and oils

There is a wide variety of different fats available for consumers to choose from. They are produced from animals, fish and vegetables. Different fats are used in food for their different properties.

Plasticity

Not all fats melt at the same temperature. Some products are designed to have a lower melting point as this gives consumers a quality in a product that they want – for example a spread that can spread straight from the fridge. This property is called **plasticity**.

Shortening

When fat is used in making rubbed-in mixtures such as pastry, biscuits, scones and cakes, it coats the grains of flour. This gives the flour a waterproof coating and prevents the gluten in it from developing. This means the finished product will have a short, crumbly texture. This is called shortening.

Aeration

When a fat and sugar are creamed together air is trapped. When the product is heated the air will expand, causing the mixture to rise.

Emulsions

An emulsion is formed when oil and a liquid are mixed together, such as in salad dressings. Often when oil and a liquid are mixed together they will separate when left to stand – you will see this when salad dressings are left to stand.

An **emulsifier** is sometimes added to these ingredients to prevent them from separating. For example, egg yolk, which contains lecithin, is used in some salad dressings, mayonnaise and low-fat spreads.

Flavour and moisture

There are many different types of fats and oils available. We use some of these because of the flavour they give to a product (for example, butter is used to provide a rich flavour in shortbread biscuits). Fats also add moisture to a product, which helps to extend the product's shelf life.

> **INVESTIGATION ACTIVITY**
>
> **Which fats produce the best pastry?**
> 1. In groups, make small batches of shortcrust pastry using 100 g flour, 50 g fat and a variety of different fats, for example butter, hard margarine, low-fat spread, vegetable fat, lard.
> 2. Produce a chart to show how the flavour, colour and texture of the products varied before and after cooking.
> 3. Write a conclusion explaining which type of fat produced the best pastry. Give reasons for your findings.

> **PRACTICAL ACTIVITY**
>
> 1. Produce a savoury pastry or scone product to show shortening property of fats.
> 2. Make a cake to illustrate the use of fats to trap air.
> 3. Fats are often used to add flavour and moisture. Make a sweet or savoury dish to demonstrate this.

> **KEY QUESTIONS**
>
> 1. What is meant by plasticity?
> 2. Why are emulsifiers added to low-fat spreads?
> 3. Explain three functions of fat in food products.

Topic link: *You will use these skills when completing your Food Investigation Task.*

> **✔ KEY POINTS**
>
> - ✔ Not all fats melt at the same temperature. This property is called plasticity.
> - ✔ When fat is used in making rubbed-in mixtures such as pastry, biscuits, scones and cakes, it coats the grains of flour and prevents the gluten in the flour from developing. This is called shortening.
> - ✔ An emulsion is formed when oil and a liquid are mixed together.

KEY WORD

Denaturation - Caused by adding acids to protein e.g. when tenderising meat, and by mechanical action e.g. whisking egg whites

Protein foods

Denaturation

When proteins are heated their chemical structure is changed. This is called denaturing. Denaturing is also caused by acids on protein and by mechanical whisking.

Coagulation

When moist or dry heat is applied to protein foods they coagulate (set). If they are overheated they become tough and more difficult to digest. Table 1.7 shows what happens to the main protein foods when they are heated.

Topic 1 Food science

Table 1.7 What happens to protein foods when they are heated

Protein	Reaction
Meat	• The muscle fibres begin to coagulate between 40°C and 60°C. • After 60°C the fibres in the meat shrink and the juice in the meat is squeezed out. • The meat changes colour from red to brown with the effect of dry heat. • Tougher cuts of meat or meat from older animals (e.g. mutton needs long slow cooking so the muscle fibres become tender). Lean cuts of meat (those with less connective tissue) are suitable for dry-cooking methods and can be cooked quickly.
Fish	• The muscles in the fish shrink as they are very short and there is only a small amount of connective tissue. • If it is cooked for too long the fibres will become tough.
Eggs	• The egg white begins to coagulate at 60°C. The egg white will change from an opaque colour to a white colour. • The egg yolk begins to coagulate at 70°C. • If the egg is heated too quickly the liquid from the egg separates out and the protein becomes tough. This is called syneresis. It is sometimes seen when cooking scrambled eggs.
Milk	• When milk is heated a skin forms on the top – this is the protein coagulating.
Cheese	• The protein coagulates.
Flour	The protein gluten in flour coagulates when cooked.

If proteins are heated too quickly, the liquid in them separates out and the protein becomes tough. This is called syneresis.

Topic link: Section A : Topic 11 Nutrients in food

Table 1.8 How coagulation is applied when preparing and cooking dishes

Reason for using	Example of dish	Explanation
Bind ingredients together	Stuffing, fish cakes, croquettes	The egg is mixed with other ingredients. When it is heated it coagulates and holds the ingredients together.
To coat products to protect when frying	Fish coated in breadcrumbs, fish in batter, scotch eggs	As the food is coated in a batter containing egg or egg and breadcrumbs the coating coagulates as soon as it touches the hot fat. This stops the fat entering the food.
To set a mixture	Quiche Lorraine, egg custard, meringues	As the egg protein is heated it coagulates and sets or thickens the mixture.

Aeration

The process of trapping air in a mixture is called aeration. When egg whites are whisked, the protein in them, **albumin**, is stretched and traps the air (for example, when eggs are whisked when making meringues). If the whisked egg whites are left to stand they will eventually collapse and become a liquid again. Once they have collapsed they cannot be whisked again.

If egg whites are heated then they will set. An example of this is in meringues. Whisked egg whites can also be called a foam, as they are a mixture of gas (air) and a liquid (egg white).

▲ Figure 1.28 The protein in the egg white stretches and incorporates air

PRACTICAL ACTIVITY

In groups, produce a range of sweet and savoury dishes to show the functional properties of eggs for example, setting, aerating and binding.

KEY WORDS

Albumin – protein in egg white
Syneresis – usually refers to eggs; if overcooked, the proteins shrink as they coagulate and separate from the watery liquid

KEY WORD

Gluten – the protein in flour

Gluten formation

When making cakes, a soft flour is used which has a low **gluten** content so that the cakes have a soft crumb. When making bread, strong flour with a high gluten content is used to provide the structure. The gluten is developed in the bread dough when it is being kneaded. Flours which have more than 10 per cent protein content are usually used for bread making.

The names of the proteins found in wheat which form gluten are:

- gliadin
- glutenin.

PRACTICAL ACTIVITY

Make a pasta dish using home-made pasta.

INVESTIGATION ACTIVITY

Investigating the gluten content of different flours

1. Mix 100 g of each of the following flours with water to form a dough. Label them 1–4:
   - white strong plain flour
   - plain flour
   - self-raising flour
   - wholemeal flour
2. Knead each piece of dough for 5 minutes to develop the gluten.
3. In turn, place each piece of dough in a fine sieve or piece of muslin and run under cold water to rinse out the starch (squeezing the dough will speed up this process). When all the starch has been rinsed out the water will be clear as it runs through the dough.
4. Squeeze out as much water as possible.
5. Label each piece of gluten, weigh and record the weight, and put on a greased baking tray.
6. Bake at 200° C for 20 minutes till risen and dry to touch.
7. Record your findings in a table like the one here.

What do your results tell you about the gluten content of the different flours?

Explain which flour you would use for the following:

- bread
- shortbread biscuits
- flaky pastry
- shortcrust pastry.

Flour	Weight before baking	Weight after baking	Appearance of the raw gluten ball	Appearance after baking	Structure of the gluten ball when cut

✓ KEY POINTS

- ✓ When moist or dry heat is applied to protein foods they coagulate (set).
- ✓ The process of trapping air in a mixture is called aeration. For example, when egg whites are whisked, the protein in them is stretched and traps the air.
- ✓ Gluten is the protein found in flour. It is developed in bread dough when it is kneaded and is used to provide the structure of the bread.
- ✓ The process of changing the structure of protein is called denaturation. Acids are often used to change protein, for example they are used to soften meat tissues before cooking meat, tenderising the meat and allowing it to cook more quickly.

Topic 1 Food science

> **KEY WORD**
>
> **Acid** – Acids are chemicals that are found in some foods
> **Denaturation** –

> **TEST YOURSELF**
>
> 1 What happens to the protein in meat when it is heated?
> 2 What is meant by synerisis?
> 3 Why does milk form a skin when it is heated?
> 4 Give four examples of dishes made with eggs which illustrate coagulation.
> 5 How is gluten developed when making bread?

▲ Figure 1.29 A range of foods that contain acids

Skills link: *You will use these skills when completing your Food Investigation Task.*

Acids

Acids are chemicals that are found in some foods. The flavour these give foods is a sour or sharp taste. Acids also have other functions when preparing foods. When acids are used to change the structure of protein in the food it is called **denaturation**.

Vinegar is a type of acetic acid. It is used to:

- tenderise meat, as the acid softens the meat tissues – this is often applied to meat before it is barbecued as it will make it cook more quickly and prevent it from becoming tough during this dry method of cooking meat.
- provide a soft texture – if a small amount of vinegar is added to a meringue mixture the centre of the meringue remains soft and similar in texture to marshmallows.

Lemon juice is also an acetic acid. It is used to:

- prevent foods going brown – foods such as apples and bananas are exposed to the air when they are cut (causing **oxidisation**). This causes them to go brown. This is called **enzymic browning**. If the fruit is put in a lemon juice solution the browning does not take place. This improves the appearance of the food.
- set mixtures that contain protein, for example, cheesecakes. Lemon juice is also added to some jams to help them set (form a gel).

> **KEY WORD**
>
> **Enzymic browning** – reaction between a food product and oxygen resulting in a brown colour (for example, potatoes or apples going brown)
> **Oxidisation** – occurs when fruit and vegetables are cut and the cells are exposed to air
> **Fermentation** – when given warmth, moisture, food and time yeast produces carbon dioxide and alcohol

> ✔ **KEY POINTS**
>
> ✔ When fruits and vegetables are cut they are exposed to the air. This often causes them to go brown. This is called enzymic browning.

Raising agents

A **raising agent** is added to a cake or bread mixture to give lightness to it. The lightness is based on the principle that gases expand when heated. The gases used are:

- air
- carbon dioxide
- water vapour.

189

These gases are introduced before baking or are produced by substances added to the recipe before baking.

Yeast

Yeast is a living organism. When yeast is given the right conditions – food, warmth, moisture and time – it can break down food to produce carbon dioxide by a process known as **fermentation**. Yeast is used to make bread. You can use either fresh or dried yeast.

▲ Figure 1.30 Yeast fermenting

PRACTICAL ACTIVITY

Make a sweet or savoury dish to illustrate yeast as a raising agent.

INVESTIGATION ACTIVITY

What are the best conditions for yeast to produce carbon dioxide?

Equipment and resources required:
- 5 test tubes labelled 1–5
- 5 balloons
- Test tube rack
- Pan test tube holder
- Teaspoon
- Salt
- Sugar
- 25 g fresh yeast or 15 g dried yeast

1. Dissolve 25 g fresh yeast or 15 g dried yeast in 150 ml warm water (37°C).
2. Divide the yeast and water mixture evenly between five test tubes.
3. Follow the instructions below for adding ingredients and where to place the test tube:

Test tube	Additional ingredient	Where to place the test tube
1	Add nothing	Stand in a warm place
2	$\frac{1}{4}$ teaspoon sugar	Stand in a warm place
3	$\frac{1}{4}$ teaspoon salt	Stand in a warm place
4	$\frac{1}{4}$ teaspoon sugar	Stand in the fridge
5	$\frac{1}{4}$ teaspoon salt	Using the pan test tube holder, stand in a pan of boiling water

4. Observe what happens to the test tubes for 15 minutes.
5. Which test tube produced the most gas?
6. How will you use this information when you make a bread dough?

Chemical raising agents

Chemical raising agents can be added to a product and produce carbon dioxide when heated. Chemical raising agents include:

- bicarbonate of soda (sodium bicarbonate) used alone (for example, in gingerbread) – a strong flavour of washing soda is produced and a dark colour, but the flavour and colour are disguised by the use of spices, such as ginger, or treacle
- bicarbonate of soda plus acid (for example, bicarbonate of soda and cream of tartar)

▲ Figure 1.31 Baking powder producing bubbles

- baking powder is a commercial preparation. The quality of commercial baking powder is controlled by law and is of standard strength. The baking powder includes an alkali and an acid. Rice flour or a similar substance is added to absorb any moisture and prevent lumps.

Self-raising flour is a prepared mixture of soft flour and a raising agent. It will give good results for plain cakes or scones, but there is too much raising agent for rich cakes. **Never** use self-raising flour for bread, pastries, biscuits or batters.

It is important that chemical raising agents are used in the correct proportion so that the product is successful. Table 1.9 shows what happens if too much or too little raising agent is used.

Table **1.9** Using raising agents

Too little raising agent	Too much raising agent
Lack of volume	Over-rising, then collapsing, giving a sunken cake, or sunken fruit
Close texture	Coarse texture
Insufficient rising	Poor colour and flavour
Shrinkage	

It is also important to:

- buy a reliable brand
- store chemical raising agents in an airtight container, in a cool dry place, to prevent loss of strength and reaction
- add and distribute moisture evenly to the mixture to ensure an even reaction.

PRACTICAL ACTIVITY

Make a cake or biscuit which illustrates the use of a chemical raising agent.

Air

Air expands very quickly. Figure 1.32 shows the different ways that air can be added to mixtures.

Whisked egg whites have the property of holding air (for example, in soufflés and meringues). Whole eggs do not hold air as easily because of the fat in the yolk.

Dishes almost entirely dependent on air as a raising agent include:

- whisked sponges
- soufflés
- meringues.

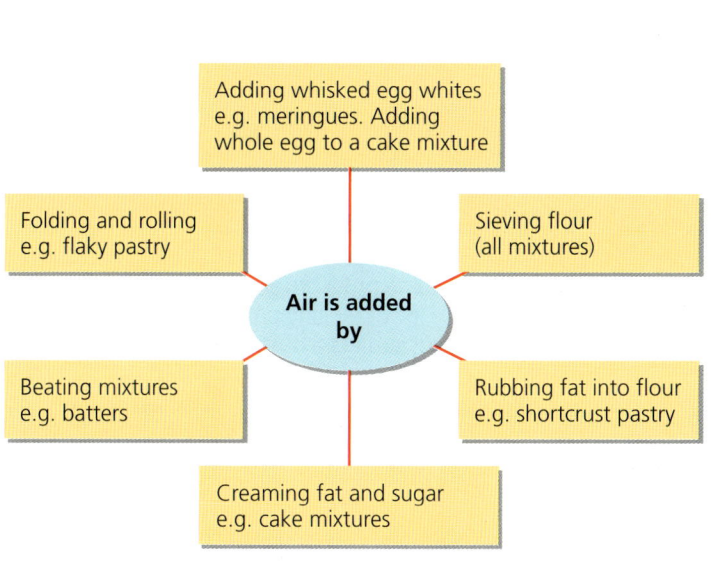

Air is added by:
- Adding whisked egg whites e.g. meringues. Adding whole egg to a cake mixture
- Sieving flour (all mixtures)
- Rubbing fat into flour e.g. shortcrust pastry
- Creaming fat and sugar e.g. cake mixtures
- Beating mixtures e.g. batters
- Folding and rolling e.g. flaky pastry

▲ Figure **1.32** Ways of adding air to mixtures

Steam

Steam is produced when products are baked, from the liquid present in the mixture. The liquids include:

- water
- milk
- eggs.

Steam is used as a raising agent in products which contain a lot of liquid for example in:

- éclairs and choux pastries
- batters
- flaky and puff pastry.

These products have to be cooked in hot ovens so that sufficient steam is produced to make the product rise.

PRACTICAL ACTIVITY

Make a pastry product which demonstrates steam being used as a raising agent.

▲ Figure 1.33 Choux pastry

Ingredient group	Working characteristic/ functional and chemical property	What happens?	How/why does this happen?
Carbohydrates	**Gelatinisation**	When flour is mixed with a liquid and heated, such as in a sauce, the mixture will thicken.	• The starch grains cannot dissolve in the liquid, so they form a suspension • As the liquid is heated the starch grains swell (at 60° C), and as more heat is applied the starch grains break open, causing the mixture to thicken (at 80° C).
	Dextrinisation	When dry heat is applied to products (such as when baking bread), it causes the product to brown.	The starch in the flour is changed into a sugar.
	Caramelisation	The colour of sugar changes from white to brown when heated.	• The sugar melts and becomes syrup • At 154° C the sugar starts to change colour • The longer the sugar is heated, the deeper the colour of the caramel and the harder it will set when it is cooled.
Fats/oils	**Shortening**	When fat is used in making rubbed-in mixtures the finished product will have a short, crumbly texture.	The fat coats the grains of flour and gives the flour a waterproof coating that prevents the gluten in it from developing.
	Aeration	The process of trapping air in a mixture to cause it to rise.	When a fat and sugar are creamed together air is trapped. When the product is heated the air will expand, causing the mixture to rise.
	Plasticity	The ability of a solid fat to soften over a range of temperatures.	Not all fats melt at the same temperature. Some products are designed to have a lower melting point as this gives consumers a quality in a product that they want – for example a spread that can spread straight from the fridge.
	Emulsification	The process of using an emulsifier (such as egg yolk) to prevent a mixture of oil and liquid from separating (such as in salad dressing and mayonnaise).	Emulsifiers attract oil and liquid and hold them together. For example, egg yolk contains lecithin, and is used in some salad dressings, mayonnaise and low-fat spreads to hold the oil and liquid together and prevent them from separating.

Topic 1 Food science

Ingredient group	Working characteristic/ functional and chemical property	What happens?	How/why does this happen?
Protein	Coagulation	When the protein in food sets.	When moist or dry heat is applied to protein foods they coagulate (set). Different protein foods coagulate in different ways.
	Foam formation	A foam is produced when eggs are whisked.	When eggs are whisked, they produce a mixture of gas (air) and liquid (egg white). The gas produced is spread throughout the liquid and the foam is produced.
	Gluten formation	When making bread, strong flour with high gluten content is used to provide the structure for the bread.	Two proteins found in wheat called gliadin and glutenin form gluten. The gluten is developed in the bread dough when it is being kneaded. This creates the structure for the bread.
	Acid denature	When acids are used to change the shape and structure of protein foods, for example to tenderise meat or provide a soft texture (e.g. when vinegar is added to meringue).	The acid causes a change in the structure of a protein. The long chains of amino acids unfold. When applied to meat, for example, it softens the meat tissues.
Fruit and vegetables	Enzymic browning	When fruit and vegetables (e.g. potatoes or apples) go brown.	The food product reacts with oxygen, resulting in a brown colour.
	Oxidisation	When fruit and vegetables are cut open and the cells are exposed to air.	A chemical reaction occurs when the cells of the fruit or vegetable are exposed to oxygen. This can cause the fruit or vegetable to turn brown (enzymic browning).
Raising agents	Yeast	A raising agent used in bread making to give the bread lightness and causes it to rise.	When yeast is given the right conditions – food, warmth, moisture and time – it can break down food into carbon dioxide by a process known as fermentation. This gives the bread mixture lightness and causes the bread to rise.
	Chemical raising agents	Chemical raising agents include bicarbonate of soda, baking powder and self-raising flour. They can be used to make baked products rise.	The chemical raising agent produces carbon dioxide when heated. This gives the food product lightness.
	Air	Used in whisked sponges, soufflés and meringues to give lightness to the mixture.	When air is incorporated into a mixture (for example, by whisking egg whites) is expands quickly to product lightness.
	Steam	Causes products that contain a lot of liquid (for example, éclairs, batters, choux pastries, flaky and puff pastry) to rise.	Steam is produced when products are baked, from the liquid present in the mixture. This causes the product to rise.

✔ KEY POINTS

✔ **A raising agent gives lightness to a cake and bread mixture by adding bubbles of gas (in the form of air, carbon dioxide or steam) to the mixture, causing it to rise. Common raising agents include yeast, chemical raising agents (for example, bicarbonate of soda, baking powder, self-raising flour), air and steam.**

Stretch and challenge

Investigate the different types of colloidal structures. Produce a chart that:

- names the type of structure
- states the two main components of the structure
- gives at least one example of a food product.

PRACTICAL ACTIVITY

In a group, make a range of products which demonstrate the use of different raising agents.

TEST YOURSELF

1 List the raising agents used in the following mixtures:
   a Yorkshire pudding
   b rough puff pastry
   c Victoria sandwich cake.
2 Why are strong spices used in a cake mixture that contains bicarbonate of soda?
3 State the conditions yeast needs in order for it to produce carbon dioxide.
4 Describe **three** ways in which air can be added to a mixture.

Topic 2 Sensory properties

→ WHAT WILL I LEARN?

By the end of this topic you should have developed a knowledge and understanding of:

→ the senses, sensory systems and the organoleptic properties of food when it is cooked
→ preferential and sensory tasting panels.

The senses (organoleptic properties) and sensory systems

We all have our personal likes and dislikes that are influenced by our senses. We use all of our five senses when we choose and eat different foods. Our senses give us information about food. The characteristics of food that affect our organs are known as **organoleptic** qualities.

The five senses are shown in Table 2.1.

Table 2.1 The senses

Sense		Explanation
	Sight	The appearance (aesthetics/aesthetic qualities) of food can make it look more or less appetising. Aspects such as colour, size, shape, age, garnish and decoration will all affect how you feel about the product.
		When you cook food the method of cooking affects what it looks like (e.g. when frying, foods become golden brown, e.g. samosa; when steaming foods retain their colour, e.g. steamed vegetables).
		The size of some foods changes (e.g. cakes rise, meat and fish shrink).
		With age the appearance will change (e.g. red meat becomes darker, as fruit ripens it changes colour).
	Sound	Some food products make sounds during preparation, cooking, serving or eating.
		For example, the crackle of popcorn, the sizzle of bacon when cooking, the crunch of crisps and raw carrot when eating.
	Smell	You can detect volatile aromas released from foods. The aroma can stimulate the digestive juices and make the food seem more appetising.
		Some aromas are pleasant (e.g. the spiciness in a curry, bread or cakes cooking). Others are unpleasant (e.g. the burning of fat, toast burning or the cooking of sprouts).

Sense	Explanation
Taste	Taste buds detect four groups of flavours: bitter, sweet, sour and salt. Umami is often known as the fifth taste; it is a savoury taste. Flavour develops when the food is combined through chewing and mixing with saliva. The ingredients we use will allow us to detect these flavours, for example: • sour – lemons • sweet – sugars in recipes • bitter – chicory and cardamom • salt – the way we add this to recipes. Figure 2.1 shows the areas of taste on the tongue.
Touch	The surface of the tongue is sensitive to different sensations, such as moist, dry, soft, sticky, gritty, crumbly, mushy. As we bite and chew food we can feel how hard or soft it is through our teeth and jaw. These qualities are known as 'mouth feel'; if they are missing, food is considered to be unpalatable. The method of cooking combined with the working characteristics of ingredients will affect the different sensations we feel, for example potatoes will be soft if they are boiled, but have a crunchy outer if they are roasted.

KEY WORDS

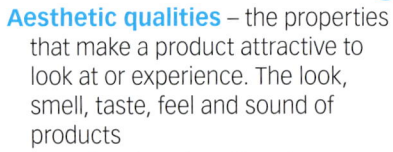

Aesthetic qualities – the properties that make a product attractive to look at or experience. The look, smell, taste, feel and sound of products

Organoleptic – describes the sensory qualities (texture, flavour, aroma, appearance) of a food product

Umami – savoury taste

Topic link:

- Section C: Topic 1 Food Science — Working characteristics and the functional and chemical properties of ingredient groups
- Section C: Topic 1 How cooking methods affect the palatability of food

RESEARCH ACTIVITY

1 For each of the different methods of cooking copy and complete the table below to show how the organoleptic (senses) properties of food may change in a dish. The first one has been completed.

Method of cooking	Example of a dish	Organoleptic property	How it is changed
Grilling	Toast	Visual Touch	Becomes brown Outside is crisp
Frying			
Boiling			
Steaming			
Baking			
Roasting			

Areas of taste

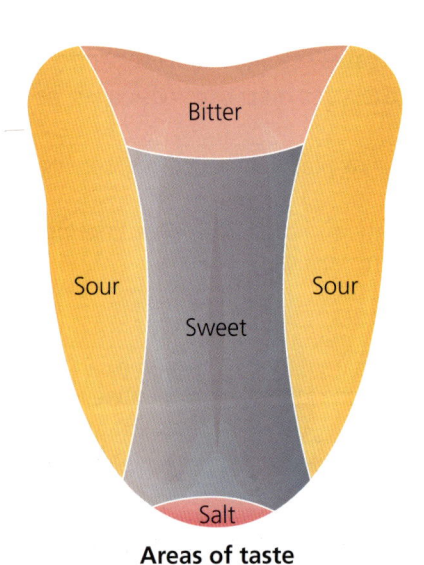

▲ Figure 2.1 Taste areas on the tongue

Topic 2 Sensory properties

PRACTICAL ACTIVITY

1 Choose a dish, savoury snack or main course dish to make.
2 Copy and complete the table below to show how the senses are stimulated as you make the product.

	Links to the senses
Ingredients	
Making the dish	
As the dish is cooking	
Tasting the dish	

✔ KEY POINTS

- ✔ The characteristics of food that affect our organs are known as organoleptic qualities.
- ✔ The appearance (aesthetics) of food can make it look more or less appetising.
- ✔ Smell and taste work together to develop the flavour of food.
- ✔ The five basic tastes recognised by our taste buds are sweetness, sourness, bitterness, saltiness and umami.
- ✔ The sensitivity of the tongue is reduced when food is either very hot or very cold.

TEST YOURSELF

1 List the five senses.
2 Give **two** examples of how cooking methods change the texture and colour of food.
3 What is umami?

KEY WORDS

Evaluating – summarising information, drawing conclusions and making judgements

Sensory analysis – tests that identify the sensory characteristics of products, that is, taste, texture, appearance, mouth feel, colour

Preferential and sensory tasting panels

Sensory analysis is used to gather information on food products to establish their most important characteristics. These qualities are called organoleptic qualities. There are several types of test, which meet British Standard BS 5929.

Evaluating dishes allows you to look at your product and to decide whether it could be improved further.

Setting up a tasting panel

It is important to use correct procedures when setting up and carrying out sensory analysis testing:

- Set up a quiet area where people will not be disturbed (do not allow testers to communicate with each other).

- Give the testers a drink of lemon-flavoured water or a piece of apple to clear the palate.
- Use small quantities of food on plain and identically sized plates/dishes.
- Use same garnish or decoration.
- Try not to give too many samples at once.
- Serve at the correct temperature for the product that is being tested.
- Use clean spoons or forks each time. Do NOT allow people to put dirty spoons into your dish.
- Use codes for the products to prevent the testers being influenced by the name of the product (this is known as testing blind). Do not use potentially biased ordering such as numerical or grade ordering.
- Have any charts ready before you begin testing.
- Make sure the testers know how to fill in the charts you are using.

Food-tasting tests

These tests are used to evaluate product acceptability by finding out the opinions, likes and dislikes of the consumer.

Ratings test

Testers give their opinion of one or more samples of food, from 'extreme like' to 'extreme dislike'. They do not give information about specific elements of a food product.

Table 2.2 Ratings test

Sample	1. Dislike very much	2. Dislike	3. Neither like nor dislike	4. Like	5. Like very much	Comments
XIB						
IBN						
DCP						
ORL						

Difference or comparison testing

These tests are used to see whether people can tell the difference between samples, for example when:

- an ingredient or quantity of ingredient is changed
- manufacturers are copying another brand, such as brands of cheese and onion crisps or a veggie burger and a beefburger.

Triangle testing is an example of this.

Triangle test

Three samples are given to the tester. Two samples are the same and the tester is asked to identify the 'odd one out'. This test is useful if you have made small changes to a product, for instance made a curry lower in fat or used more economical ingredients (e.g. changing from using chicken breast to chicken thighs).

Topic 2 Sensory properties

Ranking test

A **ranking test** is used to sort a variety of foods into order, for example different-flavoured crisps made by one manufacturer. A set of coded samples is presented to the tester. The tester has to rank the samples in order of either:

- a specific attribute (for example, sweetness, saltiness)
- a preference on a hedonic (enjoyment) scale or ranking.

Table 2.3 Ranking test

Taste the samples and put them in the order you like best		
Sample code	Order	Comments
AX		
DF		
TG		
YH		

Table 2.4 Ranking test with descriptor

Ranking according to flavour	
Sample code	Creaminess choice
X 1	2nd
B 1	1st
Z A	4th
C V	3rd

Profiling tests

Profiling tests can be used to find out what people particularly like about a food product, to help build up a profile according to a range of **sensory qualities**, such as saltiness, smoothness, crispness, flavour. Testers are asked to give a score out of five (where one is the least and five is the best). The scores for each quality are totalled and divided by the number of testers. This will give average scores. The results can be presented in a table, as shown in Table 2.5.

KEY WORDS

Profiling test – sensory evaluation test to identify specific characteristics of a product
Ranking test – a method of putting in order the intensity of a particular characteristic of a product
Sensory analysis – tests that identify the sensory characteristics of products, that is, taste, texture, appearance, mouth feel, colour
Sensory qualities – the look, smell, taste, feel and sound of products
Triangle test – used to tell the difference between two products

Table 2.5 Profile of a fruit mousse

Tasting words	Scores by tasting panel (1 = poor, 2 = average, 3 = good, 4 = very good, 5 = excellent)					Total	Average
	Taster 1	Taster 2	Taster 3	Taster 4	Taster 5		
Strawberry flavour	4	4	5	3	4	20	4
Light airy texture	1	1	2	1	2	7	1.4
Strawberry colour	3	4	1	5	2	15	3
Smooth – no lumps	3	2	1	2	3	11	2.2

Star profile

This type of analysis asks testers to describe the appearance, taste and texture of a food product on a star chart. When the food is tasted, the taster assesses the identified areas and marks the star diagram as required. The marks on each point are joined together to identify them clearly.

Topic link: *You will evaluate your products when you complete your Food Preparation task.*

When you carry out sensory analysis of your product this will involve you:

- *looking at the product*
- *smelling the product*
- *tasting the product.*

Results from sensory analysis will be used as evidence when identifying where further improvements could be made in the dishes.

Figure 2.2 shows an example of a student's use of star profiles for sensory analysis testing which was completed for the evaluation section of the Food Preparation Task

PRACTICAL ACTIVITY

1. Make a savoury main course dish suitable for your family.
2. Produce either a star profile or a profile chart to record the opinions of the tasters.
3. Write a paragraph explaining the strengths of the dish and areas which could be improved. Explain how you would adapt the recipe and/or method to make the improvements.

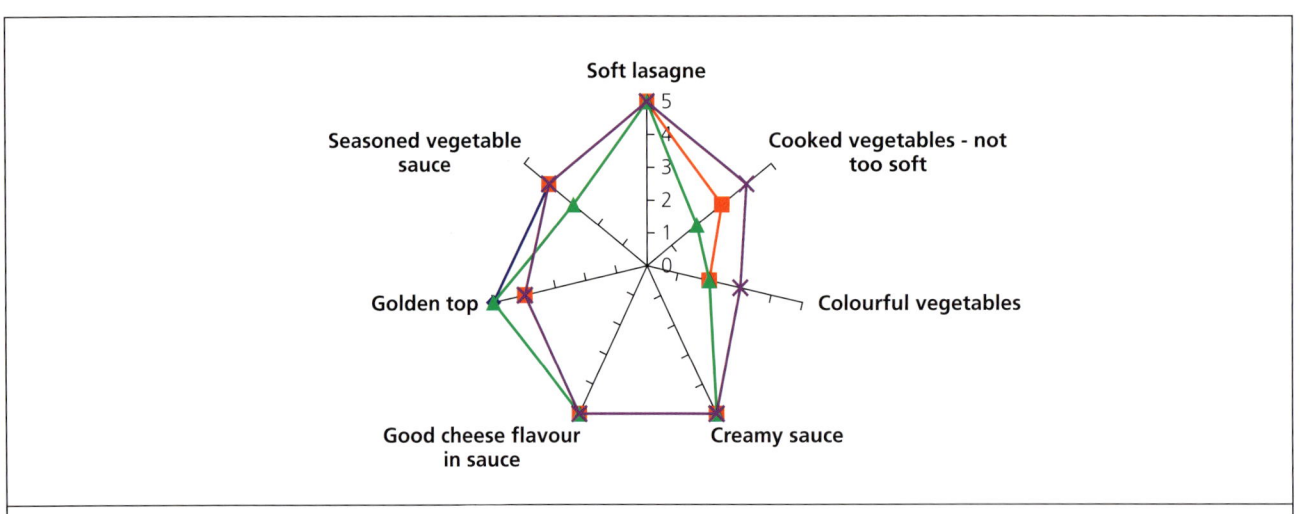

Scale

5 – Strongly agree
1 – strongly disagree

Taster comments

Taster 1 – It looked great and the sauce was excellent in consistency and really cheesy. Try to add some other colourful vegetables so it is not all red – spinach or sweetcorn, or use green peppers as well.
Taster 2 – You need to use some other vegetables to make it more colourful, also try to improve the vegetable sauce – more seasoning and do not cook the vegetables as much they were a bit too soft.
Taster 3 – I think you could leave the vegetables in bigger pieces so they are not too soft. Also, I think the vegetable sauce needs some more flavour and colour. The cheese sauce was perfect.
Taster 4 – The colour on the top of the lasagne was good. It was a pity you could not tell what vegetables were in the sauce as they had all mixed into each other. Do not cook the vegetables for so long and try to improve the flavour of the vegetable sauce.

▲ Figure 2.2 Example of sensory testing profile

Topic 2 Sensory properties

> ### ✔ KEY POINTS
>
> - ✔ Sensory analysis is used to gather information on food products to establish their most important characteristics.
> - ✔ In rating tests testers give their opinion of one or more samples of food, rating them from 'extreme like' to 'extreme dislike'. They do not give information about specific elements of a food product.
> - ✔ Ranking tests are used to sort a variety of foods into order. A set of coded samples is presented to the tester. The tester has to rank the samples in order of either a specific attribute or a preference on a hedonic (enjoyment) scale.
> - ✔ Profiling tests are to find out what people particularly like about a food product to help build up a profile based on sensory qualities. Testers are asked to give a score out of five (where one is the least and five is the best). The scores for each quality are totalled and divided by the number of testers. This will give average scores.
> - ✔ A star profile asks testers to describe the appearance, taste and texture of a food product on a star chart.

TEST YOURSELF

1. Why is it important to carry out sensory analysis tests?
2. When would you use a triangle test?
3. Explain what is meant by a rating test.
4. Explain what is meant by a ranking test.
5. Explain how you would set up a sensory analysis test.

Topic 3 Food safety

> **→ WHAT WILL I LEARN?**
>
> By the end of this topic you should have developed a knowledge and understanding of:
> → the conditions and control for bacterial growth
> → growth conditions and control for mould and yeast production
> → the signs of food spoilage
> → the helpful properties of micro-organisms in food production
> → buying of food – including labelling and date marks
> → storing food safely
> → preparing food – with particular reference to preventing food poisoning and cross-contamination
> → cooking and serving food.

Food safety is important so that we all remain healthy and can enjoy the food we eat. If food is not stored correctly it will **deteriorate** quickly and become unfit to eat. You can preserve foods to make them last longer and therefore they remain safe to eat.

Topic link: *You have learned about preserving foods in Section B: Topic 2 Food Processing and Production – food processing and preserving methods industrial and domestic.*

Micro-organisms and **enzymes** can cause changes in food. Changes are caused by the following micro-organisms:

- yeasts
- moulds
- bacteria.

In this section you will learn about these different micro-organisms.

The conditions and control for bacterial growth

Not all **bacteria** are harmful (see 'Helpful properties of micro-organisms in food production' in this topic). However, some are harmful because the food still looks, tastes and smells as it should while those bacteria are present. This makes them dangerous to eat. These bacteria are called **pathogenic bacteria**. Figure 3.1 shows bacteria which cause food poisoning and food-borne disease.

Bacteria are:

- active in warmth, moisture, food and oxygen (optimum conditions). These conditions are found in **high-risk foods**. (See Table 3.7 High-risk and low-risk foods.)

KEY WORDS

Deteriorate – start to decay and lose freshness
Enzymes – proteins that speed up chemical reactions
Micro-organisms – tiny living things such as bacteria, yeasts and moulds which cause food spoilage; can only be seen through a microscope
Bacteria – single-celled organisms present in the air, soil, on animals and humans
High-risk foods – foods which are the ideal medium for the growth of bacteria or micro-organisms, e.g. chicken and shell fish
Pathogenic bacteria – harmful bacteria which can cause food poisoning

Topic 3 Food safety

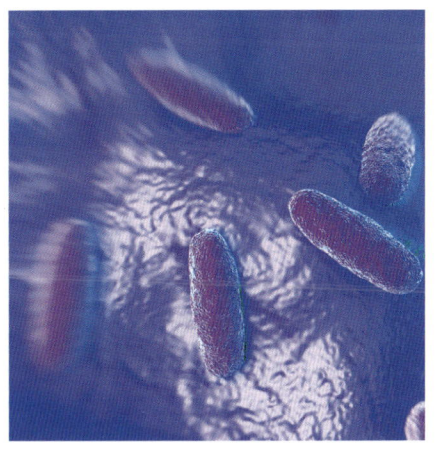

▲ Figure 3.1 Pathogenic bacteria

- able to reproduce rapidly by dividing in two, and in two again every 10 minutes (binary fission).
- able to grow rapidly in neutral **pH** conditions. Most pathogenic bacteria are unable to grow in acid or alkaline conditions, for example beetroot preserved in vinegar.
- most active in a temperature range of 5–63° C. This is known as the **danger zone**. Ambient room temperature is usually 20–25° C. The optimum temperature is 37 ° C; that is, the human body temperature. Below 0° C bacteria will become dormant. Most cannot survive at temperatures of 70° C or above.
- able to form spores that can lie dormant. If the right conditions are provided the spores will germinate.
- can grow **aerobically** and **anaerobically**.

✔ KEY POINTS

- ✔ Bacteria require food, warmth and moisture to multiply.
- ✔ Bacteria multiply quickly between 5°C and 63°C. This is called the danger zone.

TEST YOURSELF

1 Name **three** types of micro-organisms.
2 What conditions do bacteria need to grow?
3 Explain what is meant by the 'danger zone'.

KEY WORDS

pH – a measure of alkalinity or acidity
Danger zone – the temperature range (5–63 °C) in which bacteria grow rapidly
Anaerobic – does not need oxygen to grow
Aerobic – needs oxygen to grow

Growth conditions and control for mould and yeast production

Moulds

Not all moulds are harmful. Some are used in food manufacture to produce specific flavours and textures (for example, the manufacture of blue-veined cheeses such as Danish blue and Stilton).

▲ Figure 3.2 Mould

▲ Figure 3.3 Blue-veined cheese

203

▲ Figure 3.4 Mould on a salami and tomato sandwich

KEY WORD

Food spoilage – damage to food caused by the natural decay of food or by contamination by micro-organisms

Moulds are:

- visible to the eye – they grow as thread-like filaments, usually on the surface of food, for example on cheese and bread; they can be black, white or blue
- reproduced by producing spores which travel in the air; spores settle, germinate and multiply into new growths
- harmful only when they produce mycotoxins, which are poisonous substances.

Conditions needed for growth

- Moulds require oxygen in order to grow.
- Grow quickly in moist conditions at temperatures of 20–30°C.
- Grow slowly in dry, cold conditions.
- Grow on food that may be dry, moist, acid, alkaline, or has salt or sugar concentrations.

Yeasts

Through the process of fermentation yeasts are used to make breads and alcohol (sugars break down into alcohol and carbon dioxide gas).

Yeasts are responsible for **food spoilage** in high-sugar foods such as fruit, jam and fruit yoghurts.

Conditions needed for growth

- Active in warm, moist conditions with food for growth and reproduction.
- Does not need oxygen to grow (anaerobic growth).

▲ Figure 3.5 Yeast

▲ Figure 3.6 Fruit spoilage

✓ KEY POINTS

- ✓ Not all moulds are harmful. You can see moulds.
- ✓ Yeasts cause food spoilage in high-sugar foods.
- ✓ Yeasts do not need oxygen to grow.

Signs of food spoilage

Fresh foods cannot be stored for very long before changes occur which affect the texture, flavour or colour of the food. Some changes are noticeable. For instance, a banana as it ripens changes from green to yellow, and eventually it will turn black.

Table 3.1 Stages of banana ripening

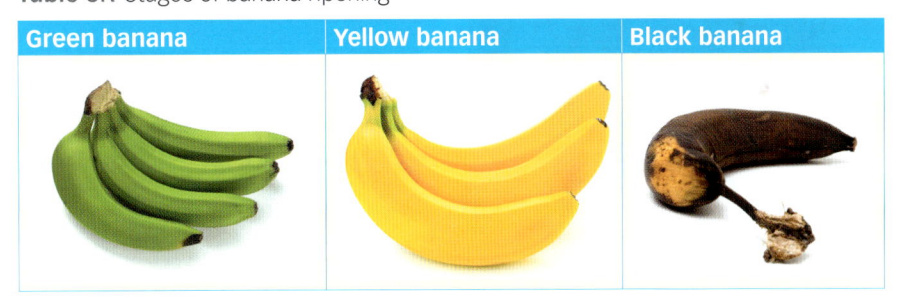

Green banana	Yellow banana	Black banana

These changes are due to the action of enzymes. They speed up ripening and natural decay, and because they are proteins they are destroyed by heat. Some of the changes that occur can often make the foods unfit to eat; this is known as food spoilage. Enzymes are found in all foods and can also cause changes in food. They are proteins that speed up chemical reactions.

Enzymes can cause 'browning' in certain foods. Enzymic browning can be reduced by:

- high temperatures, for example, blanching cut vegetables in boiling water
- acidic conditions, for example, dipping cut fruit in lemon juice.

Food spoilage bacteria can cause food to deteriorate but do not usually cause food poisoning.

> **KEY WORD**
>
> **Food-spoilage bacteria** – bacteria that cause food to go bad but do not usually cause food poisoning

Helpful properties of micro-organisms and enzymes in food production

Not all bacteria are harmful. Some bacteria are used in food manufacture, for example making cheese and yogurt. The lactic acid bacteria cultures used in these products are not harmful.

Enzymes are used in a wide range of manufacturing processes:

- bread and brewing – enzymes present in yeast are active in the fermentation process
- cheese – enzymes speed up the ripening stage.

Topic link: Section B: Topic 4 Technological developments to support better health and food production.

Buying food

Food is in danger of becoming infected by yeasts/moulds/bacteria at each stage of its production, from the farm to the table. If poor hygiene practices are followed food can easily become contaminated and this could lead to food poisoning.

▲ **Figure 3.7** Local specialist shop

Buying from reputable suppliers

When buying food you need to make sure that you buy from a reputable shop. This may be a small local shop, local market, farm shop, specialist shop or national supermarket. Many people also buy their food on the internet. There are advantages and disadvantages of shopping at each of these.

RESEARCH ACTIVITY

Make a list of the advantages and disadvantages of buying food from:
- small local shops
- local markets
- farm shops
- specialist shops
- national supermarkets
- the internet.

When buying food you need to check the following:
- Is the shop clean?
- Is the food stored in the correct condition?

Visual checks

When buying food you need to check the following:
- the food looks fresh
- the food is within date either best before or use by date
- the packaging is not damaged.

Labelling and date marks

Information found on food labels can provide important information about when the foods should be used by, storage and cooking information. This information should be followed to reduce the risk of contamination.

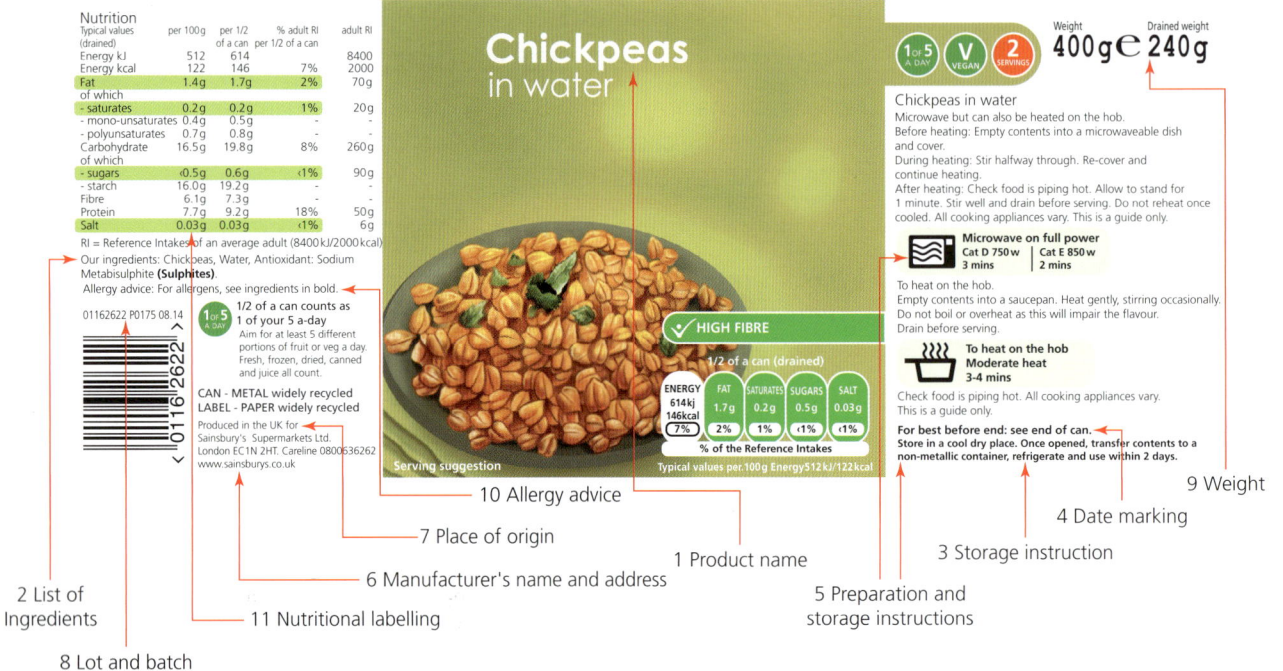

▲ **Figure 3.8** Food label

Labels on the food label:
- 1 Product name
- 2 List of Ingredients
- 3 Storage instruction
- 4 Date marking
- 5 Preparation and storage instructions
- 6 Manufacturer's name and address
- 7 Place of origin
- 8 Lot and batch number on the can
- 9 Weight
- 10 Allergy advice
- 11 Nutritional labelling

Topic 3 Food safety

New food regulations came into force in 2011. These cover all aspects of food labelling. The main change is that nutritional labelling will be compulsory on all pre-packed foods from December 2016.

The information listed in Table 3.2 is required by law.

Table 3.2 Information required by law on food labels

Information	Explanation
1 Product name	• Inform the consumer what the product is, for example cornflakes, apricot jam. • Differences between similar products must be clearly identified, for example fruit-flavoured yogurt and raspberry yogurt. • Any pictures used must not be misleading, for example strawberry-flavoured ice cream must not show pictures of strawberries on the packaging. • If a food has been processed then it must be included in the name of the product (e.g. smoked salmon, dried banana).
2 List of Ingredients	• To inform consumers exactly what ingredients are contained in the product. • All ingredients must be listed in descending order of weight, with the largest amount of ingredient first. • Food additives and water must be included.
3 Storage conditions	• Informs the consumer how to store the product in order to prevent food spoilage. • Temperature guidelines are important(e.g. keep refrigerated, suitable for home freezing).
4 Date marking	• Informs the consumer of the length of time the product can be kept. • **Use by date** for high-risk foods, for example raw and cooked meat, chilled foods (perishable foods). The date and month will be shown; after this date the food may not look or taste different, but it will be unsafe to eat and it should be thrown away. • **Best before date** for **low-risk foods** (e.g. biscuits, crisps) or foods that are processed and packaged to have a long **shelf life** (e.g. UHT milk). The date, month and year will be shown. After this date the food will start to deteriorate in terms of flavour, colour, texture or taste.
5 Preparation and storage instructions	Preparation, cooking and heating instructions inform the consumer as to how the product should be used.
6 Manufacturer's name and address	So that a product can be returned if faulty, or a letter of complaint can be made in writing.
7 Place of origin	Informs the consumer the place the food has come from (e.g. 'Product of Spain').
8 Lot or batch number	• This is not part of the EU Regulations but is required by UK law. It identifies a product if it needs to be recalled. • A date mark is sometimes used as a lot mark.
9 Weight or volume	• Most pre-packed food is required to show the net weight or volume, within a few grams of the weight. If not sold pre-packed, most foods have to be sold either by quantity or number. Some foods are sold in standard amounts. This allows consumers to compare products in terms of value for money. • A large 'e' placed alongside the amount shows that it is an average quantity.

KEY WORDS

Best before date – used on low-risk foods

Low-risk foods – foods which have a long shelf life, such as dried foods

Shelf life – how long a food product can be kept safely and remain of high quality

Use by date – used on high/risk foods

Information	Explanation
10 Allergies	Informs the customer about any ingredients that may cause reactions in people with allergies. The following foods need to be highlighted in bold or in a different font: • milk • eggs • peanuts • tree nuts • fish • molluscs (e.g. mussels, oyster) • shellfish (e.g. crab, shrimps, prawns) • soybeans • cereals containing gluten (wheat, barley, rye, oats) • lupin • celery • mustard • sesame seed • sulphur dioxide sulphites.
11 Nutritional Labelling	From December 2016 nutrition labelling must be shown on the back of packet foods. They must include the following per 100 g/ml: • energy value kcal/kJ • fat • saturated fat • carbohydrate • sugars • protein • salt.
Genetically modified (GM) ingredients	• Products and ingredients from genetically modified sources must be labelled. • You do not need to label foods such as milk which have been fed on genetically modified food.

Manufacturers may put additional information onto the packaging; this is usually to help the shop with managing their stock control or to help consumers make food choices.

Table 3.3 Example of how the nutritional labelling of chickpeas in water will appear from December 2016

	Per 100g
Energy	512 kJ/122 kcal
Fat of which saturates	1.4 g 0.2 g
Carbohydrates of which sugar	16.5 g <0.5 g
Protein	7.7
Salt	0.03 g

RESEARCH ACTIVITY

Look at a range of food packaging. Identify labelling which has been displayed on packaging which is not required by law. Suggest why you think it may be on the label.

Copy and complete the table below:

Labelling	Reason why added to the packaging

Stretch and challenge

Investigate the type of nutritional labelling manufacturers may put on the front of food packages. Explain how this may help consumers when choosing foods.

> ✓ **KEY POINTS**
> - ✓ Use-by dates are displayed on high-risk foods.
> - ✓ Some information is required on food packaging by law.
> - ✓ You should buy food from a reputable supplier.
> - ✓ The correct freezer temperature is −18°C

> **TEST YOURSELF**
> 4 Make a list of the **12** pieces of information required on food by law.
> 5 State **five** foods which would have a use-by date.

Storing food

Food must be stored correctly at all times to prevent spoilage.

Refrigerators

There are many different types of refrigerators. These include:

- larder refrigerators, which just refrigerate
- fridge freezers, which combine a fridge and a freezer.

A domestic refrigerator should be between 0°C and 5°C. Refrigerators provide safe storage of food with less risk of food poisoning. Growth of food-poisoning bacteria is slowed down in a refrigerator.

Sensible use of your fridge

- Avoid opening the door regularly – warm air enters every time you open the door.
- Avoid putting in hot food – this raises the temperature and fills the inside with steam, which condenses on the shelves and lining and so raises the temperature of other foods.
- Cover food.
- Maintain a consistent temperature. Increasing the temperature inside the fridge could lead to bacterial growth.
- Keep raw and high-risk foods away from other foods and store on the bottom shelf of the refrigerator.

Freezers and freezing

During freezing foods become frozen as the water content in the food becomes solid. The freezer 'star' rating indicates the temperature range of the freezer section in the refrigerator and the length of time you can store foods.

A domestic freezer should be kept at −18°C.

A freezer box within a fridge cannot be used to store fresh foods – it can only be used to store already frozen foods.

Table 3.4 Freezer star ratings

Star rating	Temperature °C	Storage times
★	−6	up to 1 week
★★	−12	up to 1 month
★★★	−18	up to 3 months
★★★★		Can be used to freeze fresh foods

Thawing and refreezing

When food is thawed the structure is damaged and there is sometimes loss of colour, flavour, texture and nutritional value. Food poisoning bacteria will not multiply in a freezer, but it must be remembered that the bacteria present are not destroyed in the freezer and will multiply when they are sufficiently warm. Frozen foods are therefore transported to businesses in temperature-controlled vehicles to keep the foods in a frozen state. On entering the supermarkets and restaurants, they are quickly packed into large freezers.

You should never refreeze food after it has thawed – bacteria grow quickly in thawed food because the cells have been damaged.

Foods that do not freeze well

Not all foods freeze well. Foods that contain a large proportion of water and have a delicate cell structure do not freeze well because ice crystals damage the cell structure, causing it to collapse.

Freezing vegetables

Most vegetables, with the exception of salad, freeze well and can be kept for up to a year. It is important to blanch vegetables before freezing to halt enzyme activity which causes changes in colour, flavour, texture and nutritional value.

Topic link:

Section C: Topic 1 Food Science – Heat transfer through cooking methods

Freezing fruit

Many fruits will freeze successfully. However, those with a high water content will not (for example, strawberries).

Freezer burn

Greyish-white marks appear on food when it has been packaged badly. The food dehydrates and, although safe to eat, will change colour, texture and flavour.

▲ Figure 3.9 Freezer burn on a piece of fish

INVESTIGATION ACTIVITY

1 Investigate what happens to the following foods when you freeze and then defrost them:
   - lettuce
   - tomatoes
   - strawberries
   - banana
   - single cream.

2 Record your results in a table using the following headings:

Fruit or vegetable	Colour before freezing	Texture before freezing	Colour when removed from freezer	Colour when defrosted	Texture when defrosted
Lettuce					
Tomato					
Strawberries					
Banana					
Single cream					

3 Explain the changes in the foods when they were fresh and when defrosted.

✔ KEY POINTS

✔ The correct refrigerator temperature range is 0–5°C
✔ At –18°C bacteria are dormant.
✔ Between 0–5°C bacteria growth is slow.

TEST YOURSELF

6 What is the highest temperature a refrigerator should be?
7 Why should raw meat be wrapped and placed at the bottom of the refrigerator?
8 What temperature should a freezer be?
9 Explain what is meant by 'freezer burn'.

Preparing food

Preventing cross-contamination

We need to take care when we are preparing food to avoid cross-contamination, which can lead to food poisoning. We must maintain high standards of hygiene when working with food.

▲ Figure 3.10 Hand washing

Rules for food hygiene

1. Wash hands thoroughly before handling food and again between handling different types of food.
2. Keep raw and cooked foods separate and use different equipment to prepare them.
3. Pay particular attention to personal hygiene and wear clean protective clothing; cover cuts and never cough or sneeze over food.
4. Keep all working surfaces and utensils clean. Use antibacterial spray.
5. Cover and cool all cooked food rapidly and refrigerate as quickly as possible. Store below 5 °C.
6. Do not put hot foods in the refrigerator as it will raise the temperature of other foods in the refrigerator.
7. Keep pets away from food preparation areas.
8. Take care over waste disposal. Keep bins covered and empty and wash them regularly.

When preparing food micro-organisms can transfer from raw to cooked foods, causing infection. This is known as **cross-contamination**.

To prevent cross-contamination you must avoid:

- allowing raw and cooked foods to touch each other, for example raw chicken and boiled ham
- allowing the blood and juices of raw foods to drip onto cooked foods, for example putting raw meat above cooked foods in the refrigerator – this is called **direct contamination**
- allowing bacteria to be transferred during handling or preparation, for example from hands, work surfaces, equipment or clothing – this is called **indirect contamination**.

▲ Figure 3.11 Would this bin be acceptable in your kitchen?

RESEARCH ACTIVITY

In commercial kitchens and in some homes people have different-coloured chopping boards. Which foods should be prepared on the following different-coloured boards?

- red
- blue
- yellow
- brown
- white

▲ Figure 3.12 Coloured chopping boards

Preventing food poisoning

The bacteria that cause food poisoning are called pathogenic bacteria. Most food poisoning is caused by bacterial contamination. Figure 3.13 shows why there has been an increase in the cases of food poisoning.

Section C: Cooking and food preparation

212

Topic 3 Food safety

Why there has been an increase in cases of food poisoning
- More people are using microwaves often means that food is not defrosted or cooked to the correct temperature.
- Increased use of cooked-chill foods which are high risk foods.
- Foods not stored at the correct temperatures.
- Food not prepared correctly.
- Poor personal hygiene practices.
- Hot foods not kept at the correct temperature above 63 °C.
- Not reheating food to the correct temperature for the correct amount of time

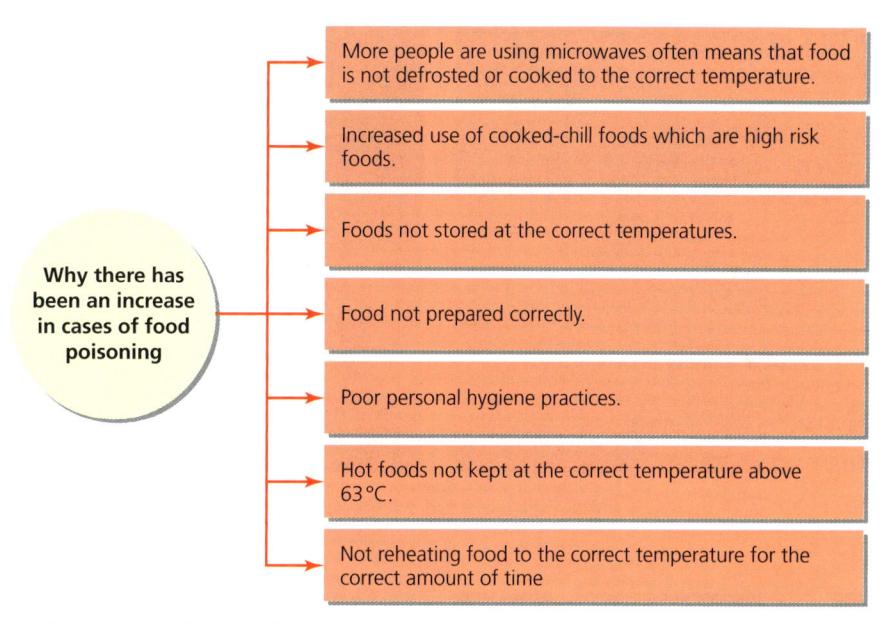

▲ Figure 3.13 Why there has been an increase in food poisoning

Figure 3.14 shows how poor preparation and cooking routines can cause food poisoning.

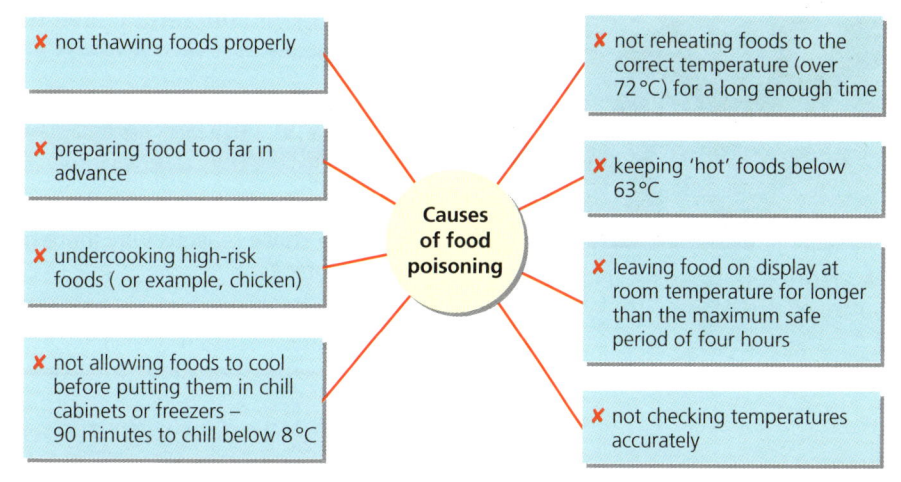

Causes of food poisoning
- ✗ not thawing foods properly
- ✗ preparing food too far in advance
- ✗ undercooking high-risk foods (or example, chicken)
- ✗ not allowing foods to cool before putting them in chill cabinets or freezers – 90 minutes to chill below 8 °C
- ✗ not reheating foods to the correct temperature (over 72 °C) for a long enough time
- ✗ keeping 'hot' foods below 63 °C
- ✗ leaving food on display at room temperature for longer than the maximum safe period of four hours
- ✗ not checking temperatures accurately

▲ Figure 3.14 How poor preparation and cooking routines can cause food poisoning

Use a temperature probe to check the temperature of food.

▲ Figure 3.15 Temperature probe

Table 3.5 Bacteria which cause food poisoning and food-borne disease

Bacteria	Possible sources
Salmonella	Poultry, eggs, meat
Staphylococcus aureus	Food handlers
Clostridium perfringens	Raw foods, such as vegetables and meat
Bacillus cereus	Cereals, especially rice
Campylobacter	Infected animals, birds and unpasteurised milk
Listeria	Raw, processed and cooked foods (e.g. soft cheese)
E. coli	Cattle, raw meat and raw milk

213

▲ Figure 3.16 Salmonella bacteria under a microscope

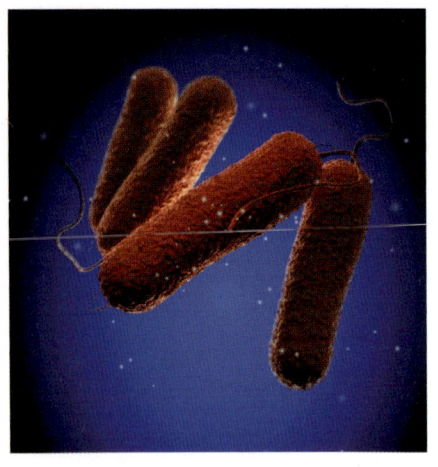

▲ Figure 3.17 Staphylococcus aureus bacteria under a microscope

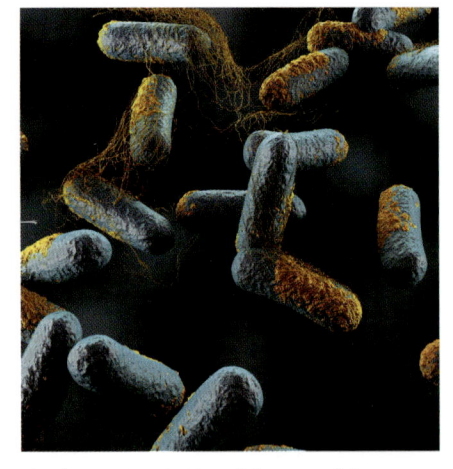

▲ Figure 3.18 Clostridium perfringens bacteria under a microscope

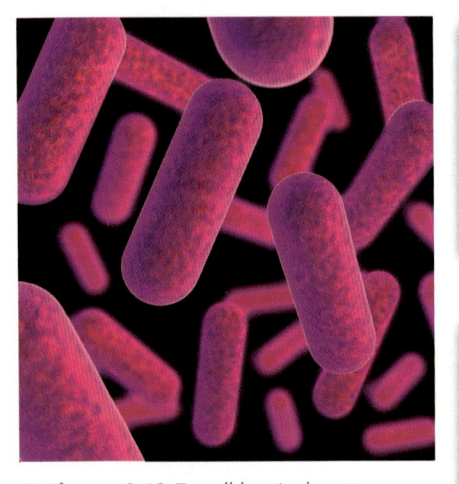

▲ Figure 3.19 E. coli bacteria seen under a microscope

✔ KEY POINTS

- ✔ You need to have good food hygiene practices to prevent food poisoning.
- ✔ Cross-contamination can cause food poisoning.
- ✔ Pathogenic bacteria cause food poisoning.

TEST YOURSELF

10 Explain what is meant by the term 'cross-contamination'.
11 State **three** reasons why there has been an increase in cases of food poisoning.
12 Why should you clean a temperature probe after each time it has been used?

Cooking and serving food

It is important when you are cooking and serving food that it is cooked to the correct temperature so that any pathogenic bacteria are destroyed. During cooking the temperature should reach 70°C for two minutes through the thickest part of the food or its equivalent.

Table 3.6 Example of temperature/time ratios

Temperature°C	Time
70°C	2 minutes
75°C	30 seconds
80°C	6 seconds
86°C or above	As an instant reading

Source: *Food Safety: The good practice guide*, Chartered Institute of Environmental Health

If food is reheated it should be to at least 75°C. If keeping food hot it must be at or above 63°C.

Topic 3 Food safety

Figure 3.20 shows the important temperatures which could be observed when cooling, storing and reheating food.

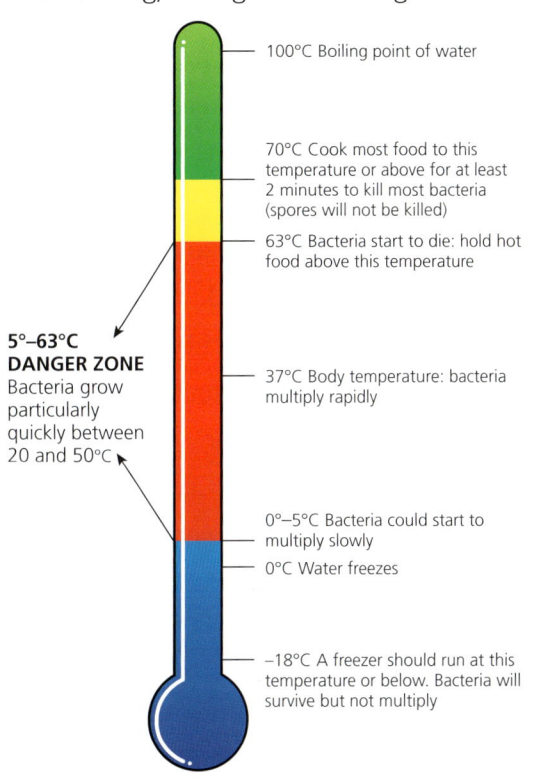

- 100°C Boiling point of water
- 70°C Cook most food to this temperature or above for at least 2 minutes to kill most bacteria (spores will not be killed)
- 63°C Bacteria start to die: hold hot food above this temperature

5°–63°C DANGER ZONE Bacteria grow particularly quickly between 20 and 50°C

- 37°C Body temperature: bacteria multiply rapidly
- 0°–5°C Bacteria could start to multiply slowly
- 0°C Water freezes
- –18°C A freezer should run at this temperature or below. Bacteria will survive but not multiply

▶ Figure 3.20 Temperature zones

Table 3.7 High-risk and low-risk foods

High-risk foods	Often have high protein and moisture content. • raw fish • dairy products • cooked meat and poultry • shellfish and seafood • gravies, sauces, stocks, soups and stews • egg products (e.g. raw egg in chilled desserts and mayonnaise) • cooked rice • protein-based baby foods
Low-risk foods	• high-acid-content foods (e.g. pickles and chutney, fruit juice) • high-sugar-content foods (e.g. marmalades, jams, fruit-packed syrup) • sugar-based confectionery (e.g. sweets, icing) • unprocessed raw vegetables (e.g. potatoes, carrots) • edible oils and fats

TEST YOURSELF

1 Give **three** examples of high-risk foods.
2 Give **three** examples of low-risk foods.
3 Explain why food should be cooked to over 70°C for two minutes.

Practice questions

1. Explain why you use soft flour when making cakes and strong flour when making bread. (2 marks)

2. Name **three** different raising agents. (3 marks)

3. State how heat is transferred when cooking the following foods:
   a. Steaming fish
   b. Stir-frying vegetables
   c. Grilling bread. (3 marks)

4. State the correct temperatures for the following:
   a. Hot-holding food
   b. A refrigerator
   c. A freezer. (3 marks)

5. Describe how to prepare and cook vegetables to reduce the loss of vitamins. (4 marks)

6. Explain what happens to the following foods when they are cooked:
   a. Eggs
   b. Meat. (6 marks)

   The quality of written communication will be assessed in the following questions.

7. Explain why some foods are cooked. (8 marks)

8. Describe how you would set up a sensory tasting panel. (6 marks)

9. Discuss how you can reduce the risk of food poisoning when preparing and cooking food. (10 marks)

   The quality of written communication will be assessed in this question.

Section D:
Skills requirements (preparation and cooking techniques)

This section includes the following topics:
- Introduction to equipment
- Topic 1: Knife skills
- Topic 2: Preparation and techniques
- Topic 3: Cooking methods
- Topic 4: Sauces
- Topic 5: Set a mixture
- Topic 6: Raising agents
- Topic 7: Dough
- Topic 8: Judge and manipulate sensory properties

Topic 1   Knife skills

> **→ WHAT WILL I LEARN?**
>
> **By the end of this section you should be able to:**
> → demonstrate accurate weighing and measurement of liquids and solids
> → grease/oil, line, flour flan rings or tins evenly
> → select and adjust the cooking process and length of time to suit the ingredient
> → test for readiness (use of temperature probe, skewer/knife, finger or 'poke' test, 'bite', visual colour or sound test)
> → use specialist equipment where appropriate (food processor, mixer, blender, microwave, potato ricer and pasta machine)
> → understand the functions of ingredients in basic recipes.

Most of your learning in this section will be through practical activities. You will be assessed on your practical making skills in Task 2 of the Non-Examined Assessment. It will be important that you demonstrate a high level of skills and present your practical work in an attractive way to score high marks. You will also be assessed on your understanding of preparation and cooking skills in your written examination.

Introduction to equipment

Using the correct equipment is essential for producing the required result in food preparation. Electrical equipment, for example mixers and processors, can take some of the hard work out of mixing, slicing and chopping, while also saving time. They cannot entirely replace hand-held equipment for efficiency, particularly for working quickly with small amounts of ingredients. During your practical sessions you need to demonstrate the correct use of equipment and look for opportunities to use a range of equipment, including labour- and time-saving items. Always read recipes carefully to ensure that you are using the correct piece of equipment for the job.

Measuring

For measuring, scales, cups, jugs or spoons may be used.

Topic 1 Knife skills

Table 1.1 Equipment used for measuring

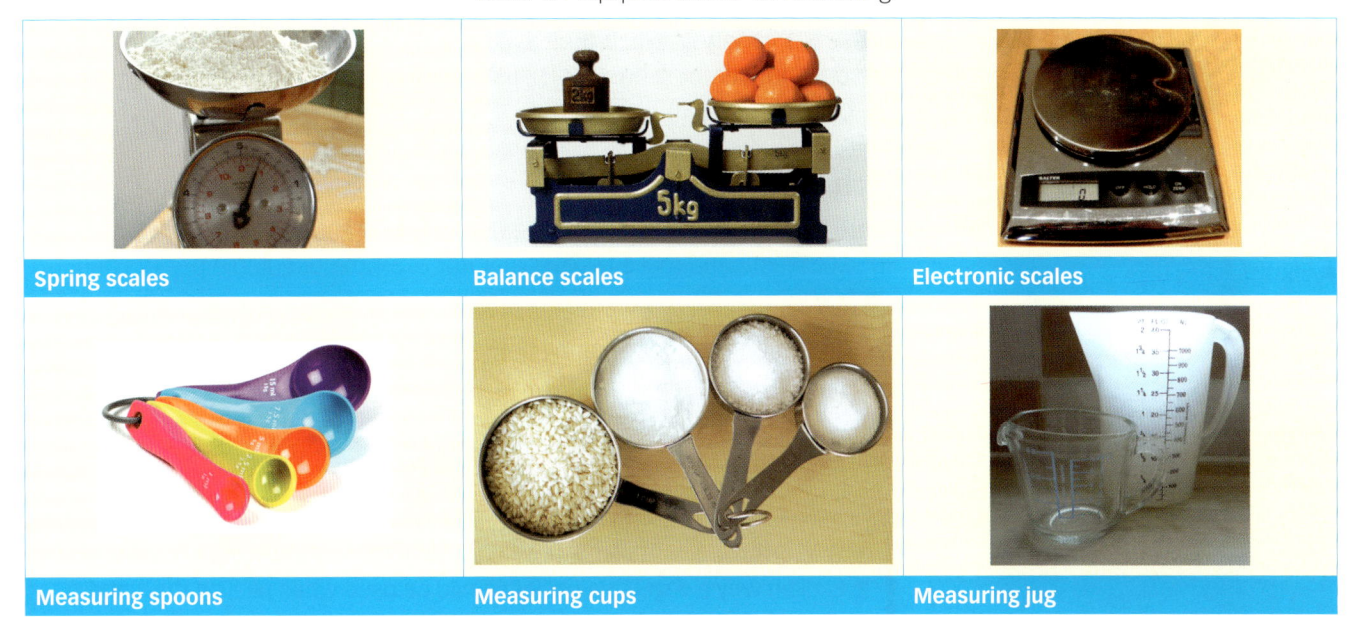

Spring scales	Balance scales	Electronic scales
Measuring spoons	Measuring cups	Measuring jug

Cutting and chopping

Knives of various types and styles are used to cut and chop. They vary in size and blade type, depending upon their use.

Graters are used for preparing cheese or vegetables. They can be round or box shaped or the rotary type (which provides a greater degree of safety).

Ceramic or nylon chopping boards are more hygienic than wood. In the catering industry different-coloured boards are used for different tasks.

- red = raw meat
- blue = raw fish
- yellow = cooked meat
- white = vegetables
- green = salad/fruit

Whisking

Whisks can be used for adding air to a mixture. Hand whisks can be balloon-shaped, coiled or rotary. Electric mixers are often used when making cake products.

Table 1.2 Different types of whisks

Coil whisk	Balloon whisk	Rotary whisk	Electric whisk

219

▲ Figure 1.1 Fish slice

▲ Figure 1.2 Spatula

Spreading and lifting

There is a variety of equipment available. Examples include spatulas (which are used for scraping out bowls), fish slices and palette knives (which can be used for lifting food).

Other equipment

More specialist equipment can be used for fruit and vegetable preparation, to save waste and make tasks easier (for example, vegetable peelers and corers).

Sieves can be used for aerating flour, and strainers for separating solids from liquids.

TEST YOURSELF

1 Why is it important that you weigh and measure accurately?
2 Explain why a vegetable peeler should be used when peeling fruits and vegetables.

When peeling vegetables and fruits (for example carrots, potatoes and apples) a potato peeler should be used to reduce food waste.

▲ Figure 1.3 Potato peeler

KEY WORDS

Bridge hold – making a bridge between your thumb and first finger and holding the food while safely cutting; used when cutting an onion in half

Claw grip – holding the end of the vegetable or fruit with your fingers and cutting the vegetables or fruit

When cutting fruits and vegetables you should use a **bridge hold** and **claw grip**.

▲ Figure 1.4 Bridge hold and claw grip

Topic 1 Knife skills

There is a range of different knives you will use during your practical lessons.

Table 1.3 Different knives and their uses

Knife	Use
Vegetable/paring knife	Cutting, slicing and shredding vegetables and fruit
Palette knife	Lifting food from trays, turning food over, mixing liquid into mixtures (e.g. pastry and scones)
Table knife	Spreading and mixing liquid into dry mixtures
Filleting knife	Has a flexible blade to make it easier to remove the flesh from the bones on fish and meat
Serrated-edge carving knives	Slicing food (e.g. bread)
Chef's knife	Cutting foods, e.g. meat

How to portion a chicken

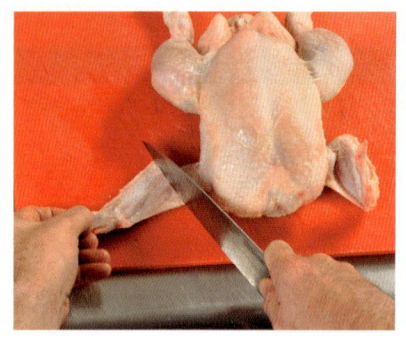

1 Raw poultry should be prepared on a red board. Remove both wings using a sharp knife.

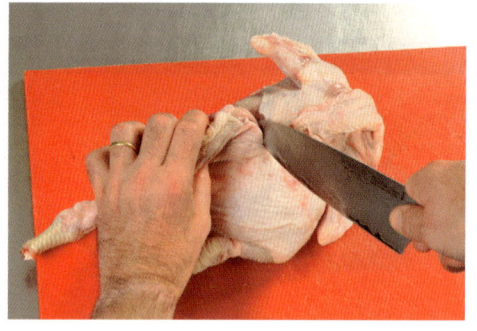

2 Remove the legs and thigh from the main carcass.

3 Remove the feet from the end of the leg.

4 Cut between the thigh and leg joint to separate the leg from the thigh.

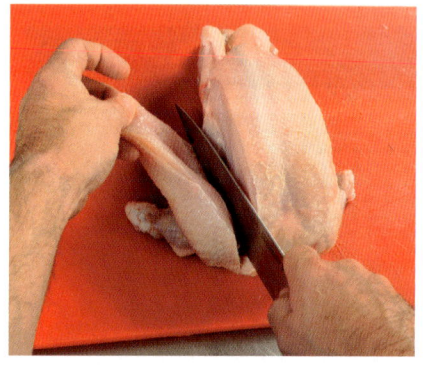

5 Remove the breast by carefully cutting it away from the main carcass.

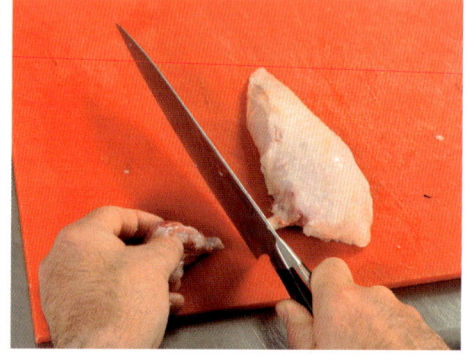

6 Cut the wing away from the breast.

7 Each breast can then be cut in half or left whole if larger pieces are required.

8 Chicken portions ready to be used (clockwise direction): thighs, chicken breast, chicken breast cut in half, legs, wings.

▲ Figure 1.5 Step-by-step cutting up a whole chicken

Topic 1 Knife skills

1 Raw fish should be prepared on a blue board. Remove the head and fins using a sharp knife and clean the fish.

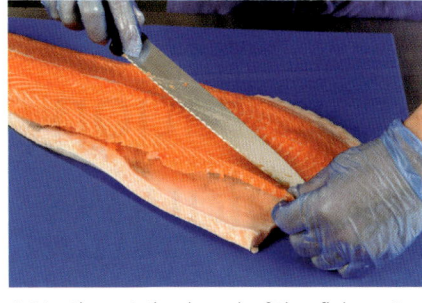

2 Starting at the head of the fish, cut down the spine of the fish with a slicing action. Keep the knife as close to the bone as possible. As you work down the fish lift the fillet so you can see where you are working.

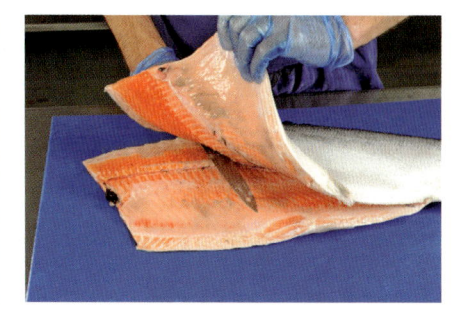

3 Turn the fish over and remove the second fillet. Trim the fish and remove any bones which are visible. Cut the fillets of fish into the required sizes.

▲ Figure 1.6 Filleting salmon

Other cutting equipment which can be used in the kitchen includes:

- Corers – used to remove the core from fruit (e.g. apples)
- Food processors – these come with a range of blades which allow you to grate, slice, puree, and mix; they can sometimes prepare foods more quickly than completing it by hand
- Graters – these are usually made from stainless steel and are available as various different types.

▲ Figure 1.7 Corer

▲ Figure 1.8 Food processor

PRACTICAL ACTIVITY

1 Some vegetables can be eaten raw.
   a Make an interesting salad using a range of vegetables and other ingredients which could be included in a packed lunch for a teenager.
   b Calculate the cost of the dish.
2 We are being encouraged to increase the amount of fresh fruit we eat.
   a Prepare, cook and serve a dish which would encourage young children to eat more fruit.
   b Give reasons for your choice of dish.

TEST YOURSELF

1 State the use of each of the following knives:
   - Palette knife
   - Vegetable knife
   - Table knife
   - Serrated carving knife
2 Give **two** advantages of using a food processor for slicing and grating vegetables.
3 Give **one** disadvantage of using a food processor for slicing and grating vegetables.
4 Explain why the claw grip and bridge hold are used when preparing fruit and vegetables.

Topic 2
Preparation and techniques

> **→ WHAT WILL I LEARN?**
>
> By the end of this topic you should have developed a knowledge and understanding of:
> - methods of preparing foods
> - equipment to use
> - basic preparation of meat, fish, fruit and vegetables
> - ingredients which can be used to marinade and flavour foods.

When food is prepared it often undergoes one or more of three manipulative processes:

- mixing (for example, beating an egg white)
- cutting (for example, grating cheese, chopping vegetables)
- forming and shaping (for example, rolling pastry, lining flan tins).

All tools and equipment used in the preparation of food will fulfil one or more of these functions. The correct tool must be selected to:

- complete the task safely, hygienically and efficiently
- achieve a consistency of finish
- achieve a quality outcome.

You will use a variety of preparation techniques when you are making different dishes.

Meat

Remember to prepare food safely and to prevent cross-contamination when handling high-risk foods. The use of coloured chopping boards can reduce cross-contamination.

A wide variety of meat, poultry and offal can be used in cooking.

Meat is classed as a high-risk food (because it contains protein and is moist), so it is important that it is processed, stored, handled and cooked correctly so that it is safe to eat.

The following is good practice and should be demonstrated when you prepare meat:

- Wash your hands before and after touching any type of raw meat.
- Keep raw meat separate from other foods. Cover and store the meat at the bottom of the fridge so that it cannot touch any other foods.

Topic 2 Preparation and techniques

- Raw meat contains harmful bacteria that can spread to anything it comes into contact with, so it is important to clean surfaces and equipment thoroughly after preparing meat.
- Raw meat should be stored at temperatures below 5°C.
- Any bacteria present in the meat will be destroyed by heat. It is therefore important to check that the meat is thoroughly cooked. This can be achieved by using a food probe or meat thermometer. The food probe should be inserted into the centre of the food to a depth of about 2 cm. Record the reading. Make sure you clean the probe thoroughly after each use.

Topic link: *for more information on preparing, cooking and storing foods safely see Section C: Topic 3 Food safety. Section 3 Topic 1 how to portion a chicken*

Fish

When choosing fresh fish:

- it should have a sea-fresh smell
- the flesh of the fish should be moist and firm
- the scales on the fish should be shiny.

Fish, like meat, is a high-risk food, and therefore the same good practices that are used when preparing meat need to be applied when preparing fish. It is also wise to thoroughly wrap fish so that the smell does not pass to other foods.

You will use a variety of different skills when preparing meat and fish dishes (and when using alternatives such as tofu or halloumi cheese), including:

- rolling
- wrapping
- skewering (for example, kebabs)
- mixing
- coating (for example, using flour, or egg and breadcrumbs)
- layering (for example, lasagne)
- shaping and binding wet mixtures (for example, falafels, meatballs or fishcakes).

Fruit and vegetables

When preparing fruits and vegetables:

- wash to remove dirt
- remove any blemishes or outer leaves
- peel if necessary; however, many fruits and vegetables can be eaten with their skin on, and peeling them will reduce the nutrient content as many of the nutrients are stored just below the surface of the skin
- prepare vegetables just before cooking to prevent loss of vitamins by the action of enzymes and **oxidisation**
- do not soak them in water as this will result in the loss of water-soluble vitamins (vitamins B and C)
- some fruits and vegetables will go brown once they are peeled and cut (for example, apples, potatoes, pears). This is called **enzymic browning**.

KEY WORDS

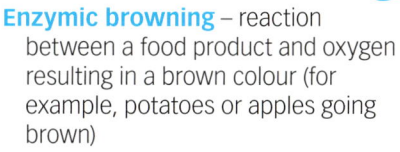

Enzymic browning – reaction between a food product and oxygen resulting in a brown colour (for example, potatoes or apples going brown)

Marinate – to soak meat, fish or vegetables in a flavoured liquid before cooling; the food absorbs the flavours.

Oxidisation – occurs when fruit and vegetables are cut and the cells are exposed to air

225

This can be reduced by
- blanching vegetables in boiling water
- dipping fruit into lemon juice
- cooking the foods as soon as they have been prepared
- handle delicate fruits and vegetables carefully so they do not get bruised.

Most fruits can be eaten raw and should be washed before they are eaten. Fruits are sometimes cooked, for instance, stewing apples or poaching pears.

You will use a variety of equipment to demonstrate different skills such as:

- mashing
- shredding
- scissor snipping
- scooping
- crushing
- grating
- blending
- peeling
- de-skinning
- de-seeding
- blanching
- shaping
- piping
- juicing
- garnishing
- segmenting

Table 2.1 Equipment used when preparing foods

Skill	Equipment used	Uses for fruit and vegetables	Uses for preparing other ingredients
Mash		To achieve smooth mashed potatoes or other vegetables	
Scissor snip		To snip herbs	To remove rind from bacon, gills from fish
Crush		To crush garlic (alternatively, the back of a knife can be used)	
Scoop			To scoop ice cream
Grate		To remove rind from citrus fruits and grate fruits and vegetables	To grate other products (e.g. cheese)

Topic 2 Preparation and techniques

Blend		To blend ingredients for a soup	To remove lumps for a sauce To make smoothies
Juice		To remove juice from citrus fruit	

Tenderise and marinate

Meat, fish and vegetables can be marinated to add additional flavour. Marinating meat or fish in an acid such as vinegar or lemon juice will change the structure of the meat and therefore **tenderise** it.

Topic link: When acids are used to change the structure of protein in meat, the protein is denatured. You will have learnt about using acid to denature proteins in Section C: Topic 1 Food science.

A wide variety of different foods can be used to add flavour and moisture. These include:

- herbs
- spices
- different oils
- rind and juice of citrus fruits.

▲ Figure 2.1 Acids which can be used to marinate meat

Stretch and challenge

Explain how the structure of meat will change if acid is added to it.

227

▲ **Figure 2.2** Ingredients which can be used to add flavour and moisture

KEY WORD
Tenderise – make it softer and easier to chew

PRACTICAL ACTIVITY

1 Fruits can be used to prepare a range of desserts. Make a dessert which makes use of seasonal fruits.
2 Traditional meat and fish dishes are often linked to different countries' cuisines. Prepare a meat dish which would be suitable for one of the countries you are studying.
3 We are being encouraged to eat at least two portions of fish a week.
   a Produce a fish dish which would appeal to either teenagers or young children.
   b Explain why your dish would appeal to your chosen group.

TEST YOURSELF

1 State **three** rules to follow when preparing fresh meat or fish.
2 What advice would you give to a student on how to prepare fruit and vegetables to:
   a maintain their nutritive value?
   b maintain their colour and texture?
3 There is a wide variety of equipment which is used when preparing foods. For each of the pieces of equipment listed below state:
   - the main use of the piece of equipment
   - a dish you could make which would illustrate the use of the piece of equipment.
   a electric hand blender
   b lemon squeezer
   c masher
4 Produce a list of **four** foods which could be used to flavour meat when making marinade.

Section D: Skills requirements (preparation and cooking techniques)

Topic 3 — Cooking methods

> **→ WHAT WILL I LEARN?**
>
> By the end of the topic you should have developed a knowledge and understanding of:
> → the methods of cooking used.

You will use a variety of different methods of cooking when making dishes. These include:

- water-based methods using the hob – steaming, boiling and simmering, blanching and poaching
- dry-heat and fat-based methods using the hob – dry-frying, pan- (shallow-) frying, stir-frying
- using the grill – char, grill or toast
- using the oven – baking, roasting, casseroles or tagines, braising.

Topic link: *Each of these different cooking methods is discussed in more detail in Section C: Topic 1 Food science.*

Ensure that you use the correct temperature when cooking and check that it is cooked thoroughly before serving.

PRACTICAL ACTIVITY

1. There are four different ways of steaming foods.
   Identify **one** dish which could be made to illustrate each method of steaming. Prepare, cook and serve one of the dishes.
2. Microwaves are often used in households to reheat foods.
   Prepare, cook and serve either a main course dish or dessert which illustrates how a microwave can be used to cook foods.
3. We are being encouraged to eat less fat.
   Make a list of dishes which could be adapted to reduce the amount of fat used during the cooking process.
   Prepare, cook and serve one of your dishes.

Name of dish	Explanation of how the method of cooking can be changed to reduce the fat content

Topic 4   Sauces

> **→ WHAT WILL I LEARN?**
>
> By the end of this topic you should have developed a knowledge and understanding of:
> - → methods of making different types of sauces
> - → faults which may occur in sauces.

There are many different types of sauces used in a wide variety of dishes.

The different starches that are often used to thicken sauces are:

- flour
- cornflour
- arrowroot.

Topic link: *Section C: Topic 1 Food Science explains what happens to starch when it is heated and therefore why it thickens sauces. This process is called gelatinisation.*

Depending on the **proportions** of the ingredient used, the thickness of the sauce varies.

Table 4.1 Proportions of ingredients used in sauces

Type of sauce	Ingredients	Description of sauce	Example of dish
Pouring	250 ml milk 15 g fat 15 g flour	Pours freely	Custard
Coating	250 ml milk 25 g fat 25 g flour	Coats the back of a spoon	Cauliflower cheese
Binding	250 ml flour 50 g fat 50 g flour	Very thick sauce that can bind ingredients	Fishcakes

KEY WORD

Proportions – relative quantities of ingredients in a recipe, expressed in numbers

Very thick sauces have a higher proportion of fat to flour than liquid when compared with pouring sauces, which have smaller proportions of fat and flour to liquid.

Methods of making sauces

Sauces can be made by three different methods:

- roux
- blended
- all-in-one.

Roux

This is the traditional method of making a sauce.

1 The fat is melted, and the flour stirred in and cooked on a medium heat.
2 The liquid is added gradually.
3 The sauce is returned to the heat and brought back to the boil, stirring all the time.

Blended

This is often used for cornflour- and arrowroot-based sauces.

1 A little of the liquid is blended with the cornflour.
2 The remaining liquid is heated.
3 The hot liquid is poured onto the cornflour mixture, stirring carefully.
4 The sauce is returned to the pan and brought back to the boil, stirring all the time.

Béchamel sauce is similar to a roux sauce. The milk is heated with onion and often a bay leaf and peppercorns. It is left to cook so that the milk is infused with the flavours. The flavourings are removed and the milk is then used to make the roux sauce.

Infused sauces – this means that the liquid used in the sauce has been flavoured examples of this include a béchamel sauce which is flavoured with onion, bay leaf and peppercorns.

Velouté sauce – this is made from chickens or fish stock and cream and is thickened with butter or flour.

All-in-one

1 All the ingredients are placed in the pan and brought to the boil.
2 Stirring or whisking is required all the time to prevent the sauce from going lumpy.

Faults in sauce making

Table 4.2 Faults in sauce making

	Roux	**Blended**	**All-in-one**
Lumpy	• fat too hot when the flour was added • the roux was not cooked enough • liquid added too quickly and not stirred sufficiently • not stirred during cooking	• cornflour and liquid not blended sufficiently • not stirred during cooking	• not stirred during cooking
Raw flavour	not cooked for long enough		
Too thick or thin	incorrect weighing and/or measuring of ingredients		
Greasy	too much fat added		

> **KEY WORD**
>
> **Reduction** – flavour is developed by reducing the liquid, which makes the flavours intensify

Reduction sauces

There are many other sauces which can be made. The following types of sauces are often referred to as **reduction** sauces:

- pasta sauces
- curry sauces
- gravy
- meat sauce.

As the sauces cook, some of the liquid evaporates; this causes the thickening and the flavour to intensify.

A tomato sauce is an example of a reduction sauce.

Table 4.3 Reduction sauce

Reduced sauce	Ingredients	Brief method	Example
Tomato sauce	• tomatoes • other vegetables such as onion, garlic, celery • herbs • stock • fat	Ingredients are sweated in the fat and then liquid is added and ingredients are cooked until soft – flavour develops through cooking and intensifies as the liquid evaporates. Sometimes the sauce is blended to make it smooth.	

Emulsion sauces

An **emulsion** is formed when oil and a liquid are mixed together.

Topic link: Emulsions are discussed in more detail in Section C: Topic 1 Food science.

The table below shows some examples of emulsion sauces.

Table 4.4 Emulsion sauces

Emulsion sauce	Ingredients	Brief method	Example
Salad dressing	• olive oil • French mustard • vinegar • salt and pepper	Ingredients are combined together. This dressing should be used and served straight away – it will separate if left to stand. Note: other flavours can be added such as herbs or changing the type of oil.	
Mayonnaise	• egg yolk • vinegar or lemon juice • salt • mustard • oil • boiling water	See Figure 4.1 for method of making	
Hollandaise	• peppercorns • white wine vinegar • cold water • egg yolks • melted butter • salt and pepper	Peppercorns are cooked in the vinegar until it has reduced. Cold water and egg yolks are added and the mixture is whisked over a pan of water until it thickens. The melted butter is then gradually whisked in and the mixture is seasoned.	

Topic 4 Sauces

The following photographs show the making of mayonnaise using a food mixer – it can be done by the same method using either a food processor or a liquidizer.

1 Put the salt, mustard, vinegar or lemon juice and egg yolks into a mixing bowl.

2 Using an electric mixer whisk until all the ingredients are combined.

3 Continue to whisk using the mixer and very gradually start to add the oil. If this is done too quickly the mayonnaise will split.

4 Keep whisking until all the oil has been added.

5 Whisk in one teaspoon of boiling water. Check the seasoning of the mayonnaise and add extra seasoning if required. Store in the refrigerator until required.

▲ Figure 4.1 Making mayonnaise

KEY WORDS

Blended sauce – usually made with a liquid and cornflour

Emulsion – a mixture of two liquids

Roux sauce – fat and flour are cooked together to form a roux. Liquid is then added gradually and it then thickens when heated. The mixture should be stirred so lumps do not form

All-in-one sauce – all the ingredients used in the sauce are added together and brought to the boil stirring all the time

PRACTICAL ACTIVITY

1 Sauces are used in many main course dishes. Prepare a main course dish which illustrates the use of a reduced sauce.
2 Pouring or coating sauces are often used in vegetarian foods as they add protein to the dish. Prepare a dish which demonstrates your skills in making a roux sauce and is suitable for a lacto-ovo vegetarian.
3 Blended sauces are often used when making desserts. Prepare, cook and serve a dessert product which demonstrates your skills in making a blended sauce.
4 Some dishes are accompanied by a sauce which is an emulsion. Prepare a dish and the emulsion sauce which serves as an accompaniment.

TEST YOURSELF

1 State **three** different methods of making a sauce.
2 Explain why some people would choose to make a sauce by the all-in-one or blended method rather than a roux sauce.
3 Explain why it is important to stir a flour-based sauce when cooking.
4 Give **two** examples of sauces which are classed as an emulsion.

Topic 5
Set a mixture

> **→ WHAT WILL I LEARN?**
>
> **By the end of this topic you should have developed a knowledge and understanding of:**
>
> → ingredients which can be used to set a mixture.

When you complete your practical work you will have many opportunities to demonstrate the setting of a mixture. Examples of this are shown below.

Using starch to set a mixture

Examples of dishes include using custards in layered desserts, and confectioner's custard (crème patisserie), which is used in many flans and tartlets and basis for soufflés.

When starches are heated with liquid, the mixture will thicken. This process is called **gelatinisation**. When this mixture is then cooled, it will set.

Topic link: *You will have learnt about gelatinisation in Section C: Topic 1 Food science.*

Using eggs to set a mixture

Eggs are also used to set a mixture. When heat is applied to protein foods such as eggs they **coagulate** (set).

Topic link: *You will have learnt about coagulation in Section C: Topic 1 Food science.*

When using eggs to set a mixture you must be careful not to use too high a temperature, as the egg will easily overcook and you can be left with scrambled eggs.

An egg custard mixture is used to set a variety of sweet and savoury products.

Table 5.1 Egg custard is used in many dishes

Savoury dishes	Sweet dishes
Quiches	Baked egg custard
Tarts	Crème caramel
Flans	Bread and butter pudding
Savoury bread and butter puddings	Queen of puddings

KEY WORDS

Gelatinisation – what happens to starch and a liquid when they are cooked together

Coagulate – to set

▲ **Figure 5.1** Desserts using a custard base

Topic 5 Set a mixture

▲ **Figure 5.2** Crème caramel

▲ **Figure 5.3** Quiche Lorraine (cheese and ham flan)

Using acid to set a mixture

Acids can be used to help set a mixture. Lemon juice is an acid and can help to set mixtures containing protein (for example in cheesecakes). Lemon juice is also added to some jams to help them set.

PRACTICAL ACTIVITY

1 Eggs are often used to set a mixture.
   Prepare, cook and serve a savoury dish to illustrate the use of eggs as a setting agent.
2 Eggs can be used to set desserts.
   Prepare, cook and serve a sweet dish to illustrate the use of eggs as a setting agent.
3 Starches are often used to set layered desserts.
   Prepare, cook and serve a layered dessert which would appeal to young children.
4 Select and make a dessert which illustrates the effect acid can have on a protein.

TEST YOURSELF

1 Explain why temperature control is important when making an egg custard.
2 Why are egg custards often cooked in a water bath?
3 Explain what happens to starches when they are used as a setting agent.

235

Topic 6: Raising agents

> **→ WHAT WILL I LEARN?**
>
> By the end of this topic you should have developed a knowledge and understanding of:
> → raising agents used in cake making
> → common faults in cake making.

A **raising agent** is added to a cake and bread mixture to give lightness to the mixture. There are three main types of raising agent:

- using air (egg [colloid foam] adds air to a mixture)
- chemical raising agents (for example, self-raising flour and baking powder)
- using steam
- using yeast which produces carbon dioxide.

Topic link: *The different raising agents and how they work is covered in more detail in Section C: Topic 1 Food science.*

Information on bread which uses yeast as the raising agent and choux pastry which uses steam as a raising agent are found on pages 240 and 242–3.

Ingredients and methods of cake making

When producing baked products it is important that ingredients are weighed accurately so that the ingredients will work correctly together.

The main ingredients used in cake making are:

- fat
- flour
- sugar
- eggs
- raising agent.

There are four main methods of cake making. Each method produces products that have a different texture.

The amount of fat in the product will determine how long the cake will stay fresh without drying out. Cakes cannot be successfully made with reduced-fat spreads, as the water content of these is too high. It is important to check on the labels of different types of fats to see whether they are suitable for cooking. The nutritional profile of the products also varies depending on the ingredients used.

Table 6.1 shows you the main information and basic recipes for the different methods of cake making. You will need to be able to adapt these recipes to make interesting and innovative dishes and products.

KEY WORDS

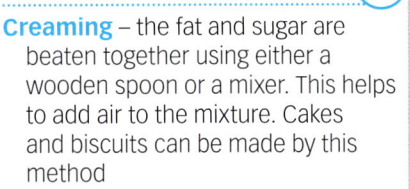

Creaming – the fat and sugar are beaten together using either a wooden spoon or a mixer. This helps to add air to the mixture. Cakes and biscuits can be made by this method

Proportions – relative quantities of ingredients in a recipe, expressed in numbers

Raising agent –

Rubbing-in method – this is when the fat is rubbed into the flour until it resembles breadcrumbs; it is used in pastry, cake and biscuit making

Whisked – when sugar and eggs are whisked together, adding air to the mixture – used when making a whisked sponge

Topic 6 Raising agents

Table 6.1 Information on methods of cake making

Method of making	Ratio of fat to flour	Raising agent	Basic recipe		Example of product
Creaming	1:1	self-raising flour contains baking powder; air is also beaten into the mixture in the creaming process	100 g self-raising flour 100 g fat (margarine or butter) 100 g sugar 2 eggs		Victoria sandwich, small buns
All-in-one	1:1	self-raising flour contains baking powder; air is also beaten into the mixture when all the ingredients are beaten together	100 g self-raising flour 100 g fat (margarine or butter) 100 g sugar 2 tsp baking powder 2 eggs		Victoria sandwich, small buns
Whisked sponge	No added fat	air steam	50 g flour 50 g sugar 2 eggs		Swiss roll, fruit flan, gateau, sponge cake
Rubbed in	1:4 in scones 1:2 in cakes	self-raising flour contains baking powder; some air is also introduced when the fat is rubbed into the flour	Cakes: 200 g self-raising flour 100 g fat (margarine or butter) 100 g sugar 2 eggs 50 ml milk	Scones: 200 g self-raising flour 50 g fat (margarine or butter) 125 ml milk	scones, rock buns
Melted	varies depending on the product being made	bicarbonate of soda in gingerbread flapjack does not contain a raising agent	varies depending on the product		flapjack, gingerbread
Batter		baking powder steam	225 g plain flour 120 ml vegetable oil 2 tsp baking powder ¼ tsp salt 1 egg 250 ml milk		muffins

If cakes are not prepared in the correct way or ingredients not measured carefully then you will not get a successful product. Table 6.2 shows some common faults in cakes.

Table 6.2 Common faults in cake making

Fault	Cause
Cake has sunk in the middle	• Too much sugar or syrup is used. This affects the gluten (protein in the flour), making it soft so it collapses. • Too much raising agent was added to the mixture and the gluten collapses. • The cake has not been cooked for enough time and the mixture has not set. • The oven door was opened and closed before the cake mixture had set.
Cake has risen to a peak and cracked on top	• Oven temperature was too high and the mixture had set on top before the cake had finished rising. • Too much mixture was used for the size of the tin. • The cake was cooked too near the top of the oven.
Has a heavy texture	• The mixture was too wet. • Not enough chemical raising agent or air was added to the mixture. • The oven temperature was too low. • When mixing, the mixture curdled and therefore could not hold as much air.
Has a hard sugary crust	• Too much sugar was used. • A coarse sugar, such as granulated sugar, was used and did not have enough time to dissolve. • The mixture was not creamed enough, so the size of the sugar crystals was not sufficiently reduced.
Has an open and coarse texture	• Too much chemical raising agent was used. • Flour had not been thoroughly mixed in.
Has risen unevenly	• Oven shelf is not level. • The cake was placed too near the heat source and it therefore rose more quickly on one side.

PRACTICAL ACTIVITY

1. A wide range of scones can be made by the rubbing-in method. Prepare a range of sweet and savoury scones which could be sold in a bakery.
2. Tray bakes can be made using a variety of different methods of cake making. Prepare a tray bake which incorporates fruit.
3. Cakes are often served at celebration events.
    a. Produce a detailed plan to explain how you will make a celebration cake.
    b. Prepare, cook and serve the cake for a celebration.
    c. Give reasons for choice of your decoration and methods.
4. Some cakes use bicarbonate of soda as a raising agent (alkali).
    a. Prepare, cook and serve a dish to illustrate this.
    b. Identify which ingredients have been used in the cake to mask the 'soapy' taste of bicarbonate of soda.

Stretch and challenge

When completing your NEA Task 2 you will need to look at the nutritional profile of your dishes.

1. Using a nutritional software program compare the nutritional profile of each of the different methods of cake making. Suggest how the recipes could be modified to improve their nutritional profile.
2. Use one of your suggested modifications to make a cake. Evaluate how successful this new dish is in terms of its sensory qualities.

TEST YOURSELF

1. Produce a mind map or chart to show the functions of ingredients used in cake making.
2. Name the raising agents used in each of the following cake mixtures:
    a. Victoria sandwich cake
    b. whisked sponge
    c. scones
    d. muffins.

Topic 7 Dough

> **→ WHAT WILL I LEARN?**
>
> **By the end of this topic you should have developed a knowledge and understanding of:**
> → different types of dough
> → ingredients used to make dough.

There is a variety of different methods of making mixtures which form a dough. These include:

- pastry
- biscuits
- bread
- pasta.

Pastry

A wide variety of different pastry and pastry products can be made.

Ingredients and types of pastry

The main ingredients in all types of pastry are:

- flour
- fat
- water
- salt.

These ingredients are combined in different ratios by different methods to produce a variety of textures and finishes.

Eggs, sugar and other ingredients such as cheese and herbs can be added to some pastries for extra flavour. The ingredients are used in different ratios and are mixed in different ways to produce a variety of textures and flavours.

Table 7.1 Functions of the ingredients used in pastry

Ingredient	Shortcrust	Flaky/Rough puff	Choux
Flour	Soft plain flour – low gluten content to produce short crumb texture	Strong plain flour – high gluten content to produce crispy, flaky layers	Strong plain flour – high gluten content which stretches to hold the expanding steam and air
Fat	Mixture of white fat and margarine/butter or butter – fat coats the flour granules to reduce the water mixing with the gluten	Mixture of white fat and margarine/butter or butter – when placed as small pieces on the dough, the fat traps air between the layers of dough	Butter or margarine for flavour
Water	Binds the rubbed-in fat and flour	Combines with gluten to form stretchy, elastic dough – lemon juice is added to strengthen the gluten	Boiled to 100° C so the heat causes the starch in the flour to gelatinise; mixes with flour to develop the gluten
Salt	Helps develop flavour	Helps develop flavour and strengthen gluten	
Egg			Helps to hold air in the starch mixture – gives a smooth, glossy finish and aids piping of the mixture

You will also notice that:

- the proportion of fat to flour varies
- the fat is incorporated into the flour in different ways.

This means that the texture of each pastry is different.

Topic link: Rubbed-in fat and flour (used in some pastry and biscuit mixtures) give a waterproof coating to the grains of flour, which prevents the gluten in the flour from developing and produces a short, crumbly texture. This is called shortening. You will have learnt about shortening in Section C: Topic 1.

Table 7.2 Information about the main types of pastry

Type of pastry	Basic recipe	Ratio of fat to flour	How fat is incorporated	Texture required
Shortcrust	200 g plain flour 100 g fat (mixture of margarine/butter and white fat or butter/margarine) water	1:2	Fat is rubbed into flour.	Light texture, crisp, short
Rough puff	200 g strong plain flour 150 g fat (mixture of margarine and or butter) 2 tsp lemon juice Water	3:4	Small pieces of fat are added to the flour and lightly mixed (not rubbed in). Liquid is added; pastry is rolled and folded 3 times, resting between each folding.	Layers of crisp pastry
Flaky	200 g strong plain flour 150 g fat (mixture of margarine and or butter) 2 tsp lemon juice Water	3:4	A ¼ of the fat is rubbed into the flour, then water added; pastry is rolled and folded, adding a ¼ of the fat each time.	Layers of crisp pastry
Choux	75 g strong plain flour 50 g butter 2 eggs 125 ml water	1:1.5	Fat is melted in the water.	Hollow inside, well risen, with a crisp texture

Making shortcrust pastry

1. Weigh the flour and sieve into a large mixing bowl. Weigh the fat and cut into small cubes and add to the flour.

2. Rub the fat into flour using your fingertips.

3. Avoid getting the mixture on the palms of your hands as these are warm and will melt the fat.

4. Continue rubbing the fat into flour until it looks like breadcrumbs.

5. Gradually add the water and mix in with a table knife or palette knife.

6. The pastry should come together as a firm but not sticky mixture.

7. Bring the pastry together into a ball – be careful not to handle the pastry too much. If you have time put the pastry into the refrigerator to relax.

8. Roll out on a lightly floured table or board.

▲ Figure 7.1 Making shortcrust pastry

Making rough puff pastry

Step 1 Sieve the flour into a large mixing bowl. Cut the butter into small pieces and add to the flour. Mix into the flour but do not rub in. Mix the water (125ml) and lemon juice together and add to the flour and fat.

Step 2 Mix to a firm but not sticky dough.

Step 3 Put pastry onto a floured board and shape to an oblong. Roll out to an oblong until it measures approximately 30 × 10 cm. Fold the ends to the middle.

Step 4 Fold the pastry in half. Cover the pastry and put in the fridge to chill.

Step 5 Remove the pastry from the fridge. Give the pastry a quarter turn and repeat step three, three more times, resting between each rolling and folding and remember to give a quarter turn before starting to roll each time.

Step 6 Put the pastry in the fridge to relax after the final folding before using

▲ Figure 7.2 Making rough puff pastry

Making choux pastry

Step 1 Put butter and water in a saucepan, heat until boiling.

Step 2 Add flour.

Step 3 Beat well, place back on heat to cook roux until it leaves the sides of the pan.

Step 4 Leave to cool for a few minutes and add the eggs a little at a time, beating well.

Step 5 Form the mixture into circles, lines or circles.

▲ Figure 7.3 Making choux pastry

Making good-quality pastry

When preparing pastry (except for choux pastry) it is important to keep everything cool.

Rolling out pastry

Rolling out the pastry has to be done carefully so that it is not spoilt.

The pastry needs to be as cool as possible. It should be of a firm consistency. You should roll out on a lightly floured work surface with a floured rolling pin. The pastry should be rolled with short, even strokes. Once you have rolled across the pastry, turn it through a quarter turn and continue rolling. You should not turn the pastry over.

Choux pastry is not rolled out – it is usually piped or spooned into the desired shapes.

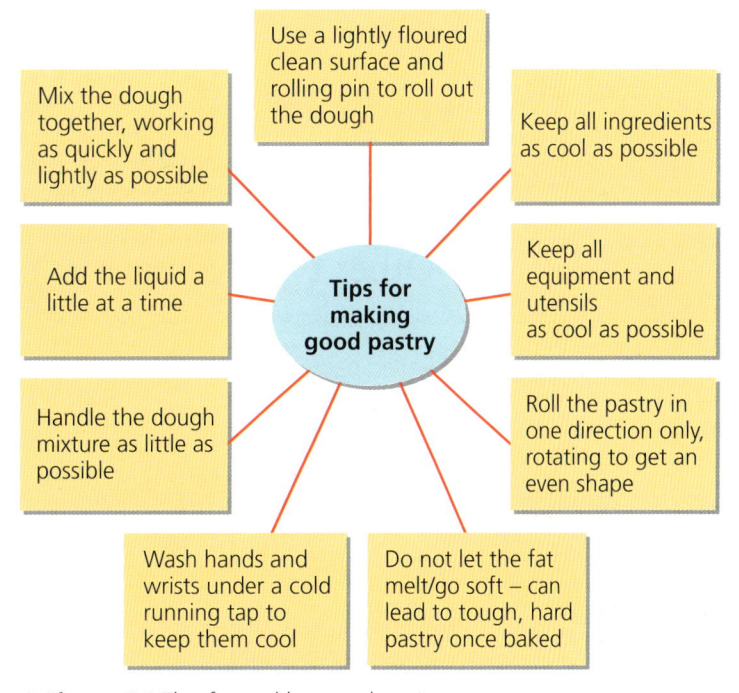

Tips for making good pastry:

- Mix the dough together, working as quickly and lightly as possible
- Use a lightly floured clean surface and rolling pin to roll out the dough
- Keep all ingredients as cool as possible
- Add the liquid a little at a time
- Keep all equipment and utensils as cool as possible
- Handle the dough mixture as little as possible
- Roll the pastry in one direction only, rotating to get an even shape
- Wash hands and wrists under a cold running tap to keep them cool
- Do not let the fat melt/go soft – can lead to tough, hard pastry once baked

▲ Figure 7.4 Tips for making good pastry

Avoiding common faults

If pastry is not prepared in the correct way, or ingredients not measured carefully, you will not achieve a successful product. Table 7.3 shows some common faults in pastry.

Table 7.3 Common faults in pastry

Fault	Cause
Pastry is soft and sticky and difficult to handle	<ul><li>too much liquid was added</li><li>a soft fat was used</li><li>the mixture has been over-handled</li></ul>
Cooked pastry is dry and crumbly	<ul><li>not enough liquid was added</li></ul>
Cooked pastry is hard and tough	<ul><li>too much water was added and the gluten in the pastry was over-developed</li><li>pastry was handled too much</li><li>too little fat was used</li><li>pastry was over-rolled</li></ul>
Pastry is soft and oily when cooked	<ul><li>temperature of the oven was too low</li></ul>
Pastry shrinks when it is cooking	<ul><li>the pastry was stretched</li></ul>
Pastry is soft and crumbly	<ul><li>too much fat was used</li><li>not much water was used</li><li>too much baking powder, if this ingredient has been used</li></ul>
Pastry blisters	<ul><li>fat not rubbed in sufficiently</li><li>too much water was used</li></ul>
Pastry is very pale	<ul><li>not baked for long enough</li><li>oven temperature was not hot enough</li></ul>
Pastry too dark	<ul><li>cooked too long</li><li>oven temperature was too high</li></ul>

PRACTICAL ACTIVITY

1 Pastry can be made into a range of interesting dishes. In small groups prepare, cook and serve a range of hand-held pastry products which could be served as part of a buffet.
2 Pastry products are often high in fat. Produce a pastry dish which shows how pastry dishes can be combined with either fruits or vegetables to contribute to increasing the amount of fruit or vegetables and fibre in the diet.
3 Making choux pastry and rough puff pastry demonstrates a high level of skills. Produce an attractive sweet or savoury dish to demonstrate one of these skills.

Other types of pastry

You can also get the following types of pastry:

- Filo pastry – this originally came from Greece. When it is cooked it becomes very crisp. The fat content in filo pastry is much lower than in other pastries. It can be purchased fresh or as a frozen product.
- Puff pastry – similar to flaky pastry. Many people buy this as either a chilled or frozen product as it is quick to use and saves a lot of preparation time.

Biscuits

The basic ingredients in biscuits are the same as those in cakes, but the proportions of fat to flour differ.

- Flour – a soft plain flour is usually used for biscuits as a strong gluten content is not required.

Topic 7 Dough

- Fat – this can be butter or animal or vegetable oils. The type of fat used will depend on the method of making and the flavour required.
- Sugar – the more sugar a biscuit contains the harder it will be. When biscuits are cooking the sugar also softens the gluten, causing the mixture to soften and spread. Some biscuits are made with a coarse sugar, such as granulated sugar, as this gives a cracked appearance on the top (for example, in cookies and gingernut biscuits).
- Eggs – these are added to some mixtures to bind the ingredients together.

Biscuits can be made by the same methods as cakes. However, they need to be shaped. This is usually done before baking and can be achieved by:

- using cutters
- piping the mixture
- putting spoonfuls of mixture on the baking tray.

Biscuits made by the rubbing-in method are usually rolled and cut into shapes.

Bread making

There is a large variety of breads made with a wide range of flours. Many types of bread are traditional to different parts of this country and to different parts of the world. They can also be made from a wide variety of different flours.

The main ingredients in bread are:

- strong plain flour
- yeast – fresh or dried
- water
- salt.

▲ Figure 7.5 Ingredients used to make bread

Other ingredients can be added to the bread to give variety to the taste and texture of the product.

Making good-quality bread

To successfully make bread, the following are important to note:

- Use strong plain flour. This contains gluten (the protein in flour), which will provide the structure to the cooked bread.
- Salt helps to improve the mixture and adds flavour.

- Yeast is the raising agent. When the warm (25–35 °C) liquid is added to the dry ingredients and yeast it must not be too hot, as this will kill the yeast and the bread will not rise.
- Kneading the dough helps to develop the gluten, which stretches to hold the carbon dioxide bubbles produced by the yeast.

▲ Figure 7.6 Kneading dough

Topic link: *You will have learnt about gluten formation, which occurs in bread making, in Section C : Topic 1 Food science.*

When making bread, if you do not follow the recipe carefully faults may occur. Table 7.4 shows the common faults that can occur in bread making.

Table 7.4 Common faults in bread making

Fault	Cause
Bread has a dense texture	- Ordinary plain flour was used, which does not have a high enough gluten content. - The yeast was killed before the bread was baked. - Too much salt was used in the mixture. - The dough was too dry, which meant it was too dry to allow the expansion. - The dough was not left to prove for long enough.
Bread has not risen well and is coarse in texture	- The dough was over-fermented/left to prove for too long. - The yeast was killed before the bread was baked.
Bread has uneven texture and large holes	Bread was not kneaded enough after the first proving.
Dough collapses when being baked	The mixture was left to prove for too long.

Topic link: *The proving process allows for fermentation. You will have learnt about fermentation in Section C: Topic 1 Food science.*

PRACTICAL ACTIVITY

1 Bread is eaten in many different countries. Produce a bread product which shows your understanding of the types of bread eaten in one of the countries you have studied.
2 Biscuits are considered a treat to most people today. Prepare a batch of biscuits which could be served as a treat.

Topic 7 Dough

Pasta

Pasta is usually made from durum wheat which has a high protein content (15 per cent). There are four main types of pasta:

- dried durum wheat pasta
- fresh egg pasta
- semolina pasta
- wholewheat pasta.

The pasta can be flavoured (for example with tomato or spinach).

There is a wide range of pasta dishes you can make to demonstrate a range of skills. These include:

- stuffed pasta dishes (for example ravioli, cannelloni)
- layered dishes (for example lasagne)
- pasta served with a sauce (for example meat sauce, pesto, tomato sauce).

You will also be able to demonstrate preparing a range of other ingredients when you are making pasta dishes; for example:

- meat
- fish
- herbs and spices
- vegetables
- nuts.

How to make fresh pasta

Ingredients
175 g pasta flour or strong plain flour
1 egg
3 egg yolks

Step 1 Sieve flour into a bowl.

Step 2 Make a well in the centre and add the beaten eggs.

Step 3 Gradually mix in the flour.

Step 4 Mix until the dough is formed.

Step 5 Knead the dough until it is smooth. Cover the dough and allow it to rest for 30 minutes.

Step 6 After resting, knead the dough again.

Step 7 Use a pasta machine to roll out the pasta.

Step 8 Different attachments can be used to cut different shapes of pasta.

▲ **Figure 7.7** Pasta-making equipment

Finishing and glazing products

You may also use a range of different pieces of equipment to help you shape products or ingredients before they are cooked or served.

Table 7.6 A range of equipment used for shaping food

Equipment	What it can be used for
Food processor	Slicing, grating and chopping foods
Cutters	Creating shapes for biscuits and pastry

Section D: Skills requirements (preparation and cooking techniques)

248

Topic 7 Dough

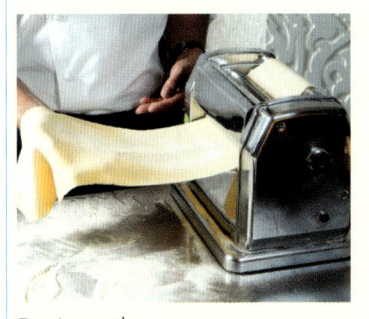

Presses	For burgers
Pasta makers	To make different-shaped pasta

The glaze is a finish usually applied to the food before it is cooked. It will help to improve the colourful appearance of the food, therefore making it more attractive to consumers. Glazes can be used on both sweet and savoury foods (see Table 8.1).

KEY WORD

Gluten formation – stretched during kneading; gluten is found in cereal foods especially wheat

Fermentation – when given warmth, moisture, food and time, yeast produces carbon dioxide and alcohol

Shortening – gives baked products a crisp texture

PRACTICAL ACTIVITY

1 A wide range of interesting dishes can be made using pasta.
   a Prepare a dish which could be served for a family meal using fresh pasta.
   b Give reasons for your choice of ingredients.
   c Evaluate how successful your dish was and identify areas which could be improved.

Stretch and challenge

Different types of biscuits use different sugars. Explain what effect this will have on the texture of the biscuits.

TEST YOURSELF

1. Explain why you would use the following flours in pastry:
   a. soft plain flour in shortcrust pastry
   b. strong plain flour in rough puff pastry.
2. When making shortcrust pastry why is it important to keep everything as cool as possible?
3. Produce a chart to show:
   - the ratio of fat to flour
   - how the fat is incorporated
   - the texture required

   for each of the following types of pastry:
   a. shortcrust
   b. flaky/rough puff
   c. choux.
4. Explain why strong plain flour is used in bread making.
5. Give **four** points which are essential for making good bread.
6. You have made a loaf of bread and it has a dense texture. Give **four** reasons why this may have occurred.

Topic 8

Judge and manipulate sensory properties

> ### → WHAT WILL I LEARN?
>
> By the end of this topic you should have developed a knowledge and understanding of:
> → how products can be finished to make them look more attractive.

First impressions play an important part in how successful a food product is going to be. Initially we rely on the senses of sight and smell when we judge a product, and then taste as we eat it. The aim when you produce food is to make it:

- attractive in appearance
- thoroughly/correctly cooked – to make it safe to eat
- appetising – mix of flavours.

It is important to taste food as you are making it, providing it is safe to do so.

When you present your food for your NEA Task 2 you will need to present it in an attractive way.

Topic links:

- *Section C: Topic 3 Food safety*
- *Non-Examined Assessment Task 2*

It is important that you taste and season food during the cooking process and before serving. The use of herbs and spices will help to develop flavours in food as will the methods of cooking you use.

The accompaniments you serve with your dishes will also help to manipulate the sensory properties. For example if you served a jus, or a reduced sauce to a dish you may be adding additional moisture to the dish, as well as colour and additional flavours.

How different products can be finished

Some products have a finish applied to them to make them more attractive. Figure 8.1 shows some different ways that foods can be finished.

▲ Figure 8.1 How different foods can be finished.

▲ **Figure 8.2** A range of garnishes which can be used on food

▲ **Figure 8.3** Piped choux pastry – chocolate éclairs

▲ **Figure 8.4** Piped potato on a shepherd's pie

Garnishing

Both sweet and savoury products can be garnished. When garnishing foods you should consider the following points:

- the neatness of the product – it should improve the appearance of the product, not dominate it
- the type of garnish – it should improve the colour, flavour, appeal and texture of the dish.

Piping

Piping can be used on both sweet and savoury products. Examples of ingredients that can be piped are:

- whipped double cream
- butter icing
- royal icing
- creamed biscuit mixtures – Viennese fingers
- choux pastry – for making éclairs and choux
- mashed potatoes
- mayonnaise.

There are different types of nozzles available. The type and shape of the nozzle used will depend on the:

- ingredient being piped
- purpose of the piping
- type of finish required.

▲ **Figure 8.5** Piping bag and nozzles

Glazing

When flour products are baked dextrinisation occurs which adds colour to the products. Adding a glaze to a product will also improve the appearance. The glaze is a finish usually applied to the food before it is cooked. It will help to improve its colourful appearance, therefore making it more attractive to consumers. Glazes can be used on both sweet and savoury foods.

Topic 8 Judge and manipulate sensory properties

Table 8.1 How different ingredients can be used to glaze products

Type of glaze	How it is used/works	Example of foods
Egg wash	Usually a mixture of egg and milk applied to the product before baking – the product will have a shiny finish.	Pastry Scones Pasty
Egg white	Used on sweet pastry products with sugar sprinkled on top – this gives the product a light golden appearance and a crunchy texture.	Sweet pastry products
Milk	Helps with the browning of the product but does not give a shiny appearance.	Bread Pastry Scones
Sugar and water	The sugar and water are boiled until syrup is formed; when the product is cooked the syrup is brushed over it – this gives the product a shiny and sticky glaze.	Sweet bread products (e.g. Chelsea buns)
Arrowroot glaze	Arrowroot is mixed with water and/or fruit juice and boiled to make a clear glaze.	Fruit flans and tarts
Jam – usually apricot or redcurrant	The jam is warmed and sieved if necessary and used to cover fruit.	French apple tart

253

Icing

Many cakes are iced to improve their appearance. They can be iced in different ways to:

- attract the customer
- suit the type of cake mixture used.

The main types of icing used on cakes are:

- glacé
- butter
- fondant
- royal
- melted chocolate.

Table 8.2 Icings used on different cakes

Glacé icing and fondant icing, used to decorate buns	Piped butter icing, used on buns	Royal icing used on a celebration cake	Melted chocolate coating biscuits

Decorating techniques

Before some foods are cooked the presentation of the dish can be made attractive. For example, when making pastry products such as pies, consider how you decorate the edges.

▲ **Figure 8.6** Attractive finish applied to a pie before glazing and baking

Enrobing or coating

Some food products can be coated with other ingredients to create an attractive finish on the product or to create a layer to separate foods.

Topic 8 Judge and manipulate sensory properties

Table 8.3 How foods can be coated

How?	Why?	What?	Examples
Applying a coating of another food	Adds texture	Batter/sugar batter	Doughnuts
	Protects delicate food	Batter	Fish
	For decoration or to improve appearance	Melted chocolate or icing	Biscuits
			Cakes
Applying layers of ingredients	Nutrition and texture	Egg and breadcrumbs	Fish cakes

Presentation and food styling

It is important when you present your food that it is attractive to the people who are going to eat it. You will also need to ensure that you serve food in the appropriate portion sizes. This will be determined by many factors including:

- the meal
- the occasion

255

- the age of the person
- other foods/courses to be served with the meal.

When you are presenting your food consider the following:

- Is the food served in the correct portion size?
- Is the food presented attractively on the serving dish?
- Are the correct accompaniments served with the food?
- Is the food being served at the correct temperature?

▲ Figure 8.7 Sausage rolls served on a contrasting coloured plate

▲ Figure 8.8 Bread rolls attractively presented on a board before serving

PRACTICAL ACTIVITY

1. Prepare to make a range of dishes which have different finishing techniques applied to them. After you have made the dishes evaluate how successful they are and suggest ways of improving the appearance of the products.
2. Piping of ingredients is often used to improve the presentation of dishes. Prepare a sweet or savoury dish to illustrate this technique.

TEST YOURSELF

1. What type of glaze could be applied to the following products:
   - cheese scones
   - apple pie
   - bread rolls?
2. You have made a chicken curry and rice. Explain how you would present it in an attractive way.
3. Give **four** points to consider when presenting food for your NEA Task 2.

Topic 8 Judge and manipulate sensory properties

Practice questions

1 Name each piece of equipment below and give **one** example of use.
(8 marks)

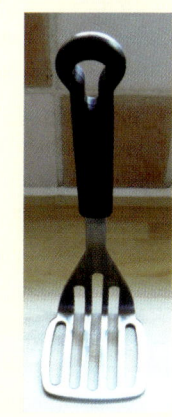

2 Give **two** reasons why meat is sometimes put in a marinade before cooking. (2 marks)

3 State **three** different methods of making a sauce. (3 marks)

4 You are making a lemon meringue pie using the following ingredients.

Pastry	Lemon filling	Meringue
Plain flour Butter Water	Cornflour Lemons (rind and juice) Sugar Egg yolk	Egg white Caster sugar

Explain **one** function of each of the ingredients used in the lemon meringue pie. (8 marks)

5 You have made a batch of bread rolls and the bread has a dense texture. Give **two** reasons why this might have occurred. (4 marks)

The quality of written communication will be assessed in the following question.

6 Food products often have a finish applied. Name and evaluate the success of the different finishes applied to the products below. (10 marks)

Preparing for assessment

In this topic you will learn about:
- Topic 1 The Non-Examined Assessment (NEA) Task 1: Food Investigation Task
- Topic 2 The Non-Examined Assessment (NEA) Task 2: Food Preparation Task
- Topic 3 The Food Preparation and Nutrition written examination

Topic 1

The Non-Examined Assessment (NEA) Task 1: Food Investigation Task

> **→ WHAT WILL I LEARN?**
>
> By the end of this topic you should have developed a knowledge and understanding of the requirements for your Non-Examined Assessment Task 1: Food Investigation Task.

The Non-Examined Assessment (NEA) consists of two different pieces of work. For both pieces of work your teacher will be sent two tasks to choose from. Topics 1 and 2 will help you to focus on what you need to do and why.

The Non-Examined Assessment is worth 50 per cent of your final marks:

- Task 1: Food Investigation Task is worth 15 per cent
- Task 2: Food Preparation Task is worth 35 per cent.

Table 1.1 gives an overview of the mark allocation for Task 1.

Table 1.1 Mark allocation for Task 1

	Marks
Plan	9
Investigation	21
Analysis	9
Evaluation	6
Total	**45**

In this task you will be required to research and investigate the chemical and functional properties of a food and to carry out investigations into the foods that have been identified in the task.

- There should be evidence of 10 hours of work.
- You should produce a report of between 1500 and 2000 words.
- It is important to be concise about what you record and how you record your work. You should use a font size of 11 if you are producing your report as a word-processed document.

The following pages will show you how to produce your work and give you ideas on presenting the results from your investigation.

Topic 1 The Non-Examined Assessment (NEA) Task 1: Food Investigation Task

Preparation of the project pages

If you are producing your task as a word-processed document, it is good practice to put the following information in a footer on each page:

- your name
- your candidate number
- your centre number.

It is also recommended to have this information on the front page of your report.

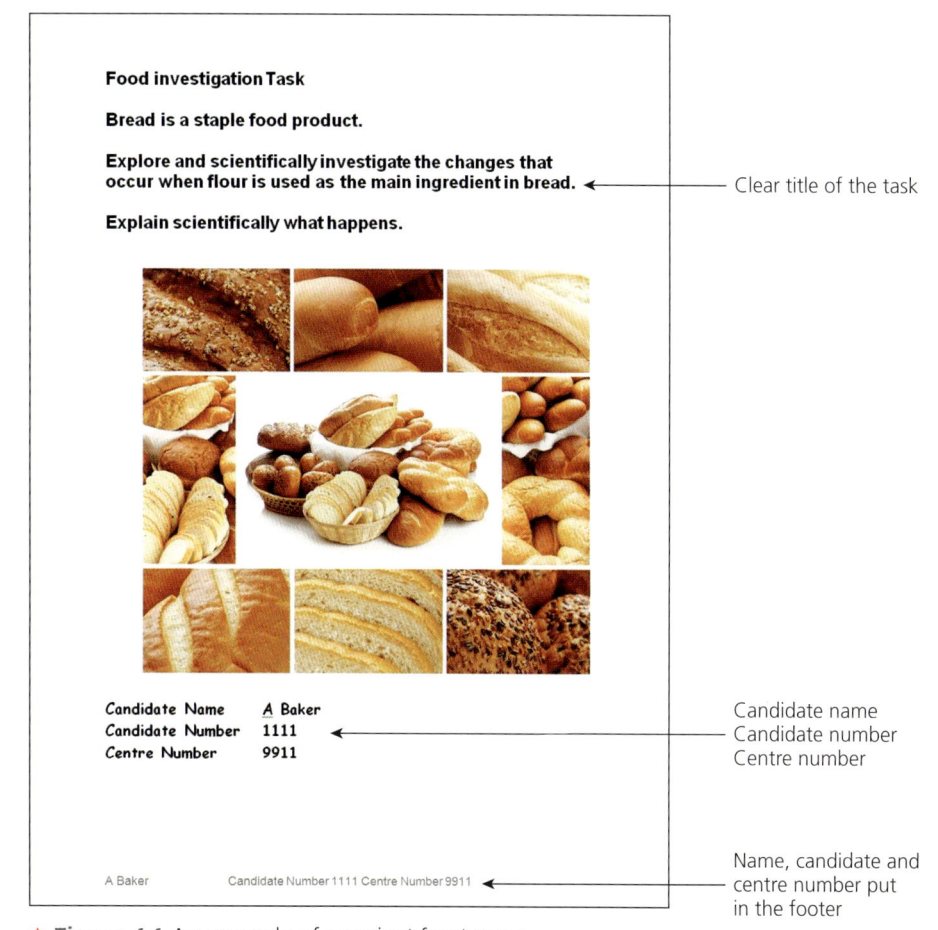

▲ Figure 1.1 An example of a project front page

It will be important to present your work in a logical order. In this section you will see how you could present your work.

Before you start planning Task 1 your teacher will have discussed how to approach the task. Figure 1.2 shows a pupil's initial ideas as notes, before starting to plan their own investigation for two different tasks.

There are lots of ideas and the pupil can then decide which ones to use for their investigation.

▶ **Figure 1.2** Initial ideas for the flour and egg investigations by two different candidates

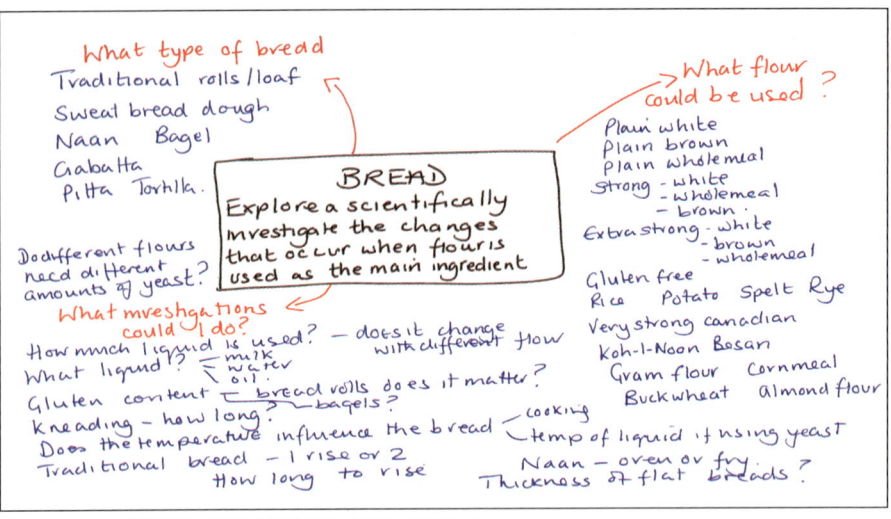

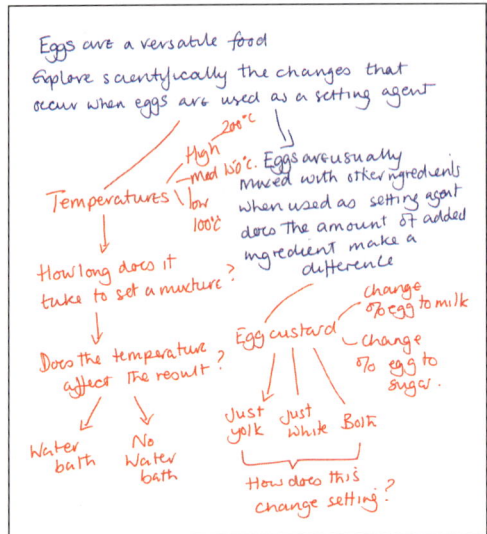

Planning

There are nine marks for the planning section. To be awarded these marks, you will need to show the following:

- How you have planned to use your time. This may include a forward plan showing how you plan to use your time
- Concise, relevant research
- Aims of the investigation
- Prediction of the investigation
- Reasons for your choice of investigations.

The following are examples of different candidates' work. Figure 1.3 shows how a high-achieving candidate placed their plans at the front of their report. Figure 1.4 shows how a candidate put their plan after completing their initial research.

- Both of these candidates have illustrated their planning by writing the methods of working for each of the investigations.
- Both candidates have recorded their research in a concise way. They are clear on what they are going to research and why.
- They have both also predicted what they think might happen.

Topic 1 The Non-Examined Assessment (NEA) Task 1: Food Investigation Task

▶ **Figure 1.3** A plan placed at the beginning of the report

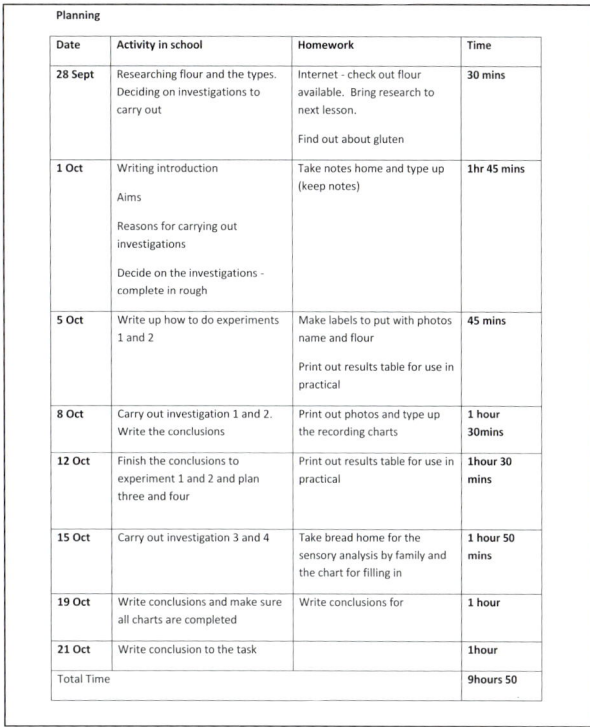

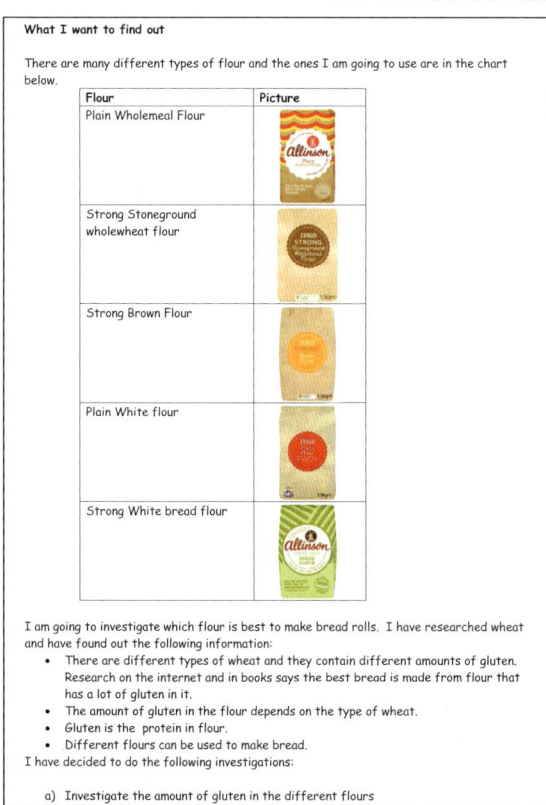

Planning

Date	Activity in school	Homework	Time
28 Sept	Researching flour and the types. Deciding on investigations to carry out	Internet - check out flour available. Bring research to next lesson. Find out about gluten	30 mins
1 Oct	Writing introduction Aims Reasons for carrying out investigations Decide on the investigations - complete in rough	Take notes home and type up (keep notes)	1hr 45 mins
5 Oct	Write up how to do experiments 1 and 2	Make labels to put with photos name and flour Print out results table for use in practical	45 mins
8 Oct	Carry out investigation 1 and 2. Write the conclusions	Print out photos and type up the recording charts	1 hour 30mins
12 Oct	Finish the conclusions to experiment 1 and 2 and plan three and four	Print out results table for use in practical	1hour 30 mins
15 Oct	Carry out investigation 3 and 4	Take bread home for the sensory analysis by family and the chart for filling in	1 hour 50 mins
19 Oct	Write conclusions and make sure all charts are completed	Write conclusions for	1 hour
21 Oct	Write conclusion to the task		1hour
Total Time			9hours 50

What I want to find out

There are many different types of flour and the ones I am going to use are in the chart below.

Flour	Picture
Plain Wholemeal Flour	
Strong Stoneground wholewheat flour	
Strong Brown Flour	
Plain White flour	
Strong White bread flour	

I am going to investigate which flour is best to make bread rolls. I have researched wheat and have found out the following information:
- There are different types of wheat and they contain different amounts of gluten. Research on the internet and in books says the best bread is made from flour that has a lot of gluten in it.
- The amount of gluten in the flour depends on the type of wheat.
- Gluten is the protein in flour.
- Different flours can be used to make bread.

I have decided to do the following investigations:

a) Investigate the amount of gluten in the different flours
b) Make gluten balls to see if I can see the difference in the amount of gluten in each flour
c) I am going to make some bread with each of the flours and see if it matters how long I knead the bread for
d) I am going to bake the bread a different temperatures to see if it makes a difference to the bread and flour.

I am doing this to see if it is true that the flours with the highest gluten content make the best bread.

This is my plan of how I am going to use the time

Date	Activity in school	Homework	Time
28 Sept	Researching flour and the types. Deciding on investigations to carry out	Find out about flour	30 mins
1 Oct	Writing introduction What I want to do Decide on 3 or 4 investigations	Take notes home and type up (keep notes)	1hr 45 mins
5 Oct	Write up the investigation on gluten and how much each flour contains - use the internet to find this out		1 hour
8 Oct	Write out how to do investigation 2, 3 and 4. Make the charts	Make labels to go with photographs. Print out a copy of charts so I can fill them in as I am working	1 hour 30mins
12 Oct	Complete the practical for investigation 2 and write up the results	Print photos out and stick under the charts	1hour 30 mins
15 Oct	Carry out investigation 3 and 4	Print photos out and stick under the charts	1 hour 50 mins
19 Oct	Write conclusions and make sure all charts are completed		1 hour
21 Oct	Write conclusion to the task		1hour
Total Time			10hours 05 mins

The ingredients I will use when carrying out these investigations are
- different flours
- yeast
- water
- salt

▲ **Figure 1.4** Plan put after the initial research

Figure 1.5 shows how a high-achieving candidate has completed the research.

- The candidate has given a clear aim for the investigation.
- They have explained what ingredients are going to be used and why.
- The candidate has also given a prediction before listing the four investigations to be completed.

263

▲ Figure 1.5 The high-achieving candidate's research

Investigation

There are 21 marks for the investigation section. In order to achieve high marks, you will need to:

- produce detailed plans and methods of working for each investigation
- follow the plans accurately
- show that the investigations are completed in a logical order
- produce records of results; these may include any of the following:
  - charts and graphs
  - photographs
  - written descriptions.

Figure 1.6 shows detailed planning for a gluten investigation. There is a detailed chart in which to complete the results as well as the method. The candidate inserted the information in the columns after carrying out the investigation.

▲ Figure 1.6 Detailed planning for the gluten investigation

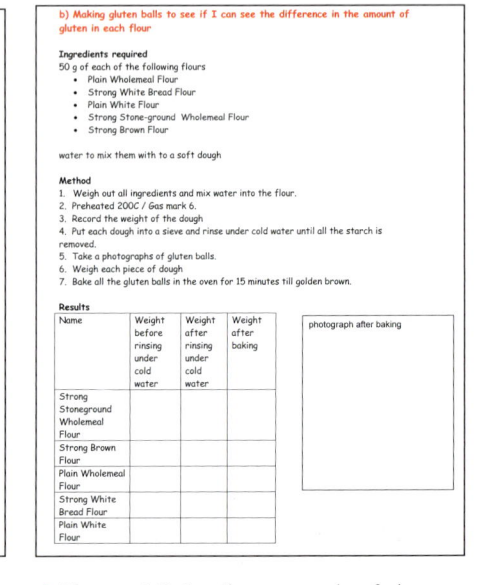

▲ Figure 1.7 Another example of clear planning for an investigation

Topic 1 The Non-Examined Assessment (NEA) Task 1: Food Investigation Task

When you are carrying out your investigation, it is a good idea to print out spare copies of your results tables so that you can accurately record what you have found out. Remember there are marks for carrying out the investigation accurately and in a logical order.

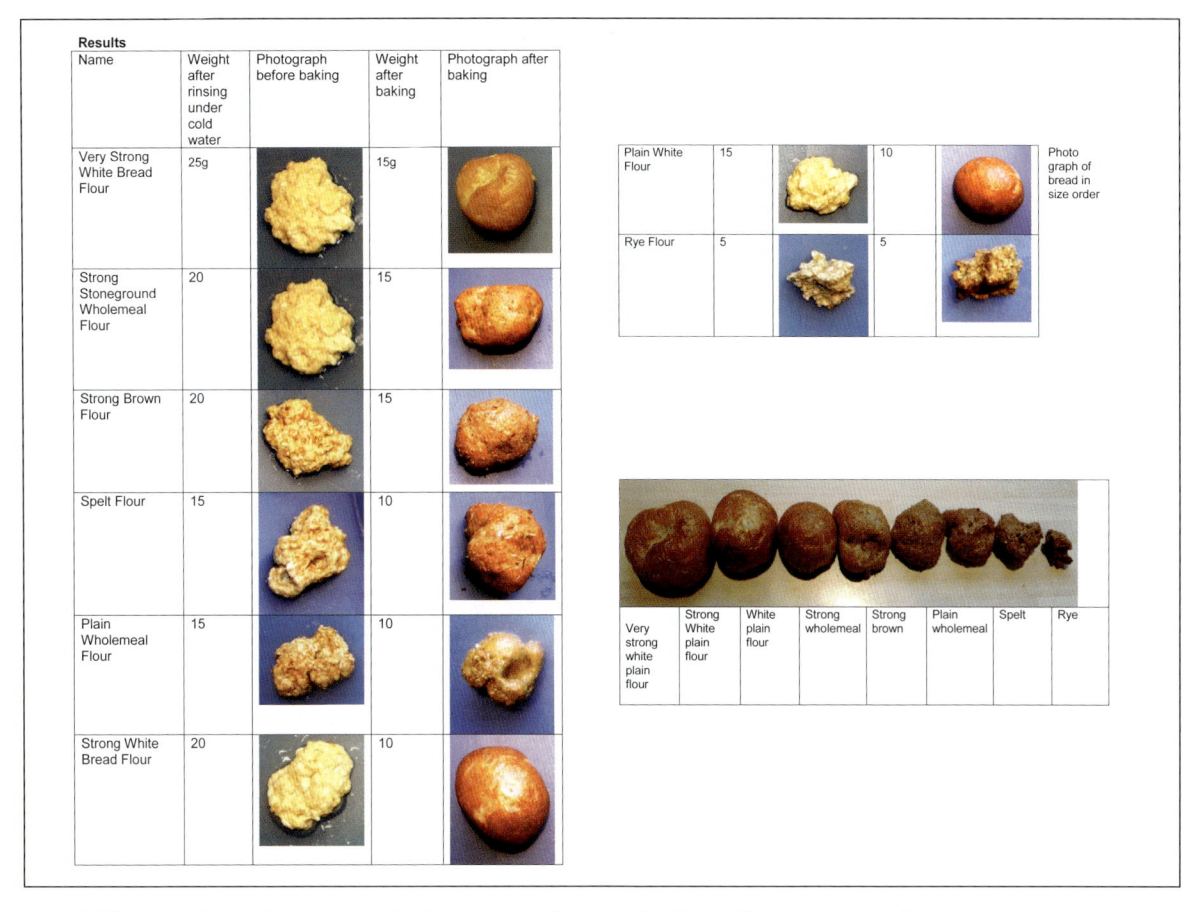

▲ **Figure 1.8** A high-level candidate's record of results for the baking of gluten balls

In Figure 1.8 the candidate took one picture of all the results and then used Word to crop them into individual photographs. It takes less time if you put all your results on one photograph, but they must be labelled so that your teacher can see your results (see Figure 1.9).

▲ **Figure 1.9** The candidate's work, labelled before photographing

Analysis

There are nine marks awarded for the analysis. When you are completing this section you need to:

- explain your findings
- ensure you use scientific explanations.

The following extract shows a high-achieving candidate's analysis from their investigation into whether the length of time bread is kneaded affects the results. It is clear that the candidate has understood what has happened and has explained this. If you read what they have written you can see they have made good use of connectives to link their ideas.

▶ **Figure 1.10** A high-achieving candidate's analysis

Analysis of results

It is clear from the photographs that the breads that were kneaded for the longest amount of time rose the most in all cases for each different type of flour. However, if you compare the rate of rising between the different types of flour the results differ. The bread made from flour which had the highest gluten content – very strong white flour – had the highest volume, followed by Allinson Strong White Bread Flour.

The wholemeal flours did not perform as well. I believe this is because they have a higher extraction rate and there is all the bran still contained in the flour. When kneading the wholemeal flour dough they did not appear as stretchy as the white flour. The spelt flour rose better than the rye flour, which rose very little either after the first prove or before putting it in the oven to cook.

The rye flour and the spelt flour did not rise as much. Again these have 100% extraction rate.

The texture of the breads differs depending on the type of flour used and the length of kneading. If you compare those kneaded for the least amount of time the texture is closer. The longer it is kneaded the larger the air pockets are in the bread and the lighter in texture. This is because the gluten was stretched and when the CO_2 is produced by the yeast it was able to stretch more due to the longer kneading.

However, again the very strong and the strong white flours produced the bread with the best textures. All the wholemeal, spelt and rye flours had very close textures.

The candidate completed this type of analysis at the end of each investigation that was completed.

Topic 1 The Non-Examined Assessment (NEA) Task 1: Food Investigation Task

Evaluation

There are six marks for the evaluation section.

You need to review your findings from the investigations and

- explain how these can be used when developing and modifying new recipes and dishes.

When completing this section of your work it is important that you link

- your findings from all your investigations together and
- explain how this will influence your future practice. Here is an example of an evaluation.

```
Evaluation
From the first two investigations where I looked at the gluten content of the
flours, those which said they contained more protein did have more gluten in
them. The only one which goes out of order is the strong white flour. There
may be several reasons for this including me not squeezing as much water out
of the mixture or not getting rid of all the starch.

I carried out the third investigation to see if the amount of time I kneaded
the dough affected the results. It is clear to see that the amount of gluten
present in the flour affects the rise of the bread. This is because it is
stretched during kneading and then when it is proving and baking the CO₂
produced by the yeast makes the bread rise. The protein (gluten) then sets,
holding the bread in its risen state. The longer the bread is kneaded the
better the structure of the bread because the gluten is elastic and is more
developed.

It is interesting that the flours which had the highest extraction rate
and also had a high gluten content did not work as well. I would suggest
the reason for this is that the bran which is in the flour must affect the
development of the gluten.

The investigations 3 and 4 link together: the white flour tended to produce
the better textured bread and these were the ones preferred by my tasters.
This is disappointing as we should be eating more wholegrain products.

Therefore my recommendations for making bread are the following:
• Use a flour with a high gluten content, or a mixture of flours with a high
  gluten content, e.g. half wholemeal and half white - this means you will
  still get fibre which is important in the diet.
• Knead the bread for a minimum of 5 minutes to develop the gluten.
• Bake the bread at the recommended temperature in your recipe.

My prediction was that: 'traditional bread recipes are made using strong
flour and the dough needs to be kneaded to develop the gluten'.

From my investigations I have found that this is true.

To develop this investigation further I would like to see what happened
when you combined different flours - would it have been possible to get a
satisfactory product which contained a higher amount of fibre?
```

▲ Figure 1.11 A high-achieving candidate's evaluation

Evaluation

From carrying out these four investigations I have found out the following results:

- Different types of flour contain different amounts of protein – gluten.
- If you knead your bread dough for a longer amount of time, you will have a bread dough which expands more as the yeast produces the carbon dioxide. This is because the gluten becomes stretchy and like elastic – see the photos for investigation B.
- When the bread is baked in a hot oven the CO_2 continues to be produced until the yeast is killed. The bread then sets in its risen state. The bread baked at the lower temperature continued to rise in the oven but some of them then collapsed. I think this was because the oven was not hot enough to set the bread.

If I make bread again I will:

- use strong plain flour, because it contains more gluten
- knead the bread for as long as possible so that the gluten becomes stretchy and can stretch when the bread is rising
- cook bread rolls at 210°C because it stops the bread from collapsing.

At the beginning of this task I wanted to find out whether it is true that the flours with the highest gluten content make the best bread. My conclusion is that it does make a difference, but you do need to knead the bread thoroughly. Wholemeal flour which had the same gluten content as the white flour did not make such a good bread product.

▲ **Figure 1.12** A middle-attaining candidate's evaluation

The candidate on the previous page has:

- given reasons for what they have said
- given recommendations for making bread
- linked the work to the prediction in the planning section.

Here is an extract from an evaluation by another candidate.

This is an evaluation by a middle-attaining candidate. Although the candidate has made reference to the investigations, they have not been linked together. The candidate has said how the investigations will influence them when bread making and has made reference to the prediction which was made in the planning stage.

When you have finished your report remember to:

- check your spelling, punctuation and grammar throughout your pages
- check your pages are in the correct order
- check your name, centre number and candidate number is clearly shown
- ensure your full title of the task is shown at the start
- you have done a word count
- included a list of books and websites used.

Topic 2

The Non-Examined Assessment (NEA) Task 2: Food Preparation Task

> **→ WHAT WILL I LEARN?**
>
> By the end of this topic you should have developed a knowledge and understanding of the requirements for your Non-Examined Assessment Task 2: Food Preparation Task.

Table 2.1 gives an overview of the mark allocation for Task 2 Food preparation task.

Table 2.1 Mark allocation for Task 2

	Marks
Plan	20
Prepare	20
Cook	25
Present	25
Analysis and Evaluation	15
Total	**105**

In this task you will be required to research and investigate the influence of lifestyles, age and culinary traditions when you develop menus and/or complete dishes for your task.

There should be evidence of 20 hours of work, and this includes the three hours you will have to prepare, cook and serve your completed dishes.

You can produce your work using a variety of different formats; for example:

- Word document
- PowerPoint presentation
- by hand.

You should use a font size of 11 if you are producing your report as a word-processed document. You are recommended to use no more than 10 pages (20 sides) of A4 or A3 paper.

If you are using PowerPoint and are printing it out to submit, please ensure that your writing can be seen and that you have not made it difficult to read with a coloured background. You should also remember if you are submitting your work electronically that a moderator will not be looking at it with a projector, so the font size needs to be able to be easily read on a computer.

Preparation of the project pages

If you are producing your task as a word-processed document, it is good practice to include the following information in a footer on each page:

- your name
- candidate number
- centre number.

It is also recommended to have this on the front page of your task (see Figure 1.1 in the previous topic).

A Baker

Candidate Number 0001

Centre Number 20220

You have invited a friend to your house for a family celebration dinner. Your friend is a lacto-vegetarian.
Plan, prepare, cook and present three dishes, which could be served for this occasion.
Analyse and evaluate your work.

Menu
Curried parsnip soup with plaited bread

Mushroom en croute
Jersey new potatoes
Cauliflower cheese
Broccoli

Rhubarb fool
Brandy snaps

A Baker	Candidate Number 1000	Centre Number 20220

▲ **Figure 2.1** Example of a front page

It will be important to present your work in a logical order. In this section you will see how you could present your work.

Before you start planning Task 2 your teacher will have discussed how to approach the task.

Topic 2 The Non-Examined Assessment (NEA) Task 2: Food Preparation Task

Plan

There are 20 marks for the planning section. To be awarded these marks you will need to show how your choice of dishes is linked to the task; detailed reasons and explanations are required. You must include:

- detailed reasons for your choice of dishes
- nutritional information for each dish
- reference to the sensory properties of the dishes
- reference to food provenance and seasonality
- a costing for each dish
- list of skills and techniques used
- a detailed plan for making the dishes – see information on page 276 for the time plan.

In this section you will be shown examples of how you could approach the task.

This extract shows a candidate's initial response to the lacto vegetarian task shown here.

> You have invited a friend to your house for a family celebration dinner. Your friend is a lacto vegetarian.
>
> Plan, prepare, cook and present three dishes that could be served for this occasion.
>
> Analyse and evaluate your work.

> In order to plan this task I need to investigate the needs of a lacto vegetarian so that the foods served are suitable for my guest. The celebration I am inviting my friend to is a birthday celebration as our birthdays are on the same day in March.
>
> I am going to make a three-course dinner; this will include a starter, main course and dessert. I will serve the accompaniments with the meal.
>
> As my friend is a lacto vegetarian, she does not eat any meat or eggs but does eat dairy produce (milk, cheese, yoghurt).
>
> As this is a celebration meal, it will allow me to use more luxury ingredients such as cream and cheeses. Although the meal does not have a nutritional focus, I will ensure that I include a range of nutrients. The nutrients I will include are:
>
> - Protein: must be obtained from dairy produce or vegetables as I am catering for a lacto vegetarian
> - Starchy carbohydrates: from pasta, rice or potatoes.
> - Fibre – from fruits or vegetables
>
> I will calculate the nutritional value for each dish and then total this at the end to compare the meal to the daily requirements.
>
> When I am making this meal I want to include a variety of interesting dishes which have a range of textures and colours. I am also going to source seasonal and local produce where ever possible.

▶ Figure 2.2 Candidate's analysis of task

▶ Figure 2.3 Initial ideas for dishes for the vegetarian task

You can see that the candidate has identified the occasion and the celebration at this early stage, because this will affect the choice of dishes. They have also shown that they are aware of the foods a lacto vegetarian can eat. The candidate has also made clear that they will include all the different elements from the marking criteria for this section.

The next stage is to identify possible dishes that you could make. When you do this, you need to think about:

- how they link to the task
- whether they will allow you to demonstrate a range of high-level skills
- whether the three dishes can be completed within the three hours
- what the cost is likely to be
- if there is a nutritional focus, are the dishes suitable?
- whether the dishes are suitable for the intended audience, e.g. a lacto vegetarian, people attending a music festival or multicultural fair, young children, etc.

Figures 2.3 and 2.4 show two different candidates' approaches. In Figure 2.3 the candidate is responding to the vegetarian task and has shown a range of possible dishes that could be included. You can see that the candidate has also started to think about the seasonality and skills in the dishes. This is important as you need to demonstrate high-level skills in the making section of your work.

Figure 2.4 shows a candidate who has produced a list of dishes suitable for the multi-cultural festival task (see box). They have also shown they have thought about the culture and the skills but these are not listed specifically.

```
We live in a multi-cultural society where we have a
wide range of food choices.

Your local area is holding a street food/music
festival. Plan, prepare, cook and present three
dishes that could be served at the festival.

Analyse and evaluate your work.
```

Preparing for assessment

Topic 2 The Non-Examined Assessment (NEA) Task 2: Food Preparation Task

Country	Skill level H	Skill level M	Skill level L	Notes	Provenance
India					
Vegetable dhal, chapatti and rice		✓		Make own chapatti	Local vegetables Traditional spices
Samosa, salad and raita	✓			Make own samosa pastry Lamb in filling	UK meat - red tractor Local veg
Chicken curry, naan bread		✓		Meat prep Bread prep	UK free range chicken
China					
Pancake rolls and dipping sauce			✓	Veg prep	UK veg where possible
Sticky duck dogs, mango slaw	✓			Meat prep - boning meat? Bread making / shaping Fruit / veg prep Food processor for making slaw	UK meat Seasonal veg
Stir fried pork with ginger and honey and rice		✓		Meat prep	UK free range pork UK honey
UK					
Homemade burger in bun with coleslaw	✓			Meat prep, bread, veg prep	UK meat and veg Local flour?
Fish gougons, potato wedges and salad	✓			Fish prep, coating, frying, salad and dressing	Sustainable fish
Chicken and veg pie	✓			Meat prep, pastry - rough puff, sauce, veg prep	UK meat Local and seasonal veg

▲ **Figure 2.4** List of suitable dishes for the multicultural festival task

The next stage is to give reasons for your choice of recipes. When you write this, you will need to refer to:

- how the dishes link to the task
- the nutritional values of the dish
- the cost of the dish
- the provenance of the ingredients
- the skills you are using.

The following extracts will show you examples of how this can be approached.

Figure 2.5 shows a candidate who is going to make a curried vegetable soup as part of the vegetarian task. The information shows that they have taken into consideration many of the points listed above. The candidate has also worked out the nutritional information and presented this later in the project.

It is important you make reference to the nutritional content in your dishes. You can use any nutritional program that you have in your school. You can also use Explore Food, which is free to use from the Food a Fact of Life website: http://explorefood.foodafactoflife.org.uk/.

Local Seasonal	Ingredients	AMT	COST/500G	ACTUAL COST	Skills
L	Parsnips	500	65	0.65	Peeling
L S	Bramley apple	100	80	0.16	Chopping
	Coriander seeds	3	1650	0.10	Sauté
	Cumin seeds	3	1150	0.07	Blending
	Oil	25	55	0.03	
L S	Onions	150	35	0.11	
	Garlic	5		0.03	
	Turmeric	3	1100	0.07	
	Ground ginger	3	1100	0.07	
	Vegetable stock cube	15	500	0.15	
			Cost	1.42	

I have chosen to serve curried parsnip and apple soup with plaited bread rolls for the starter. I have chosen this because I can use local and seasonal ingredients. The parsnips are still in season and the apples and onions are also UK produce. I decided on a curried soup to add an interesting flavour which comes from the use of spices. The bread rolls will add an alternative texture to the starter as they will have a crisp crust. I am aware that the soup and bread will both be similar in colour but I will also put some chopped parsley or coriander on the soup to add colour and serve it in a colourful dish for contrast.

The labels below show the main nutrients present in the soup. The protein in the dish comes from the vegetables which means it is LBV. As there is a range of dishes being served there will be a range of proteins in the meal. There is fat in this dish because I needed to sauté the vegetables. I used corn oil rather than butter as the saturated fat is lower. I decided to do this as I want to use butter in the pastry in the main course and there is also cream in the dessert.

The cost of the dish is 36p per portion which is cheap and I am pleased with this as some of the other dishes are expensive.

▶ **Figure 2.5** Example of reasons for choosing a particular dish

Figure 2.6 shows how a candidate used the program and commented on the nutritional value of a dessert product that was made. This product was high in fats and sugars and this has been explained. The candidate has also linked the nutrients in this product to the nutritional content of the other dishes being served, and to the context, that it was a special occasion.

Nutrition Information Typical Values

	Per 100g	Per portion (13g)
Energy (kJ)	1852	244
Energy (kcal)	443	58
Fat (g)	26	3.5
Saturates (g)	17	2.2
Carbohydrate (g)	51	6.7
Sugars (g)	26	3.4
Fibre (g)	1	<0.5
Protein (g)	3.4	<0.5
Salt (g)	0.7	0.09

Brandy Snaps — Energy 244kJ 58kcal 3%, Fat 3.5g 5%, Saturates 2.2g 11%, Sugars 3.4g 4%, Salt 0.09g 2% of an adult's Reference Intake. Typical values per 100g: Energy 1852kJ/443kcal

Nutrition Information Typical Values

	Per 100g	Per portion (125g)
Energy (kJ)	590	738
Energy (kcal)	141	176
Fat (g)	6.8	8.6
Saturates (g)	4.2	5.3
Carbohydrate (g)	19	24
Sugars (g)	16	20
Fibre (g)	<0.5	0.5
Protein (g)	1.8	2.3
Salt (g)	0.07	0.09

Fruit Fool — Energy 738kJ 176kcal 9%, Fat 8.6g 12%, Saturates 5.3g 27%, Sugars 20g 22%, Salt 0.09g 2% of an adult's Reference Intake. Typical values per 100g: Energy 590kJ/141kcal

The nutritional information for the fruit fool and brandy snap biscuit is shown above. Although the recipe for the fruit fool used skimmed milk instead of whole milk and also whipping cream instead of double cream the fat content is still high per portion (12.1g). As this meal is a celebration and is this type of dessert is not eaten every day I think it is suitable. I could have changed the cream to yogurt but this would have affected the flavour of the dish. Also, other dishes in the menu are much lower in fat.

▶ **Figure 2.6** Nutritional information about a chosen dish

Topic 2 The Non-Examined Assessment (NEA) Task 2: Food Preparation Task

You will need to prepare a detailed time plan for your practical task. You have a maximum of three hours to prepare your dishes. When you prepare your time plan, it is important to include:

- the time taken for each task
- the method of making, including important information, for example consistency of mixtures, how to tell if it is cooked, special finishes
- timings for processes, e.g. length of cooking time, chilling time
- food hygiene procedures.

You will need to ensure that you serve all the dishes at the correct temperature, and that they are ready to be eaten.

Here is an example of a candidate's menu for the vegetarian task.

▶ Figure 2.7 Example of a menu

Starter: Parsnip and apple soup with bread rolls

Main course: Mushroom en croûte with new potatoes, broccoli and cauliflower cheese

Dessert: Rhubarb fool with brandy snaps

You will only need to serve one portion of each course. This means you do not need to cook the full quantity of vegetables, since they do not reheat very well; however, you still need to show the full quantities in the ingredients lists, nutrition and costing.

You will need to plan the order carefully. Figure 2.9 shows how a candidate has completed some initial planning before starting to write the plan. The candidate printed the methods out on different-coloured pieces of paper, cut them up and then arranged them on a piece of paper in order for the three-hour practical. This was then used to write the final plan.

Figure 2.10 shows part of a candidate's plan at the start of the three-hour practical task. The candidate has continued to make use of colours, with different-coloured fonts for each dish, as this will make it easier to know which dish is being worked on at a specific time.

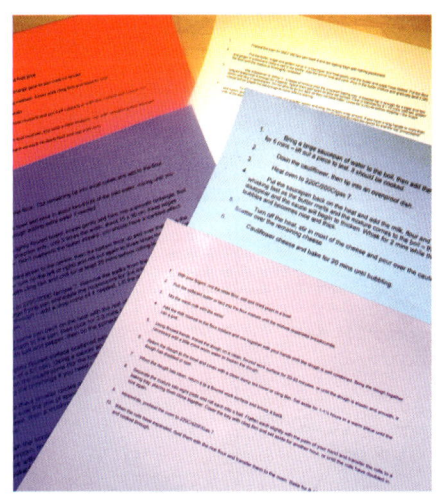

▲ Figure 2.8 Recipes printed on coloured paper

Remember to allow time to arrange the food on plates and to do your washing up.

Time	Method		Special Points	Photo
9.00	Organisation ← self food storage			
9.10	With your fingers, mix the white flour, salt and dried yeast in a bowl.			
	Mix the warm milk with the water.			
	Add the milk mixture to the flour mixture and mix together with your hands until the dough is well combined. Bring the dough together into a ball.		Soft consistency	✓
	Using floured hands, knead the dough on a clean, floured work surface for 20-25 minutes, or until the dough is elastic and smooth. If necessary add a little more warm water to loosen the dough.			
	Return the dough to the bowl and cover with a clean damp tea towel or cling film. Set aside for ~~1½~~ hours in a warm place until the dough has doubled in size. 30-40 mins+		Leave to rise 30-40 mins	
9.20	Make pastry		Breadcrumbs	✓
	1. Rub in ¼ fat into the flour. Cut remaining fat into small cubes and add to the flour		Soft not sticky dough	
	2. Make a well in the bowl and pour in about two-thirds of the cold water, mixing until you have a firm rough dough adding extra water if needed.			
	3. Turn out onto a lightly floured board, knead gently and form into a smooth rectangle. Roll the dough in one direction only, until 3 times the width, about 15 x 30 cm. Keep edges straight and even. Don't overwork the butter streaks, you should have a marbled effect.			
	4. Fold the top third down to the centre, then the bottom third up and over that. Give the dough a quarter turn (to the left or right) and roll out again to three times the length. Fold as before, cover with cling film and chill for ~~at least 20~~ mins ~~before rolling to use~~.		Rest 20 mins fridge 5°C	✓
9.30 Washup				
9.40	1. Wash and chop rhubarb.			
	2. grate rind from orange and fruit juice.		approx 10 mins Low heat lid on	
	3. Add rhubarb, sugar and orange juice to pan cook till tender.			
9.45	1 heating a small frying pan and dry roasting the coriander, cumin and cardamom seeds – this is to toast them and draw out their flavour.		2-3 mins change colour	

9.55 Washup — Prepare veg for soup onions chop a parsnip.

- Parsnip 2cm dice
- Soft – remove from heat – dish to cool.
- 5 mins to soften.

9.50 Check rhubarb cooked ✓

2 After 2-3 minutes they will ~~change colour and start to jump in the pan~~. Remove them from the pan and crush them finely with a pestle and mortar.

3. Heat the butter and oil in a saucepan until the butter begins to foam, then add the onions and gently soften for about 5 minutes before adding the garlic. Let that cook, along with the onions, for another 2 minutes, then add all the crushed spices, along with the turmeric and ginger, stir and let it all continue to cook gently for a few more minutes while you

10.00 4. ~~peel and chop the parsnips into 1-inch (2.5 cm) dice~~. Add the parsnips to the saucepan, stirring well, then pour in the stock, add some seasoning and let the soup simmer as gently as possible for 1 hour without putting on a lid.

— cook 1 hr. (11.00).

Washup

10.05 Make custard - blending method. Cover with cling film and leave to cool.

Coating consistency put in bowl to cool.

10.10 When the dough has risen, return it to a floured work surface and knock it back.

shape to plait

Separate the mixture into ~~eight~~ parts and roll each into a ball. Flatten each slightly with the palm of your hand and transfer the rolls to a baking tray, placing them close together. Cover the tray with cling film and set aside for another ~~hour~~ or until the rolls have doubled in size again.   30

Oven on 180°C.

Put the butter, sugar and golden syrup in a saucepan and heat gently until the butter and sugar have melted. Put the flour and ginger in a bowl and make a well in the centre. Add the lemon zest and juice. Pour in the butter mixture and gradually beat it into the flour until the mixture is thoroughly combined.

Use a teaspoon to dollop 3 - 4 heaps of mixture onto the prepared baking tray. A heaped tsp is enough for a cigar and two heaped teaspoons is enough for a basket. Space them well apart as they will spread. Cook in batches for 8 – 10 mins until set, golden brown and lacy in appearance. Do not allow to go too dark as they will taste bitter. Leave for a minute before shaping – the snaps should still be pliable but set enough to move without tearing.

Wash up - while checking on brandy snaps ✓

To make cigars, oil the handle of a wooden spoon and wrap the brandy snap around. If you have a long handle or more than one spoon, you can do a few at a time. The base of the biscuits should be the bit that touches the spoon so that the top 'presentation' side of the biscuit is seen. Transfer to a cooling rack.

5. Heat oven to 220C/200C fan/gas 7. Remove the stalks from the mushrooms. Heat half the oil in a large frying pan and sizzle the mushrooms for 3-4 mins on each side until golden and cooked through – add a drop more oil if needed. Lift the mushrooms out onto kitchen paper to drain.

▲ Figure 2.9 Initial time plan using coloured paper

Topic 2 The Non-Examined Assessment (NEA) Task 2: Food Preparation Task

Time	Method	Special points	Photo
9.00	Personal organisation - hair tied back, apron on Washed hands		
9.05	Organise all ingredients. All high risk foods in fridge - milk, cheese, Butter, cream. Other ingredients on separate trays for each course **Soup** - parsnips, apple, onion spices, garlic stock cube **Bread** - strong plain flour, dried yeast **Mushroom Wellington** - strong plain flour, butter, mushrooms, milk, Vegetables - potatoes, cauliflower, broccoli, flour. Rhubarb fool and brandy snap biscuits - flour, sugar, rhubarb, custard powder, almonds	Fridge 5ºC Oven on 150 ºC	
9.10	Wipe down work surface	Use sanitiser	
9.10	Make bread dough - strong plain flour, salt and yeast mixed together. Add 125 warm water. Mix together Knead for 5 mins on floured board Put bread in bowl, cover with cling film. Place in warm area to prove.	38 ºC Soft consistency. Till smooth Till double in size - 20 mins.	✓
9.20	Wash up and wipe table down		
9.25	Make rough puff pastry. Rub 1/4 fat into flour Chop remaining butter into small pieces and add to flour mix. Stir in. Add **cold** water and mix with knife. Roll to oblong - fold in thirds - quarter turn and repeat.	Looks like bread crumbs. Soft but not sticky consistency. Floured table. Wrap in cling film and chill - fridge	✓ ✓

▲ **Figure 2.10** Example of a time plan

As part of your evidence of your practical work, you need to take at least two photographs of techniques you are using in your work. It is a good idea to plan these in advance. This candidate chose to show them on the time plan.

Method of working

There are 20 marks for the Prepare section. Your teacher will assess how you work while you are completing the practical work. To achieve high marks, you need to:

- have high standards of personal and food hygiene
- work in an organised manner
- follow the time plan
- work independently
- complete all the dishes within the three hours
- complete successful dishes with their accompaniments.

Cook

There are 25 marks for the skills and cooking section. Your teacher will assess this while you are carrying out your practical work.

You need to have thought about the marking of this section when you make your choice of dishes to cook. You will gain marks in this section if you:

- successfully prepare and cook dishes that include a high level of skills
- use a range of tools and equipment safely and correctly
- use correct cooking methods and have good cooker management.

Remember

You need to take at least two photographs of skills or techniques you have used during making of your dishes, as well as the final photographs of your dishes. Table 2.2 shows how a candidate planned the photographs to be taken. After the practical cooking, they then inserted the photographs into the table in their project document.

Table 2.2 Planning for photographs

Photo	Skill
	Rolling out samosa pastry
	Filling samosa
	Finished samosa with dip and salad
	Preparing meat for curry
	Mixing naan bread
	Naan bread served with curry

▲ Figure 2.11

Present

There are 25 marks for the presentation of your dishes. This includes how your dishes taste. This will be assessed by your teacher.

When you present your food it should be:

- served at the correct temperature
- plated as one portion in a suitable way for the context
- garnished/finished so that the dishes look attractive.

Figures 2.11 to 2.14 show how dishes have been presented for one portion.

▲ Figure 2.12

▲ Figure 2.13

▲ Figure 2.14

Topic 2 The Non-Examined Assessment (NEA) Task 2: Food Preparation Task

Analysis and evaluation

Topic link: Section C: Topic - 2 Sensory properties

There are 15 marks for this section. To achieve high marks you need to show you have completed detailed sensory analysis for all your dishes.

You will need to make reference to:

- the different sensory qualities you wanted in your dishes
- justification of all your choices
- evaluate how successful your dishes have been in meeting the task
- give details of improvements and modifications you could make.

You can record your sensory analysis using a variety of different methods including charts and star profiles.

Figure 2.15 and 2.16 show how two different candidates have recorded the tasters' opinions of a main course meal for vegetarians. You can see they have given the tasters very clear criteria to assess which to assess the dish against. This means that the candidate will be able to use the information in the when they need to identify areas for improvement.

It is also a good idea to ask your tester how the product can be improved. You will then be able to use this information when identifying areas for improvement.

You must also evaluate the whole of the task this means looking back at all of the decisions you have made. Make sure you make reference to the following:

- your choice of dishes
- the nutritional and sensory information
- costings
- the effectiveness of your planning and making of the dishes
- improvements and modifications you would make

Tasting of the mushroom en croute served with new potatoes, broccoli and cauliflower cheese.

Mushroom en croute

Taster	Golden pastry	Crispy Pastry texture	Moist filling	Balanced seasoning	Cheese flavour	Ration of mushrooms to spinach to cheese	Portion size	Total (35)
1	3	5	5	4	3	5	5	30
2	3	4	5	3	3	5	4	27
3	3	5	5	4	4	5	5	31
4	4	4	5	4	3	5	5	30
Total (20)	13	18	20	11	13	20	19	

Vegetable accompaniments

Taster	Potatoes cooked	Texture of broccoli	Texture of cauliflower	Creamy texture of cheese sauce	Strength of cheese sauce	Attractive presentation with the mushroom en croute	Overall portion size of meal	Total (35)
1	5	5	5	5	5	5	5	35
2	5	4	4	5	5	5	4	32
3	5	5	5	5	4	5	5	34
4	5	5	5	5	5	5	5	35
Total (20)	20	19	19	20	19	20	19	

As you can see for the table above the mushroom en croute was generally successful. The average score for the completed dish was 29.5 (out of 35). There are some elements of the dish I would not change because they scored full marks (moist filling and ratio of the mushrooms to spinach to cheese). I would however look at improving the following elements the golden pastry, the seasoning and the cheese flavour as these all scored lower marks.

If you then look at the scores for the vegetables which were served with the mushroom en croute you can see that these scored highly. Only one of the tasters thought the vegetables were too soft and that the cheese sauce was too strong. One person also thought the size of the meal was slightly too small. In all these cases they only missed the top score by one mark.

▲ **Figure 2.15** Record of taste testing for samosa with salad and yogurt dressing

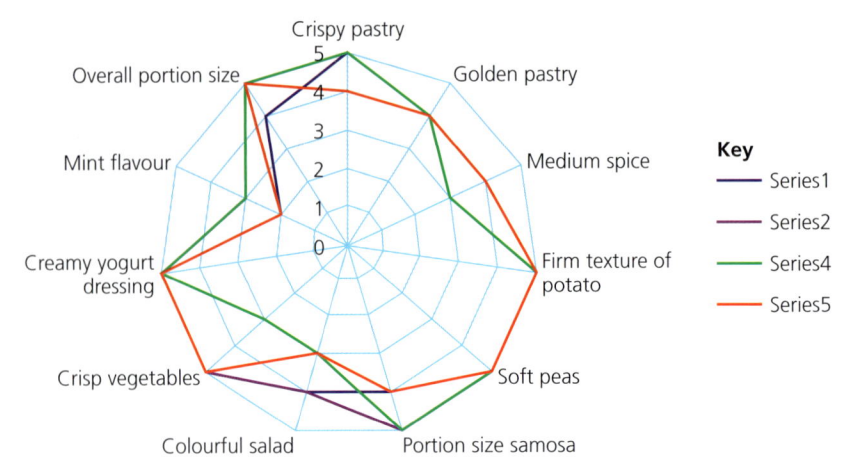

▲ Figure 2.16 Star profile for samosa with salad and yogurt dressing

To gain high marks it is important that you give reasons for what you say. Look at the example below from a candidates work.

```
Improve the cheese flavour - I used a cheddar cheese and this was not very strong
I will change this to a stronger cheese in future. This will have an effect the
cost of the dish as strong cheese is more expensive.
```

The candidate has said what will be changed – cheese to a stronger flavour one.

The effect improved flavour and also an increase in cost.

The following extract is part of an evaluation, it focuses on the dishes.

You will notice that the candidate has given reasons for what has been said and has backed this up with reasons.

▼ Figure 2.18 Evaluation

```
Evaluation of the dishes
I am now going to evaluate how successful my meal for the vegetarian birthday
celebration was and suggest improvements.
I am pleased with how the dishes were served. As you can see from the photographs
the dishes are all presented in an attractive way and the comments from the
tasters show this as well.
```

- 'All the dishes were presented in an attractive way, the way you served foods on coloured plates made them look attractive and you also garnished the food to make it look attractive'.
- 'All the food was attractive, I particularly liked the plaited bread rolls. The brandy snaps also added colour and texture to the fruit fool'.

I would have liked there to have been more colour in the soup, but because I wanted to use seasonal ingredients parsnips was a good choice. If I was making this again I would add some carrots or make a carrot and coriander soup which would still have an interesting spicy flavour. The bread was attractive because I plaited it. If I was to make this again I may add either sesame seeds of poppy seeds to the top to make them look more attractive and to add additional colour.

Preparing for assessment

280

The main course was successful, however there are some changes I would make. The pastry was not as golden as I would have liked but I could not use egg as the glaze as my friend is an lacto vegetarian and does not eat eggs. However improvements I would make are:

Improve the seasoning – add some herbs to this for example thyme goes well with mushrooms and to add a little salt and pepper to the mushroom.

Improve the cheese flavour – I used a cheddar cheese and this was not very strong I will change this to a stronger cheese in future. This will have an affect the cost of the dish as strong cheese is more expensive.

The vegetables which I served with the mushroom en croute were all successful so I will not make any changes to this.

I was pleased with the rhubarb fool and brandy snaps. I had to use a blended sauce for my custard as my friend does not eat eggs. The consistency of the rhubarb fool was creamy. I did not mix all the rhubarb into the fool and put some as a layer in the middle of the fool and some on top. This provided a contrast in taste between the creamy custard and the slightly sharp rhubarb and also made it look more attractive.

If I were to make this dish again I would need to improve my brandy snap biscuits as they were not all the same size. I need to be more careful when putting the mixture onto the baking tray. When I rolled them round the spoon I did not get them all the same size either. This was because some had cooled too much and were not as easy to shape. This could have been averted if I had put fewer on the baking tray or I had worked more quickly.

If you look at the nutritional values of the different dishes (see nutritional profiles in planning section) you can see that the main course and dessert are both quite high in fat. This is because I have used butter, cream and cheese. As this is a special occasion meal and not the type of meal eaten every day I feel that this is justified. I could have changed the butter to a vegetable fat but this would have affected the taste of the pastry and brandy snaps and I do not think I would have had such good scores for the taste and texture of the dishes. It has already been pointed out to me by the tasters that the cheese flavour was not strong enough so if I reduced the amount to reduce the fat content the flavour would have been affected even more.

The overall cost of the meal per portion is good:

- Soup and bread per portion – 45p
- Mushroom Wellington with vegetables £1.67
- Rhubarb fool with brandy snap biscuit £1.26

This is a total of £3.38 per person. This is an economical meal even though it is a celebration meal.

I stated at the start of this task that I wanted to use local and seasonal foods and have done this by using foods which are in season e.g. rhubarb, parsnips, onion, and early new potatoes. I have also sourced products which are produced in the UK rhubarb, parsnips, onions. The early new potatoes were imported from Jersey though.

The cheese is from the UK and has the farm assured mark on it meaning that they cows were kept in good conditions. All of this also helps to support UK farmers.

I planned my practical work carefully. The use of the different colours meant it was clear for me which dish I was working on. The timings were generally accurate and this meant I had completed all three dishes on time. I lost some time when I was making the pastry for the dessert however I was able to gain back time later on when it did not take me as long to prepare the fruit and to do some washing up. The details in the plan enabled me to work methodically as it included information on finishing techniques such as glazing pastry putting the thicknesses of mixtures and cooking times meant I did not forget things. I was able to work safely and hygienically as I had included important information such as when foods needed to be put in the fridge, reminders about using different chopping boards for raw meat.

If I was to do anything different in the planning next time it would be to put more information on how to tell if the dishes were cooked or not. I would also have made my pastry earlier so that it had longer to relax in the fridge before I needed to roll it out.

The Evaluation above shows part a on a candidates evaluation which is where they are evaluating how they worked when carrying out the practical activity. Again this candidate has said the changes they would make and why they would make them.

On completion of your task

Once you have completed your task you should:

- check your spelling, punctuation and grammar throughout your pages
- check your pages are in the correct order
- check your name, centre and candidate number are clearly shown
- ensure the full title of your task is shown at the start
- include a list of websites and books web.

Topic 3

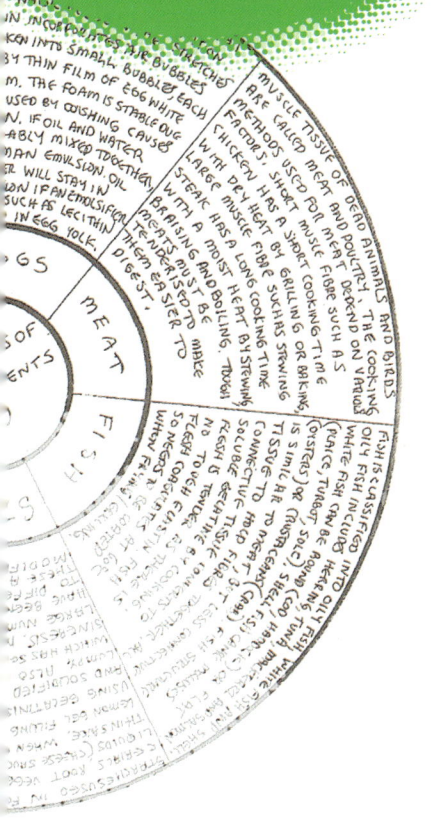

The Food Preparation and Nutrition written examination

→ **WHAT WILL I LEARN?**

By the end of this topic you should have developed a knowledge and understanding of:

→ the requirements of the written examination
→ how to approach your exam paper.

Introduction to the examination

The Food Preparation and Nutrition written examination is 1 hour 30 minutes and is 50 per cent of your GCSE marks. It is externally marked and is taken at the end of your course.

The paper will have questions from the four areas of the specification:

A Nutrition
B Food provenance and food choice
C Cooking and food preparation
D Skills – preparation and cooking techniques.

There will be a variety of styles of question. Some of these will be short-answer questions and others will require a longer response. The quality of your written response will be marked in questions marked with an asterisk (*).

Achieving examination success

Examination success depends on a variety of factors:

- Your folder/book throughout the whole course should be kept in an organised way so that you can use it for revision. This includes all notes, handouts, research, tests and homework:
  - Use section dividers and use the chapters from the book as a guideline.
  - Make sure that you know the key points from each topic that you study. You could keep a separate notebook for revision and list the key points throughout the course.
- Revision is very important. There are many ways that you can make this more interesting, and there are some suggestions in this chapter.
- Take every opportunity to practise examination questions. This will develop your examination technique. Practice questions are included at the end of each section in this textbook.
- Make sure that you understand the words that are used in examination papers.

How can I remember the key facts?

After you have covered a topic in lessons, make a summary of the facts. A useful way of doing this is to a make a few points under the headings shown in Table 3.1.

Figure 3.1 is an example of a revision card.

Table 3.1 Headings for revision

Topic:	
Points I must know	(2–3 vital facts that are really important)
Points I should know	(4–5 additional pieces of key information)
Points I could know	(Extra information to help your understanding)

DIETARY FIBRE

Key facts I must know:

1. Dietary fibre is found mainly in cereal foods, beans, lentils, fruit and vegetables.
2. Dietary fibre cannot be broken down by human digestive enzymes.
3. Dietary fibre helps to prevent constipation and lower blood cholesterol and glucose levels.

Facts I should know:

1. In the UK most people do not eat enough fibre. The recommended intake for adults is currently 18 g per day, may be changing to 30 g.
2. A low fibre intake is associated with constipation and some gut diseases such as diverticulitis and bowel cancer.
3. Foods and food products that contain 6 g fibre per 100 g or 100 ml may be labelled as a 'high-fibre' food.

Facts I could know:

1. There are two types of fibre: insoluble and soluble.
2. Soluble fibre is found in oats, fruit, vegetables and pulses (beans, lentils and chickpeas). Insoluble fibre is found in wholegrain cereals and wholemeal bread

---

▲ Figure 3.1 Example of a revision card for dietary fibre

REVISION ACTIVITY

Produce a revision card for how heat is transferred.

Revision techniques

Charts

A simple revision method is to put your facts into charts. It is much easier to remember visual information.

Table 3.2 shows part of a revision chart for nutrients and would be a good way of recording your information in the first place.

Topic 3 The Food Preparation and Nutrition written examination

Table 3.2 Example of a revision chart for nutrients

Nutrient	Function	Source	Deficiency / Excess
Carbohydrates			
Starch	Energy Extra is stored as fat	Cereals (wheat and rice) Root vegetables (potatoes)	**Lack of energy** **Obesity**
Sugar	Energy, but not essential	Sweet fruit, honey, sugar, treacle	**Heart disease** **Linked to cancers** **Diabetes** **Sugar: tooth decay**
Dietary fibre	Helps to pass faeces easily	Fruit and vegetables Wholegrain cereals	**Constipation, haemorrhoids (piles)** **Diverticular disease**
Protein			
Many different types, e.g. • Gluten • Collagen • Albumin	Growth and repair Secondary energy	Animal, e.g. meat: high biological value (HBV) Plant, e.g. cereals, pulses: low biological value (LBV) Pulses (peas, beans, lentils) Nuts	**Body tissue repair affected** **Stunted growth**
Fats			
Vegetable fats (oils) Animal fats	Energy Protection of organs Warmth Provides fat-soluble vitamins A, D, E and K and essential fatty acids (EFAs)	Seeds (sunflower), olives, soya beans, nuts	**Reduced energy intake can lead to weight loss** **Vitamin deficiency** **Obesity** **Heart disease** **Linked to cancers** **Diabetes**

Brace maps

On a brace map (see Figure 3.2) you can record key information. Figure 3.3 shows an example that has been completed while revising fish.

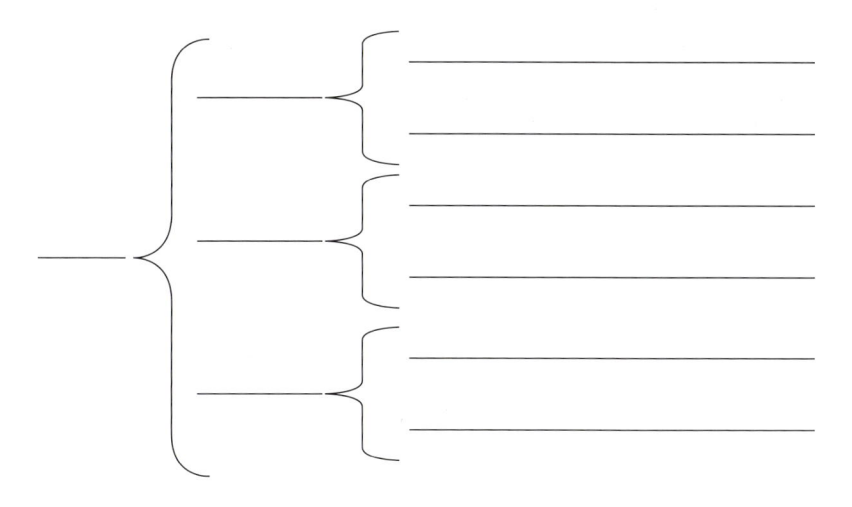

▲ Figure 3.2 Outline of a brace map for revision

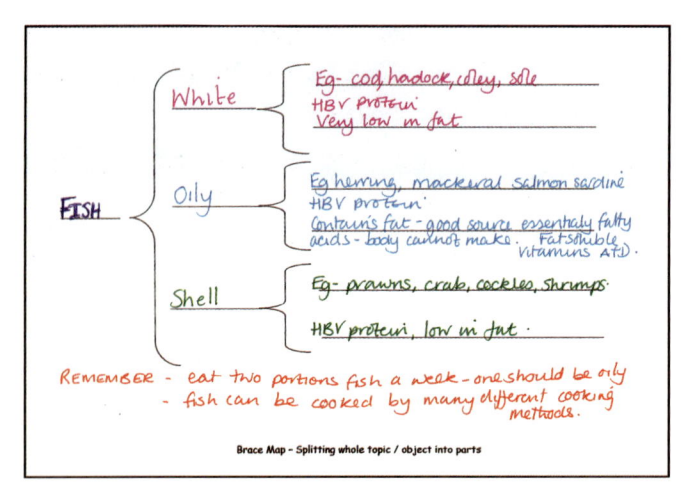

▲ Figure 3.3 Revision of fish shown on a brace map

REVISION ACTIVITY

Use a brace map to record a revision guide to a topic. You could work in groups and choose a topic such as preservation. Each one of you could cover a different aspect and then you could share your results.

Circle maps

Write the topic in the middle and then put all the information you know around the outside. Some candidates find it more useful to put the very important points at 12 o'clock, 3 o'clock, 6 o'clock and 9 o'clock, and then complete the rest.

Circle maps are sometimes a good way of planning exam answers, especially for the longer response questions.

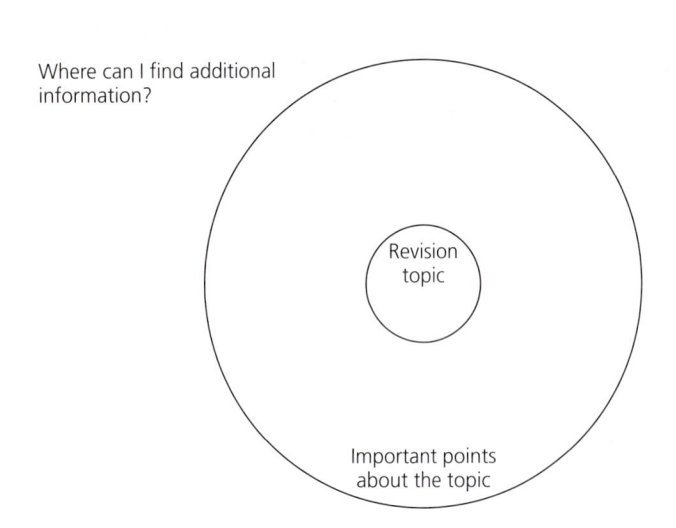

▲ Figure 3.4 Outline of a circle map for revision

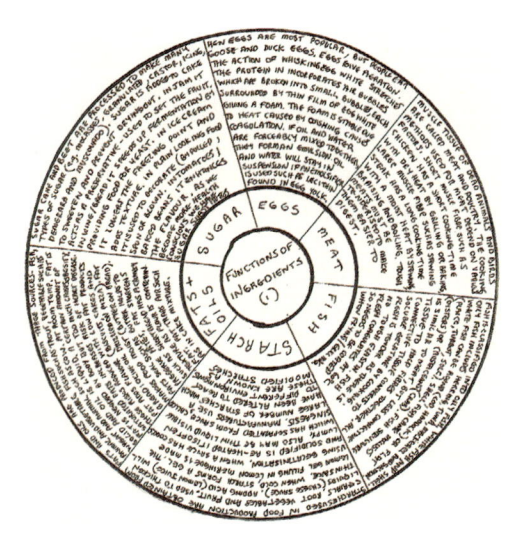

▲ Figure 3.5 Revision of the functions of ingredients shown on a circle map

REVISION ACTIVITY

Use a circle map to revise methods of cooking.

Topic 3 The Food Preparation and Nutrition written examination

Bubble maps

Some topics have a lot of information that is important. In this case, a bubble map is useful.

Figure 3.7 shows a bubble map completed by a student on factors affecting food choice. You will notice that the candidate has extended the diagram, adding other important information that they wanted to remember.

▲ Figure 3.6 Outline of a bubble map for revision

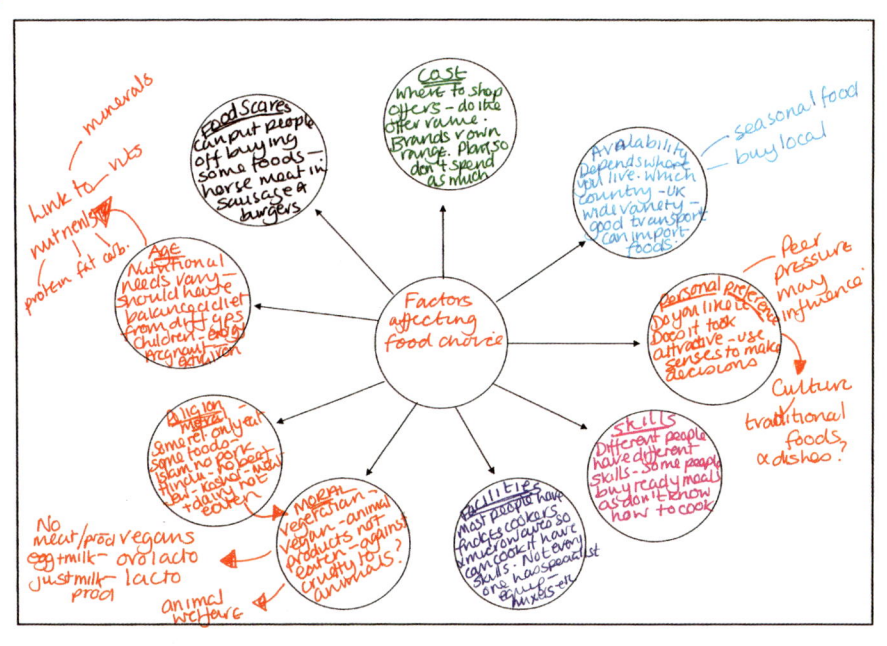

▲ Figure 3.7 Revision of the factors affecting food choice, shown on a bubble map

REVISION ACTIVITY

Use a bubble map to make revision notes on food contamination.

Double bubble maps are useful for evaluating information, looking at the advantages and disadvantages of a topic or theme, or comparing and contrasting. Figure 3.9 shows a student's work looking at the similarities and differences between ovo-lacto vegetarian and a vegan.

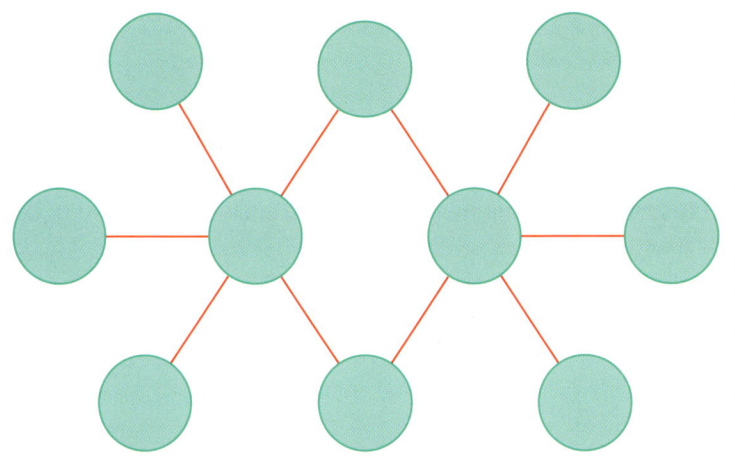

▲ Figure 3.8 Outline of a double bubble map

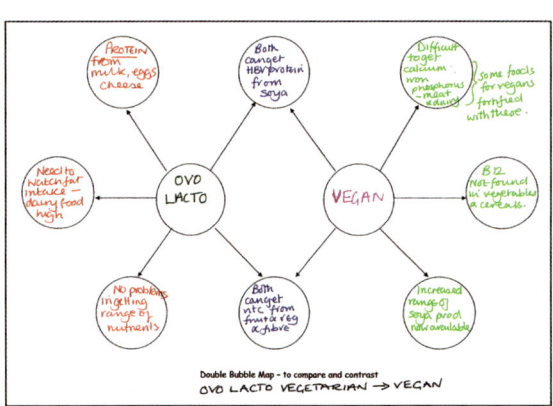

▲ Figure 3.9 Comparison of two vegetarian diets, shown on a double bubble map

287

Understanding the terms used in an examination paper

The language that is used in an examination paper is very important and many candidates lose valuable marks because they have not completed what they were asked to do.

State

'State' is a simple instruction and will be worth only one mark. It is the very rare occasion where a one-word answer may be accepted but it depends on the question. Here are some examples:

1 State the name of the equipment that is used to check the temperature of cooked meat. (1 mark)
   Food probe. (1 mark)
2 State **two** functions of protein in the diet. (2 marks)
   Growth (1 mark)
   Repair. (1 mark)

Give

'Give' is often used as an introduction to a question and it may also ask for a 'reason' or a 'way'. Here is an example:

3 Give **two** reasons why we should reduce the amount of fat in the diet. (2 marks)
   To reduce the risk of heart disease. (1 mark)
   To reduce the risk of obesity. (1 mark)

If a candidate just wrote 'heart disease' or 'obesity' in answer to this question, they would not get any marks because they are not saying why, they need to say 'to reduce the risk of …'.

Reasons

A question requiring reasons will usually start with 'give' or 'state'. The question often requires a one-sentence answer. You should justify and give examples for what you are saying. Here is an example:

4 Give **two** reasons why organic vegetables have become more popular. (2 marks)
   They do not use any artificial chemicals or pesticides. (1 mark)
   Some people think they have a better flavour than other vegetables. (1 mark)

Examples

If you are asked to give more than one example in an answer they need to be different. A poor example of this is:

5 Give **two** ways that a manufacturer could promote their product. (2 marks)
   On television (1 mark)
   Adverts (0 marks)

Topic 3 The Food Preparation and Nutrition written examination

These are both the same so can get only 1 mark. A correct answer for the second mark would have been: 'Giving away taster samples in a supermarket'.

Another poor example is:

6 Give **two** ways that dried fruit could be used to reduce the sugar in a recipe. (2 marks)
  Cakes (0 marks)
  Biscuits. (0 marks)

This answer is not specific enough and therefore did not get any marks. Correct answers for one mark each would include 'You could put sultanas in an apple crumble' and 'Dried apricots could sweeten cereal bars'.

Explain

To answer an 'explain' question, full sentences must be used, including a *reason* or *justification* and an *example* if it helps. Here is an example:

7 Explain **two** nutritional benefits of eating a variety of fruits and vegetables each day. (4 marks)
  Fruits and vegetables do not contain any fat, (1 mark) *therefore if people eat more fruit and vegetables this will help reduce their fat intake.* (1 mark) *Fruits and vegetables contain vitamin C* (1 mark) *which protects the body against infection* (1 mark) *and prevents scurvy.*

You can see that the candidate has given clear reasons for what they have said and has earned all four marks.

Function

The word 'function' is asking you to explain the function (job) that an ingredient or tool performs. It is a more difficult part of a question and therefore needs a detailed answer. Here is an example:

8 Preservatives and emulsifiers are added to some food products. Explain **one** function of preservatives and **one** function of emulsifiers in food products. (4 marks)
  Preservatives help to keep food safe for a longer shelf life. (1 mark) *because they protect the food against the growth of micro-organisms.* (1 mark) *Emulsifiers are used to help substances that contain oil and water mix together.* (1 mark) *These would normally separate, for example mayonnaise.* (1 mark)

Describe

If you were in an English examination and were asked to 'describe', you would plan and carefully think out what you were going to write. Too often, candidates put one- or two-word answers for a describe question. Here is an example of a 'describe' question, and several possible answers that would each be worth one mark:

9 Describe how freezing increases the shelf life of vegetables. (2 marks)

Cold temperature means the bacteria do not multiply, but does not destroy the bacteria. (1 mark)
Bacteria need warmth to multiply and a freezer does not provide warmth. (1 mark)
Water becomes unavailable for the bacteria to reproduce as it forms ice crystals. (1 mark)
Chemical changes in the food are slowed down because of the cold temperature. (1 mark)

Advantages and disadvantages or benefits and limitations

When answering about advantages and disadvantages, or benefits and limitations, you need to make sure you do not just say opposites. Here is an example:

10 Give **two** advantages and **two** disadvantages of buying Fairtrade products. (4 marks)

Advantages:
Workers are paid a fair price for the work they do. (1 mark)
There is now a wide range of products to buy which are fairtrade. (1 mark)
Disadvantages:
The products are sometimes more expensive than other products. (1 mark)
They are imported so they will have a higher carbon footprint. (1 mark)

This candidate has given four different points for four marks.

REVISION ACTIVITY

List the advantages and disadvantages of:
- freezing
- chilling
- drying
- canning

fruits and vegetables.

Evaluate

When answering an 'evaluate' question, you should write from two points of view, for example the consumer and the manufacturer, or the supermarket and the manufacturer.

You will have had experience of evaluating in other parts of the course and need to remember these skills when completing exam questions. You could use the double bubble map shown in Figure 3.8 to practise answering evaluation questions.

Often the response to these types of questions will be marked with an *. This means that the quality of your written communication will be assessed.

Topic 3 The Food Preparation and Nutrition written examination

You should write your answer in full sentences and use paragraphs. Answers should be well organised and clearly presented.

Here is an example:

11 A 14-year-old boy's packed lunch consisted of:
- Cheese sandwiches on white bread
- Packet of crisps
- Chocolate bar
- Apple
- Can of Coke.

Evaluate the packed lunch.

The advantages of this packed lunch include that the cheese contains calcium needed for strong bones and teeth and protein required for growth and repair, although it is high in fat. A diet high in fat is linked to obesity and heart disease. White bread contains some fibre but there would have been more if it had been wholemeal bread. However, it is fortified with calcium.

The apple is providing some vitamin C and some fibre, which is required for a healthy digestive system and helps to prevent constipation.

The weak points about the packed lunch are that it is high in fat from crisps and chocolate bar as well as the cheese. It is high in salt from the crisps; we should be reducing the amount of salt eaten.

The sugar content is high due to the chocolate bar and the Coke; again we should not have a diet high in sugar because it can be linked to obesity and also tooth decay. It is low in fibre apart from the apple.

The packed lunch could easily be improved by removing the crisps and replacing with an unsalted snack or vegetable such as salad; this reduces the fat and lowers the salt levels. Change white bread for wholemeal, therefore increasing the fibre. Replace Coke with water. Do not include the chocolate bar or replace with a fruit-based cake (muffins).

A candidate will gain high marks in this question if they have recognised most of the healthy eating issues and have made sound comments to improve the menu.

Discuss/analyse

When you are asked to 'discuss', you must give well-reasoned points and explanations. Adding examples will often help to show the examiner what you are thinking and support your answers.

One-word answers or a list are not acceptable. Look at the number of marks awarded to identify how much to write.

You need to practise these types of questions as they may have as many as 12 marks and the quality of your written communication may also be taken into account.

Table 3.3 is a grid you can use to practise answering this style of question. Remember to make use of connectives to link your points together. Figure 3.10 is an example of a student's work.

Table 3.3 Grid for 'discuss', 'explain' and 'analyse' questions

Statement	Connective word	Explanation	Connective word	Example

Question: Explain what advice you would give to consumers when buying and storing food when on a limited budget

Statement	Connective word	Explanation	Connective word	Example
BUYING Buy in season foods	because	these are usually cheaper - especially if from UK - transport costs	an example	strawberries in July parsnip November
Buy suitable amounts	therefore	you will avoid waste - shopping list - plan menu	for example	avoid buy one get one free if not in your menu plan or can freeze it
Check date marks		to avoid food waste make sure - have as long as possible.	should	Use by - high risk eg meat Best before - tins/dry
STORING First in first out	this means	stock rotation so you use oldest food first again avoid waste	therefore	Put new food to back of fridge/ bottom of freezer
Check temp. of freezer/fridge	because	bacteria multiply more quickly if not correct temperature. If freezer not -18 - defrosts	this	means fridge 4°C or less.
Follow storage instructions	because	food will last longer	eg	jam in fridge after opening - often says this on packets.

▲ Figure 3.10 Example of a completed answer planning grid

REVISION ACTIVITY

Draw a grid as shown in Table 3.3 and then answer the question below. There are 10 marks for the question.

1 There are concerns in the UK that the number of obese adults is rising. Assess the factors that can contribute to the rise in adult obesity.

How can I achieve my best in the examination?

Many candidates do not achieve their best in the examination for a variety of reasons even though they know the correct answers.

Here are a few guidelines to help you get those valuable marks:

- Read the instructions on the front of the paper.
- Read each question carefully and highlight the key parts of each question. Lots of candidates answer what they think the question is about instead of the actual question. For example, on a question about hygiene when taste-testing food, many candidates just put hygiene rules. Nothing to do with tasting!

Topic 3 The Food Preparation and Nutrition written examination

- Look to see how many marks are allocated to the parts of the question.
- It is rare to have a question that requires a one-word answer. The examiner will have allowed the number of lines they think is needed for you to answer the question to gain the marks.
- Make sure you give an answer to the question and do not just reword the question. A good example of this is:
  How can you improve the colour? Answer: Use different colours. (0 marks)
  How can you improve the flavour? Answer: Use different flavours. (0 marks)
  Correct answers would be:
  Improve the colour by adding chopped green peppers and yellow sweetcorn.
  Improve the flavour by adding mixed herbs.
- There are a number of words frequently used in answers that will not gain you any marks because they are not qualified or explained. Examples of these are:
  - healthier
  - quicker
  - longer
  - faster
  - because it's healthy
  - cheaper
  - easier.
- Finally, when you have completed your examination, you must always read and check your answers. Check to see where you think the examiner is going to be able to award you marks.

Glossary

Accelerated freeze-drying (AFD) a technique where food is frozen and then dried

Acid acids are chemicals that are found in some foods

Additives substances added to food in small amounts to improve colour, flavour, texture or to make the food stay safe for longer

Aeration the process of trapping air in a mixture

Aesthetic qualities the properties that make a product attractive to look at or experience; the look, smell, taste, feel and sound of products

Albumin protein found in egg white

Amino acids the smallest units of a protein

Anaemia deficiency disease caused by lack of iron in the diet

Anaerobic does not need oxygen to grow

Anaphylactic reaction an extreme reaction to a substance, needing immediate medical treatment

Animal sources meat, fish, poultry and dairy products

Antioxidants substances that stop fat from going rancid

Aseptic sterilised; preserves foods without using preservatives or chilling

Bacteria single-celled organisms present in the air, soil, on animals and humans

Balanced diet a diet that provides adequate amounts of nutrients and energy

Basal metabolic rate (BMR) amount of energy we need for all bodily functions

Best before date used on low-risk foods

Blast-freezing a quick-freezing method; small ice crystals form and there is less damage to the food than in slow freezing

Blended sauce usually made with a liquid and cornflour

Bridge hold making a bridge between your thumb and first finger and holding the food while safely cutting; used when cutting an onion in half

Buddhism a religion; most Buddhists are vegetarian

Bulk sweeteners have a similar level of sweetness to sugar

Calcium a mineral element that is essential for strong bones and teeth

Calorie a unit of energy that is used to give the energy yield of foods and the energy expenditure by the body

Caramelisation process of changing the colour of sugar from white to brown when heated

Carbohydrate the major source of energy in the body

Carbon footprint a measure of the impact human activities have on the environment in terms of greenhouse gases produced through the outlet of carbon dioxide; the amount of carbon emissions produced in the growing, processing, production, distribution and disposal of food

Carbon offsetting planting trees to absorb carbon dioxide

Carotene vitamin A

Casein protein found in milk

Chemical raising agent baking powder or bicarbonate of soda are examples of chemical raising agents

Claw grip holding the end of the vegetable or fruit with your fingers and cutting the vegetables or fruit

Coagulate to set; the change in structure of protein brought about by heat, mechanical action or acids

Coeliac disease a medical condition caused by an allergy to the protein gluten present in the cereals wheat, barley and rye

Collagen protein found in meat

Colloidal structure when two substances are mixed together

Complementary proteins mixing different low-biological-value proteins to supply all the essential amino acids

Conduction where heat is transferred from one molecule to another

Glossary

Connective tissue surrounds the muscle fibres

Contamination when food is affected with micro-organisms

Convection where warm molecules rise and the cooler molecules fall closer to the source of heat

Creaming the fat and sugar are beaten together using either a wooden spoon or a mixer (this helps to add air to the mixture); cakes and biscuits can be made by this method

Cross-contamination when micro-organisms transfer from raw to cooked foods, causing infection

Cryogenic freezing food is immersed or sprayed with liquid nitrogen

Danger zone the temperature range (5–63° C) in which bacteria grow rapidly

Dehydrating removing water

Dehydration a medical condition resulting from insufficient water in the diet

Denaturation when acids are used to change the structure of protein in food

Deteriorate start to decay and lose freshness

Dextrinisation when dry heat is applied to flour and it browns as the starch is changed into a sugar

Diabetes a metabolic disorder caused by the poor absorption of glucose. This can be due to the failure to produce insulin (in Type 1 insulin-dependent diabetes) or the poor response of tissues to insulin (in Type 2 non-insulin-dependent diabetes). Type 1 diabetes mellitus develops in childhood. The onset of Type 2 is usually in middle age onwards.

Dietary fibre material from plants, which is not digested by humans but which absorbs water and binds other residues in the intestine, thus aiding the excretion of waste material from the body

Dietary guidelines advice from the government on recommended food intake in order to achieve dietary goals

Dietary reference values (DRVs) estimates of the amounts of nutrients needed for good health

Direct contamination allowing blood and juices of raw foods to drip on to cooked foods

Disaccharide two monosaccharides combined

Diverticular disease a disease caused by lack of fibre in the diet

Diverticulitis a condition which affects the large intestine

E number a number given to an additive to indicate that it has been approved for use in the EU

Eatwell Guide a healthy eating model, to encourage people to eat the correct proportions of food to achieve a balanced diet

Eco footprint measurement of our actions on the environment

Elastin protein found in meat

Emulsifier a substance that stops oil and water separating (for example, lecithin in egg yolk)

Emulsion a mixture of two liquids

Energy balance the relationship between energy input and energy used by the body

Enzymes proteins that speed up chemical reactions; can affect the flavour and shorten the shelf life of products

Enzymic browning reaction between a food product and oxygen resulting in a brown colour (for example, potatoes or apples going brown)

Essential amino acids amino acids that cannot be made by the body

Essential fatty acids small unit of fat that must be supplied in the diet

Estimated Average Requirements (EARs) the average amount of a nutrient needed

Evaluating summarising information, drawing conclusions and making judgements

Extraction rate how much of the whole grain is used

Extrinsic sugar sucrose added to a product

Fairtrade guarantees that disadvantaged farmers get a fair deal

Fats are solid

Fat-soluble vitamins dissolve in fat

Fermentation when given warmth, moisture, food and time, yeast produces carbon dioxide and alcohol

Folate or folic acid important in the diet of pregnant women for the development of the foetus

Food combining mixing different low biological value proteins to supply all the essential amino acids

Food intolerance becoming ill after eating certain foods

Food miles distance food travels from farm to plate

Food security considers availability, accesses and utilisation of food

Food spoilage damage to food caused by the natural decay of food or by contamination by micro-organisms

Food-spoilage bacteria bacteria that cause food to go bad but do not usually cause food poisoning

Fortification the addition of nutrients to a food product to improve its nutritional value

Fortified when a nutrient is added to a product to improve its nutritional value

Free sugars added to foods and drinks by manufacturers, cooks or consumers and found naturally in honey, syrups and fruit juice

Fructose simple sugar

Functional foods have extra health benefits

Gelatinisation this is what happens to starches and water when cooked together

Genetically modified describes crops where the genetic structure of the crops has been changed

Globalisation process by which different parts of the globe become interconnected by economic, social, cultural and political means

Gluten the protein in flour

Gluten formation stretched during kneading; gluten is found in cereal foods, especially wheat

Halal meat meat and poultry slaughtered in a particular way so that no blood remains

HBV high-biological-value protein

Hermetic airtight

High-biological-value (HBV) proteins proteins that contain all the essential amino acids

High-risk foods foods which are the ideal medium for the growth of bacteria or micro-organisms (e.g. chicken and shellfish)

Hinduism Hindus will not eat any meat from cows

Homogenisation involves forcing the milk at high pressure through small holes; this breaks up the fat globules in order to spread them evenly throughout the milk and prevent separation of a cream layer

Hydrogenation the process of adding hydrogen to oils to make them into solid fats

Imported food that is grown in a different country and brought to the UK

Indirect contamination allowing bacteria to be transferred during handling or preparation

Insoluble fibre absorbs water and increases bulk, making it easier to pass faeces through the digestive system

Intense sweeteners examples are saccharin and aspartame

Intensive farming large amount of produce is generated from a relatively small area of land

Intrinsic sugar contained within the cell walls of plants

Invisible fats foods containing fat which cannot be seen

Iron a mineral present in the blood and stored in the liver; prolonged lack of iron leads to anaemia

Islam a religion where people do not eat any pork or pork products; they only eat halal meat

Judaism a religion where they eat kosher food; pork, meat and dairy products are not eaten in the same meal

Kilocalories (kcal) and kilojoules (kJ) measurements of energy in foods

Lacto vegetarians do not eat eggs, meat of dairy products

Lacto-ovo vegetarians do not eat meat, fish of dairy products

Lactose a type of sugar found in milk

Lactose intolerance not able to digest milk sugar lactose

LBV low biological value protein

Lecithin found in egg yolk; it is an emulsifier

Lipids another name for fats and oils

Glossary

Locally produced grown or reared close to where it is purchased

Low biological value (LBV) proteins proteins that do not contain all the essential amino acids

Low fat 3 g fat or less per 100 g

Low salt 3 g of salt or less per 100 g (or 0.1 g sodium)

Low sugar 5 g fat or less per 100 g

Low-risk foods foods which have a long shelf life, such as dried foods

Macronutrient nutrients needed by the body in large amounts

Maillard reaction this happens when foods containing proteins and carbohydrates are cooked by dry methods

Malnourished an unbalanced diet when health suffers

Marinate flavouring meat by soaking in a liquid mixture

Micronutrient nutrients needed by the body in small amounts

Micro-organisms tiny living things such as bacteria, yeasts and moulds which cause food spoilage; can only be seen through a microscope

Milling the process of making flour from grains of wheat

Minerals micro-nutrients needed by the body in small amounts

Modified atmosphere packaging (MAP)

Monosaccharide simple sugar

Monounsaturated fats a fat molecule with one hydrogen space

Multicultural several cultures of ethnic groups within society

Mycoprotein is produced from micro-organisms

Myoglobin the colour pigment that gives red meat its red colour

Non-starch polysaccharide (fibre) the part of food that is not digested by the body

Nutritional value nutrients contained in product

Obese excessive fatness, measured as ratio of weight to height

Oils are liquid

Organic grown or reared without the use of artificial aids, fertilisers, pesticides and antibiotics

Organoleptic describes the sensory qualities (texture, flavour, aroma, appearance) of a food product

Osteomalacia caused by lack of vitamin D in adults

Osteoporosis a disease in which the bones start to lose minerals and their strength and break easily

Ovo vegetarians do not eat dairy products, meat or fish

Oxidisation occurs when fruit and vegetables are cut and the cells are exposed to air

Palatable pleasant to taste

Pasteurisation the process of prolonging the keeping quality of products such as milk by heating to destroy harmful bacteria

Pasteurised a method of heat-treating milk to kill harmful bacteria

Pathogenic bacteria harmful bacteria which can cause food poisoning

pH a measure of alkalinity or acidity

Physical activity level (PAL) the energy used for all types of movement

Plasticity lower melting point for product, e.g. allowing a customer to use a spread straight out of the fridge

Pollution contamination of soil, water or atmosphere by harmful substances

Polysaccharide complex carbohydrate, either starch or fibre

Polyunsaturated fats a fat molecule with more than one hydrogen space

Preservatives substances that extend the shelf life of a product

Primary processing changing a basic food to preserve it or prepare it for sale or cooking

Productivity amount of food produced

Profiling test   sensory evaluation test to identify specific characteristics of a product

Proportions   relative quantities of ingredients in a recipe, expressed in numbers

Prove   when the yeast fills the dough with gas, causing it to rise and aerate

Radiation   where heat is passed by electromagnetic waves from one place to another

Ranking test   a method of putting in order the intensity of a particular characteristic of a product

Rastafarianism   a religion where people only eat clean food

Reduction   flavour is developed by reducing the liquid so that the flavours intensify

Reference Nutrient Intakes (RNIs)   the amount of a nutrient that is enough for most people in a group

Retinol   vitamin A

Rickets   caused by lack of calcium and vitamin D in children

Rubbing-in method   this is when the fat is rubbed into the flour until it resembles breadcrumbs; it is used in pastry, cake and biscuit making

Satiety   feeling full after eating

Saturated fats   each atom is combined with two hydrogen atoms

Secondary processing   using a primary processed food to make it into another product

Sensory analysis   tests that identify the sensory characteristics of products (i.e. taste, texture, appearance, mouth feel, colour)

Sensory qualities   the look, smell, taste, feel and sound of products

Shelf life   how long a food product can be kept safely and remain of high quality

Shortening   when fat coats the flour grains and prevents the gluten from developing and absorbing water, resulting in a crumbly mixture

Sikhism   Sikhs have similar eating patterns to Hindus

Soluble fibre   slows down digestion and absorption of carbohydrates and helps control blood sugar levels

Stablisers   help to prevent mixtures separating

Staple food   food that forms the basis of a traditional diet (for example, wheat, barley, rice, maize, rice)

Sterilisation   a method of heat treatment used to kill harmful bacteria; used when canning food

Sucrose   simple sugar

Sustainability   this means reducing the impact of a product on the environment

Sustainable   the resource will not run out

Sustainable resources   resources which will not run out

Syneresis   usually refers to eggs; if overcooked, the proteins shrink as they coagulate and separate from the watery liquid

Tenderise   changing the structure of meat by adding a marinade

Thickeners   modified starches are often used as thickeners in food products

Tofu   is made from ground soya beans

Traceability   can track the product back through all stages of production

Triangle test   used to tell the difference between two products

Ultra heat treatment (UHT)   high-temperature, short-time sterilisation of products such as milk; known as long-life milk

Umami   savoury taste

Unsaturated fats   fatty acid with at least one double bond in acid chain; can be monounsaturated or polyunsaturated

Use by date   used on high-risk foods

Vegans   strict vegetarians who will not eat any animal products

Visible fats   fats that can be seen

Water intoxication   having too much water

Water-soluble vitamins   dissolve in water

Whisked   when sugar and eggs are whisked together, adding air to the mixture; used when making a whisked sponge

Yeast   raising agent used in bread

Yoghurt   made from fermented milk

Picture credits

p1 © Innovation Works UK Ltd/Alamy Stock Photo; p3 © Crown copyright. Public Health England in association with the Welsh government, the Scottish government and the Food Standards Agency in Northern Ireland; p4 © Crown copyright; p5 *b* © Crown copyright; p17 © Olga Koronevska/iStock/Thinkstock; p19 © botazsolti/iStock/Thinkstock; p24*a* © rez-art/iStock/Thinkstock; p26 © Courtesy of Coeliac UK; p36 © Innovation Works UK Ltd/Alamy Stock Photo; p38 *t* © fotokostic/iStock/Thinkstock, *b* © imtmphoto/iStock/Thinkstock; p51 *b* © Monkey Business – Fotolia; p54 *t* © ia_64/iStock/Thinkstock; p65 © Sally and Richard Greenhill/Alamy Stock Photo; p66 and p68 © Fuse/Corbis/Getty Images, *m* © Thomas Northcut/Photodisc/Thinkstock; p69 and p78 *t* © camij/iStock/Thinkstock; p79 *tl* © thodonal/iStock/Thinkstock; p79 *tm* © shakzu/iStock/Thinkstock; p79 *tr* © Comstock/iStock/Thinkstock; p81 *tl* © naito8/iStock/Thinkstock; p81 *tm* © egal/iStock/Thinkstock; p87 and p92 *tl* © lzf/iStock/Thinkstock; p88 *t* and p94 © songdech17/iStock/Thinkstock; p88 *br* © jomoba/iStock/Thinkstock; p89a © tropper2000/iStock/Thinkstock; p89b © andegro4ka/iStock/Thinkstock; p89c © HaraldBiebel/iStock/Thinkstock; p89d © Okea/iStock/Thinkstock; p89e © ratmaner/iStock/Thinkstock; p89f © PicturePartners/iStock/Thinkstock; p90 *ml* © Perytskyy/iStock/Thinkstock; p90 *bl* © dionisvero/iStock/Thinkstock; p96 *t* © Courtesy of Red Tractor; p96 *m* © Courtesy of RSPCA Assured; p97 *t* © Courtesy of Soil Association Certification; p97 *b* © Courtesy of Abel & Cole; p98a © IrenaSimunic/iStock/Thinkstock; p98b © Elena_Danileiko/iStock/Thinkstock; p98c © HasseChr/iStock/Thinkstock; p98d © nito100/iStock/Thinkstock; p104 © Courtesy of Marine Stewardship Council; p103 and p113 © BRINGARD Denis/Hemis/Alamy Stock Photo; p110 *tl* © popovaphoto/iStock/Thinkstock; p110 *bl* © Courtesy of East End Foods plc; p115 *t* © Ingram Publishing Company/Ultimate Food Photography; p119 *ml* © akova/iStock/Thinkstock; p120 *tl* © metinkiyak/iStock/Thinkstock; p120 *bl* © Ernesto Solla Domínguez/iStockphoto; p122 and p127 © umenie/iStock/Thinkstock; p123 © Rklfoto/iStock/Thinkstock; p124 *t* © Courtesy of Fairtrade Foundation; p124 *b* © Mike Greenslade/Alamy Stock Photo; p125 © anelina/123RF; p126 *t* © nathan4847/iStock/Thinkstock; p126 *b* © Courtesy of Carbon Footprint Ltd.; p131 © Anjes/iStock/Thinkstock; p134 © Anjes/iStock/Thinkstock; p134 © Ingram Publishing Company/Ultimate Food Photography; p139 © travellinglight/iStock/Thinkstock; 141 © grafvision/iStock/Thinkstock; p143 *l* © olgna/iStock/Thinkstock; p143 *r* © Paul_Brighton/iStock/Thinkstock; p144 © karandaev/iStock/Thinkstock; p145 © foodandstyle/iStock/Thinkstock; p146a © Cathy Yeulet/iStock/Thinkstock; p146b © travellinglight/iStock/Thinkstock; p146c © Vladimir1965/iStock/Thinkstock; p146d © highviews/iStock/Thinkstock; p147a © benhammad/iStock/Thinkstock; p147b © chameleonseye/iStock/Thinkstock; p147c © Amandaliza/iStock/Thinkstock; p147d © Muralinath/iStock/Thinkstock; p147e © Mohammed Anwarul Kabir Choudhury/123RF; p147f © heinteh/123RF; p147g © Darkkong/iStock/Thinkstock; p148 © arraymax/iStock/Thinkstock; p149 *tl* © popovaphoto/iStock/Thinkstock; p149 *tm* © urbanbuzz/Alamy Stock Photo; p149 *tm* © urbanbuzz/Alamy Stock Photo; p150 and p160 *tl* © egal/iStock/Thinkstock; p152 *tl* © Ingram Publishing/iStock/Thinkstock; p152 *bl* © Claudiad/E+/Getty Images; p153 *ml* © fotokostic/iStock/Thinkstock; p154 *tl* © shironosov/iStock/Thinkstock; p154 *ml* © Digital Vision/iStock/Thinkstock; p155 *tl* © Alex Segre/Alamy Stock Photo; p159 *tl* © Courtesy of Vegetarian Society; p160 *m* © Wiktor Rzeźuchowski/iStock/Thinkstock; p160 *b* © Wavebreakmedia Ltd/iStock/Thinkstock; p163 © olgakr/iStock/Thinkstock ; p164 *m* © RafalStachura/iStock/Thinkstock; p166 © dianazh/iStock/Thinkstock; p167 © Joseph Belanger/123RF; p168 *tm* © GYRO PHOTOGRAPHY/amanaimagesRF/Thinkstock; p177 *bl* © Arnaud-h/iStock/Thinkstock; p178 *bl* © Reload_Studio/iStock/Thinkstock; p178 *bm* © OLEKSANDR PEREPELYTSIA/iStock/Thinkstock; p178 *br* © Oleksandr Perepelytsia/Alamy Stock Photo; p182 *tl* © olgakr/iStock/Thinkstock; p182 *bl* © angorius/iStock/Thinkstock; p179 *t* © karelnoppe/iStock/Thinkstock; p179 *ml* © Digital Vision/iStock/Thinkstock; p179 *mr* © George Tsartsianidis/123RF; p179 *bl* © maxsol7/iStock/Thinkstock; p183 *ml* © William Berry/Fotolia; p183 *m* © Elena Elisseeva/Fotolia; p183 *mr* © Elena Elisseeva/Fotolia; p190 *tl* © audriusmerfeldas/iStock/Thinkstock; p192 © yasuhiroamano/iStock/Thinkstock; p195a © mishooo/iStock/Thinkstock; p195b © Design Pics/iStock/Thinkstock; p195c © RusN/iStock/Thinkstock; p196 © AntonioGuillem/iStock/Thinkstock; p202 © John Carey/Photolibrary/Getty Images; p203 *tl* © royaltystockphoto/iStock/Thinkstock; p203 *br* © AlexPro9500/iStock/Thinkstock; p204 *tl* © dziewul/iStock/Thinkstock; p204 *m* © EYE OF SCIENCE/SCIENCE PHOTO LIBRARY; p204 *br* © oleshkonti/iStock/Thinkstock; p205 *tl* © nikitos77/iStock/Thinkstock; p205 *tm* © Maksym Narodenko/iStock/Thinkstock; p205 *tr* © Zoonar RF/Zoonar/Thinkstock; p206 *tl* © Ryan McVay/Photodisc/Thinkstock; p210 *bl* © rep0rter/iStock/Thinkstock; p212 *tl* © Purestock/Thinkstock; p212 *ml* © IngaNielsen/iStock/Thinkstock; p212 *bl* © John Carey/Photolibrary/Getty Images; p214 *tl* © Eraxion/iStock/Thinkstock; p214 *tm* © decade3d/iStock/Thinkstock; p214 *tr* © decade3d/iStock/Thinkstock; p214 *ml* © Chris Dascher/iStockphoto; p219 *tl* © Fuse/Corbis/Getty Images; p219 *tm* © AnnaDudek/iStock/Thinkstock; p219 *ml* © Diana Taliun/iStock/Thinkstock; p219 *m* © Fuse/Corbis/Getty Images; p219 *bl* © Alexey Bragin/iStock/Thinkstock; p219 *bl* © rclassenlayouts/iStock/Thinkstock; p219 *br* © Agatha Brown/Fotolia; p219 *br* © Grosescu Alberto Mihai/iStock/Thinkstock; p220 *tl* © Viacheslav Krisanov/Hemera/Thinkstock; p220 *m* © popovaphoto/iStock/Thinkstock; p222 © Andrew Callaghan/Hodder Education; p223 *t* © Andrew Callaghan/Hodder Education, *ml* © MichaelJay/iStock/Thinkstock; p226 *bm* © PinonRoad/iStock/Thinkstock; p226 *bm* © Keith Bell/123RF; p226 *bm* © Aleksandr Ugorenkov/Fotolia; p232 *tr* © margouillatphotos/iStock/Thinkstock; p232 and 233 and 234 *t* © Andrew Callaghan/Hodder Education; p234 *bl* © Simone Van den berg/Hemera/Thinkstock; p235 © Andrew Callaghan/Hodder Education; p236 and p253*b* © zhekos/iStock/Thinkstock; p246 © Monkey Business/Fotolia; p248 *ml* © spinetta/Fotolia; p248 *m* © Denisa V/Fotolia; p248 *mr* © Constantinos/Fotolia; p249 *tm* © rgbdigital/istock/thinkstock; 249 *m* © meral yildirim/istock/thinkstock; p217 *bl* and 252 *bl* © Svetlana Kolpakova/Hemera/Thinkstock; p253a © Andrew Callaghanl; p253b © zhekos/iStock/Thinkstock; p253c © vetas/iStock/Thinkstock; p253d © Monkey Business Images/Monkey Business/Thinkstock; p254a © Ruth Black/Fotolia; p254b © RuthBlack/iStock/Thinkstock; p254c © Anna Yakimova/123RF; p254d © Tuned_In/iStock/Thinkstock; p255 © Andrew Callaghan/Hodder Education; p256 © Andrew Callaghan/Hodder Education; p258 *tl* © Siede Preis/Photodisc/Getty Images; p258 *tm* © evgenyb/Fotolia; p258 *tr* © Ingram Publishing Company/Ultimate Food Photography; p258 *ml* © Anna Yakimova/123RF; p258 *m* © Elena Elisseeva/Fotolia; p258 *mr* © Ruth Black/Fotolia; p258 *bl* © Monkey Business/Fotolia; p278 *tr* © Lilyana Vynogradova/123RF.

l = left; *r* = right; *m* = middle; *t* = top; *b* = bottom

Except where stated above, photographs are by Val Fehners.

Index

accelerated freeze-drying (AFD) 119
access to food 123
acetic acid see vitamin C
acid denaturation 193
acids, in cooking 120, 189, 227, 235
activity levels, and energy requirements 41, 153
additives 131–7
adolescents
   energy requirements 29, 40
   nutritional requirements 23
adults
   energy requirements 29, 40
   nutritional requirements 24, 29–31, 55
advertising 155
aeration 183, 185, 187, 191, 192, 193
AFD (accelerated freeze drying) 119
agriculture 96–7
albumin 187
alcohol 40
all-in-one cake method 237
all-in-one sauces 231
allergies 26–7, 208
amino acids 43
anaemia 19–20, 65
animal fats 4, 83, 84, 110
animal welfare, in food production 95–6, 161
antioxidants 133, 138
aromas from food 195
arrowroot 181, 231, 253
aspartamine 135
availability of food 122–3, 152
babies
   energy requirements 40, 41
   nutritional requirements 21–2, 44
bacillus cereus 213
bacteria 202–3, 212–15, 224, 225
   beneficial bacteria 138, 205
baking 170–1
   biscuits 244–5
   bread making 245–6
   pastry 239–44, 254
baking powder 191, 193, 237
balanced diets 2–12
   functional foods 137–8
   see also diets; healthy eating; malnutrition; weight loss
barley 89
basal metabolic rate (BMR) 39
batters 170, 187, 237, 255
beans
   nutrients 5, 43, 45, 56, 60
   poisons 165
   portions 11
   preservation methods 116–17, 118
   vegan protein substitute 80–1

béchamel sauce 231
Benecol products 138
best before date 207
beta carotene see vitamin A
bicarbonate of soda 190, 193, 237
binding sauces 230
biscuit making 244–5
blanching method 169
blast chilling 116
blast freezing 118
blended sauces 231
blood pressure 16
BMI 39
BMR 39
body mass index (BMI) 39
boiling method 169, 175
bone health 18–19, 23, 59
bone mass 18, 64
braising 171
bread
   additives 20, 64
   food investigation task 261–8
   gluten content 27
   nutrients 4, 20, 36, 63, 69–70
   processing 108–9
   salt content 35
   see also flour
bread making 108–9, 245–6
breakfast cereals 19, 88, 89, 119, 129
breastfeeding mothers, nutrition 24
bridge hold 220
brown flour 105
browning 183
Buddhism 157
butter 4, 83, 84, 110
buying food 205–9
   see also marketing
cake making 236–7
calcium
   functions 64
   health needs 18, 23, 63
   sources 72, 74, 76
calorie controlled diets 14
campylobacter 213
cane sugar 53
canned fruit and vegetables 11, 92
canning (food preservation) 11, 92, 115
CAP (controlled atmosphere packaging) 120
caramelisation 183, 192
carbohydrates
   effect of cooking 177
   energy source 39, 40
   food group 4
   functions 52, 54, 55
   sources 29, 53, 54, 55, 70, 72, 74, 81
   types 52–4, 55

   see also bread; pasta; potatoes; rice; starchy carbohydrates; sugar
carbon footprint 94, 126–7, 152
carbon offsetting 127
cardiovascular disease 15–16, 49
casserole method 171
celebrations and food 146, 154, 272–3
cereals 4, 56, 69–70
   production and use 88–90, 136, 141, 157
   see also rice
Channel Island milk 74, 107
cheese 75–6, 112–13, 140, 160, 187, 204
chemical raising agents 190–1, 193
chicken 5, 77, 222
children
   energy requirements 9, 29, 40, 41
   nutritional requirements 2, 7, 21–3, 29–31, 44, 55, 64
chilling process 116
Chinese cuisine and culture 141, 142, 143, 144, 147, 148
cholecalciferol see vitamin D
cholesterol 15–16, 48, 49, 138
chopping boards 219, 224
choux pastry 192, 240, 242–3
Christian food customs 146, 157
claw grip 220
clostridium perfringens 213, 214
coagulation 186, 193
coatings 187, 230, 254, 255
cobalamin (vitamin B12) 61, 177
coeliac disease 26
   see also gluten
coffee 6, 119, 121, 124
comparison testing 198
complementary proteins 43
conduction cooking 167, 169, 170, 171, 172
controlled atmosphere packaging (CAP) 120
convection cooking 168, 169, 170–1, 172
convenience foods see ready-made foods
cook-chill foods 116–17
cook-freeze methods 119
cooking methods
   dry methods 170–1, 172–4
   functions of ingredients 180–93
   heat transfer 167–8
   meat and fish 178–9
   moist methods 169–70, 171
   potatoes 70
   to reduce fats 36–7
   see also baking; cuisines; equipment; food preparation; food science
cornflour 181, 231
coronary heart disease 15, 48
cost saving on food 151, 155

Index

cream 4, 111
creaming method 237
cross-contamination, prevention 211–12, 224–5
cryogenic freezing 119
cuisines 139–43, 146, 157–8
culture, cuisines and customs 146, 154, 157
cutting equipment 219, 221
dairy alternatives 4, 75, 80, 111
dairy products
    fat source 34, 51, 74
    food processing 105–7, 110–13
    in healthy diet 4
    minerals source 63, 64, 74
    protein source 43, 74
    and vegetarianism 159–60
    vitamin source 58, 59, 60, 61, 74
    see also lactose intolerance
Danone products 138
decoration of food 254–5
deep-frying 173
dehydration (food preservation) 119
dehydration (lack of water) 67
denaturation 186, 189
dental health 19, 54
dextrinisation 181, 192
diabetes 14, 17, 48
Dietary Reference Values (DRVs) 28–31
dieting 14
diets
    gluten-free 26
    recipe modification 32–7
    see also balanced diets; veganism; vegetarianism
difference testing 198
digestive problems 17, 55
disaccharides 53
diverticulitis 17, 55
dough 108–9, 239–44, 245–6
dredging (fishing) 99
dried foods 119, 148
    dried fruit 4, 11, 63, 124
drinks see hydration
DRVs 28–31
dry-frying 172
drying methods 119
E. coli 213, 214
E numbers 131
EARs 28, 29
eating patterns 148, 153–4
Eatwell Guide 2–5, 10, 37
egg custards 234
eggs
    allergy to 26
    in cooking 187, 193, 232, 234, 240, 245, 247, 253
    nutrients 5, 45, 59, 60, 63, 80
    preservation 120
    production 96
    structure 80

eight tips for healthy eating (DoH) 10
emulsifiers 135, 136, 183, 192
emulsion sauces 232
energy
    nutritional sources 39–40, 50
    requirements 8–9, 38, 40, 41
enrobing 254–5
enzymes 205
enzymic browning 189, 193, 205, 225–6
equipment 147, 153, 218–21, 223, 226–7, 233, 248–9, 252
essential amino acids 43
essential fatty acids (EFAs) 49, 50
Estimated Average Requirements 28, 29
examination questions, terms 288–92
factory farming 96, 99, 100, 161
Fairtrade 123–4
farming methods 95–7, 100–1, 124, 161
fat-soluble vitamins 58–9, 82
fats
    effect of cooking 177
    energy source 39, 40, 50
    functions 49–50
    high-fat foods 6, 6–7
    as ingredients 185, 192, 236, 237, 240, 245
    interpreting food labelling 33
    lowering fat intake 4, 34, 36–7, 50, 76, 77, 83, 84
    nutritional requirements 29, 50
    sources 51, 70, 76, 78, 79, 80, 81, 82
    structure 47–9, 82
    see also oils; saturated fats; spreads; unsaturated fats
females
    energy requirements 9, 29, 40
    nutritional requirements 29–31
fermentation 193, 204
fertilisers, use 96
fibre 15
    daily requirements 29, 55
    functions 17, 55
    sources 36, 56, 70, 72
    and veganism 160
filo pastry 244
finishing of food 251–6
fish
    macronutrients 5, 43, 45, 49, 51, 78, 82
    micronutrients 59, 63, 64, 79
    preparation and cooking 178, 179, 187, 223, 225, 227
    preservation 118, 120
    production 98–9
    salt content 36
    types 98
fish farming 100–1
fishing methods 99
five-a-day campaign 10–11
flaky pastry 240
flavour of food, enhancing 134, 180, 185

Flora products 138
flour
    in cooking 181, 187, 237, 240, 245, 246
    in food investigation task 261–8
    fortification and additives 64, 129, 130
    nutrients 70
    processing 103–5, 108–10
    types and uses 105, 191
fluidised bed drying 119
fluidised bed freezing 118
foam see whisking
folic acid (vitamin B9) 24, 61, 177
food accessibility 123
food additives 131–7
food availability 122–3, 152
food choices, influences 150–6
food colouring 134, 166
food combining 43
food costs 151
food hygiene 212
    see also food safety
food intolerance/allergies 26–7, 208
food investigation task 260–8
food labelling
    additives 132
    energy content 14
    legal requirements 207
    nutritional information 6–7, 8, 12, 155, 275
    production information 125, 161
    storage and cooking information 155, 206–8
food miles 127, 152
food poisoning, prevention 212–15
food portions 11, 37, 79
food preparation
    assessed task 269–82
    equipment 219–21, 223, 226–7, 233, 248–9, 252
    fruit and vegetables 225–6
    meat and fish 224–5, 227
    safe practices 211–15
    see also cooking methods
food preservation 114–21, 165, 189
food processing 103–21
    food additives 131–7
    food tasting panels 197–201
    fortification 130
    preservation methods 114–21, 165, 189
    primary food processing 103–7
    secondary food processing 108–13
    see also cooking methods
food processors 223, 233
food safety
    food poisoning avoidance 202–3, 205, 210, 211–15, 224–5
    moulds and yeast 203–4
    sale of food 205–9
    storage of food 209–11

food scares 156
food science
    effect of cooking 177–80
    function of cooking 164–6
    heat sources in cooking 167–8
    ingredient functions 180–93
    see also cooking methods
food security 122–8
food spoilage 205
food storage 152, 207, 209–11
food tasting panels 197–201
food-tasting tests 198–200, 279
food waste 125–6
fortification of foods 20, 64, 84, 129–30
free sugars 6, 7–8, 53
freezer burn 210
freezers 152, 209–10
freezing techniques 92, 117–18, 210
fructose 52
fruit
    categories 91
    cell structure 91
    effect of cooking 193
    Fairtrade production 124
    farming methods 96–7
    in healthy diet 4
    nutrients 26, 36, 49, 51, 56, 61, 67, 72, 138
    portions 11
    preparation 220, 225–6
    preservation methods 115–16, 118, 119, 120, 210
    seasonal availability 93–4
    sugar content 35, 52, 53, 72
fruit juices 4, 6, 11, 19, 130
frying 172–3, 175
functional foods 137–8
garnishing 252
gelatinisation 181, 192
gelling agents 136
genetically modified (GM) foods 125, 208
glacé icing 254
glazing 249, 252–3
glucose 52
gluten
    in cooking 105, 187, 188, 193, 246, 249
    food investigation task 264–8
    gluten free diet 26
GM foods 125, 208
grilling 173–4, 175, 178
hand washing 212, 224, 243
harpooning (fishing) 99
health problems
    effect of diet 6, 7, 8, 12–19, 50, 55, 154
    effect on energy 41
    food intolerance and allergy 26–7
    healthy eating 16, 17, 19, 19–20, 154
    nutrient deficiencies 45, 59, 64, 65
healthy eating
    balanced diets 2–12
    fibre 18, 55
    government guidelines 10–11
    for health problems 16, 17, 18, 19–20, 154
    malnutrition 123
    pregnancy and breastfeeding 19, 24, 64, 65
    recipe modification 32–7
    unsaturated fats 16, 48–9
heart disease 15–16, 48
herbs 35, 119, 138, 145, 165
high biological value (HBV) proteins 43
high blood pressure 16
high-risk foods 202, 207, 215, 224, 225
Hindu food customs 146, 158
history of food 139
hollandaise sauce 232
homogenised milk 105–6
honey 90
hydration (drinks) 6, 8
    see also water
hydrogenated glucose syrup 135
hydrogenation of fats 49
hydroponics 94
icing 254
illness see health problems
imported foods 93
Indian cuisine and culture 141, 142, 143, 144, 145, 146, 147, 148
infused sauces 231
ingredients
    in cooking 180–93
    on labels 207
    ready-prepared 148, 152
insoluble fibre 56
intensive farming 96, 99, 100, 161
international cuisines 142–5, 146, 148
invisible fats 51
iron in diet 19–20, 24, 63, 65, 72, 77, 80
Islam, food customs 146, 158
Italian cuisine 142, 144, 145, 147, 148
jam 189, 253
Jamaican cuisine 143, 144
Jewish food customs 158
jigging (fishing) 99
Judaism, food customs 158
kneading method 246
knives 219, 221
lacto vegetarians 160, 270–2, 274–7, 279–82
lacto-ovo vegetarians 159
lactose 53, 74
lactose intolerance 27, 75
    see also dairy alternatives
lecithin 135
legislation and regulations 116, 134, 207
lemon juice 189, 227, 235
lifestyle, eating patterns 148, 153–4
listeria 213
locally produced food 92–3, 161, 273, 274
long-grain rice 89
low biological value (LBV) proteins 43, 81

low-fat products 4, 34, 76, 77, 83, 84, 130
low-fat spreads 130
low-risk foods 207, 215
Lower Reference Nutrient Intakes (LRNIs) 28
macronutrients 28
    see also carbohydrates; fats; proteins
Maillard reaction 183
maize 70, 89, 136, 181
males
    energy requirements 9, 29, 40, 41
    nutritional requirements 29–31
malnutrition 123
maltose 53
MAP (modified atmosphere packaging) 120
maple syrup 90
margarine 84
marinating 227
marketing, effect on consumers 155
mayonnaise 232, 233
mealtimes 148, 153
measuring equipment 218–19
meat
    classification 95
    farming methods 95–6, 97, 161
    in healthy diet 5
    nutrients 20, 34, 51, 60, 61, 63, 77
    poultry preparation 222
    preparation and cooking 178, 187, 224–5, 227
    preservation methods 118, 120
    salt content 36
    structure 77
    vegetarianism 159–60
meat alternatives see textured vegetable protein
melting (cake method) 237
men see males
metabolic rate 39, 41
Mexican cuisine 142, 143, 144, 145
micronutrients 28
    see also calcium; iron; minerals; vitamins
microwaving 174, 175, 213
milk
    effect of heat 187
    in glazing 253
    in healthy diet 6
    nutrients 73–4
    preservation methods 115, 119
    production processes 105–7, 110–13
    types 106–7
milling of flour 103–4
minerals 63–5
    fortification of foods 20, 64, 129, 130
    functions 63–4, 65
    health needs 18, 19–20, 31
    sources 63–4, 70, 74, 77
    and veganism 160
    see also calcium; iron; phosphorus
mixtures, setting 234–5

Index

modified atmosphere packaging (MAP) 120
monosaccharides 52–3
monosodium glutamate (MSG) 136
monounsaturated fats 48
moulds 114, 203–4
MSG 136
Muslim food customs 146, 158
mycoprotein (Quorn) 81, 160
niacin (Vitamin B3) 60, 74, 177
non-dairy foods 4, 75, 80, 111
non-free sugars 7, 8, 53, 54
non-starch polysaccharides see fibre
noodles 143
nutrient sources
    carbohydrates 29, 53, 54, 55, 70, 72, 74, 81
    fats 51, 70, 76, 78, 79, 80, 81, 82
    fibre 36, 56, 70, 72
    minerals 63–4, 70, 74, 77
    proteins 43, 45, 70, 74, 76, 78, 79, 80
    vitamins 59, 60–1, 70, 74, 76, 77, 79, 80
nutrients
    definition 28
    on food labelling 208
    functions 29, 43, 44, 49–50, 54, 55, 59, 60, 63–5
    see also carbohydrates; fats; minerals; nutrient sources; proteins; vitamins
nutritional requirements 28–31
    adolescents 23
    adults 24, 29–31
    babies 21–2, 44
    children 7, 21–3, 29–31, 44, 64
    function of nutrients 29, 43, 44, 45, 49–50, 54, 55, 59, 60, 63–5
    older people 24
    in pregnancy 19, 24, 61, 64, 65
    see also balanced diets; health problems, effect of diet; healthy eating
nuts 26, 124, 138
oat milk 75, 89
oats 70, 89, 136
obesity 12–14, 41, 54
    see also weight gain
offal 77
oils
    Fairtrade production 124
    hydrogenation 49
    as ingredients 185, 193
    nutrients 5, 59
    sources of 82
    structure 48–9, 82, 84
    white fats 83
oily fish 5, 19, 49, 51, 59, 78, 79, 99
older people, nutritional requirements 24
Omega-3/Omega-6 49
organic farming 97, 124
organic milk 107
organoleptic qualities of food see senses
osteomalacia 59
osteoporosis 18–19, 59, 64

oven-drying 119
ovo vegetarians 160
oxidisation of fruit 193
pasta
    fresh pasta making 247–8
    nutrients 4, 36, 56, 69–70
    production and use 88, 110, 141
pasteurisation 106, 115
pasteurised milk 106
pastry
    techniques 241–4, 254
    types 239–43, 244
pathogenic bacteria 202, 202–3, 212–15, 224, 225
pesticide use 96
phosphorus 23, 65, 74, 76
physical activity level (PAL) 39
phytochemicals 138
piping (decoration) 252, 254
plant sterols 138
plasticity (fats) 185, 192
plate freezing 118
poaching (cooking) 169
polysaccharides 54–6
polyunsaturated fats 49, 70
portion size 11, 37, 79
potatoes
    cooking methods 36, 70
    nutrients 4, 61, 70
    potato flour 181
poultry 5, 77, 222
pouring sauces 230
prebiotic foods 138
pregnancy
    energy requirements 40
    nutritional needs 19, 24, 61, 64, 65
preparation of food see food preparation
presentation of food 255–6, 278
preservatives 133, 183
preserving methods 114–21
    advantages and disadvantages 114
    chemical preservatives 119, 133, 183
    controlled atmosphere methods 120–1
    drying methods 119
    temperature methods 115–19
primary food processing 103–7
probiotic foods 138
processed meat 5
profiling tests 199
proteins
    energy source 39, 40
    food combining 43
    food groups 4, 5
    function 44, 45
    ingredient in cooking 186–8
    non-meat/non-dairy alternatives 80–1, 111
    nutritional requirements 43, 44
    sources 43, 45, 70, 74, 76, 78, 79, 80
puff pastry 244
pulses

nutrients 5, 19, 43, 45, 51, 61
    portions 11
Quorn 81, 160
radiation cooking 167, 168, 173–4
raising agents 189–92, 193, 235–8
ranking tests 199
Rastafarian food customs 158
ratings test 198
raw meat and fish 212, 219, 222–3, 224–5
ready-made foods 11, 136, 244
    preservation methods 116, 118
    ready-prepared ingredients 148, 152
    see also cook-chill foods; cook-freeze methods
recipe modification 32–7
red meat, nutrients 5, 19, 20, 77
Red Tractor mark 96
reduction sauces 231–2
Reference Nutrient Intakes 28, 29, 30, 44
refrigeration of foods
    chilling process 116
    storage 152, 209
reheating food 213, 214–15
religion, cuisines and customs 146, 157–8
retinol see vitamin A
revision techniques, written examination 283–7
riboflavin (vitamin B2) 60, 74, 76, 80, 177
rice
    nutrients 4, 36, 43, 56, 70
    production and use 89, 124, 141
rice flour 181, 191
rice milk 75
rickets 59, 65
RNIs 28, 29, 30, 44
roasting 171
roller drying 119
root vegetables 72, 181
rough puff pastry 240, 242
roux 231
royal icing 254
RSPCA Assured mark 96
rubbed in method 237, 240
rye 89
saccharin 135
salad 11
salad dressing 232
salmonella 213, 214
salt
    daily requirements 30
    food labelling 33
    high-salt foods 36
    reducing in diet 8, 35
    used in preservation 119
saturated fats 7, 15, 47–8
    food labelling 33
    sources 70, 76, 79, 80, 81
sauces 230–3
sea ranching 100
sea reared fish 100

303

seasonal availability 93–4, 152, 273, 274
secondary food processing 108–13
self-raising flour 191, 237
semi-skimmed milk 74, 106
senses
   appeal of food 195–6, 251–6
   sensory tasting panels 197–201
setting mixtures 234–5
shallow-frying 173
shaping food 248–9
shelf life 207
shellfish 5, 79, 99, 119
short-grain rice 89
shortcrust pastry 240, 241
shortening 185, 192, 240, 241
Sikh food customs 158
simmering method 169
skimmed milk 74, 106
smoking (food preservation) 120
smoothies 4, 6, 11
sodium 74, 76
   see also salt
Soil Association 97
soluble fibre 56
sorbital 135
soya beans 80, 81
soya milk 75, 130
soya products 45, 75, 80, 81, 111, 130, 138
Spanish cuisine and culture 142, 144, 148
spelt 89
spices 35, 124, 144, 165, 190
spoilage of food 205
spray drying 119
spreads
   butter 4, 110
   low-fat 15, 84, 110
   margarine 84
   nutrients 5
stabilisers 135
staphylococcus aureus 213, 214
staple foods 141, 157
star profiles 200, 280
starchy carbohydrates 4, 54
   ingredient in cooking 180–2, 234
   modified starch 136
   nutrients 69–71
   see also bread; pasta; potatoes; rice
steam, as a raising agent 191–2, 193
steaming 170, 175, 178
sterilisation (food preservation) 106, 115–16
sterilised milk 106
stir-frying 173
storage of food 152, 207, 209–11
sucralose 135
sucrose 53
sugar
   content in foods 70, 81, 85
   Fairtrade production 124
   in food labelling 33, 85
   in food preservation 119

glazing 253
high-sugar foods 5–6
   as ingredient 183, 237, 245
   low-sugar products and recipes 4, 35
   recommended amounts 7
   sources of 53, 90
   and tooth decay 19, 54
   types 52–3, 182
   see also sweeteners
sugar beet 90
sugar cane 90
sun drying 119
sustainable farming methods 96, 97, 99, 124, 126, 127, 161
sweeteners 135
synthetic additives 132
tapioca 181
taste, detection 196
tea 6, 20, 64, 119, 124
teeth 19, 54, 64
temperature
   for bacterial control 203, 213, 214–15
   in cooking methods 169, 170, 172, 234, 246
   mould growth 204
tenderising 227
textured vegetable protein 80–1, 130, 160
thawing food 210
thiamine (vitamin B1) 60, 72, 74, 76, 177
thickeners 136
tinned food 11, 92, 115
tocopherol (vitamin E) 59
tofu 81
tomato sauce 232
tongue, taste areas 196
traditional foods 139–43, 146, 157–8
Traidcraft 124
trans-fatty acids 49
trawling 99
triangle test 198
TVP 80–1, 130, 160
Type 2 diabetes 16
UHT (ultra heat treatment) milk 106, 115
umami 196
unsaturated fats 5, 15, 48–9, 70, 76, 79, 80, 81
use by date 207
utensils 219–20, 226
   see also equipment; knives
vacuum packing 121
veganism 160
vegetables
   effect of cooking 193
   Fairtrade production 124
   fibre source 36, 56, 72
   freezing 210
   in healthy diet 4
   intensive farming 94, 96
   nutrients 19, 49, 59, 60, 61, 63, 72, 82, 138, 225
   portions 11

preparation and cooking 193, 220, 225–6
preservation methods 115–16, 118, 119, 120
seasonal availability 93–4
structure 92
sugar content 52, 53
types 92
water content 67
vegetarianism 20, 159–61, 270–2, 274–7, 279–82
velouté sauce 231
vinegar 120, 189, 227
visible fats 51
vitamin A 58, 59, 72, 74, 76, 80, 130, 177
vitamin B1 60, 72, 74, 76, 177
vitamin B2 60, 74, 76, 80, 177
vitamin B3 60, 74, 177
vitamin B9 (folic acid) 24, 61, 177
vitamin B12 (cobalamin) 61, 177
vitamin C 20, 58, 61, 65, 72, 130, 177
vitamin D 18, 24, 58, 59, 64–5, 74, 76, 130
vitamin E 59
vitamin K 58, 59
vitamins
   effect of cooking 177, 225
   effect of preservation methods 116
   fortified foods 129, 130
   functions 59, 60–1
   health needs 18, 20
   sources 59, 60–1, 70, 74, 76, 77, 79, 80
   type 58, 60
   and veganism 160
   see also names of vitamins e.g. vitamin A
waste (unused food) 125–6
water
   function and requirements 6, 66–8
   sources 67–8, 79
water intoxication 67
water-soluble vitamins 60–1
weight, body mass index 39
   see also obesity; weight gain
weight gain 13–14, 24, 41
weight loss, in illness 41
wheat
   nutrients 69–70
   production and use 88, 136, 141, 157
whisking 186, 187, 191, 193, 219, 233, 237
white fats 83
white fish 5, 79, 99
white flour 105
whole milk 74, 106
wholegrain foods 36, 56, 61, 69, 70, 138
wholemeal flour 36, 56, 105
women, pregnancy/breastfeeding needs 19, 24, 40, 61, 64, 65
   see also females
yeasts
   food production 190, 193, 246
   food spoilage 204
yoghurt 76, 111, 138